PEOPLE *of* TERRA NULLIUS

PEOPLE *of*

BETRAYAL AND REBIRTH

TERRA

IN ABORIGINAL CANADA

NULLIUS

BOYCE RICHARDSON

Douglas & McIntyre
Vancouver/Toronto

93 94 95 96 97   5 4 3 2 1

Douglas & McIntyre Ltd.
1615 Venables Street
Vancouver, British Columbia V5L 2H1

Canadian Cataloguing in Publication Data

Richardson, Boyce.
  People of Terra Nullius

  Includes bibliographical references and index.
  ISBN 1-55054-118-8

  1. Indians of North America – Canada – Government
relations –1951- . 2. Indians, Treatment of – Canada.
3. Indians of North America – Canada – Politics and
government. I. Title.
E92.R53 1993   323.1'197071   C93-091629-8

Editing by Roy MacSkimming
Design and type by George Vaitkunas
Jacket design by Barbara Hodgson
Map by Fiona MacGregor
Printed and bound in Canada by D.W. Friesen and Sons
Printed on acid-free paper ∞

Acknowledgements

The author wishes to acknowledge the help of many people in the process of bringing this book to fruition, particularly his editor Roy MacSkimming, both a friend and a professional adviser of high quality; Peter Quaw, of the Lheit Lit'en nation; Charles Wagamase, of Kenora; Sakej Henderson and Marie Battiste, of Eskasoni; Andrew Chapeskie, of Kenora; Marion Ironquil Meadmore, of Winnipeg; and David Nahwegahbow and Russell Diabo, advisers to the Barriere Lake Algonquins, who were all generous with their help; and to *Reader's Digest*, Montreal, for providing the budget for much of the travel involved in researching the book. Of course, none of the above is responsible for the views expressed here.

Dedication

This book is dedicated to the many aboriginal people who have welcomed me to their land and communities, and have been so generous with their time when I have turned up with my questions. Especially to the memory of Job and Mary Bearskin, a wonderfully wise and gentle couple; Ronnie Jolly; Abraham and Shirley Voyageur; Malick Blacksmith; and Billy Bearskin, who all appeared in films I made, and have, as aboriginal people say, passed on to the spirit world;

And to Sam and Nancy Blacksmith, vigorous, good-humoured and skilled hunters, still in excellent health in their seventies; Isaiah Awashish, a member of the last generation of those hunters who have attained spiritual power from their close association with and extraordinary knowledge of animals; his late son Willie, already a spiritual force at the time of his untimely death at the age of seventeen; and especially to Philip Awashish, a valued and admired friend for many years, who has devoted himself unreservedly to the cause of his people.

Three Notes

1

Terra Nullius, a land that is empty of people. This is a legal concept used by Europeans when they first arrived in North America. They wanted to justify their claim to own all the land, pretending that no one else had been here first.

2

Many aboriginal people in Canada prefer not to be known as "Indians". I have used the expressions "native people", "aboriginal people" or "First Nations" wherever possible. The word "Indian" is still in regular use, however, even among the aboriginal people themselves, and remains, in certain contexts, the most appropriate term. I have also used it where the historical context demands.

3

It is difficult to know what to call the society that surrounds the aboriginal people. "European" describes its culture and ethos, but is an inaccurate description of its people, most of whom have never set foot in Europe. "Canadian" is too all-embracing, for there is a sense in which it includes everyone who lives here, including aboriginals. I have settled for "Euro-Canadian", meaning a society whose values derive from Europe. This is not ideal, for Canada is not as European as it once was, but I feel the term most closely approximates the reality of Canada as it relates to aboriginals.

CONTENTS

CONTENTS

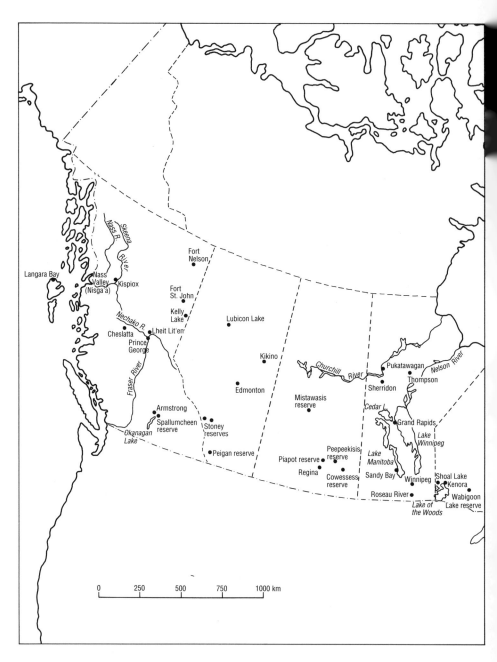

This map shows the places mentioned in this book, including many aboriginal communities that are normally omitted from maps used by Canadians. The map illustrates the wide geographic distribution of aboriginal people, who populate every part of the country, and provides a perspective on Canada very different from that given by the usual maps built around major population centres. Although once called *Terra Nullius* in order to justify the dispossession of the aboriginal people, Canada has always been a far from empty land.

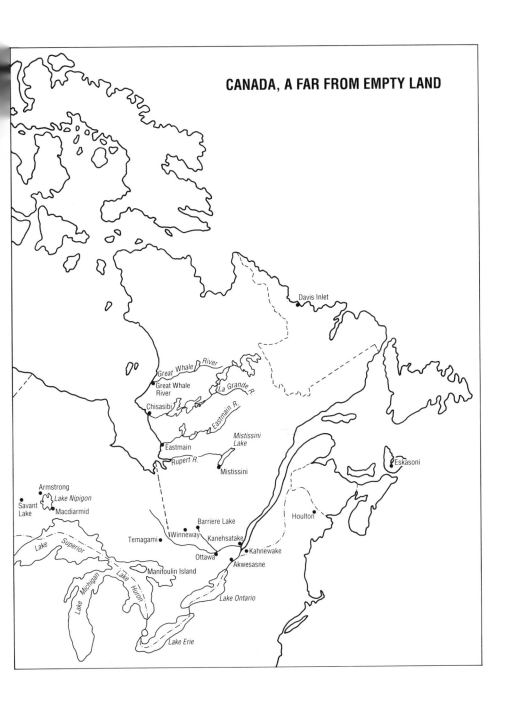

CANADA, A FAR FROM EMPTY LAND

Davis Inlet

Great Whale River
Great Whale River
Chisasibi
La Grande R.
Eastmain R.
Eastmain
Rupert R.
Mistissini Lake
Mistissini
Eskasoni

Armstrong
Lake Nipigon
Savant Lake
Macdiarmid
Houlton
Lake Superior
Temagami
Barriere Lake
Winneway
Kanehsatake
Kahnewake
Lake Michigan
Lake Huron
Ottawa
Akwesasne
Manitoulin Island
Lake Ontario
Lake Erie

1

Celebrating survival

In November 1991, indigenous peoples who have somehow survived the 500-year holocaust brought from Europe gathered in Ottawa, Canada. They came from throughout the Americas – from the Arctic islands in the north through Mexico in the centre to Patagonia in the south.

They came to attend the Indigena 500 conference, convened to discuss the United Nations-sponsored celebration in 1992 of the arrival in their world of Christopher Columbus – something that none of them wanted to celebrate, given what has happened since. Aztec, Iroquois, Mayan, Ojibway, Inca, Algonquin, Carib, Cree, Cheyenne, Mapuche, Seminole, Moskito and dozens of others, adorned in their brilliant colours, wrapped in their *sarapes*, helmets, hats and embroidered tunics, speaking their many languages, joined together for a few days in this cold, grey northern capital. Ostensibly, they came to make plans for counteracting the Columbus celebrations, but they didn't do much decision-making. Instead, as one watched and listened, one had the feeling that these representatives of many peoples had come together mainly for the warmth of knowing that they all still exist.

For five days in the Canadian Museum of Civilization, they celebrated the symbols and practised the rituals that have held them distinct from the societies that have overrun them. From north to south their beliefs, rituals and values are similar. The elders and shamans found space in a museum corridor big enough to allow them to meet in a circle. But when they discovered that other groups – youth and women and political leaders – were meeting elsewhere, lined up behind desks in conference rooms, white-man's fashion, the elders sent out a peremptory message that all such meetings must cease,

1

and everyone must gather in a circle to talk together. For non-aboriginal observers like me, the symbolism of the circle, one of the most beautiful and profound ideas in the aboriginal universe, came to dominate the conference. The Oglala Sioux holy man Black Elk wrote, many decades ago:

> The Sun comes forth and goes down again in a circle, the Moon does the same, and both are round. Even the seasons form a great circle in their changing, and always come back again to where they were. The life of a man is a circle, from childhood to childhood, and so it is in everything where power moves.[1]

The Indigena 500 delegates came to celebrate the fruits of Earth (referred to in almost every speech as "our Mother Earth"). They prayed frequently, beat drums, blew horns, danced, chanted and sang at any time of the day they felt appropriate, holding up coca leaves, corn, potatoes – sacred objects in their religions. Each morning they invoked the blessing of smoke from sweetgrass before they did anything else, because they felt they had to make an offering to the Earth before they could start a meeting.

They spoke mystically of dreams and prophecies, and of tasks assigned through the mysterious power of these prophecies. They spoke of symbols – the four directions, the four seasons, the four colours of mankind. They spoke of obscure forces that somehow had brought them all to Ottawa. They all believed that each person follows a preordained path on his or her brief passage through life to the spirit world.

They spoke of things they had not done because "the time has not been right", and of things they must do because "only now has the time come". Only now is the time coming, they said, for fulfilment of the prophecy that was the symbol for the conference. That prophecy holds that the people started as one and were then dispersed, and that only when the northern eagle and the southern condor meet will they again be strong.

The conference was a rivetting experience, even for a white urban sceptic. These were people whose very survival was put in question from the moment we arrived in North America with our aggressive European technology, cultural arrogance and fanatical proselytizing religion. It is now believed that there were between 90 and 110 million aboriginal people in the Americas, of whom 90 per cent were killed or died in the first century after European contact – incomparably the most appalling holocaust in human history.[2]

For many native Americans, their survival is still in question. Every day, somewhere in this hemisphere, some of their people are being killed. One could understand when they expressed an almost naive euphoria: their conference validated for them the fact of their common survival.

Sure, the sceptic could not help asking questions. Are there not pompous, self-serving elders, portentous and dreary, as well as wise, profound and loveable ones? Of course, and some of them were there too. Can this aboriginal unity they all trumpet be as profound as they claim? Surely not, for as they moved on the last day to make decisions, bitter divisions emerged among them. Is not much of their indigenous religion, in which they now invest such hope, already heavily influenced by the very Christianity that tried so hard to destroy them, and came so close to succeeding? Of course: their prayers and chants carry Christian overlays, and many of their elders and leaders, so keenly espousing native values, are also practising Christians.

The ironies were evident from the opening ceremony in the museum's Great Hall, a spectacular architectural achievement, 100 metres from one end to the other, fifteen metres from floor to ceiling, with vast windows looking towards Parliament Hill across the Ottawa, a river that for centuries was the lifeline and heartbeat of the proud Algonquins, until they were driven off by European settlers not so very long ago. In this structure that Canadians have built especially to preserve the relics of a culture that for 200 years we tried vigorously to destroy, Rufino Paxi Limachi, an Aymara sacerdote from Bolivia, wrapped in a colourful embroidered robe, delivered up prayers and invocations from an Andean religion that has existed for thousands of years. While he chanted and sprinkled with flicking fingers the sacred liquid from the coca leaf, behind him stood a reconstructed nineteenth-century aboriginal house from British Columbia bearing this inscription:

> In memory of Chief Clelaman, who died July 1893, aged fifty years. He was honest and well-disposed, and respected by both whites and Indians. In December 1892 he gave away, with the help of his sons Alexander and Johnny, property in blankets, canoes, etc., valued at $14,000, this being his eighth large Potlatch and feast that he had held.

The inscription should say – but does not – that when Clelaman held his ceremony, the Potlatch was illegal. It had been banned by the Canadian government at the urging of missionaries and officials – even though it was the central institution of government and social order among west-coast aboriginal nations. Many were sent to jail for practising it. This was a cruel law, based on ignorance and prejudice. But like Limachi's Aymara religion, the Potlatch never disappeared. It merely went underground, until the law was repealed in 1951 after seven decades of desultory failure.

The inscription makes a point, although not the one intended. That it should stand unblushing in this immense building, into which the Canadian nation has poured its own wealth and genius, suggests the insouciance with which Canadians regard their past mistreatment of those who were here first. Our nation, it seems, is in need of a history lesson.

"After 500 years we are going to be reborn, dear brothers and sisters," cried Limachi. Then, to summon up the spirits, he blew a long, melancholy blast on an animal horn that he carried everywhere he went.

Half a dozen musicians from Ecuador, neat in white shirts and pants, black *sarapes* and little hats, sang of the oppression their people still suffer. Six young northern men, the Red Spirit Singers, sang and chanted a song about flight. Their dress: contemporary t-shirts and jackets bearing legends such as "Ocean Pacific" and "Ottawa West", and pictures of cyclists and basketball players. The contrast between Latin Americans and North Americans is striking, even among indigenous peoples.

Ovide Mercredi, a Cree from northern Manitoba and National Chief of Canada's Assembly of First Nations, told the visitors that as indigenous peoples of the western hemisphere they share a common destiny. The colonizing forces from Europe introduced imbalance to the hemisphere, he said. Those same forces today are pushing the world close to ecological disaster. Indigenous teachings about the need for balance within nature must be adopted soon if humanity is to survive into the twenty-first century.

Mercredi quoted the Cree Chief Poundmaker when he was released from prison in 1887 following the Riel rebellion in western Canada:

Our old way of life is gone. But that does not mean we should become imitation white men. Our beliefs are good. No man has yet shown me anything better.

"Right now," said Mercredi, "we are confused. We are struggling.... It is necessary to create change, but power is not something we should strive to possess. The experience of others shows that power possesses those who seek it."

Black Elk said:

In the old days when we were a strong and happy people, all our power came to us from the sacred hoop of the nation and so long as the hoop was unbroken the people flourished.

"We are not alone," said Mercredi. "Today we find fellow human beings who share our spirit for peace, justice and equality between peoples. The children of our ancestors and the children of our colonizers will have to join hands."

Black Elk said:

And I saw that the sacred hoop of my people was one of many hoops that made one circle, wide as daylight and as starlight, and in the centre grew one mighty flowering tree to shelter all the children of one mother and one father.... The flowering tree was the living centre of the hoop, and the circle of the four quarters nourished it. The East gave peace and light, the South gave warmth, the West gave rain, and the North with its cold and mighty wind gave strength and endurance.[3]

For a week in Ottawa, they talked about all this. While impatient younger spirits hungered for decisions and action, the older people chanted and smoked and thought about the world. They reaffirmed the circle.

"I am the circle," said Wilfred Pelletier, an Odawa from Wikwemikong, Manitoulin Island, in Lake Huron, who has lived in Ottawa for many years. "I have always been here. I will always be here, always. I live in each child. I have no beginning and no end."

At this remarkable international meeting, aboriginal Americans reaffirmed values that for generations they have secretly guarded against all attack. And they expressed their confidence that they can help all of us, all human beings on Earth, to find our way to a viable future.

2

The education of
a white man

This book distils one man's education in twenty-five years of meeting, talking to and learning from aboriginal people in Canada. It is an education that relatively few Euro-Canadians have had. I have been fortunate. The experience has enriched my life immeasurably.

The book's structure is based on two interwoven strands. One describes aboriginal people I have met in their communities across the country, and what they have shown and told me about their history and about the way they think and live. The second documents prejudiced policies that, since the first days of the European invasion, have been wrapped around the aboriginal people like the tentacles of an octopus, squeezing the life out of them. I have found, in discussing this with Canadians, that it is sometimes hard for us to accept that such painful things have happened here. When one group in our society has been treated for so long as an amorphous, distant, mysterious mass, it requires an effort to realize that in fact they are just like the rest of us, but with the distinction that they have survived terrible trials imposed on them by history. At long last they are emerging into a new era of self-determination and into the political consciousness of Canadians, helping to point us in new directions.

My own experience began towards the end of 1968, when I was assigned by the now-defunct *Montreal Star* to write a series of articles investigating the conditions, said to be desperate, of Indians living in some of the inaccessible villages of northwestern Ontario. I had met few Indians before, and had never been in an Indian community. Like most Canadians, I had heard that native people were in a poor way, and historically had suffered gross injustices. But to know this, and to witness it, are very different things.

When I returned to Montreal, I reported that without ever leaving Ontario I had been on a journey through the pages of a nineteenth-century Russian novel. Maybe some day, I wrote, an Ojibway Tolstoy, a Cree Dostoevsky, an Iroquois Gorki would arise, because lying at hand in the Canadian hinterland was human material as rich in drama, as complex in character, as intense in gaiety and sadness as anything those great novelists wrote about.[1]

Something like this has, in fact, happened. In the last ten years there has been an explosion of books, plays, poems, music and works of art by aboriginals, much of it of very fine quality, part of that great rebirth of native spirit which I try to describe in this book.

Introduced to the double standard

On my first trip in 1968, I went to Armstrong, Ontario, a small village north of Lake Nipigon, inaccessible by road. At one end of town, the federal government maintained a spiffy radar station as part of the mid-Canada warning system of that time; at the other end, a group of Ojibway people, with the official status of squatters, were huddled in a collection of appalling tarpaper shacks. Both communities were the responsibility of the federal government. One had mess halls and recreation facilities and comfortable houses and all the comforts that money could buy; the other was totally neglected. Thus, in my first visit to an aboriginal community, I was exposed in the most unforgettable way to the double standard Canadians applied in their dealings with aboriginal people.

In giving me this assignment, my editor, the late Frank Walker, had suggested that I should not write just one series and then drop the subject, but should follow it up. He had once worked with the Hudson's Bay Company, and unlike most editors, had had many dealings with native people and had visited many of their communities. I was happy to follow up the story. In two decades as a reporter, I had seen how disadvantaged people – the poor, the blacks, the Indians, the immigrants, the maimed, halt and lame – were repeatedly used by the press as raw material to build circulation, or, in slow periods, to fill up space with gripping, heart-rending stories. A newspaper's concern was seldom – one could almost say never – with the amelioration of the conditions being described. The customary thing was to knock off a quick, bleeding-heart piece about the raw deal given to Indians, their shocking housing, their dreadful poverty, their high death rates and chronic diseases. The reporter would go away, but maybe another would return in a year or two, to find the same conditions unchanged, ready and waiting for another bleeding-heart series.

In the ensuing years, I wrote dozens of articles and a couple of books about native people across the country, and made films about and with them. I travelled to native communities in northern Quebec, the Northwest Territories, northern Alberta, Manitoba and British Columbia. At first, of course, I was appalled by living conditions on the reserves, and indignant at the unjust way aboriginals had been, and were being, treated. But within a year or two, I began to transcend the Euro-Canadian, liberal conception of aboriginals as classic victims. Wherever I went, I began to talk to the elders. I came in touch, for the first time in my life, with people who had lived their lives in intimate connection with nature. The hunting communities were full of old men and women who had spent their lives at work in the bush every winter, but were now, because of failing health, confined to the villages by order of the public health nurse. This was deeply disorienting for them. They themselves had pulled their own fathers behind them on sleds in the days when no one was considered too old to go into the bush. Even when they couldn't hunt themselves, the experience and wisdom of the elders had always been the guiding spirit in the hunting camp. Now, to meet the needs of health and education systems introduced into their communities from outside, the elders were left behind in the village, effectively emasculated in their function as teachers and advisers. When I approached them, I found they were delighted to be asked about their lives, and loved to talk. The shy, suspicious, taciturn aboriginals of the stereotype disappeared, replaced by talkative, amusing, warm and welcoming people. As I began to appreciate the extraordinary depth of their knowledge, the fact that aboriginals had for so long been treated by Canadian society as more or less worthless became for me the very exemplar of our cultural arrogance.

Just as I became involved with aboriginal people, they themselves were beginning to organize seriously as a political force. In 1968 the Liberal government of Lester B. Pearson had just concluded a nationwide consultation of aboriginal people about their wishes for the future. This was the first major effort by a Canadian government to canvass native opinion. The proceedings of the many meetings were recorded in thirty or so red-covered volumes, and it caused some amusement in the Department of Indian Affairs when I asked for copies of all of them. Because I was able to set my own working hours at the *Star*, I had time to read all thirty volumes, and then write a very long story about them. It was unheard-of at the time for a major newspaper to give so much space to such esoteric material; the bureaucrats at Indian Affairs were astonished. Even more astonished several months later were the aboriginals, when the newly installed Trudeau government proposed to end the federal trustee relationship with them and transfer the responsibility to the provinces. In all the consultation meetings designed to discover Indian opinion, no one had asked for this. Talk about cultural arrogance!

All these years later I am still following up the aboriginal story. I'm not sure if it has chosen me, or I have chosen it. I am a white, middle-class guy from the cities. I have never hunted in my life, have little interest in tramping the wilderness, and am nervous in canoes. Aboriginals were just one of many subjects that I covered in my newspaper career. I began as a sports reporter; later wrote a column from London on the English theatre; became a specialist in urban problems and planning; and from 1968 wrote a great deal about development and pollution – the environment, as it is now called.

So, before going any further, I feel I should explain where I am coming from, as they say nowadays, and why I have written this book.

An egalitarian upbringing

Since I was a youngster, I have always been concerned with social issues. Newspapers do provide a window on society, and I started to work in print journalism when I left high school in 1945 in Invercargill, a small town in the South Island of New Zealand. Itchy feet took me to Australia, India, England, Scotland, Ontario and Manitoba before I wound up in Montreal. I was always painfully aware – in fact it became an article of faith with me – that the newspapers I worked for were owned by rich people who used them as vehicles to represent the interests of their class, and to oppose, usually with great vehemence and even viciousness, the interests of working people and the disadvantaged. I had been brought up in an egalitarian society, in an egalitarian time, and that early conditioning has stuck with me. My view of politics is that it is a never-ending struggle between the haves and the have-nots, with all the artillery in the hands of the haves.

Given these attitudes, there were built-in limits to my career in newspapers. In 1971 I quit *The Montreal Star* to become a freelance journalist. Perhaps I had been following up the aboriginal story too assiduously; in any event, my bosses shed no tears at my departure. They knew, as well as I, that I was always in a state of internal rebellion against the worldview of whatever newspaper I was working for.

These attitudes may explain why I hung in, as it were, on the aboriginal story; and why it came as no surprise to me in 1968 to find that the Indians, then a seemingly helpless and largely invisible minority, had always been, and were still being, treated with the most casual brutality. Among the many victims of a capital-owning industrial society, the Indians were, and are, the least fortunate of all. Like other disadvantaged groups, they suffer discrimination on grounds of race, colour and class; but they are also singled out for distrust and contempt because of the unaccommodating strangeness of their culture, economy and value system. When I began to read extensively about them, I realized that for nearly two centuries Canadian society had not needed Indians for anything, and had made every effort to shove them aside, out of sight and out of mind. Even to abolish them, get rid of them. History proves it.

Thus I was predisposed to protest when, in 1971, the Quebec government of Premier Robert Bourassa decided to build a huge hydroelectric project in the hunting territories of the James Bay Crees. I had visited these people on assignment a year or so before, and had described how their land rights had been violated. When the James Bay Crees suddenly came into the news, I was almost the only reporter extant who even knew they existed. A week after Bourassa's announcement, I was invited to appear on television and say what I thought of the project. I said the Indians should go to court to stop it. Later, the Sierra Club asked me to write a book about the proposed development. I travelled to the area again, producing some articles about the Crees' opposition to the project. The book was published, *James Bay: The Plot to Drown the North Woods*, a root-and-branch onslaught on the proposal. Then, in the summer of 1972, the Indians of Quebec Association suggested I might like to make a film around a scientific task force they were sending into the region.

With two friends and a camera, I travelled to Fort George and up the La Grande River in the middle of summer. Only one of us had ever made a film before. We were short of money, equipment and expertise. We stumbled around in the bush from one mistake to another, a comic and even farcical experience. But somehow we managed to get a film made called *Job's Garden*. The film was built around a wonderful couple, Job Bearskin and his wife Mary. Neither had ever been to school; neither could speak French or English; neither had ever been anywhere much, except up and down their beloved river every year of their lives.

Job talked always of the wilderness as being "like a garden", a place where plants, animals and people grew and prospered every year. In contrast, a young helicopter pilot who had been flying around the area for Hydro-Quebec for eighteen months told us that the area was "one of the most barren in the world today, scraped clean by glaciers centuries ago, and virtually nothing has grown here since". The cultural divide between the Indians, with their profound knowledge of the country and the way it worked, and the engineers, who saw in it only megawatts of electrical generating capacity, could not have been more neatly encapsulated.

In those days, whenever Indians appeared on television they would go unnamed, simply regarded as members of an anonymous and mysterious group that was usually creating some kind of problem, while every non-Indian would be identified by name and function. This was a visible symptom of a cultural disease, and now that I had the chance, I determined to turn it on its head. In *Job's Garden* every Indian on screen or on the sound track was identified, while the few white people in the film remained as anonymous as the machines they were driving. I have never made the pretence, then or since, of being "objective", as it is laughably called. I figure, as I have all my life, that the people in charge have no trouble getting their message out, and I have no intention of helping them do so. *Job's Garden*, for all its technical crudeness, was very much liked by the Crees of James Bay because for once they had a chance to say their piece. And making the film had a big effect on me: having met the Crees, young and old, having been exposed to the gentle wisdom of Job and Mary Bearskin, and their profound understanding of the human role on this Earth, it became for me a decent objective to do whatever I could – not that it was much – to help them defend their way of life.

For the next three years, while the Crees battled valiantly against the project that would destroy their homeland as they had known it, most of my energies went into making a pair of films for the National Film Board about the Cree hunting life and the aboriginal rights of native people across Canada. This time we did not lack money or expertise. I was teamed as co-director with a superb NFB cameraman, Tony Ianzelo, who generously taught me how to make a film.

For the Cree film, a hunter called Sam Blacksmith agreed to let us spend time with him on his territory far north of Chibougamau, in the wilderness east of James Bay. We made two visits, one before freeze-up in the autumn, as the hunters took the census of the animals on their territory (approaching the task with the precision of scientists), and another in March, as they struggled out of a hard season in which big game had been notably absent. We were able to show in impressive detail the personalities of the individuals in the hunting camp; Cree Hunters of Mistassini, distinguished as it is by Tony's wonderful photography, became one of the most popular films on Indians ever made in Canada. It has been broadcast on television all over the world, and is still being used in school and university courses almost twenty years later.

During pauses between filming and editing, I was able to witness much of the Crees' momentous court battle, in which they sought and won – for only one week – an injunction to stop the James Bay project. When the court case was over I wrote another book, this one about James Bay Cree life, Strangers Devour the Land, published in Canada and the United States. By that time I had become irrevocably linked with the James Bay Crees. They were quite different from any people I'd ever met, and I had come to admire and like them enormously.

A long learning process
It took time to open my mind to the aboriginal style of life and values. I can remember the exact moment when I began to get the hang of what they were all about.

On my first visit to Mistassini, I had met a young woman, Edna Neeposh, a social worker in Chibougamau, who had attended college. Edna told me that she had just returned from the bush with her family, and how wonderful it had been. I marvelled that anybody could possibly enjoy being in a tent in forty-below-zero weather, and I don't think I really believed her when she said she loved it. But I finally understood two years later, when a friend, Phillip Awashish of Mistassini, took me one February into his father's hunting camp. We flew into one of the hundreds of tiny, snow-enshrouded lakes north-west of the enormous Mistassini Lake. Their camp was visible from the air mainly because of the smoke curling up from a tent snuggled into the vast, trackless wilderness. We walked up from the shore past the animal bones hanging in the trees, the piles of split firewood, the sleds and snowshoes lying around.

We picked up the tent flap that served as a door, and walked from that frozen and overpowering winter world into the warmest, cosiest, sweetest-smelling place you could imagine. The spruce boughs freshly laid on the floor every three or four days filled the tent with a wonderful aroma, compounded by the smell of cooking beaver hanging all day by a string from the roof, beside the radiating heat from the wood stove. The family lay around on blankets and rugs, exuding an air of contentment and leisure which was immediately captivating. The children, the freest children I have ever seen in Canada, ran around playing joyfully but with what seemed an inbred discipline. This camp was not only their playground, but their school and their workplace. Suddenly I knew what Edna had been talking about; I knew what Indians meant when they said that they felt really at home only in their own environment. I knew that out here they were the masters, and that in the cities, even in the villages, they were diminished. This was the moment when my education in the realities of aboriginal Canada began. From that moment, I knew there was a different dimension to Canadian life than anything I had understood before, and that it was something of inestimable value.

Until I met aboriginals, I had never thought of human beings as participants in a natural system that is endlessly recycled, with every element dependent on every other element. I had always behaved as if society were perfectible; had never given thought to life as a natural continuum, in which we also are called upon to act as stewards for future generations. Gradually, I began to understand that all of my assumptions about social progress, personal achievement and human control over the hostile forces of nature are not necessarily proper measures of a meaningful human existence.

I also began to understand that for aboriginals, my Western-based attitudes were mere alien baggage. Concern about their material conditions, their housing, poverty and health, although important, somehow did not touch them where it mattered. Approached only with these considerations in mind, Indians inevitably appeared a helpless, almost hopeless lot, always at a disadvantage compared to the aggressive, successful people who surrounded them. When I was able to set aside these assumptions, aboriginal people no longer appeared to be so helpless. Wise, perhaps, would be closer to the mark. Calm. Contemplative. Patient. Although, admittedly, sad.

Between the late 1970s and mid-1980s, I moved on to other interests. For some years my energy was absorbed in making documentary films about China for the National Film Board. For another NFB assignment I investigated the history of the Aluminun Company of Canada (ALCAN) and its behaviour in various parts of the world as a typical multinational resource corporation. The ALCAN film got produced, but received limited distribution. The NFB was not comfortable with the film; it contained too much of my disenchantment with the wealthy and powerful. Through all these years, my interest in aboriginals remained. I was commissioned to write an overview of Canada's native people for publication in Mexico by the journal of the Interamerican Indian Union; this set me off on a round of intense reading that deepened my knowledge of the subject. Later I received a commission from the Canadian Council on Children and Youth to write a non-stereotyped history of native people for use in high schools. I wrote the book, but the Council could not find a publisher for it. I cannot say with certainty that it would have improved education in Canada, but I do know that writing the book was important for my own education about the historical treatment of natives in this country.

A new generation of aboriginal politics

During the 1980s a new generation of Canadian aboriginal leaders came into office. Gradually, they were beginning to make their voices heard as an integral part of political discourse. Aboriginal and treaty rights were recognized in the Canadian Constitution of 1982, certainly a step forward; but in practice, the willingness of society to improve the state of aboriginal people was still honoured more in the breach than the observance. There were changes, especially in the quantity and level of education that aboriginals were receiving. But living conditions on many reserves remained desperate, and the Métis people continued to be grossly disadvantaged. The many thousands of aboriginal people who drifted to the cities in the '70s and '80s had to struggle against blatant discrimination that reduced them to economic and social inferiority.

The federal government said it was willing to deal with aboriginal land claims, but the claims procedure dragged along so slowly that by 1987 the assembled chiefs decided it was time for their people to take more direct action. No longer willing to watch passively as immense wealth was taken from their lands and they were left behind in poverty, aboriginal people across the country began to hold sit-ins, blockades, demonstrations and marches in defence of territory that they still had a stake in, but that was being despoiled for industrial purposes by the dominant society. Lubicon Lake, Temagami, Haida Gwai, and many other names joined James Bay in the news, becoming familiar to non-native Canadians as causes worthy of their support.

I again became more actively involved when the Assembly of First Nations asked me to edit a book, *Drumbeat*, written by various chiefs describing their conflicts with the government. In 1988 I began to make a film about the struggle of a group of Algonquins who live at Barriere Lake, in the headwaters of the Ottawa River, to defend their way of life by bringing clearcut logging to a halt. The name of that film describes my viewpoint on this subject. We called it *Blockade: Algonquins Defend the Forest*, which suggests that the native people are doing our job for us. I was busy with that film when the series of events occurred that transformed, probably forever, the relationship between aboriginals and other Canadians.

The first of these events was the action by Elijah Harper, a Cree member of the Manitoba legislature, to prevent singlehandedly the province's ratification of the Meech Lake constitutional accord in June 1990. For the first time in modern Canadian history, native people were able to intervene decisively in a matter of essential importance to all non-native Canadians. The intervention was so much in line with the feelings of ordinary Canadians about the accord, and was carried out with such dignity and intelligence, that the image of aboriginal people as a political force was transformed at a single stroke.

At about the same time, the Quebec government cranked up its James Bay hydro project once more, this time with an even more grandiose scheme for spending some $48 billion on completing the work of damming the Crees' traditional rivers. Although the atmosphere in the country was now more favourable towards aboriginal claims, and various governments were protesting their willingness to meet aboriginal needs, their sincerity was severely tested in the renewed James Bay case. Both the Quebec and federal governments had committed themselves in the James Bay and Northern Quebec Agreement of 1975 to conducting intensive social and environmental assessments of any further development within the territory; but now both went to court to argue that they were not bound to fulfil these undertakings. Once again – the record is wearisomely familiar from history – the aboriginal people were left to conclude that Canadians and their governments could not be trusted to keep their word. The Crown arguments were so weak that one judge described them as "ludicrous": with their loss in court, the governments were forced to honour their legal responsibilities. This delayed the construction schedule for the damming of Great Whale River by several years.

I was asked by a production company in Toronto to make a film bringing the story up to date as part of a television series, *As Long As the Rivers Flow*, dealing with aboriginal self-government. So once again, after an interval of fourteen years, I travelled north to James Bay, talked to many old friends, heard their concerns about the impact of the hydro dams on their way of life, and recorded the many environmental, social and psychological changes that they have had to contend with. The film, *Flooding Job's Garden*, was shown on educational networks across the country.

This time the James Bay Crees had the resources to fight the government's proposal; with the support of New England environmentalists, they waged a superbly orchestrated public-relations campaign in the United States, which resulted in the cancellation of the huge Hydro-Quebec contracts to supply power to New York state.

Through these events, the place of aboriginals in Canadian society was gradually transformed: but by far the most decisive event came in the summer of 1990, with the armed resistance of the Mohawks of Kanehsatake (Oka) and Kahnawake, near Montreal, to the takeover of a piece of land they regarded as sacred. This time, non-native opinion was less favourable than to the scuttling of the Meech Lake Accord. Understandably, many people had severe reservations about armed insurrection as a means of obtaining political goals in a modern nation. Yet whatever one's reservations, it is impossible to deny that with this action, the aboriginals finally broke through into the consciousness of the mass of Canadians. Now it became clear to everyone that things were desperately wrong among the aboriginals, and that at last serious action to deal with their problems was imperative.

This change of status explains why the election in 1991 of Ovide

Mercredi, an articulate Cree lawyer, as National Chief of the Assembly of First Nations was greeted with such interest and enthusiasm; and why, at Mercredi's urging, such a prominent place was accorded to aboriginals in the constitutional negotiations leading up to the Charlottetown Accord of 1992. Aboriginal leaders were included in the negotiating process, something that had previously been denied to them. In the accord itself, the native peoples' inherent right to self-government was recognized, and it was proposed that they should become a third order of government, alongside the provinces and the federal power. This was regarded by most people as a tremendous breakthrough. Even those who opposed the accord on other grounds usually went out of their way to say that they favoured the change in the status of aboriginals. Something, however, happened on the way to the polling station. While the Métis, non-status Indian and Inuit leaders claimed their people voted in favour of the accord, Indians on the reserves decided overwhelmingly to reject the proposals. Although Prime Minister Mulroney threatened before the vote that the aboriginals would never get another such agreement (and therefore would be cutting off their nose to spite their face by opposing it), many other people believed that the Charlottetown proposals for native self-government could be reintroduced without recourse to a constitutional amendment.

The genesis of this book

Like my other involvements with aboriginal issues over the years, my decision to write this book grew out of things I was already doing. Because of the intense interest generated by the Elijah Harper action, the Oka crisis, and the election of Ovide Mercredi, *Reader's Digest* magazine asked me early in 1991 to travel across the country and write two articles on the native people of Canada. The *Digest* financed a generous travel schedule that took me among the Mikmaqs of Nova Scotia, the Ojibway and Algonquins of Ontario and Quebec, the Crees of Manitoba, the Métis of the west, the Carriers and Gitksan people of northern British Columbia, and the urban Indians of Winnipeg and Regina. Since I could use in the magazine articles only a fraction of the material I gathered, I determined to write a book, combining my information with other materials gathered over the past quarter-century.

What most impressed me in my travels across the country was the great social and spiritual revival underway among aboriginal people. Everywhere I found them recovering from the traumatic disease of alcoholism, turning back to aboriginal rituals and ceremonies, undergoing native healing processes, espousing the beliefs they inherited from their forebears, and asserting their independence in an entirely healthy way. That is a story well worth telling in itself. But it is also true that Canadians do not understand what has been done to aboriginal people in our name, especially in the last century, and that if we are to redress the wrongs of the past, we can do so only in the knowledge of what has happened in history.

Hence my book based on my trip for *Reader's Digest* gradually became more complex. I found myself drawing on the memories of past journeys to aboriginal communities. I found it essential to include the history of the various nations I have visited as they themselves have experienced it, for this is a history never taught in our schools; just to know it changes our concept of our country. I then saw the need to explain as clearly as I could exactly where Canada's past Indian policy came from, how it originated in a prejudiced view of aboriginal people, and how our legislatures and laws have been used to attack everything of importance to the first inhabitants. This is the formidable national legacy that we must now work to overcome, if we are at last to include aboriginal people as full partners in Canadian society.

I have met many wonderful aboriginal people over the years, and have much to thank them for. In spite of everything they have suffered and are still suffering, the natives of Canada retain inherited values such as sharing, foresight, restraint, tolerance and co-operation, which are exactly the qualities most needed today if the human race is to survive in good order.[2] The aboriginal people themselves are aware that they have much to offer as humanity struggles to handle the rampaging technologies that are so dramatically degrading that "fragile miracle we call the biosphere"[3] – the air, waters, soils and vegetation that we all depend on.

I believe we have come to a critical moment in our evolution as a society. The aboriginal people are just at the beginning of a great rebirth of everything that is best in their values, qualities and beliefs. And it is time for us, too, to understand and accept responsibility for what we have done, and to work with them for a better future.

3

Snapshots from
past and present

The story of aboriginal life as told to me over a quarter-century has retained an essential consistency. When I first went out to aboriginal reserves and communities in 1968, I met many people who were suffering – indeed, who had been traumatized by their suffering; and when I returned in the 1990s, many of the stories I heard were strikingly similar. The kind of people I met, and the things they told me, are not things one can easily forget. It seems from what I have seen and heard that in Canada, aboriginals are the people who have been chosen to suffer the most. That terrible knowledge has always informed everything I have written about aboriginal life.

Past: in a tavern an old man sat

In a tavern in the village of Armstrong, Ontario, in 1968, an old man sat propped against the wall, his eyes cast to the ground. They said that in his younger days he'd been one of the best trappers in the north. He had a leathery, weather-worn face, high cheekbones, a withdrawn sort of dignity. He took the occasional swig from a bottle, but appeared oblivious to everyone around him.

My friend Willie John called over to him gently. "Did you ever know Sagan Kushkan?"

"Sagan Kushkan?" asked the old man, looking up. "No," he said, in Ojibway. "I never met him. I heard of him, but I never met him."

"Sagan Kushkan – appearing from the clouds," said my friend. "That was my Dad."

My friend turned away from the old man and muttered, "He has buried his sixteen children."

The whole community – the Ojibway community, that is; their white neighbours knew nothing of this – was heavy with the old man's tragedy. The last of the sixteen, Johnny, a steady worker, a quiet and decent boy, had been killed a few days before by another quiet and decent boy in a drunken brawl.

The police had arrested the killer and taken Johnny's body south to Fort William, 300 miles by rail and road in those days, for an autopsy. There, their examination finished, the police had released the body, although there was no one to take care of it. The old man had to borrow $78 to get someone to send his son's body back.

When the tavern closed, the old man stood up. He had one leg shorter than the other. He'd been like that since birth. Some of the younger people took him home, for he had nowhere else to go. Next morning we went to see him in the tiny shack where he'd spent the night. Willie John, then working for the Company of Young Canadians, a federally-funded youth corps of development workers, took all the particulars and promised to help him get the money back.

Later that day, all three of us left town on the same train, headed back east towards Longlac. When we came to a place called Mud River, just a railway hut in the bush, the old man climbed down and headed for his own little shack, where he lived by himself, alone with his memories of his dead wife and sixteen children. The last I saw of him – an unforgettable image – he was hobbling away along the railway line, disappearing into the trees, rock and snow of the northern wilderness.

A story from Gorki, for sure.

Present: Foster child

Contemporary Indian life is still charged with intense drama.

On April 16, 1991, I talked with Wayne Christian, a Shuswap and former foster child, now director of the Round Lake Addiction Treatment Centre near Vernon, British Columbia.

"One day in 1966 when I was twelve, I returned to my home in the Spallumcheen reserve [just north of the Okanagan Valley] from a trip with some friends to the United States, and found our house really quiet. My mother was there. She told me the welfare had taken the kids and were coming back for me. There were ten of us kids, and we were all taken.

"I still don't know what the circumstances were. Our people used

20

to go across the border into Washington state to Oroville or Omak, to pick apples.They would leave the children with their grandparents, but in our communities, if there were not two parents at home at all times, non-native social workers interpreted that as neglect.

"My mother was not a drinker. She was not really assertive or verbal, she had no recourse even to say 'I can look after them.' I was devastated. I still harbour a lot of anger about it.

"I was placed in local communities. Myself and some of my brothers and sisters were put into homes in Armstrong [B.C.], a few miles south of the reserve. I was in three different homes. I stayed there from the age of twelve to eighteen. At thirteen I contemplated suicide. I could not understand why my mother allowed this.

"I went to school in the Armstrong system. It was tough. I used to fight a lot. I always had to prove my toughness. I began to hang around with a crowd who accepted me for who I was. We came into conflict with the law. We stole motorcycles, guns. I ended up in jail for four weeks. I decided I didn't want that kind of life.

"I was in jail in August and returned to school in September hoping to take my finals. The principal was not going to let me in. My foster parent intervened on my behalf, talked to the school board chairman and got me back in. That was a turning point for me. It's hard to explain what happened. It changed my attitude. I felt I owed it to them to try."

From then on Wayne Christian did well in school, but by the time he entered university, he had not had much to do with his own people for many years. Mainly through the native student union, he was able to get back in touch with his identity as a Shuswap.

He became involved in native issues. He took part in a nine-day occupation of the Indian Affairs offices in Vernon, and committed himself to the native cause. The band brought him back to the reserve to work in education. He became a councillor, then the chief. Because of his personal experience, his priority was to get control over child welfare.

Others of Wayne's family came back to the reserve but they did not all survive the pounding as well as he had. "On December 10, 1978, my brother committed suicide. He was seventeen or eighteen at the time. He had been away for so long. I had a hard time trying to help him. He had tried to kill himself before, but this time, he killed himself with my rifle.

"I woke up that morning. He was gone. Twenty-five yards away I found him. It was snowing. I was totally devastated.... It was not from drinking. Friends had tried to help him. He used to walk for miles and miles. He was really tortured by something, and we could never find out what it was.

"That completely disoriented me. It caused me to re-evaluate my whole attitude. Right when that happened, one of our mothers was in the process of having four boys apprehended by the provincial government. Each member of council had a similar story within their own family. But this was the '60s. We looked into the statistics and found out that from our community of 300, 100 children had been taken and put in non-Indian homes. We now call it 'the '60s scoop'.

"At the time we had lots of kids running away from foster and group homes, coming back to the reserve, searching for their identity. They came with all sorts of horror stories of physical and sexual abuse. They were lost. A lot of them did not even know who their blood relations were."

Wayne Christian decided to move into action. He organized a march of more than a thousand Indians on Victoria, the provincial capital, demanding that natives be permitted to control their own children.

Within two years, under his leadership, Spallumcheen declared its own jurisdiction. They simply told the federal and provincial governments, "We are running this from now on." Rather mysteriously, the governments went along with it. The Minister of Indian Affairs and Northern Development has forty days to disallow any bylaw that an Indian band might pass. He disallows hundreds every year, but for some reason the minister at the time, John Munro, neither disallowed the Spallumcheen by-law, nor allowed it. As a result, the band still has the only native child-welfare system in Canada that has not been delegated from a white jurisdiction.

In the early '80s, Wayne Christian became a leading organizer of the constitutional express that descended on Ottawa from all parts of the country, moved across to Britain and Europe, and succeeded finally in entrenching aboriginal rights in the 1982 Constitution.

Eventually he moved from his chieftainship to become director of the Round Lake Treatment Centre, not far from his home reserve. This is a beautiful, tranquil place on an isolated lake, where native staff work with native addicts, using traditional ceremonials and methods to connect their disoriented patients with their heritage.

At the age of thirty-seven, having survived the worst that Canadian society can do to him, he has become one of the significant native leaders in the country. Is his story, with its mixture of private triumph and public tragedy, not worthy of Thomas Hardy?

Past: Cecilia Kwandibens

I remember Cecilia Kwandibens from 1968. I could never forget her. While we were in Armstrong, Ontario, she came to see Willie John. A heavy, slow-moving, painfully shy woman, she held two or three envelopes she'd received from some government office or other, containing stuff that she really couldn't get quite clear in her head.

She lived in a shack at Ferland, forty miles to the east on the CNR tracks, right at the head of Lake Nipigon, five or ten miles along from Mud River. She was thirty-three, a mother of five, and looked fifty. Her husband, forty, had broken a leg that had failed to mend, and could work only fitfully. They had no electricity. Cecilia had to carry her water from a local creek half a mile away, and had nothing large to store it in.

She tucked her feet under the chair and spoke to Willie in a voice so soft he could hardly hear. She had come to town to pick up her welfare cheque, $105 a month. It came in those days in the form of a voucher cashable only for food or clothing at one of the two local stores. This was a measure designed by the people who controlled Indians to prevent them from spending their money on liquor. But no control was placed on the prices the stores could charge. This voucher was the only income Cecilia had for her entire family. Since she had no cash, she had to get money from her father-in-law for the train fare to come to town.

When Cecilia's children had been away at residential school, the monthly family allowance cheque went to the school. Now the children were going to school in Ferland, where she lived, but the family allowance cheques had not resumed. Presumably the money was still being sent to the school. That was what the letters were about that she fingered so gingerly. Willie showed her what to sign, and she went off, more or less relieved.

Cecilia Kwandibens was Number 266 in the Whitesands band, reserve number 81, somewhere along the western shore of Lake Nipigon. During the Second World War, when there was nothing to do at the reserve, the people had left and gathered in tents and huts

23

around the whistle stops along the CNR line – Armstrong, Ferland, Mud River, Auden. Once they had left the reserve, they were regarded by the government as squatters on land they had always thought was theirs. Later, when I asked the Indian agent in Thunder Bay to look up the history of that reserve and tell me about it, he refused to do so. He evidently thought it better not to talk too much about stuff like that.

Present: Street drunk

I spoke to Randy Councillor, now director of the detoxification centre in Kenora, Ontario, on February 22, 1991:

"I was a street drunk for twenty-two of my forty-two years. I drank all over the towns and cities of this area – Thunder Bay, Winnipeg, American cities.

"My family on one side was Métis out of Red River; my father's side was very traditional Ojibway. My mother was a staunch Catholic; my father was a medicine man. At age five I had visions that I would be a medicine man, and belong to my father's society, but I became very confused between the two teachings. At the age of eight my grandfather and my father took me on a sixty-mile journey, gave me a little blanket and a pipe, flew my eagle feathers, and left me there. I was scared. I cried for four days and nights alone, nobody within sixty miles of me. After eight days and nights without eating, they picked me up again. They put me through special ceremonies to revive me, gave me a cup of soup, allowed me to sleep, and held a sweat lodge.

"When I reflect on it I can see that I was scared to be a medicine man. At thirteen I became a very troubled child. I walked out of high school. My father said, 'Now you have decided you are not going to continue your education, you must be man enough to fend for yourself.' I hated my father for that.

"I left home with the most meagre belongings. I drifted to Thunder Bay. An Italian family adopted me. I got my education, but I was hanging around with flower children. I began to drink. I got my pipefitter's certificate, and a job as a welder in the shipyards. I would work in the day, but get drunk at night. I was eight years out there like that.

"I was searching but I did not know what I was searching for. I went to pow-wows. When I look back at it, I have come to believe I was ashamed to be an Indian. When asked, I would say I was a half-breed. Why I was ashamed, I do not know.

"The only reason I became sober, thirteen years ago, is that I lost two brothers, very dear to me, eleven days apart. One committed suicide, the other drowned. Both were non-drinkers. I tried to get help from my father, the medicine man, but he was in the process of mourning, and could not extend help to me. He advised me to quit drinking, and I took his advice.

"When I finally came back to my father, I was tired. I found the answer to my search in my community. The key was held by my father. I could not run away from what they had set out for me to be. So I had to quit fighting it, and accept it. My father started to teach me the principles, ethics, way of life of our own people. I knew what I needed to do. I was fortunate my mother was still alive to support me. I started learning.

"I have since been practising to be a medicine man. My family tree descends from the medicinal society. I am working with people almost every day. It is something you are gifted with. But what my father did, I cannot do a lot of those things.

"Today I have five ceremonial drums, three left by my father, the other two are my own. They are very sacred to us. We do not take them to contemporary pow-wows, but keep them for use in special rites within the community.

"Each tribe seems to be engulfed by cultural displacement. Sometimes I wonder if it is not a design by the general society to wipe out something. If you look at it as a native person, from our own culture, we have to compete with the academic system, seven hours a day, and with TV at home. So we have left only an hour and a half a day, and in that time you cannot teach a child his own language. Our language is dying, that is the first sign of deterioration.

"Our native style of life has to be based on four elements – heritage, culture, values, language – and if you take one away it begins to break down. Then we have the symptoms of this breakdown, alcoholism and abuse. We have been blinded by money, new ideas, electoral systems that are breaking up our communities, but more and more, we are reverting to our customs. The whole trend of the new generation is focussed on that.

"We have to take responsibility for ourselves. All these problems we face were not only created systematically, but we allowed it all to happen. Only recently have we started to make some sort of movement to bring it all to the public's view. It is very sad for me at my age to see something that has happened in my lifetime, such as the abuses in the residential school system, coming to the forefront, when we know all that should have been dealt with twenty years ago. I guess we had to go through that agony and pain. We seem only now to have come to the ability to cut off those chains that imprisoned us from talking about it. Society was not ready to accept that something like this could exist in Canada.

"My personal goal has been to understand this Canadian culture that has devastated our way of life. I felt I would be able to understand society in general, and be able to forgive a lot of these things we were suffering.

"Something is going to come out of all this that will be a mixture of both societies. Then perhaps we can learn to live side by side without saying, 'You are Indian,' and 'You are white.'

"I hope to see the day when we acknowledge each other as persons."

4

We're civilized, you're savage

The entire history of Europeans in North America has been built on the assumption that we are superior to the people who were here when we arrived. This assumption seems to have come to us easily, and early. In 1496 Henry VII of England described John Cabot's task, when he commissioned him to sail across the Atlantic, as "to conquer, occupy and possess" the lands of "heathens and infidels".[1]

We haven't changed. As recently as 1991, Chief Justice Allan McEachern of the British Columbia Supreme Court, after an exhaustive inquiry, concluded that before Columbus the aboriginal nations were barbarous, primitive, and unequal to any nation of Europeans.[2]

On arriving as settlers, our forebears had to invent language capable of describing what they were doing so that they wouldn't feel bad about it. The aboriginal inhabitants had to be demonized in the minds of all right-thinking men and women. It took about fifty years to pull off this trick, which has turned out to have been one of the most important and lasting achievements of the colonizers, influencing public attitudes throughout the Americas to this day.

Even before they arrived, the prospective settlers had already equated the idea of civilization with their own way of life; yet it was still not normal English usage to apply the word "savage" to human beings, and, when it was so used, no pejorative sense was implied. A 1566 description of the destruction of a Huguenot colony in Carolina mentioned "savages", but added that they were "kind and gentle". An account of Florida at about the same time also described the Indians as gentle, and did not even mention savages. In 1580, John Florio, who translated Jacques Cartier's account of his voyages into English, identified "savage" with wilderness and animals, but not with human beings.³ As late as 1609 "wild and savage people" were said to live in the colony of Virginia, but they were described as "very loving and gentle".⁴ At that time, the word "savage" connoted naturalness, or the wildness of nature, and many writers referred to the Indians as "the naturals".

In the interests of permanent conquest, this benign conception of aboriginals had to be changed, and it soon was. Following an Indian uprising in Virginia in 1622, John Smith, who had once described "the Salvages" as "poore innocent soules", now described Indians as "cruell beasts", and "savages with a more unnaturall brutishness than beasts".⁵ In the circumstances, this was just what the Europeans were looking for. Within a few years, it had become normal for virtually all Europeans to characterize aboriginals as wild, roaming beings, almost like animals, whose wasted, uncultivated ground could be improved only if the Europeans performed their duty by settling and developing it. Such attitudes quickly made their way into all subsequent histories of North America, became the accepted ideology of the colonies, and impregnated the judgments of their courts.

Even many of those who wrote sympathetically about the natives nevertheless clung to this assumption that their own culture was superior. Historian Francis Jennings traces such comments through an astounding range to the present day. John Marshall, whose nineteenth-century judgments in the United States Supreme Court have been interpreted as sympathetic to the Indians, wrote: "The tribes of Indians inhabiting this country were fierce savages, whose occupation was war...."⁶

In our own day, the eminent British historian Hugh Trevor Roper has dismissed

> barbarous tribes in picturesque but irrelevant corners of the globe: tribes whose chief function in history, in my opinion, is to show to the present an image of the past from which, by history, it has escaped.⁷

Jennings summarizes, with mordant humour:

> The logic is simple, faulty and compelling.... Civilization is that quality possessed by people with civil government; civil government is Europe's kind of government; Indians did not have Europe's kind of government; therefore Indians were not civilized. Uncivilized people live in wild

anarchy; therefore Indians did not have any government at all. And therefore Europeans could not have been doing anything wrong – were in fact performing a noble mission – by bringing government and civilization to the poor savages.[8]

Operating within such a worldview, North American and European legal experts have tied themselves into knots to find an intellectual justification for the invasion of the Americas and the seizure of lands owned and occupied by the original inhabitants. One of the first ideas was that North America, legally speaking, was vacant territory, *terra nullius*, to which Europeans could freely take title. This European right was held to derive from the act of "discovery", or from a symbolic act (such as planting a cross or flag), or from effective occupation (such as creation of settlements).[9] Some have held that rights of ownership were obtained by European powers through conquest, although this is not put forward by Canada or the United States as the basis for their assumption of title.

A basic idea has been to deny that there was ever any pre-existing social or legal order; to assert that those already here did not have sovereignty over their territories, because they were nomadic hunters with no political or legal organization. (I report in some detail in Chapter 20 a fascinating and elegant refutation of this argument by an aboriginal jurist, Sakej Henderson.) The Europeans did not bother to be consistent: while arguing that they themselves had obtained valid title, the British, for example, would refuse to accept that the French had obtained valid title by the same means. This did not stop them from arguing, when it suited them, that they had received title from another European state – for example, Britain claimed, and Canada still does, that it received title to Mikmakik, the home of the Mikmaqs, from France with the signing of the Treaty of Utrecht in 1713, and that somehow, by that time, the aboriginal title had magically disappeared, even though the French themselves said this had not happened. This is still part of the Canadian government's case against aboriginal title in the Maritime provinces: the native claim is held to have been "superseded by law" – in other words, laws made by Europeans since their arrival have simply brushed aboriginal title aside.

Not all jurists have been able to bring themselves to make this extraordinarily self-serving argument: even Mr. Justice Marshall, who held that European title derives from "discovery", admitted in his judgments that discovery did not end pre-existing Indian territorial or political rights. The moment that the existence of such rights is admitted, all the other European rationalizations fall to the ground, evidently indefensible.

In recent years, many experts in jurisprudence – for example, Professor Brian Slattery of York University in Toronto – have exposed the absurdity of all this elegant reasoning in defence of the indefensible.[10] It is a fundamental principle, Slattery writes, that all human beings have rights to life and the necessities of life. Wherever they are, they secure this by making individual and collective use of their territory; and naturally any group of people has a right to protect the well-being of its members in their territory. Therefore, North American aboriginals, like other people, must have had a right to the territories in which they lived; and these rights held good against all other groups, including Europeans. To assert that the rights of aboriginal Americans were outweighed by the needs of Europeans implies that European lives were more valuable than those of aboriginals. Thus, since the beginning, all European claims to ownership of North America have been based on an essentially racist argument.

"The doctrine of *terra nullius*," writes Professor Douglas Sanders, "is widely recognized as racist."[11] He adds that the question of the pre-existing rights of indigenous peoples is far from settled in favour of the invaders, and is still the subject of litigation in Sweden, Norway, Australia, Malaysia and Canada.

Here in Canada, the idea that European society is civilized, while aboriginal society is savage, continues to affect government policy and legal judgments as it has for the last two centuries. The unfavourable judgment of Chief Justice Allan McEachern of the British Columbia Supreme Court, referred to earlier, was reached after the Gitksan-Wet'suwet'en, who have always lived along the Skeena River in northern British Columbia, spent four years trying to educate the Chief Justice about their sophisticated and ancient methods of government, centred around the Feast, or Potlatch.[12] They were unable to shake the prejudices of a highly educated lifetime: his judgment (now partially set aside after being appealed) reflects the basic Eurocentric assumptions prevalent long ago when the invasion of the Americas occurred.

5

Mikmaqs: in the path of the invaders

The Mikmaqs[1] were the first of Canada's aboriginal peoples to be in regular contact with Europeans. They first appear in the written history of North America on a July day in 1534, when Jacques Cartier, a master mariner from St. Malo, sailing along the coast of what is now New Brunswick, entered the Bay of Chaleur, and came upon two groups of Mikmaqs in some forty to fifty canoes. They "held up furs on the ends of sticks to indicate that they wished to trade,"[2] but made so much noise that they alarmed the French, who fired at them to frighten them off.

The next day, only nine canoes approached the French, and a profitable trade was undertaken. On the third day, the Mikmaqs greeted the visitors warmly and offered them seal meat. Then 300 of them bartered their furs for iron kettles, knives and other goods. McGill University anthropologist and historian Bruce Trigger believes the Mikmaqs were already so accustomed to trading that they had brought their furs to the coast hoping that some Europeans might turn up with whom they could do business.

Cartier left a favourable account of the Mikmaqs. He described their country as "the most beautiful a man could see" – level and flat, covered with trees, wild wheat, peas "as thick as though sown and cultivated", grapes, strawberries, mulberries and roses, and with "many fair meadows and good grasses, and lakes full of salmon".

The Mikmaqs welcomed the newcomers. Cartier wrote:

We saw a group of women...who were knee-deep in the sea, dancing and singing. The others...came freely to us, rubbing their arms with their

31

hands, and thereafter raised them to heaven, leaping and making many signs of gladness, and grew so intimate with us that they ended by bartering all that they had from hand to hand, in such wise that they kept nothing save their stark naked bodies, for they gave us everything which they had, though its value was but small.[3]

The Europeans immediately identified these friendly people as prospective religious converts. "We recognized that this folk could easily be converted to our faith,"[4] remarked Cartier. The aboriginals were also receptive to the iron goods brought by the Europeans, and in the coming decades traded eagerly for them all along the east coast.

In this way the Mikmaqs enter history as written by us.

Visit to Mikmakik [5]

In February, 1991, when I was preparing the articles for the *Reader's Digest* mentioned earlier, I decided to visit the Mikmaqs. A friend in Ottawa suggested I contact Mikmaq legal advisor Sakej Henderson in Eskasoni, Nova Scotia, the biggest Mikmaq community, and when I did so Sakej invited me to stay with his family for a few days.

I drove south from Sydney through the rolling countryside of Cape Breton along the shore of frozen Bras d'Or Lake towards Eskasoni. Twenty-five miles from Sydney, the highway turns imperceptibly into the main street of a rambling community that wanders along the lakeshore in an undisciplined fashion, as if built by accident. I learned later that many Mikmaqs call this highway Welfare Road,[6] because they believe it was paved in 1960 for the sole purpose of allowing Sydney businessmen to come into the village and capture the welfare dollars that the federal government had begun to hand out.

The site of Eskasoni between the lake and the surrounding hills is spectacular. Out on the frozen lake the tiny figures of schoolchildren were playing pick-up hockey. I passed the white steeple of the Holy Family Catholic Church, standing sentinel on a grassy hill above the road; then a post office, a general store and gas station; and on the other side, near the lake, two large new schools that dwarfed everything around them.

Halfway through the village, I turned down towards the lake where I found a cluster of houses, a neighbourhood known as Apuamek. Here Sakej Henderson lives in a house that looks, as some houses often do, as if it is in the process of always growing. And across from him lives Alex Denny, Grand Captain of the Sante' Mawi'omi wjit Mi'kmaq (the Mikmaq Grand Council), a central figure in the Mikmaq revival of the last two decades.

Sakej turned out to be a delightful man. He quickly settled me at a dining table overlooking the lake, and patiently began to answer my questions. Plump, friendly and comfortable, he clearly enjoyed talking about his legal work for the Grand Council, about the unbroken history of the Mikmaq nation, and their vigorous programme for asserting their continuing rights.

I am not sure what I expected to find in Eskasoni, but I certainly did not expect that the man running their legal affairs would hold a doctorate of jurisprudence from Harvard; or that his wife, Marie Battiste, curriculum director in the village school, would have a doctorate in education from Stanford. In 1978 they were working at the University of California in Berkeley, when Alex Denny appeared one day and told Marie she was needed in Eskasoni. "To do what?" she asked. "Run the school," Denny replied. Sakej had already been giving the Grand Council legal advice for a couple of years, and Denny now wanted him to devote himself completely to that task.

Both were ready for the move. Marie, a self-made Mikmaq scholar, had been brought up mostly in Maine, but her roots were in Mikmaq life in Cape Breton. Sakej, part-Chickasaw, part-Cheyenne, was a lawyer whom she had met and married at Harvard, a specialist in the aboriginal law of North America. Marie finished her doctorate in 1984 and they moved north, where they immediately embarked on an intellectual adventure that many of us would consider quixotic: for Marie, the revival of a language spoken by an estimated 4,000 people, and only fitfully by many of those; for Sakej, the use of the full panoply of international law to prove that this handful of people remain a bona fide nation, whose ancient agreements supersede their more recent incorporation into the Canadian state. As I soon learned, they have pursued these objectives with high seriousness and great success.

As seen from Mikmakik

To gather his thoughts, my host would occasionally get up from the table and wander around the house. On one of these excursions, he produced a document that he said would help explain what was happening: the complaint entered in 1986 by the Mikmaq Grand

Council to the United Nations Human Rights Commission, accusing Canada of racism, discrimination and denial of the Mikmaq right to self-determination.[7]

Although written by lawyers, the Mikmaq document begins in the mists of mythological time, when Niskam, the Creator, brought down Nakuset, the sun, to light the Earth and create all living things. That first world was destroyed by earthquakes and floods, and when the land finally dried, the people of Mikmakik found themselves joined together by a single tongue and spirit.

The document describes how Mikmaqs discovered Europeans, not vice-versa. It is a long story. Once during a terrible famine, an old man was approached in his sleep by a young man bearing three crosses, which he said would protect the Mikmaqs in time of conflict and hunger, see them through long sea voyages and among strange peoples, and give them wisdom in council. When the old man awoke, he drew these three crosses on birchbark and explained them to all the people.

Many generations later, about 600 years ago, Mikmakik was invaded by Haudenosaunee (Iroquois) from the west; fighting under the symbol of the three crosses, a Mikmaq force drove the invaders out. The Mikmaqs then reorganized under a new constitution that divided their country into seven great districts (sakamowti), each with many clans, and each clan with its sakamow (chief), sa'ya (spiritual leader), and keptin (war leader). Together they formed one national council, the Sante' Mawi'omi (holy gathering, or Grand Council), which exists to this day.

A hundred years later (that is, five centuries ago), a Mikmaq woman dreamed one night that a small island covered with bare trees and black bears sitting in the branches was floating towards Mikmakik. She told her dream to the elders, but none could interpret it. Many years later, a sailing ship full of black-bearded Europeans landed; and when they planted a cross of wood on the shore, the Mikmaqs saw that the strangers, too, belonged to the cross, and welcomed them.

Those Europeans may have been the company of John Cabot, sailing out of Bristol in western England, who in 1497 explored the sakamowtis of Ktamkuk, Unimaki, and possibly Kespikiok (later known as Newfoundland, Cape Breton Island and the Gaspé). Cabot returned a year later, ran as far south as Chesapeake Bay, and was the first to establish for Europeans that there was a huge and fruitful continent on the other side of the Atlantic.[8] Fishermen wasted no time in following up his discovery: the first cargo of Newfoundland fish was unloaded in England in 1502, only four years after Cabot's second voyage.[9] Within ten years Basques, Portuguese, Normans and Bretons were fishing regularly off the shores of Mikmakik. By 1504 Basque fishermen were summering among the Mikmaqs in Unimaki (Cape Breton).

So when Cartier stopped thirty years later to trade in Kespikiok (the Bay of Chaleur, between Gaspé and northern New Brunswick), he was not altogether strange. He sailed in among people who, through dreams, legend and actual experience, had already comfortably fitted his like into their cosmology.

That is the story of how the Mikmaqs discovered the Europeans, as told by their Grand Council to the UN Commission on Human Rights in 1986.

The stamina of a long-held tradition

I soon discovered that Sakej Henderson deeply reveres his neighbour Alex Denny. Alex was a young man of twenty-eight when, in 1968, he was appointed by the elders of the Grand Council to the lifetime job of Grand Captain. Sakej compares him with the trickster, or juggler, of Mikmaq mythology. "He can blend into any situation," Sakej told me admiringly, "he's never lost for a word; he has no problems of self-confidence, no doubts. He knows where he wants the people to go."

The Grand Council is a self-perpetuating body that has existed in an unbroken line since the time before contact with Europeans. It is based on the authority of Mikmaq families, and the Grand Captain's duty as executive head of the Council, working under the leadership of the Grand Chief, is to keep in touch with every family, and to "watch over", as Sakej put it, "the whole spiritual universe". A great deal of the decision-making in Eskasoni takes place informally as families exchange visits and through constant discussion arrive at a consensus about what should be done. "We handle all the correspondence through the homes," said Sakej, a fitting method for a council that has no budget or formal authority and whose officers cannot accept money.

For generations, the Grand Council stubbornly refused to accept the system of elected band councils that the Canadian government tried to force on all native peoples across the country. Consequently, the Mikmaqs weren't registered or organized into bands until 1960, when their powerful old chief, Gabriel Sylliboy, lost his struggle with the Indian agents. In 1969 the Grand Council called into being the Union of Nova Scotia Indians, finally putting the Mikmaq political organization into a form the government could understand.

I wondered how the Grand Council leaders were able to get by when they were unpaid. "Alex is singularly unconcerned with money," said Sakej. "He does what he has to do. He might pick blueberries in Maine. He introduced us to the market in Boston for Christmas trees and wreaths. He is a carpenter. He might live on welfare. He might work for the government. He had a building-supply company, made it work, and then turned it over. To build his house, he became president of the Union for four years, and then stepped down and turned over power to others. And his wife also works."

At the moment Alex was at a *salite*, or village auction. A woman had died, and people had gathered that morning according to custom to auction off the possessions of the deceased. "It is the Grand Captain's duty to start the auction. If you're interested, we could drop in on it."

I was interested for sure. So we wandered down the icy village road along the shore of the lake, past a straggling line of plain wooden houses to an unmarked hall, where most of the villagers were sitting around two long rows of tables.

A meal had been served, and the atmosphere was relaxed and cheerful. People were in their everyday clothes, laughing and joking quietly, exchanging gossip. Every few minutes a young man walked the length of the hall, holding up items for auction and accepting bids. In the Mikmaq tradition, all the events surrounding death (and birth) involve the whole community; and since this death a few days earlier, the women of the Grand Council had been cleaning the deceased's house and keeping the family constant company. From the moment of death, someone from the community stays with the family until after the funeral; no visitor can leave until another arrives.

Attendance at funerals is one way in which Mikmaq families keep in touch. Most people attend every funeral in Eskasoni; about half will go to funerals on the other four reserves on Cape Breton Island; as many as a quarter might go to funerals in mainland Nova Scotia reserves, and some might even go as far as Restigouche, Quebec, about 500 miles away, to take part in the obsequies for a deceased Mikmaq.

Alex Denny was lounging at one of the tables. He is an open-faced, friendly man with the manner of an ordinary worker, but carrying nevertheless an air of quiet authority. He immediately put me at ease, in that way Indians have, by not taking any particular notice of me. I was grateful, for I already felt somewhat conspicuous in this gathering of intimates. I was surprised at the lack of solemnity in the hall. Alex joked a lot with the people around him, and aroused a good deal of laughter by bidding $12 – "that's all I've got," he said – for every item that was carried past. He lost every bid.

Alex told me people bring items they are expected to buy back, if possible. "My wife has a pair of towels that must be worth $10,000 by now, she's bought them back at so many auctions." The people in the hall appeared to have accepted this death almost matter-of-factly, but their very presence indicated their concern. Perhaps we, too, were once this way, in less complicated times; but few of us still are. For the Mikmaqs, a *salite* is a final demonstration of community support for one of their own. Proceeds, which I was told can sometimes amount to many thousands of dollars, go to the family of the deceased. "It pays for the funeral expenses. It is our way of dealing with wills and probate and all that," said Sakej.

On my first excursion into a Mikmaq village, I had found an ancient tradition still very much alive in everyday life.

A 500-year timeframe

At the time of my visit, Sakej Henderson was busy drawing up a paper recommending that on October 14, 1992, the 500th anniversary of the arrival of Columbus, an international jury should assess the effect of Columbus' "discovery" on the aboriginal peoples of the Americas. For several hours he paced the house nervously, feeling tense, he said, as he always does when confronted with writing his thoughts down on paper. Eventually he emerged from wherever he was doing his thinking into the central part of the house and handed me a paper to examine – "an early draft," he called it, sitting down and waiting for my reaction. In face of Sakej's evident erudition, I was almost as nervous in reacting to his paper as he was in showing it to me. The paper had the air of having been hastily hammered out on a typewriter, and was full of minor grammatical and spelling errors. Sakej obviously was an instinctual, rather than meticulous, writer. I tentatively mentioned a couple of minor errors, but he waved my comments aside. "It's always like that at first," he said. "These things will come right with time." For him, writing a paper was not an overnight thing.

The purpose of his proposed international inquiry would be to determine whether the Spanish Crown, in the person of King Juan Carlos, should apologize to the Indians of the Americas. Such an apology had first been suggested by Father Bartolome de las Casas in 1550, and Sakej thought the time had come for its delivery.

The way Sakej sees history is that two realms of human civilization developed, which existed independently of each other until 500 years ago: Pangea, the realm of the Euro-Asian-African landmass and its connected subcontinents and islands; and Indigena, consisting of the Americas, Australia and the Pacific Islands.

"You see, when the rulers of Pangea discovered Indigena, they had a problem," Sakej said. "The fact is, both realms were spiritually dominated in various ways. Pangea's spiritual transcendency was based on a God, a person just like us, who was the source of all knowledge, given in the Bible.

"The problem was that the Bible did not cover the entire world. So when they discovered a whole new continent, with people, plants and animals totally missing from the Bible, their knowledge, once considered universal, became particular to themselves only."

The first Papal Bulls in 1493 declared that Indians were human, even if infidels. "They were still guided by Aristotle's paradigm, man at the top, beasts and animals second, devils third. That was the entire category covering their world. But the Pope rushed to judgment. In 1537 a Papal Bull said we were 'truly men' and should not in any way be enslaved. That gave us certain rights," remarked Sakej: "aboriginal rights."

In 1550, Las Casas, who had protested against the brutality of the Spanish conquest, was accused of treason by the Spanish landowners in America, and summoned to defend his attitude before the most learned scholars of Spain.[10] In the debate, Sepulveda, Spain's leading philosopher, representing the viewpoint of the Spanish aristocrats, came up with the idea, said Sakej, "that Indians were inferior (beasts), because we were so strange. His whole idea was to argue for enslavement. But when the Crown concluded that we could not be enslaved, it took the word 'conquest' out of their doctrine, and introduced the idea of treaties."

Sakej's paper suggested the proposed inquiry concern itself with correcting false historical assumptions, rediscovering the contribution native peoples of the Americas have made to the world, acknowledging the tragic consequences of the encounter, and rekindling a dialogue between the "vast solitudes" that still exist between the two realms. "The issues involved in the Inquiry are limited to the standards of civilization, Christian conversion, necessity, genocide, ethnocide, racism, colonialism and violations of human rights." He proposed that a jury of respected scholars examine these charges, as had been done in the 1550 debate, under procedures established by the International Court of Justice.

Sakej said: "Most people don't know that agricultural produce imported from America saved Europe, whose crops at that time were all above the ground. The European civilizations had never advanced beyond throwing out seeds and letting the wind spread them. In the Americas agricultural scientists had developed 300 forms of potato. The plough only became really important in Europe after they found out the crops they brought from America required planting in the ground."

I was finding out that Sakej has a mischievous sense of humour. He loved to toss off this sort of surprising information, to shock me out of my Euro-Canadian complacency. Then he sat back and smiled at me with a look of great satisfaction, like a cat with cream.

Christ help us; Mary pray for us

The story of how the Mikmaq Grand Council became the Holy Council is an extraordinary one. Within forty years of the debates in Spain, and before any European colonies had been established in Canada, a Mikmaq chief, Messamouet, had been to France and had stayed for a year at the house of the governor of Bayonne.[11] There he had learned about the controversies that had raged in France and Spain about the best way to treat the inhabitants of the New World.

So when the French arrived in 1604, with Samuel de Champlain as navigator, geographer and draughtsman, the Mikmaq chief Membertou was ready for them. From the first, Membertou was friendly towards the French, and in 1610, only six years after their arrival, he was baptised a Christian and named Henry after the late French king.[12]

As related by the Mikmaq document submitted to the UN, "A

covenant was made to protect the priests of the Church, and the French who brought the priests among us.... A great wampum belt two metres in length records this concordat [with the Vatican], and has ever since then been kept at the Collegio di Propaganda Fide in Rome."[13] The meaning of the belt is plain from its imagery. On the left are the symbols of Catholicism; on the right, symbols of the power of the Grand Council. In the centre, a priest and a *sakamow* hold a cross, and in the hand of the *sakamow* is the holy book. "Over the course of the seventeenth century the whole Mikmaq people became Catholics and took St. Ann as their patron."

From that day to this, the Mikmaqs have been loyal, practising Catholics. It is part of their striking originality that the motto of their Grand Council, whose policies today are based entirely on preserving and reviving Mikmaq traditions, language and beliefs, is still, "Christ Help Us; Mary Pray for Us."

Their submission to the UN states: "Although we loved the French for living peacefully and usefully among us, learned their language and shared their religion, we did not wish to become part of their country. They found this strange. 'They consider themselves braver than us,' one of our first priests, l'abbé Biard, complained of us, 'better than us, cleverer than us, and, difficult to believe, richer than us.' But one of our Gaspésian *sa'ya* [spiritual leaders] spoke well in 1690 when he told the French visitors, 'If France as thou sayest is a little terrestrial paradise, art thou sensible to leave it?' "

Membertou did not have authority to bind his allies in the Wabanaki confederacy to his concordat with the Vatican, so he sent his sons out to consult the other tribes about the new alliance. Not all agreed to join. The Beothuks of Newfoundland, although allied to the Mikmaqs, did not want to become Catholic. The Montagnais and Maliseet[14] wanted to remain totally independent, although the Maliseet later became Catholic, thus giving rise to their name, which, in Mikmaq means "bad speakers", or people who can't make up their minds.

How have the Mikmaqs succeeded in making so viable a synthesis between their traditions and Catholic doctrine? It was easy for them to remain friendly with the French, because French settlements were so small that for more than 200 years the Mikmaqs remained the majority in the Maritime provinces. But when the British began to arrive as settlers, they claimed ownership of Mikmakik, as the French had never done; so the Mikmaqs long opposed the British with arms. Although they made peace with the British after their last battle in 1758, they remained Catholics, and to this day hold the annual feast of St. Ann in the last week of July on Chapel Island in Bras d'or Lake.

Like much of Mikmaq life, this assembly has an ancient lineage. Mikmaq *sakamows* had always held general assemblies at which "they resolve upon peace, truce, war or nothing at all".[15] Over the years, these gatherings became the central Mikmaq ceremony, drawing people from throughout the eastern seaboard. Although the pilgrimage fell out of favour in the first half of this century, when the Mikmaqs were in decline, somehow it never quite died out. In 1932, in the depths of the depression, the *Halifax Herald*[16] reported that for the first time in 200 years, the annual St. Ann's mission had been called off by the major chiefs. Only five days later, the newspaper reported that the people had turned up anyway, in greater numbers than ever.

Ten or fifteen years ago, the gathering was attracting only a few of the older people and their immediate families. It is evidence of the recent revival of the Mikmaq spirit that in 1991, Chapel Island was again covered with a sea of tents, as some 3,000 people crowded together to immerse themselves in the language, rituals and beliefs that lie at the centre of their collective personality. On the final Sunday, the great procession is led by a statue of St. Ann supported by the most respected persons in the community, followed by the priests from each Mikmaq reserve, the chiefs in tribal regalia, the elders singing the traditional songs honouring the saint, the youngest children and new communicants, and then the whole assembly of Mikmaqs.

This is an authentically Christian occasion, but its significance is not only religious. It is held on an island where there are no modern houses, no laws, regulations or policemen, and removed from all non-native influence. Mikmaqs believe the spirits of the people who have been buried on Chapel Island look after them while they are there.[17] With such protection from the ancestors, they allow their children to roam and play freely without supervision, and no child has ever drowned there, although they are constantly playing around water. Many Mikmaqs believe the islands around Chapel Island are inhabited by *Wigguladummooch*, or Little People, who live in the forests, as the Mikmaqs did long ago. Some report having seen them along the shores in the early morning, and others say they have met and talked to them. One Eskasoni woman sets out food for the Little People in the winter, and others say they have received moccasins and ribbons from them. The Christian churches frown on such superstitions. Dr. Marie Battiste has written: "To me, the Little People are real."[18]

The intimacy of the extended family

That evening we walked across to Alex Denny's home at 9124 Apuamek. It is the only numbered house anywhere around, and when I asked why, I begin to appreciate Alex's deadpan humour. A few years before, the band council decided to identify houses with numbers, and streets with letters, just as in white communities. Alex would have none of it. He advised the council that his street would have a Mikmaq name, and his house would be number 9124, after section 91 (24) of the British North America Act, which gives the federal government responsibility for "Indians and Lands reserved for the Indians". And so today his house reminds everyone who passes that Canada has inherited from the British Crown the promises made to the Mikmaqs in ancient treaties.

Alex's house was full of people, as it apparently is on most nights, most of them members of his or his wife Janet's family. Janet has "a network of eleven sisters and brothers," Sakej told me, "and they all know what each of them is doing every day." Janet and Alex have five children, two of them adopted; the eight brothers and sisters of Janet's family still living in Eskasoni have twenty-five children in all, and many of them were present that evening.

Some food appeared (it seemed to be ready at all times), and over the meal there was a great deal of laughter, and encouragement for Janet's success in losing thirteen pounds after five weeks on a diet. Like all family gossip, the conversation was extraordinarily specific and impenetrable to an outsider. Gossip, from which no one is exempt, is the Mikmaqs' main form of social control.[19] In the daily round of visiting, everything that happens on and off the reserve, even as far away as Boston, is worked over in detail, and in the process families gain honour, respect, prestige, disgrace or shame. Anyone who has done anything wrong is not allowed to forget it for a long time, although gradually he or she will be allowed to return to the social network.

All this is integral to the Mikmaq way of politics and information. "The place runs on gossip," Sakej told me. "Alex will visit the elders

42

in the morning. Very quickly what he says will go the rounds of the village, and feedback will come in by the afternoon."

Over a kitchen table I talked to Alex for a long time, and then we drifted back to Sakej and Marie's house, where Joe Gould, an addiction counsellor by day and a young man with considerable presence, took up his guitar and in a beautiful voice sang Mikmaq songs for almost an hour. Between songs Marie told me about that day's funeral. The woman who had died, Myrtle Christmas, had been the wife of Peter Christmas, director of the Micmac Association of Cultural Studies, which works to maintain "the language, beliefs, chants, dances, prayers and customs of our traditions". Because of Peter's work, many younger people like Joe Gould now have a fund of stories and songs in the Mikmaq language which they are always willing to share. Peter's father, Ben Christmas, was a famous educator, writer and storyteller. "He was the sort of man who could do anything," said Marie. "I'll tell you a story about him."

When Ben was chief, many decades ago, she said, a Baptist missionary named Silas T. Rand appeared among the Mikmaqs and tried to persuade them to learn to read and write English. The Catholic clergy did not want this; they told the Mikmaqs to stick to their hieroglyphic text. But Chief Ben Christmas supported the missionary. "If the Mikmaqs had known how to read and write," he said, "the whites would not have stolen our land." So Mikmaqs did learn to read and write. Silas Rand went around proselytizing for a long time, but in the whole Mikmaq nation, Ben Christmas and his wife Susan were the only converts Rand ever made to Protestantism. And even they, it is said, called for a Catholic priest in their dying hours.

Centuries of neglect

When the first Europeans arrived, the Mikmaq population is believed to have been between 35,000 and 50,000, although some estimates run up to 100,000 (depending, it seems, on how many allied groups are included).[20] The subsequent experience of the Mikmaqs certainly supports the modern view that huge numbers of American aboriginals were wiped out within a century.

By 1616 there was already a decline in numbers, attributed by the priests to alcohol and the adoption of French foods. A massive epidemic, possibly of bubonic plague,[21] that swept through coastal New England between 1616 and 1619 also had its effect, but modern research suggests that dietary changes were the most important factors in weakening Mikmaq resistance. Within little more than a century, only 15,000 Mikmaqs were left, and by the middle of the nineteenth century, a mere 1,300 remained.

Almost as deadly as disease and diet was the very presence of the settlers, who occupied Mikmaq lands and denigrated and suppressed Mikmaq knowledge, traditions and capacities. Like other aboriginals throughout the Americas, the Mikmaqs were held by the newcomers to be worthless, a people without spiritual or even human qualities. As a result, the Mikmaqs became social pariahs with the status of squatters in their own lands.

Our own historical record shows that the Mikmaqs were reduced to desperation by the Europeans' failure to carry out promises made to them in eighteenth-century treaties. After many years of war between Britain and France, Mikmakik (or Acadia, as we call it) was ceded by France to Britain in the treaty of Utrecht in 1713; much of the current disagreement over Mikmaq rights arises from the meaning of that treaty. The French said the Indians had been their allies, but not their subjects. The British claimed the treaty transferred title to all of Nova Scotia, unencumbered by any native claims, and that the natives were henceforth their subjects.[22] The Mikmaqs, having been told by the French that they were not mentioned in the treaty, considered themselves an independent people.[23]

As they began to settle New England in the eighteenth century, the British came into conflict with the aboriginal nations, and a number of treaties were signed. Of these the most important for Nova Scotia were signed in 1725 and 1752. It is a lesson in the subjective nature of history to read the conflicting interpretations placed on these treaties by the contending parties, now represented by the Canadian government and the Mikmaq Grand Council.

The Canadian version is that these agreements were not signed between equals, and therefore were not treaties at all, but documents of surrender by the Indians.[24] The clause in the 1752 treaty which gave the Indians "free liberty of Hunting and Fishing as usual..." does not, according to Canada, imply an aboriginal right, but rather a favour granted at the pleasure of the Crown. Furthermore, after the treaty was signed, Canada now says, the Mikmaqs returned to hostilities against the British. In the Canadian government's view, these hostilities were an act of rebellion by British subjects, not an act of warfare by an independent nation. The government position now is that these hostilities abrogated all the treaties between New England, Nova Scotia and the Maritime Indians signed between 1693 and 1752.

Following Britain's conquest of New France in 1759, the military invited settlers to occupy aboriginal lands. This happened less than a decade after the Mikmaqs had been promised that they would be able to continue to use their lands. So many settlers began to pour into Nova Scotia and the other seaboard colonies that the authorities in Britain became alarmed. They ordered colonial governors to remove settlers from land claimed by Indians, and told them to apply to London for permission before authorizing any further Crown land grants.[25]

The governor of Nova Scotia, Jonathan Belcher, carried out these instructions, reserving to the Mikmaqs most of the Maritime seacoast – about two-thirds of Nova Scotia as it then existed. But the small Nova Scotia business community would have none of it. They attacked Belcher as an incompetent, and succeeded in having his proclamation annulled. By the 1790s Mikmaqs were starving,[26] and by 1824 missionary John West reported the Mikmaqs "fast diminishing in numbers as they wander, like those of New Brunswick, in extreme wretchedness and detached parties, throughout the Province".[27]

Repeated petitions to the British authorities to stop the occupation of Mikmaq land elicited no response until 1841, when the *Kjisakamow* [Chief] Louis-Benjamin Peminuit Paul petitioned the new Queen Victoria:

> My people are in trouble. I have seen upwards of a Thousand Moons. When I was young I had plenty: now I am old, poor and sickly too. My people are poor. No Hunting Grounds – No Beaver – no Otter – no nothing. Indians poor – poor for ever. No Store – no Chest – no Clothes. All these Woods once ours. Our fathers possessed them all. Now we cannot cut a tree to warm our Wigwam in Winter unless the White Man please.... Pity your poor Indians in Nova Scotia.... Let us not perish....[28]

This plea persuaded the Colonial Office to admit that the Mikmaqs had "an undeniable Claim to the Protection of the Government as British Subjects", so Nova Scotia set aside 123,000 acres for reservations, on which they invited chiefs to settle.[29] Most chiefs were unwilling to give up the land they had always lived on, merely to be herded onto land chosen for them elsewhere. But they need not have worried: only half of the reserved land was ever set aside. Instead of expelling the squatters from Indian lands, as their own legislation required, the province feebly ordered the squatters to pay for the land they had taken. Few ever did. The wildlife was hunted out, the Mikmaq farms were taken, and the people were reduced to living as itinerant woodcutters and handicraft peddlers.[30]

Reported Rev. John Sprott of Musquodoboit in 1846:

> The better days of the Indians have long gone by. They are only the ghost of what they were – few in number, and poor in circumstances...the mere fragment of nations which have passed away.... The approach of the white man, and the march of improvement, have sealed their doom, and compelled them to fly from mountain to mountain to seek a resting place.... They cannot live when the wild animals are frightened away, and their hunting grounds are destroyed.[31]

Wrote Abraham Gessner, Indian Commissioner, to the Legislative Assembly of Nova Scotia in 1848:

> Almost the whole Micmac population are now vagrants, who wander from place to place, and door to door, seeking alms.... They are clad in filthy rags. Necessity often compels them to consume putrid and unwholesome food. The offal of the slaughterhouse is their portion....[32]

On February 8, 1849, nearly a century after the signing of the 1752 treaty, the Mikmaq chiefs addressed a remarkable petition to the governor of Nova Scotia. Even in the depths of their decline, the chiefs remembered the treaty well, and had a clear understanding of its meaning:

> ...A long time ago our fathers owned and occupied all the lands now called Nova Scotia.... Tired of a war that destroyed many of our people, almost ninety years ago our Chief made peace and buried the hatchet forever. When that peace was made, the English governor promised us protection, as much land as we wanted, and the preservation of our fisheries and game. These we now very much want....
>
> Good and Honorable Governor, be not offended at what we say.... But your people...came and killed many of our tribe and took from us our country. You have taken from us our lands and trees and have destroyed our game. The Moose yards of our fathers, where are they....

You have put ships and steamboats upon the waters and they scare away the fish. You have made dams across the rivers so that the Salmon cannot go up and your laws will not permit us to spear them.

In old times our wigwams stood in the pleasant places along the sides of the rivers. These places are now taken from us, and we are told to go away. Upon our camping grounds you have built towns, and the graves of our fathers are broken by the plow and harrow. Even the ash and maple are growing scarce. We are told to cut no trees upon the farmer's ground, and the land you have given us is taken away every year....[33]

The chiefs said that by 1849 there were only about 1,300 of their people left, reduced from 6,000 ninety years before. In spite of their desperate condition, they did not beg. Instead, as Peter Christmas observes, "they ask for freedom to develop their own resources and govern them accordingly." [34]

We have resolved to make farms, yet we cannot make farms without help. We will get our people to make farms, build houses and barns, raise grain, feed cattle and get knowledge. Some have begun already. What more can we say? We will ask our Mother the Queen to help us...in our distress...that we may at last be able to help ourselves.[35]

Old men remember

Even in the despair in which the Mikmaqs entered the twentieth century, the memory of those old treaties, and the sense of the Mikmaqs as an independent nation, endured in the minds of the elders. In 1928, only a year after the House of Commons had contemptuously dismissed aboriginal land claims as "more or less fictitious", the Mikmaq chief Gabriel Sylliboy attempted to have his people's treaties confirmed by the Canadian courts. Charged with illegally hunting outside the season imposed by Nova Scotia law, he argued that his right to hunt was protected by the treaties of 1725 and 1752. When the case came to court, an old man, Joe Christmas, a former chief (grandfather of Peter Christmas, already quoted), testified as recorded in rough notes of the proceedings:

Heard that according to treaty we had right to hunt and fish at any time. I cannot read. Heard it from our grandfathers. Heard that King of England made treaty with Micmacs, with the whole tribe (Objected to). Remember hearing that goods were given – blankets – under treaty (Objected to).[36]

47

Chief Sylliboy testified that for thirty-four years he had always started trapping muskrats at Hallowe'en, and had never been interfered with before. He had been hunting for four days and killed fourteen muskrats when the skins were taken by the officer.

Since I was boy heard that Indians got from King free hunting and fishing at all times. Still believe treaty good. When officer took pelts I told him I had treaty. He said he knew nothing about that. I said let me go and I'll show you copy of treaty.

Sylliboy and other witnesses said that for as long as they could remember, Mikmaqs had received blankets, seed, spears, coats, hides, flour, gunpowder and other items as payment under treaty. "Remember my grandfather going to Sydney," testified Francis Gould, aged seventy-four. "...He told me he got these from the King. Under the treaty. We promised to keep treaty and got these things in return. That is what my grandfather told me."

Ben Christmas, who was then chief of the Sydney band, told the court that nothing had ever been paid to Indians to cancel or revoke the treaty. "Still believe we have rights of hunting and fishing at all times," he said.

But in 1928 the justice system paid no heed to these memories, or to the certified copy of the treaty produced from the Nova Scotia archives. Sylliboy lost the case. The judge ruled against him on very narrow grounds. He found that in 1752, the treaty had been signed with only a small band of Mikmaqs inhabiting an area near the Schubenacadie River, and since Sylliboy was from Cape Breton, he could not claim protection of the treaty. The judge ruled that the document was not a treaty, but "a mere agreement made by the Governor and council with a handful of Indians giving them in return for good behaviour, food, presents and the right to hunt and fish as usual". He reiterated the long-held British view of the meaning of the treaty of Utrecht:

The savages' rights of sovereignty and even of ownership were never recognized. Nova Scotia had passed to Great Britiain not by gift or purchase from or even by conquest of the Indians, but by treaty with France, which had acquired it by priority of discovery and ancient possession; and the Indians passed with it. [37]

48

The Mikmaqs, of course, view this treaty in a completely different light. As Alex Denny explains, George III agreed "to protect our Catholic nation and lands against foreign nations and individuals, and we agreed to honour the treaties of our southern allies, the Wabanaki Confederacy, and to bring the other Mikmaq districts into the union".

The 1752 treaty is known to the Mikmaqs as the Elekewaki treaty ("in the King's House", meaning that in the Mikmaq view they had agreed to come within the purview of the British Crown). The Mikmaqs believe that the treaty reserved all Mikmaq territory for their own use, but allowed the small British settlements of that time to remain on their land. "We were guaranteed that our way of life could continue according to our desires, either by hunting and fishing or by entering into trade with the British." The Mikmaqs agreed to take their disputes with the British to His Majesty's civil courts, but to enforce tribal law in Mikmaq disputes; while the Crown promised that the law would be similar to "a great hedge about our rights and properties".

Denny says that the Crown itself has never denied its treaty obligations. Queen Elizabeth affirmed them as recently as 1973. But, he says, the Mikmaqs have had to fight the Canadian bureaucracy unremittingly for many years, and the arbitrary measures taken by the federal and provincial governments "bring shame and dishonour on the Crown". He adds: "I am impressed that Mikmaqs are never more loyal to the Crown than when we fight for our promised rights."

The aboriginal memory is long. Sixty years later, as we shall see, the Mikmaqs again entered the courts to challenge the 1928 decision that had brushed their treaty rights aside, and this time they experienced considerably greater success.

6

Colonials, and the policies they made

The laws governing our relations with aboriginal people still embody the arrogant and racist attitudes that were the colonial norm in the early nineteenth century. Unfortunately, most Canadians do not realize this. When Canada became a nation in 1867, the existing British colonial laws were simply consolidated into the Indian Act. Passed in 1876, the Act consigned the aboriginal people to the status of minors, and treated them as if they were wards of the state. The main thrust of this Act has never changed. It is essential for us today to understand where the Indian Act came from, to acknowledge the attitudes it embodies, and to ask how a modern nation like Canada comes to have such a thing still on its books.

The Indian Act did not spring full-blown from the minds of the Fathers of Confederation, but evolved gradually throughout the previous hundred years. Aboriginals had begun to give ground to the colonists long before Confederation, especially in the years after the American Revolutionary War, when United Empire Loyalists flocked into Canada from the United States. These newcomers needed land; in the thirty-six years between 1786 and 1822, the colonial authorities signed nineteen treaties with different groups of aboriginals, covering the most favourable agricultural lands of southern Ontario. The objective was to clear the land of the underlying Indian title.

The impetus for these treaties came from a Royal Proclamation issued by King George III in 1763, after Britain emerged victorious from the Seven Years' War with France. In the Proclamation, the Crown undertook that Indian lands should not be settled or developed without the agreement of "the several Nations or Tribes of

Indians with whom we are connected, and who live under Our Protection", that this agreement could be granted only "at some Publick meeting or assembly" of the Indians with the colonial authorities, and that "no private persons" should be permitted to buy Indian lands. This measure was designed, said the Proclamation, to avoid repetition of the "great Frauds and Abuses" that had already occurred in the purchasing of Indian lands.

This treaty-making was not an orderly process.[1] The Indians did not initiate the treaties, and did not much influence their terms. Their title was alienated, and it was simply assumed that they would retreat from advancing settlement into more remote hunting territories.

Most of the surrenders in southern Ontario were a great bargain for the colonists.[2] For example, two million acres of what are now Kent, Elgin and Middlesex counties (where the cities of London and Chatham have since been built) were surrendered by Ottawas, Chippewas, Pottawatomies and Hurons in 1790 for £1,200 (less than $5,000); and three million acres of Norfolk and Haldimand counties (west of the Niagara peninsula) were surrendered by Mississaugas two years later for even less. In 1796 Chippewas (also known as Ojibway) gave up most of four counties for £2,000-worth of goods. And so the tale goes on: for example, Etobicoke, York, Vaughan and other townships now part of Metropolitan Toronto were surrendered by Mississaugas on September 23, 1787 "for divers goods and valuable consideration" – ten shillings, although with some provision for additional future payments.

Some aboriginals moved into southern Ontario during these years, as others were being removed. After the Revolutionary War, the Indian allies of the British had felt betrayed by the terms of the peace settlement, in which vast Indian lands were surrendered to the new American state; hence room had to be found in Ontario for the 1,500 Iroquois who had fought for the British under Joseph Brant, and had been promised land in British America. In the 1780s surrenders of land were negotiated at the Bay of Quinte near Kingston, and along the Grand River in southwestern Ontario, for Iroquois settlement; but the transactions were bungled because the Governor General granted to the Iroquois land that was not his to dispose of. More than 130 years were to pass before this mess was sorted out. The Grand River tract granted to the Six Nations comprised more than a million acres, but eventually some of this land was withheld because it had not been properly ceded by its Mississauga owners; then Brant himself almost immediately sold half of his people's entitlement, including some of the best land in the province, along the Grand River from Fergus south to Paris.[3] During these years, too, some Delawares, Ottawas and Wyandots crossed the border from the United States, and a number of Ojibway filtered south from the north and west.

A turning point for all aboriginals came in 1814, when the war for possession of the North American continent finally ended. In Canada, the War of 1812 saw the last great armed stand of the eastern Indians, when the forces gathered by Tecumseh, a Shawnee born not far south of Lake Erie, fought beside the British against the American invasion. Tecumseh, regarded by many as the greatest aboriginal leader in North American history, dreamed of creating an Indian nation. He worked all his life to unite aboriginals from Canada to the Gulf of Mexico, but his effort was too late. He died in battle at Moraviantown in 1813, and his body was never seen again, spirited away from the field, most historians believe, by his followers.[4]

Until 1814, Europeans had always needed the Indians, first in the fur trade, and then in war, and so had tried to maintain alliances with them. With the ending of the war, the priority for the British colonists, as for the Americans, became to occupy, populate and develop the countryside. Henceforth, the Indians stood in the way of that enterprise.

The colony of Upper Canada had 80,000 settlers by 1812, and tens of thousands more poured in after the war's end. As the treaty-making process continued, Indians were removed from more and more lands. In the year 1818 alone, many treaties were negotiated: the Chippewas surrendered more than 1,500,000 acres for a £1,200 annuity; the Mississaugas gave up 650,000 acres for £522-worth of goods; all of the area from Oshawa through Peterborough and beyond, nearly two million acres, was given up by Chippewas for annual payment of goods worth £740; and when Lanark and its surrounding counties were needed to accommodate the soldiers demobilized after the war, the Mississaugas surrendered 2,748,000 acres in consideration for goods worth £632 a year. As the Algonquins and Nipissing were later to discover, Mississaugas surrendered land to the north of them that was not really theirs to surrender.

To any charge that they were exploiting the Indians, the settlers and administrators answered that the land was of little value so long as it was used only for hunting. Only the pressure of hard-working, productive Europeans added value to the land.

Having cleared the Indians out of the way of settlement, the colonial authorities could plot their next move. In the thirty years after 1820, the main lines of public policy towards the Indians were established. The Indian Act as we know it today evolved from the debate in those years about whether to protect the Indians from the advance of European settlement, or to assimilate them into mainstream colonial society through education, religion and agriculture.

From 1822 onwards, a veritable hailstorm of letters, memos, reports and recommendations about Indian policy passed back and forth across the Atlantic between the British and colonial authorities. To put it bluntly, the authorities who formulated these policies were contemptuous of aboriginals, and determined that they should not interfere with the process of European settlement.

In 1826 the British authorities asked Major-General H.C. Darling to write the first official report ever produced about Indian conditions in Canada. Darling reported that there were 18,000 Indians within the jurisdictions of Upper and Lower Canada (now Ontario and Quebec). This figure included only aboriginals living on reserves or in settlements close to the colonial towns, but not the nomadic forest-dwellers known in those days as "wandering" or "wild" Indians – Algonquins, Ojibway, Crees, Montagnais, Naskapi – who lived in the Hudson's Bay Company territories in what is today northern Quebec and Ontario. Since those people did not stand immediately in the path of settlement, Indian policies of the day did not take them into account. Their numbers were put at 3,000, an extremely low estimate.[5]

Darling recommended that Indians should be collected "in considerable numbers" and settled in villages; they should be provided with "religious improvement, education and instruction in husbandry", and helped with "housing, rations, and necessary seed and agricultural implements". The British government liked these ideas, but did not want to pay for them; in 1830 it transferred Indian administration from the military to the civil authority, thus making the payment of treaty annuities a charge against the colonial revenues.

In announcing this decision, the Secretary of State, Sir George Murray, said that earlier policy had failed to reclaim the aboriginals "from a state of barbarism", and provide them with "the industrious

and peaceful habits of civilized life".[6] This failure was understand-
able, he said, since the Indians were disposed to cling to their original habits and mode of life, while "the new occupants of America"
tended "to regard the natives as an irreclaimable race, and as incon-
venient neighbours whom it was desirable ultimately wholly to remove". Murray accepted Darling's suggestion that Indians should
now be "settled in townships or upon detached lots of land in a manner similar to the European settlers", and should be encouraged in religious knowledge and education.

Creating the ideal Indian

An examination of official statements about Canada's Indians from
Darling in 1828 to Prime Minister Sir John A. Macdonald in 1880 (and
beyond), shows that aboriginal people were considered praiseworthy
only to the extent that they adopted European values, beliefs and habits.

For the public men of the nineteenth century, the ideal Indians
were those on the Quebec reserves, long settled in villages under the
leadership of priests. Hurons had become established at Loretteville
in 1650, Mohawks at Caughnawaga in 1667, and Mohawks, Nipissing
and Algonquins at Oka from 1717. These people were praised in the
official accounts because of their many intermarriages with whites,
their large families, regular church attendance, success in agriculture,
and abandonment of their "pagan" ceremonies and beliefs. (Ironically, 160 years later, the descendants of these supposedly acculturated people took to armed resistance in defence of their aboriginal
land claim during the 1990 Oka crisis.)

One of the main aims of colonial governments was to extend this
model from Quebec's village Indians to the many "wild and wandering" Indians of Ontario. Schools and missions were opened in various
places in southern Ontario, where missionaries and teachers – including such native Christians as the Ojibway Methodist, the Reverend
Peter Jones – worked assiduously towards the end of settling Indians
on their own land so that they could be "civilized".

An experimental reserve was established at Coldwater, near Lake
Simcoe, with the intention of making Indians into Christian farmers.
Although the Indians were apparently anxious to make this experiment
work, it failed because of inferior equipment, incompetent staff, and
rivalries between competing missionaries and government agencies.[7]

When the eccentric Sir Francis Bond Head arrived in 1836 to become Lieutenant-Governor of Upper Canada, a certain schizophrenia entered official attitudes towards Indians. Head had had a colourful career in South America, where he had written travel books about his forays into the Andes, and had no inhibitions about announcing as soon as he arrived that the policy of turning Indians into farmers was already a complete failure. "The greatest kindness that could be done to these intelligent, simple-minded people is to remove them as much as possible from all communication with whites," he said.[8] His solution was to gather as many Indians as possible on Manitoulin Island, at the north end of Lake Huron. After all, the island was uninhabited by whites, and "appears to have few temptations to invite them thither".

Head immediately obtained surrender of the island and its extensive archipelego from the few wandering Ottawas and Ojibway who used it from time to time, his object being to free it for settlement by other Indians. At the same time, Head told the Ojibway of the Bruce peninsula (separated from Manitoulin by the twenty-five mile channel between Georgian Bay and Lake Huron) that the government could not protect them from incoming settlers, and persuaded them to surrender a huge area of land, and move either to Manitoulin or to the barren north end of the peninsula.[9]

The Aborigines' Protection Society, formed in London in response to the deteriorating condition of aboriginal people throughout the British colonies, thought Head's scheme hypocritical. The Society said he was merely trying to get the Indians out of the way of settlement by banishing them on to "twenty-three thousand barren islands, rocks of granite perfectly useless for every purpose of civilized life", where they were doomed to live on berries and the few fish they could catch from the shallow waters of the lake.[10] In return Head had obtained, they said, three million acres of rich lands.

What happened on Manitoulin Island was not much different from the Coldwater experiment. In twenty-five years, only 1,000 people arrived, and only 3,000 acres were improved.

These first attempts at "settling and civilizing" the "wandering" Indians of Ontario were a failure. But the Quebec example remained strong, and the idea that Indians should be confined to reserves and acculturated to European ways began to win the day. Gradually, the ideas put forward by Major-General Darling in 1828 were written into official policy. By 1838 the Colonial Secretary said the first object should be to locate Indians "in compact settlements, apart, if possible, from the population of European descent...to gain them from a wandering to a settled life". To give native people a sense of permanency, "they should be attached to the soil by being taught to regard it as reserved for them and their children by the strongest securities."[11] Their land should be granted to them "forever". No creditors should be able to claim against these lands, which should not be sold without the agreement of the Lieutenant-Governor, the principal chief and the resident missionary.

Here we see the genesis of policies that remain largely unchanged to this day. Six years later, in 1844, the Bagot commission of inquiry formalized these attitudes, and laid out an agenda that from 1850 onwards was translated into legislation and law. The main principles enunciated by the commission were:[12]

• Indians should be gathered in settlements, instructed in agriculture, and placed in the hands of teachers "of strictly moral and religious character" who would gradually elevate them to the standards of Europeans. (This became the reserve system.)

• Indian parents had too much influence on their children, so a system of "labour or industrial" schools should be created, where the children could live all the time. (These became the residential schools, which lasted until the 1970s, and are remembered with such bitterness by so many native people of our own day.)

• Since Indian life was thought to be so degenerate, an escape hatch should be offered to those who could earn it. Any Indian "qualified by education, knowledge of the arts and customs of civilized life and habits of industry and prudence" should be given a limited title to up to 200 acres of communal Indian lands, and at the same time a once-and-for-all payment in furniture, stock or tools. In return for this, he would forfeit all future claims to the communal property of the tribe. (This was the genesis of the policy of "enfranchisement", under which Indians were later divided into two classes, judged by the level of their acculturation into European styles of living. The ultimate objective was to admit them to the status of full citizens, provided they would renounce their race and deny their culture. This policy, conceived in 1844, lasted for more than a century.)

• All land not handed over to individuals in this way should be surrendered to the government, to be sold for the benefit of the tribe. Obviously, the commission had in mind that within a few years,

Indian reserves would no longer exist. (This was merely the first of many schemes that eventually stripped Indians of more than a third of the lands later granted them as reserves.)

• The annual gifts paid to Indians in compensation for land surrenders, and for loyalty during the colonial wars, should be discontinued: something the colonial authorities had been trying to achieve for the previous two decades. The Indians had always objected strenuously to this. "Father, these presents (since we are taught to call them by that name), are not in fact presents," the Six Nations had protested ten years before. "They are a sacred debt contracted by the government, under the promise made by the Kings of France to our forefathers, to indemnify them for the land they had given up, confirmed by the Kings of England since the cession of the country and up to this time punctually paid and acquitted." [13]

It is extraordinary that the perceptions of the Bagot commissioners, and the officials who appointed them, remained enshrined in Canadian laws until the 1980s. In a real sense, we have been trapped for a century-and-a-half in the prejudices of Victorian Englishmen. Here are some of the opinions held by influential law-makers:

Lord Sydenham, the colony's Governor General when the commission was established, said in 1841 that the attempt to combine "a system of pupilage" for the Indians with their settlement "in civilized parts of the country" was embarrassing for the government, expensive, a waste of resources, and was not helping the Indians. [14]

Unleashing a classic anti-Indian diatribe in a letter to the Colonial Secretary, Sydenham wrote:

Thus circumstanced, the Indian loses all the good qualities of his wild state and acquires nothing but the vices of civilization. He does not become a good settler, he does not become an agriculturalist or mechanic. He does become a drunkard and debauchee, and his females and family follow the same course. He occupies valuable land, unprofitably to himself and injuriously to the country. He gives infinite trouble to the government, and adds nothing either to the wealth, the industry, or the defence of the province.

It was only a quarter-century since Tecumseh had fallen in battle in defence of Canada, but in the view of the colonial authorities, the Indians had become useless people, occupying valuable land.

The Bagot commissioners took their cue from the Governor. They posited two types of aboriginal people: an ideal type, whom Europeans, by definition, never had dealings with; and a degenerate type, whom Europeans saw on a daily basis. In his native state, they wrote,

> the red man...[is] a person of the finest description.... Height, beauty of proportion, nobility of carriage, activity, strength and suppleness are [his] general characteristics.... In his native state the Indian is simple-minded, generous, proud and energetic, docile...of a lively and happy disposition...and very hospitable. An Indian brave would rather die than commit an act derogatory to his character as a warrior....

Unfortunately, the onset of civilization and settlement gave rise to the second type:

> In his half-civilized state [the Indian] is indolent to excess, intemperate, suspicious, cunning, covetous and addicted to lying and fraud.

This was a comfortable dichotomy, providing the colonists with a cushion on which to rest their prejudices: Indians with whom they were in contact were degenerate, corrupt and untrustworthy; only those whom they never met were admirable. The people of whom these views were held had already been stripped of their economy, were being harried out of their lands, were denied political and civil rights, and were subject to laws in the making of which they had no say. But even the commissioners had to admit that the poor condition of "the red man" was not entirely his own fault:

> The game is exhausted in his old hunting grounds and has become scarce in those far distant to which he is obliged to have recourse. He now hunts for the sake of the fur alone, to produce which he is often pledged to the trader.... His expeditions become long and distant; his success precarious; his supply of food is often exhausted, and he is frequently exposed to the horrors of starvation, both by hunger and cold....

Diseases such as tuberculosis, rheumatism and scrofula easily took hold among these weakened people, exhausting their strength and "laying the seeds of disease and degeneration in their descendants". Not surprisingly, figures gathered by the commission indicated that the number of Indians in their limited census had fallen in fifteen years from 18,000 to 12,000.

Even though the Bagot commission realized that laws were needed to prevent Europeans from squatting on Indian lands, the preoccupation of the period was expansion, not justice. The commission accepted the inevitability of development, and rejected arguments that the Indians had been unjustly dispossessed and inadequately paid for their land:

> It would have been as impossible to resist the natural laws of society and to guard the Indian Territory against the encroachments of whites as it would have been impolitic to have attempted to check the tide of immigration. The alternative would have been "the horrors of a protracted struggle for ownership," which could have had only one result: the occupation of Indian lands "without any compensation whatever."

In other words, *force majeure* had the strength of natural law. We are still hearing the same arguments in Canada today, sometimes from the most distinguished of judges.

Ideas become actions

Embodying these perceptions, the Indian Act took shape in the two decades before Canadian Confederation. Settlers were now moving into the lands of "wandering" Indians as the colonies slowly spread west and north. In 1850 the decision was taken to set aside areas of reserved land for displaced Indians. In Lower Canada, 230,000 acres of land were set aside for Indian reserves; and in Upper Canada, the Robinson treaties, covering the land north of Lake Superior, established reserves for the first time in return for the surrender of Indian title.

These land grants, as they were called (although the Indians have always wondered how land could be granted to them which had always been theirs), were proposed as protective measures for the Indians, and so they appeared to be. But they had an obverse motive: the new reserves were motivated as much by the colonial need to clear the Indians from the path of settlement as to protect them. The Robinson treaties were signed only because minerals had been discovered in Ojibway lands. In Lower Canada, the Temiscaming and Maniwaki reserves, established under the 1850 land grants, were designed by priests and officials as collecting grounds for the Algonquins in the Ottawa Valley being dispossessed by the lumber industry.

In fact, many of the supposedly protective measures introduced in the next two decades severely restricted the freedom of aboriginal people. For example, in 1850 two acts were passed for the protection of Indian lands from trespass and injury in Upper and Lower Canada. These decreed that Indian lands could not change hands without the consent of the Crown – a protective measure. But they also allowed the Crown to lease Indian lands, collect rents, license the cutting of timber on them, and put the money into a fund to be administered on behalf of the Indians, something that no non-natives would ever have accepted.

The Indians themselves had no say over how this money was spent. For many years, the authorities used it to build schools, in spite of repeated protests by the Indians. The Six Nations complained:

> As our white brethren are provided with the means of education at the public expense, we do not think we ought to be called upon to give up a portion of our small allowance for these purposes. [15]

This became a permanent policy, and survived for so long that when David Crombie was appointed Minister of Indian Affairs and Northern Development in 1984, he asked his bureaucrats if it was still existing practice for the Crown to use Indian funds "to pay the costs of programmes which are regularly available to the Canadian public?" Crombie's question was never answered before he was removed from office.[16]

The 1850 acts prohibited Indians from exchanging goods for liquor – a protective measure – but also made it illegal for them to sell property they may have derived from government presents and annuities – a repressive measure.[17] These presents and annuities could be compared with modern-day social-security entitlements, except that the government took control of how they were spent. It was almost as if, in our own day, old-age pensions were seized and spent on building drop-in centres for the aged.

In 1850 the authorities also attempted for the first time to define an "Indian". The lawmakers felt a definition was needed so that they could know who held a stake in "Indian lands". The Upper Canada definition included all persons of Indian blood, reputed to belong to a particular body or tribe of Indians, and their descendants; all persons intermarried with such Indians and living among them, and their descendants; all persons living among such Indians whose parents were Indians and members of the same tribe; and all persons adopted in infancy by such Indians, and living in their village or on their lands, and their descendants.

In Lower Canada, the definition excluded non-Indian men married to Indian women, but not non-Indian women married to Indian men.

Thus began the division into "status" and "non-status" Indians, which has weakened aboriginal society ever since.

Summing up the effect of these acts, the historian J.R. Miller recently identified 1850 as the moment at which Canada "found itself on the slippery slope that led from the moral heights of protection to the depths of coercion".[18]

Working up to the Indian Act

In spite of the opportunity offered them in 1850, the Indians did not flock en masse to live as Europeans. Disappointed, the authorities called into being in 1856 yet another commission of inquiry to explain the failure. This commission wrote in its report:

> There is no inherent defect in the organization of the Indians which disqualifies them from being reclaimed from their savage state. The attentive eye will observe a progress, slow it is true, but not the less steady, towards improvement.... With sorrow, however, we must confess that any hopes of raising the Indians as a body to the social or political level of their white neighbours is yet but a glimmer and a distant spark.[19]

In 1857, the drive to assimilate Indians was given expression in an Act whose title tells all: "An Act for the Gradual Civilization of the Indian Tribes of the Canadas". Its object was to remove all legal distinctions between Indians and other Canadians. This time the authorities entered the game of enfranchisement with a vengeance. The 1857 Act spelled out in detail how aboriginal people could be detached from their community, their nation and their race, and become honorary whites.[20] Henceforth, a commission comprising a visiting superintendent, a missionary and one other person appointed by the Governor could determine whether a male Indian who was twenty-one or over (and willing to be enfranchised) fulfilled the criteria: ability to speak, read and write English or French, good moral character, and freedom from debt. If they found him so, they could recommend to the Governor that such a person "shall no longer be deemed an Indian" within the meaning of the Act. Even a person who could not read and write could be enfranchised after a three-year probation.

This extraordinary measure, declaring a person to be of another race than the one into which he had been born, was probably unique in the history of the world. It embodied not only an insulting view of

aboriginals, but encouraged them to think so poorly of their own race that only by embracing the values, beliefs and habits of another race could they feel that they were living a decent life. As an encouragement to enfranchisement, the law allowed up to fifty acres of reserve land to be given to enfranchised Indians "in fee simple", and in addition a sum of money equal to the annuities and other yearly revenues received on their behalf by the tribe. Symbolically, at least, the granting of this bureaucratic power to "deem" someone to be a non-Indian was a turning point in Canadian history: no longer were natives and non-natives, who had once worked so closely together in trade and war, engaged on a common journey as they developed the country.

The controls taken over Indian lands, property and lives were tightened by an Enfranchisement Act in 1859, Lands Acts in 1860 and 1866, and by various statutes passed in the colonies of Nova Scotia and British Columbia. So when the new nation of Canada took over responsibility for "Indians and lands reserved for the Indians" in 1867, the die was already cast. Theoretically, this brave new country embarking on a brave new future could have fully recognized the dignity, status and equality of aboriginal societies. But given the attitudes that had been developed over the previous half-century, this was never likely. The seeds had already been sown for the tragedy that overcame the native people in the following century.

For a decade, the new government poured its energies into establishing control over the huge country inherited from Britain. Getting hold of Indian lands was a major part of this effort. In 1869, an Enfranchisement Act introduced a system of elected chiefs to replace the traditional chiefs, and individual Indians were again encouraged to take private ownership of their lands.[21] This Act also provided that an Indian woman who married a non-Indian would lose status, band membership and annuities, as would her children. The General Council of Ontario and Quebec Indians asked for this law to be amended so that "Indian women may have the privilege of marrying when and whom they please without subjecting themselves to exclusion or expulsion from the tribe."[22] Their request was ignored. This measure, which remained law until 1985, led to the absurdity of tens of thousands of aboriginal people being defined as non-Indian although they lived as Indians, spoke Indian languages, and held to Indian beliefs and values, while thousands of European women who married Indian men were defined as status Indians. Blandly, the government said, in the words of one bureaucrat, that these measures were "designed to lead the Indian people by degrees to mingle with the white race in the ordinary avocations of life".[23]

In 1870, Canada acquired the Hudson's Bay Company lands, and Manitoba joined Confederation (the legislation provided a land settlement, never satisfactorily fulfilled, of 1,400,000 acres for the Métis). In 1871, the first of the Canadian Indian treaties was signed in Manitoba, and British Columbia joined Confederation. By 1875, five treaties had been signed extending west to southern Saskatchewan, and in 1876 Interior Minister and Superintendent-General of Indian Affairs David Laird introduced the Indian Act in the House of Commons. The Act's main purpose, Laird said, was to consolidate all previous legislation passed in the various colonies regarding Indians.[24]

Laird warned that "Indians must either be treated as minors or as white men," but a memorandum issued by his Deputy Superintendent-General, Lawrence Vankoughnet, four months after the Act was passed, put the issue of Canada's future policy beyond doubt: "The legal status of the Indians of Canada is that of minors, with the government as their guardians," Vankoughnet declared.[25]

The Indian Act, with its 100 sections, most of them left to the discretion of the minister, confirmed that henceforth Euro-Canadians intended to exercise full control over every aspect of the lives of native people, whom they were steadily herding into small reserves so that they could no longer stand in the way of white settlement. The full onslaught on the aboriginal people was just beginning; the primary weapon, the Indian Act, was ready for use.

Seeking status: an Indian Act comedy

The Canadian race-classification system invented in the nineteenth century is still alive and well 150 years after it was created. This national embarrassment appears to have defied all efforts to abolish it. In 1985 Parliament passed Bill C-31, restoring Indian status to people who had lost it during the many years of the nightmarish enfranchisement policy. But eight years later, the cure appears to have been almost worse than the disease; the new law has actually intensified the race-classification system, and in some respects has carried it to new heights of lunacy.

Down the street from my home in Ottawa lives a native artist, Claude Latour. Born in Ottawa, Claude always knew that his family roots lay in the Maniwaki Algonquin reserve, north of Ottawa, although when he was growing up neither his parents nor grandparents had Indian status. His grandmother was born in 1898 in Maniwaki but had lost her status. Under Bill C-31 she applied for, and won, reinstatement, and so did Claude's mother. He decided to apply as well. He found himself engaged in an incredible historical paper-chase, as he tried to comply with the arcane regulations established by the government to administer C-31.

The story begins with an Orkneyman named William Budge, who came to Canada with the Hudson's Bay Company and in 1863 married a full-blooded Algonquin woman, Cecile Okitchikijik, Claude's great-great-grandmother. As Claude tells it, the Department of Indian Affairs had no trouble believing that Cecile was an Indian, but since she was never registered as such, never signed a treaty, and died, as they say, an infidel (that is to say, was never baptised), she was merely a "bush" or "savage" Indian, ineligible to be considered an Indian under departmental regulations. If Claude could prove that Cecile had ever received an annuity payment of some kind from the government, he could have his status. That is, shall we say, Route One.

William and Cecile Budge had seven children. Their son Tom, being the son of a white man and an Indian woman without status, is today race-classified as 6.2 F, code for a Métis with native blood from the female side, but legally speaking, as far as the department is concerned, a white. Tom married a woman called Mary-Ann, the daughter of Suzanne, who was a registered Indian with a band number, and therefore classified as a 6.1. Mary-Ann's father was a wealthy white businessman who had engaged in an affair with Suzanne, so a false surname was used on Mary-Ann's documents. As the daughter of a white man, Mary-Ann has been classified as a 6.2 F. A quirk of the regulations, however, provides that she could inherit her mother's 6.1 classification, if it could be proved that she was the illegitimate daughter of an unmarried woman. Such could be extremely difficult to prove, since Suzanne was married four times. But for Claude, that could be Route Two.

In any case, Mary-Ann lost her status with the department when she married Tom Budge, legally a white man. Although they did not have status, Tom and Mary-Ann lived on the Maniwaki reserve and had seven children. One of them was Claude's grandfather, Lloyd Budge. He married Marguerite, a 6.1, in 1919, and they had fourteen children. By this marriage to a 6.2 F, Marguerite lost her status. However, as fully recognized members of the Maniwaki band, Lloyd and Marguerite and their children were admitted to status by the band in 1928, with the full agreement of the government.

In 1943 the baleful name of Malcolm McCrimmon, an Indian Affairs accountant, appears on the family record. For many years McCrimmon was the official in charge of "cleaning up" band membership lists. As described by author John Goddard in his book *The Last Stand of the Lubicon Cree*, McCrimmon's action in removing hundreds of names from band lists in northern Alberta became a major element in the 1980s argument between the Lubicons and the government. Evidently McCrimmon was actively doing the same work in other parts of the country. On his recommendation, Lloyd and Marguerite Budge and their children were removed from Indian status in 1943. Eventually they were kicked off the reserve, and moved to Ottawa in 1952.

To get his status, Claude had to prove that his grandfather Lloyd was an Indian. He could do that only by finding the evidence needed to upgrade the classification of Cecile or Mary-Ann from 6.2 F to 6.1. Route Three would be to collect affidavits from people in Maniwaki who could testify that Lloyd and Marguerite had always been Indians.

Route Four would have been simply to proceed through the agreement of the chief and band council. But, as in many reserves where restoration of lost band members is unwelcome because it creates pressure on overtaxed resources, this approach had already been refused.

The affidavit route would have been the simplest, but it would deal only with Lloyd and Marguerite. Claude preferred to try to win status for his whole family – there are hundreds of Budges by this time, he says – by proving the credentials of Cecile Okitchikijik.

So he hired an archivist to come up with this proof.

As nearly as I could figure it, Claude has 37.5 per cent Indian blood. I asked him why he was bothering with all this. "I make my living as a native artist, and there are still some First Nations who insist on seeing your card before they will accept you as a participant in a show. Otherwise, they just have my word for it.

"But I also want the government to admit that an injustice was done when my grandparents were kicked out of status in 1943."

Did he think he could win? "Yes, I do. I will win because I have chosen the most difficult and honourable route," he told me.

In the end, Claude's confidence was justified. Early in 1993, he was advised that his application for status had been approved. He had submitted proofs covering Routes One, Two and Three. What the department accepted was that Mary-Ann, Claude's great-grandmother, was the illegitimate daughter of a union unsanctified by marriage. So Claude is, so they now say, an Indian after all.

7

Mikmaqs: the trauma of government help

The trauma of the Mikmaq people, described in Chapter 5, did not end when Chief Sylliboy failed to reaffirm their treaty rights in 1928. Later, they had also to survive the trauma of government help. Even today, the people of Eskasoni are coping with the consequences of ill-conceived government schemes that were supposed to put them back on their feet.

Marie Battiste was born in Houlton, Maine, after her parents fled the appalling conditions created by the federal government's decision in the 1940s to centralize all Mikmaqs in just two reserves – Shubenacadie on the Nova Scotia mainland, and Eskasoni in Cape Breton. Only seven or eight families had been living at Eskasoni at the time, most of them farming, but Mikmaqs from other parts of Cape Breton were promised that if they would move there, they would be helped to become farmers, or to find other work.

The authorities claimed their intention was "to have the Indians live in well-organized and completely self-sufficient communities".[1] The purpose of the policy was "to enable the Indians...to make a living for themselves and thus become increasingly less a burden on the taxpayers of Canada". But the scheme turned out to be a disaster, with more than a thousand people crammed onto land that could support only half a dozen families.

"My parents left Chapel Island in 1946 and came to Eskasoni, intending to stay," Marie told me. "Some people moved with just tents, and lived through the winter. But my parents moved in with my mother's cousin, which at least gave far more protection than a tent. My mother had three children, her cousin five. It was quite typical to have three families staying in one house.

"During centralization the government built only the shells of the houses, but not the interiors, and there was no insulation. It was a very cold house, heated by a wood stove. People put mattresses on the floor. My aunt did not have any finished flooring, and from up-stairs you could look down to the kitchen between the boards. For many years the house never got fixed up; her husband became so angry about it all that he would never fix it, and eventually when his son was grown, he finished it."

The Mikmaqs have many links with New England, at least as far south as Boston, and have always crossed the border freely to pick up seasonal work. So to escape the rigours of Canada's improvement schemes, Marie's father and mother went south as migrant farm workers to pick potatoes. Eventually they decided to stay in Houlton, a village 480 miles almost directly west of Eskasoni, just across the border from Woodstock, New Brunswick.

"I grew up right on the Main street of Houlton, 'Paddy-holler' they used to call it. I was always very conscious of being Mikmaq, and of the racism and prejudice that were so much a part of Houlton's men-tality, directed against the many Mikmaqs who came through every season looking for work.

"The seasonal work could get you enough money to buy your boots and your car payment, and if everyone in the family worked hard, they would have enough money to pay off their bills until the time came for pulping blueberries and making reed baskets. My par-ents lived in a tarpaper shack beside the potato house. My mother cared for the kids and picked potatoes.

"In Houlton, my father and mother never fraternized with the local folks. We stayed to ourselves. There were not many other Indians in the Houlton area, no Indian village, for example, but some people were scattered around, and we did visit with some Maliseet families.

"My father had a sense that things were never good in Canada, that people were poor, there were no jobs, and no educational op-portunities. He believed that if we stayed in Maine, we would have a chance for a better education, so I worked towards that, towards ful-filling their anticipation."

This negative perception of Canada was confirmed by the experi-ence of Marie's older sister, Eleanor, who lived for three years at the Catholic residential school on the Shubenacadie reserve. In 1947, the authorities were very proud of this school, "the only large school of its type east of Ontario [that] provides for orphan and neglected Indian children from the three Maritime provinces":

> The school has faciliites for the teaching of crafts such as pottery and woodcarving...agricultural pursuits, including stock-raising and dairying, and owns some excellent pure-bred stock. Girls are taught homemaking and domestic sciences, weaving and other handicrafts.... The training and care given the pupils are adequate to enable them to get that good start in life which they might not otherwise have.[2]

Marie's sister had a somewhat different experience. "My aunt wrote that Eleanor was not doing well, that she could not read or write, could not speak English, was full of lice, and in fact refused to speak at all. In that school the punishment for refusing to eat porridge was to be put in a darkened room for up to three days. My sister has spent many, many years since then trying to cope with the damage that was done to her. Eventually she went to Boston, worked in factories, and now she has three children of her own; but she was a psychological victim of boarding school."

Statistics for the time show that throughout the Maritimes and eastern Quebec, school places were available for only 75 per cent of Indian children between the ages of seven and sixteen. In retrospect, the decision of Marie's father to seek education for his children in the United States was probably a wise one.

"I decided to become a teacher," Marie explained, "and went to the University of Maine. I got scholarships and grants, and worked my way through school in the kitchen. In the third year the State of Maine provided free education for Mikmaqs and Maliseets. When I graduated, I worked at the university in a federal upgrading programme for disadvantaged youth."

When her family moved to Boston, Marie was able to enter the Harvard Indian Education Programme. A few years later she moved with Sakej Henderson to California and found herself living, as she put it, in a totally alien environment, dominated by dog-eat-dog ideas of individual gain, in which children were "precocious, demanding, ugly". She wanted children of her own, but decided this was no place to bring them up.

Although reared in Maine, Marie had spent a lot of time back in Eskasoni. The family had come north for the annual St. Ann's mission, and "when somebody died, we would get in the car and come to the funeral." At the same time, she felt she had been deprived of the "gathering, social bonding, and linking that epitomizes the strength of Mikmaq culture", so when Alex Denny appeared in 1978 to urge her to return to Cape Breton, she was ready to go.

Denny had become Grand Captain in 1968; the Mikmaq people were demoralized then, confused by all the changes that had been forced on them. It was only four years since Gabriel Sylliboy, their unchallenged leader since the late 1920s, had died. (Although Silliboy was a towering figure among the Mikmaqs, his death at the age of ninety passed almost unnoticed in Nova Scotia, recorded only in a perfunctory three paragraphs at the bottom of page fifteen of the Halifax newspaper.)[3] In a heroic, bloody-minded, last-ditch attempt to assert the continuing existence of the Mikmaq nation, Sylliboy had opposed every government effort to assimilate Mikmaqs into the mainstream of Nova Scotia life. His death left the Mikmaqs leaderless and rudderless as they confronted a major dilemma: to assimilate as government wanted them to, or retain their identity as a distinct people?

The elders turned to Alex as a man young enough to communicate with the new generation, and traditional enough to defend the long-accepted values of the nation. He accepted that his mandate was to pick up where Sylliboy had left off, to reassert the nationhood of the Mikmaqs, and ensure that the international community understood their plight. "Our treaties were signed nation-to-nation," he told me over the kitchen table. "I had to prove that beyond a reasonable doubt."

The modern consequences

The Mikmaqs have always tried to adapt to meet the demands of the Canadian economy, but whatever they have done has never seemed to be enough. First they adapted by becoming traders instead of hunters, but soon found themselves eliminated from the trading networks. They adapted by becoming farmers, only to be relocated and dispossessed of their farms.[4] They adapted by becoming industrial workers; they were then squeezed out of their jobs by the racism entrenched in the economic system.

In 1991, unemployment on the reserve was an estimated 85 to 90 per cent. It was scarcely worth their while, said Alex Denny, to look for work in Sydney, because they were almost never hired. "You have to be three times better than any non-Indian if you are to get a job.

70

You have no chance of getting a job if your uncle or brother doesn't work within the system." Not surprisingly, the Mikmaqs nurse a long-held sense of grievance over the way they have been treated.

Alex recounted his own experience with a mixture of bitterness and mordant humour: "I worked as a government employment and relocation officer, and I can tell you that every economic development project started on the reserve was doomed to failure. The Indian Affairs bureaucracy always sent in people to run things who couldn't make it on the outside." On one occasion the officials brought into the reserve a huge bulldozer, built a garage for it designed by an engineer from Ottawa, and held a grand opening. "Their opening fell flat when the bulldozer wouldn't fit into the garage." Alex's expression wavered between anger and incredulity.

"Once they started an oyster farm. It went well, but then the oysters started to die off. They brought in two scientists from Ottawa, then two oceanographers from Halifax, to discover what had gone wrong. I asked an old man in the reserve. He said, 'If you put a cow on the field, it does well. What happens when you put a hundred cows on the same field?' It took the scientists two years to figure out the oysters were starving."

Really, it was no laughing matter. Nor were the Mikmaqs amused when a successful factory they had started for making doors, windows and coffins was closed by the government as soon as two Sydney businessmen complained that the Mikmaqs were taking away their business.

The consequence of these blunders has been that, much against their will, the Mikmaqs have been orced to exist on welfare, "fool's gold", as Alex calls it, with occasional supplements from "lazy Indian projects": fifteen-week make-work jobs such as cutting brush, or digging holes and then filling them in, all of them terribly destructive to the spirit and morale of the people.

On the basis of these experiences, Alex analyses all the works of Euro-Canadian society with a sardonic realism. In Eskasoni, he told me, people have to exist on welfare payments of $104 a week. But in the steel mills in Sydney, which have never made a profit and have always been subsidized, the workers are paid $28 an hour. "Workers on welfare," he snorted.

"I was a civil servant for twelve years. In 1972 I went into my office every day for three months and wrote two letters. I was making

$28,000 a year, but if that is not stealing, I don't know what is. One thing I am not is a thief, so I quit."

His biggest problem during his years as Grand Captain, he said, has been to prevent his people from being bought, "even when they aren't being paid for it". He has come to believe that the key to preserving Mikmaq life and culture is to develop people within their families. "It's important to try to keep the families together," he told me. "It's not all that easy, but what is life without a struggle?"

Enough work for decades

Marie Battiste today is a handsome, cheerful, friendly, formidably intelligent woman, a real presence, one senses immediately, in the lives of everyone she touches: a woman who gives everything she is capable of giving to her family, village and nation, yet who really seems to feel that she receives more than she gives.

When she arrived back in Cape Breton in 1984, Marie found herself in a community whose people had for generations been subjected to what we would call, if it had happened in any other country, brainwashing. "When I brought Marie back, I told her it would take fifteen to twenty years for her to be accepted," said Alex Denny. "First, we had to eradicate what was instilled in the minds of our people."

Herded together on lands that could not support them, discouraged from speaking their own language and practising their own rituals and culture, systematically shut out of the economic benefits promised by Canadian society, the Mikmaqs had had their confidence in themselves shattered. Their knowledge of their past was at a nadir. The values of ordinary white Canadians had been held up to them as the ideal for so long that being white itself had become desirable: newborn babies were praised above all for the fairness of their skin.

In both the federal Indian and public schools, the Mikmaqs' language was ignored, and their history and culture treated as irrelevant. There was no agreement within the communities on the language issue: some wanted Mikmaq to be revived, but others feared this would worsen their already shaky command of English, and lessen their already poor chances of making it in mainstream society.

When Marie Battiste began the discouraging and painstaking work of cultural revival, the school dropout rate was more than 90 per cent. Few ever made it through grade ten. From 1950 to 1967, only three Mikmaqs had graduated from university. The children from reserves such as Shubenacadie and Membertou were sent to public schools, which received up to $6,000 per student from the federal government, but gave the Mikmaq people no say in the curriculum, no representation on the school board, and no classes in their own language. In fact, the province had no policy at all for native education.

First, Marie took over the tiny, twenty-eight-pupil Mikmawey school on Chapel Island. She and the two other teachers spent their own money putting together Mikmaq texts. They began by assuming that the Mikmaq language is more than a means of communication: it is an instrument that holds all knowledge of the ancestors and of the Creator given to Mikmaq people for their survival and development as human beings. In other words, the language is central to the Mikmaqs' sense of themselves.

From the first, Marie and her colleagues decided the children and staff would breakfast together, then pray together in Mikmaq, establishing that food, sharing and prayer are essential aspects of the Mikmaq worldview. Mothers and grandmothers were brought in to teach Mikmaq, integrating their considerable experience into the school day. Students were given up to forty-five minutes a day of Mikmaq instruction in reading and writing, and in the traditions and customs of their people.

Soon, people from Eskasoni were asking to send their children to the school. When a survey was taken in the summer of 1985, 96 per cent of the parents asked for Mikmaq instruction for their children. The small demonstration project had turned public opinion around, and in 1988 Marie Battiste became curriculum co-ordinator in the large, 660-pupil band-operated school in Eskasoni.

She is still not satisfied with the amount of Mikmaq instruction given, but feels it is getting there. Written and electronic curriculum materials have been developed by her office in Eskasoni, and the spirit has spread to other reserves. The small reserve of Wagmatcook, where about 400 people live on St. Patrick's Channel near Baddeck, has developed a full immersion programme – "much more progressive than ours," according to Marie. In Membertou, a reserve within the city limits of Sydney, parents have been threatening to withdraw their children from the public schools so that they, too, can be instructed in their own language.

"We are becoming more aware," Marie told me, "of what we have missed out on, of all the potential we have been robbed of for growth as individuals, communities and as a nation, and all so that we can have a mythical place in the Canadian nation! People now are beginning to realize there is no place for us, it is denied to us." She spoke without bitterness, but with calm and total conviction. However much I wanted to protest that there has to be a place in Canada for her people, her experience has persuaded her otherwise.

Everyone I spoke to who cares about the Mikmaq language emphasized its unusual beauty and depth. "It is a verb-oriented language," said Marie. "The reason it is so beautiful is that it constantly deals with relationships and processes. Any noun can be made into a verb, which carries the weight of the whole conversation. It is always describing people doing, acting, being. It has little to do with accumulation and objects."

Having been brought up in a non-Mikmaq environment, Dr. Battiste says she is herself still reaching for a strong language base, still trying "to reach into myself and pull it out...." Although she now writes stories in Mikmaq, "ten years ago I could not say anything in it. Now I am versatile, but not fluent. I still have to release myself from all English bondages...." Her three children speak it among themselves, as do many other children in the village. "There is now a great deal of parent pressure on kids to speak it. The sort of thing, 'Either you play together in Mikmaq, or you don't play over there.' "

The Mikmaq language has revived to the point where the band council, the largest employer, recently announced it will hire only bilingual people: a remarkable event in a place where only a few years ago, the English language was rolling over everything.

Mikmaq people are also taking to higher education in much larger numbers than ever before. In 1991, more than a hundred were attending the University College of Cape Breton alone. In 1984, the College graduated twenty-two teachers of the Mikmaq language (but the successful programme was immediately cancelled by the authorities, an academic version of the closed joinery factory of the 1950s); and in 1990, twenty-five social workers graduated. All are now working in Mikmaq communities. Today Eskasoni has "the best-educated welfare clientele in the country", as the community's director of operations, Peter Stevens, told me wryly.

So far, this Mikmaq revival has been more spiritual than material, but it is no less real or influential for that. At Sunday morning mass, the sounds of ancient Mikmaq chants and songs now ring out across

74

Eskasoni from the parish church on the hill, sung by a congregation that is usually filled with young people, who a few years ago were in the habit of ignoring church. "You have to realize," said Alex Denny, with a satisfied smile, "that in the early '70s a priest told people who were singing the Mass in Mikmaq, 'I don't want any of that trash in my church.'"

Setting the stage for takeoff

Once I had gained some understanding of the psychological framework within which the Mikmaq leaders are operating, my investigation of the administrative machinery of the village – the budgetting of the band council, the control of social services, the upgrading of educational skills, the formation of development schemes – was relatively brief. I was easily persuaded of the importance of the Mikmaq spiritual revival; I had long ago realized that the solutions to the problems of aboriginal communities are to be found in spiritual and psychological change. My hosts in Eskasoni had talked almost entirely about cultural, spiritual and psychological matters, and I felt that through them I had touched the essence of what was happening in the village. When I talked to the administrators, they too acknowledged that spiritual revival was the key to creation of a renewed Mikmaq society.

It is significant that, in spite of the high unemployment rate, shortage of housing and low average income, only about 125 of more than 2,500 Eskasoni band members live off the reserve. This is an extremely small number compared to some reserves in western Canada, where more than half the people have left, despairing of ever having the chance to create a viable life. The Mikmaqs stay in Eskasoni mainly for the emotional and spiritual support they find there.

Operations director Peter Stevens is typical: he returned after years away, and is glad he did so. "There is security here, a lot of emotional and financial support. The extended families are quite elaborate. Here my child can run in freedom, without fear of being harrassed."

The conversation of the village administrators is riddled with phrases of renewal. They talk of "unlocking the minds" of Mikmaq people from their psychology of dependency, of taking the people back to "the social, economic, political and spiritual order we had before the coming of the white man".

The administrators of the band believe the communal values of the

Mikmaqs conflict with the individualism forced on them by the federal and provincial governments, and look to the building of a "completely new society" based on what Peter Stevens called "humanist values". But like many Indian bands across the country, in Eskasoni they are also buzzing with schemes for material improvements – groceries, banks, supply and hardware companies – and even of grandiose plans for hotels, marinas, ski trails and golf courses on the surrounding islands, lakes and hills. The Eskasoni Economic Development Corporation, set up in 1986 by the band council, dreams of making Mikmaq-owned and -operated business into a major force in aquaculture through the production of salmon and trout in Bras d'or Lake.

Alex Denny was less than enthusiastic about such schemes. He has always emphasized small enterprises that strengthen the family and prevent Mikmaqs from being dominated by the bottom-line thinking of large corporations. Predictably enough, in the following year the Eskasoni development schemes ran into trouble, necessitating million-dollar borrowings, mass firing, and a local political crisis.

In the social agencies, there was also a hopeful spirit. After sixteen years of struggle, the addiction counsellors could at last see "a light at the end of the tunnel", having finally realized that drugs and alcohol are not the real problem, but merely symptoms of landlessness, overcrowding and unemployment. "Right now the violence is internal," said Peter Stevens. "But we are territorial beings. With a higher population every year, our land base is getting smaller. If it goes on, it could turn into anger, violence and chaos."

For the recent improvements almost everyone credits the psychological revival based on reaffirmation of traditions that is now underway. Most of the people treated for addictions are under thirty; when the treatment ends, they now bring drummers and cultural counsellors to their graduation ceremonies, something they never did a few years ago.

Old men's memories vindicated

Half a century after Sylliboy's defeat in court, the Mikmaqs went to court to fight the battle again, and in 1985 they won a great victory. Still convinced that their treaty was valid, the Grand Council in 1980 chose James Matthew Simon, a resident of Shubenacadie, to mount a test case by hunting outside the boundaries of his reserve in defiance of Nova Scotia law. Simon was charged with possession of a type of shotgun and shells not permitted under the Nova Scotia Lands and Forests Act. The provincial Attorney-General argued, as in 1928, that Mikmaq treaty rights have been extinguished. The court agreed, and Simon was convicted. The Nova Scotia Supreme Court upheld the conviction; but the Supreme Court of Canada overturned the judgments of the lower courts, thus confirming a gradual change in the interpretation of aboriginal rights by the highest court in the land.

The Supreme Court ruled that the treaty of 1752 is still a binding and enforceable agreement between the Crown and the Mikmaq people, and that its protection of Mikmaq hunting rights overrides provincial legislation interfering with those rights. The court held that interpretation of treaties must take into account changes in technology and practice, so that Mikmaq hunters could not be limited to using spears and handmade knives, as Nova Scotia had asked. Furthermore, their rights extend not only to subsistence hunting, but to hunting for commercial purposes.[5]

Chief Justice Brian Dickson rejected the finding in the Sylliboy case that the Mikmaqs were savages incapable of making valid treaties with the British sovereign. Such language, Dickson wrote, "reflects the biases and prejudices of another era of our history...is no longer acceptable in Canadian law, and indeed, is inconsistent with the growing sensitivity to native rights in Canada".[6]

This success came nearly twenty years after Alex Denny joined the Grand Council with the intention of confirming Mikmaqs' treaty rights, and a decade after Sakej Henderson became their legal advisor. Following the decision, the Mikmaqs themselves formally ratified a set of hunting guidelines based on an ancient concept, *Netukulimk*, which urges that Mikmaqs must be "mindful of the Creator, the consent of the animal and other resources used, and the responsibility of sharing among the human community".[7] The guidelines assume that the rights of Mikmaqs override provincial laws related to seasons, quotas, licences, tagging, hunting gear and methods, but they also provide that only those Mikmaqs who observe the guidelines will be protected by the terms of the 1752 treaty.[8]

"I hear people say that we've always had the treaties," Alex Denny told me. "But years ago, when we started down this road, nearly everyone had forgotten the treaties, and many people didn't even know they exist." He believes it is largely because of the Mikmaqs' steadfast fight, which they undertook with little money and deep doubts, that aboriginal and treaty rights are now entrenched in the Canadian Constitution, and have become an essential part of the new vision of Canada.

Unfortunately, Nova Scotia carried on attacking the hunting rights of the Mikmaqs as if the Supreme Court judgment had never been made. In 1987, six Mikmaqs were charged for fishing illegally and twenty-three for hunting deer and moose. Three years later, Nova Scotia issued 200 licences for the annual moose hunt, only two of them to Mikmaqs. In a direct challenge to the provincial government, the Mikmaqs organized their own hunt, carried out under their own hunting guidelines. Fourteen hunters were arrested and charged with violations of the provincial Wildlife Act, and the province announced that any hunting carried out pursuant to the 1752 treaty would be prosecuted.[9] In 1991, the aboriginal right to fish and hunt was confirmed by the Nova Scotia Court of Appeal. The Crown then had to admit it had no chance of establishing a *prima facie* case, dropped all charges against the hunters, and left the Union of Nova Scotia Indians and Native Council with legal bills for $350,000!

So Chief Sylliboy's long struggle is not quite over.

8

The land is
lifted, nimbly

In the late 1960s, when I first ventured among aboriginal people, our Euro-Canadian assumption that our rights are superior to those of aboriginals still dominated relations between the two groups, with disastrous results for the aboriginals. For example, in northern Quebec I found that whenever Euro-Canadians arrived wanting to start a business, open a tourist lodge, sink a mine, or build a town, the Crees who had lived there for thousands of years were systematically pushed aside. And yet, as I soon discovered from my reading, the aboriginals had well-founded rights, even in terms of Euro-Canadian law.

The obligation not to occupy Indians' lands without their agreement was undertaken by Britain, but transferred to Canada in 1867 under Section 91 (24) of the British North America Act. By that time, most of the Maritimes, and much of Quebec and Ontario, had already been occupied by Euro-Canadians without any reference to aboriginal rights. But from 1870 onwards, with a view to gaining peaceful control over the westward expansion of the new nation, the Canadian government signed treaties with Indians in Ontario, the Prairies and the Northwest Territories, in fulfilment of the undertaking given in the Royal Proclamation of 1763. The process was not extended to British Columbia (except for a small part in the northeast of the province); from its creation in 1871, the provincial government rejected the idea that aboriginals had any rights to the lands they were occupying when Europeans happened along.

Quebec, too, had been bypassed by the treaty-making process, but that had not stopped Euro-Canadians from occupying it. The Crees I visited had always been forced to step aside, even in their own hunting territories, to make way for outsiders. The application of the Royal Proclamation in this area was not quite as straightforward as in other parts of Canada. Northern Quebec had been part of the vast territory owned by the Hudson's Bay Company, which was exempted in 1763 from the provisions of the Royal Proclamation. But when the Company sold its lands to Canada in 1870, the Canadian government undertook to recognize Indian rights throughout those lands, and formalized that intention in an Order-in-Council.[1]

From 1870, therefore, Canadian law provided that all Indians, whether they lived on the Hudson's Bay Company lands or elsewhere, were to be treated in the same way: that is, they had a legal interest in their land, which required a treaty to effect its surrender. It was on that basis that the western treaties were signed, also covering land once owned by the Hudson's Bay Company. So when the time came in 1912 for Canada to transfer what is now northern Quebec to the authority of the provincial government, the transfer took place under the specific condition that Quebec must "recognize the rights of the Indian inhabitants in the territory to the same extent, and obtain surrenders of such rights in the same manner, as the government of Canada has heretofore recognized such rights and has obtained surrenders thereof...."[2] This was never done. As a result, Jimmy Mianscum, whom I met on my first trip to the Cree lands, and whose family for generations hunted and trapped on the land where the town of Chibougamau was built, was expected simply to move aside to make way for the town, in spite of all the solemn undertakings given by Britain and Canada. Jimmy was living with a group of other displaced Crees not far from Chibougamau, in a tent settlement called Doré Lake, a small neglected community that over the years was moved seven times to make way for various industrial developments.

In 1971, the Quebec government decided to dam all of the major rivers in Eenou Astchee (as the Crees call their homeland), without even advising the Crees of this intention. The documented existence of Cree rights may have seemed conclusive to a layman like me, but when the Crees went to court to try to stop the project, the high-priced lawyers of the Quebec government would have none of it. They argued that there was no case to answer, since Indian title was meaningless, and its nature unspecified. They said that, even in the unlikely event that Indian title had some application elsewhere in Canada, it had no relevance to northern Quebec. The Crees' lawyers rattled off a long list of legal instruments in which Indian title had been specifically confirmed – the 1760 Articles of Capitulation, the 1763 Royal Proclamation, the instructions to Quebec governors in 1763 and 1775, the Imperial Order-in-Council of 1870, the Quebec Boundaries Extension Act of 1912. But the government lawyers almost jovially claimed that these instruments did not mean what they appeared to mean. Perhaps the documents recognized a moral obligation of some kind, they said, but certainly no legal rights. They went a step further: documents in which the Crown had negotiated the surrender of rights in other parts of the country did not imply that Indians had any rights to surrender. This was an extraordinary argument: essentially, that promises made to Indians were meaningless. These amiable men put it forward with an air of the greatest good humour, as if refuting some kind of simplistic foolishness dreamed up by children.

Among these men, we were far away from the world of Jimmy Mianscum.[3]

A century of persistence

While the Crees' case was being argued in Montreal, the Nisga'a people of northern British Columbia had managed to get their claim as aboriginal owners of the Nass River valley heard by the Supreme Court of Canada. The Nisga'a had stubbornly insisted on this claim ever since British Columbia had been created, and had done so against an impenetrable miasma of bureaucratic double-talk and legalese. For decades, the official attitude had been that aboriginal rights were a fiction, and that aboriginals showed concern about their rights only when whipped up by white agitators.

Through more than a century the Nisga'a refused to accept that somehow or other, by means that were never explained to their satisfaction, strangers had magically become the owners of their lands. When a federal-provincial inquiry in 1887 visited the Nisga'a in the Nass valley, an old blind man called Neis Puck listened for some time, then interrupted:

> I am the oldest man here and I can't sit still any longer and hear that this is not our fathers' land. Who is the chief that gave this land to the Queen? Give us his name, we have never heard it....[4]

Another Nisga'a chief, David Mackay, said:

What we don't like about the government is their saying this: "We will give you this much land." How can they give it when it is our own? We cannot understand it. They have never bought it from us or our forefathers. They have never fought and conquered our people and taken the land in that way.... It has been ours for thousands of years.[5]

In 1906 and 1909, British Columbia Indians sent representatives to London to present their aboriginal claims to the King. In 1911, they persuaded the Prime Minister, Sir Wilfrid Laurier, to submit the question to the Supreme Court without the agreement of British Columbia, but Laurier was defeated in an election before he could do so.[6] In 1913, the Nisga'a unsuccessfully petitioned the British Privy Council, which was then the final court of appeal in constitutional matters; and in 1927, as members of the Allied Indian Tribes of British Columbia, they pressed their claims before a federal parliamentary inquiry in Ottawa. The Reverend Peter Kelly, one of the province's outstanding native leaders, told the committee:

It has taken us between forty and fifty years to get where we are today.... If this committee sees fit to turn down what we are pressing for, it might be another century before a new generation will rise up to get where we are today.

These were prophetic words.

The Indian argument was treated with contempt by the parliamentarians of the day, who described the claim to aboriginal rights as "more or less fictitious", and blamed white agitators for stirring up trouble. In one of the most undemocratic measures ever enacted by a Canadian legislature, Parliament quickly passed an amendment to the Indian Act making it illegal for any Indian to pay anyone for support "in the prosecution of any claim".[7] This law resulted in the virtual collapse of organized native opposition; until it was repealed in 1951, Indians were, in effect, forbidden by law from pursuing their legal rights. It was almost half a century before the Nisga'a were able again to get a hearing.

In 1967, the Nisga'a began yet another action to affirm their aboriginal right to their land.[8] The political climate was unfavourable. As their case was moving through the courts, Prime Minister Pierre Trudeau unequivocally denied the validity of aboriginal rights, and even of the treaties signed by Canada with aboriginal nations.

Federal policy was that the government would not consider any further claims even to the land that had been illegally occupied by Euro-Canadians. This included, of course, such claims as were being made by the Nisga'a and later by the Crees of Quebec.

The Nisga'a were, as usual, beaten in the lower courts, where they encountered the contemptuous view of aboriginal cultures held by so many jurists throughout Canadian history. For example, the Chief Justice of the British Columbia Appeal Court, H.W. Davey, held: "The Nisga'a were undoubtedly at the time of settlement a very primitive people with few institutions of civilized society, and none at all of our notions of private property."

But when the case came to the Supreme Court of Canada, Nisga'a persistence was rewarded at last. Although the Nisga'a lost the case on a technicality, six of the seven judges affirmed the concept of aboriginal title. Three of the six held that the Nisga'a had aboriginal title before the arrival of Europeans, and it had never been extinguished; the other three judges ruled that such title did exist once, but had been extinguished in colonial times. As a result, the Trudeau government surrendered, admitting the validity of the aboriginal claim to much of Canada, and creating a mechanism, the land-claims policy, to deal with it.

To this immense aboriginal victory was added, shortly afterwards, a judgment in favour of the Quebec Crees by Mr. Justice Albert Malouf of the Quebec Superior Court. Malouf found that the Crees had been exercising their right to hunt, trap and fish in their territory since time immemorial, and that outside interference with their way of life compromised their existence. He therefore ordered Quebec to cease trespassing on the Cree lands. For a brief, giddy moment, the Crees' claim to ownership of Eenou Astchee was given credence. But the Canadian legal system could not abide such an outlandish idea; Malouf's judgment was hastily overturned by the Quebec Appeal Court a week later. But by this time, the political climate towards aboriginal rights had been transformed. Just as the Nisga'a judgment forced a change in Canadian government policy, so the Malouf judgment forced the Quebec government to negotiate with the Crees about their land rights, something it had never intended to do.

As natives began to research their claims, preparatory to submitting them to government, they began to realize that their rights did not flow from the Royal Proclamation, or any other act of a non-

Indian legislative body, but from their immemorial occupancy and ownership of their land. History showed that the surrenders by which aboriginal people had lost much of their land had been deviously obtained, inadequately explained, and sloppily administered. So a new determination grew among aboriginals not to agree to any further surrenders.

Ever since, this has been a major point of friction between governments and aboriginals. The governments enter land negotiations determined to alienate Indian title, as laid down in the Royal Proclamation of 1763. The aboriginals, who had accepted that legal structure from the time of Confederation, now seek a different set of arrangements, on the grounds that their rights were not created by European or Canadian statutes, but are inherent in their immemorial occupancy of the country.

By 1975, when the Crees surrendered their rights over most of Eenou Astchee in the James Bay and Northern Quebec Agreement, in tacit acceptance of the system laid down in the Royal Proclamation, aboriginals elsewhere in Canada were vigorously affirming that they would never again surrender rights. The federal government has since treated the James Bay agreement as a model to be followed everywhere; but in protracted negotiations in the Yukon, the Northwest Territories and elsewhere, the aboriginals have tried mightily – although so far unsuccessfully – to avoid further surrenders of title.

9

Algonquins: at the heart of Canada's history

From time to time during the last quarter-century, I have been in touch with the Algonquins of the Ottawa Valley. As with the Crees, I came to admire these people; eventually I became involved in making a film about their struggle to halt the clearcutting of their traditional forests, and thus to defend their way of life.

I had my first contact with Algonquins in July 1969. As a reporter for *The Montreal Star*, I made a trip far up the Ottawa Valley, in company with an Algonquin chief called Mike McKenzie, to visit some of the scattered communities in the enormous territory that has always been the Algonquin homeland.

I had spent most of the previous decade working as an international correspondent out of London, England; in a very real sense, this plunge into the forested hinterland northwest of Ottawa reintroduced me to Canada. The trip covered 1,200 kilometres, a distance that in Britain would have taken me from London far into the north of Scotland, or, in another direction, clear across France, Germany and beyond, through hundreds of ancient towns and cities, heavily settled countryside and cultivated landscapes.

How different is Canada! Almost within spitting distance of our major cities lies a wilderness only fitfully tamed, sparsely settled by whites, yet long occupied by a small number of very private people who have managed to retain their way of life despite – or perhaps because of – having been shoved aside by an invading civilization.

The landscape these people have always called home is impressive for its sheer immensity, but even more so for a brooding sense of the permanency of Earth, and the relative insignificance of the many

85

creatures, including humans, that roam across it. This idea that we are merely one of many insignificant creatures that inhabit Earth was an entirely new one to me.

Before Europeans arrived, Algonquins had lived here for thousands of years, their lives taking their pulse from the seasonal fluctuations of the Ottawa, the great river that first took Europeans into the Canadian interior. Those newcomers had been bent on exploration, commerce and change; but as they penetrated deeper inland, they found an aboriginal hunting civilization that had developed its own concepts of space and time, its own relationships to natural and spiritual forces, and that, in its own way, was every bit as wonderful as the civilization of the invaders. Unfortunately, however, the newcomers did not understand much, or perhaps any, of this.

Mike McKenzie's family had once properly been called Amikendizie (beaver's gizzard). But four generations before, some teacher or priest could not be bothered writing this beautiful name properly, and so he anglicized it. Recently, the Algonquins had given him a new name, Makadaomakwa (Black Bear).

Forty-six at the time of our trip, Mike had spent his early life hunting and trapping with his family. Later, he served in the Canadian Army, and then for twenty years worked in the paper mill in Temiscaming, Quebec. He became chief of his Algonquin band simply by taking an interest. He was not well educated, but he was experienced. In this he was typical of the tough and determined leaders, many of them manual or semi-skilled workers, who in the late '60s undertook the task of initiating – against great odds – an aboriginal revival.

The purpose of Mike's trip was to sign up members for the Indians of Quebec Association, of which he was vice-president. In this he would be only sporadically successful. The Algonquins were in transition at the time. Those who lived in or near the towns around Lake Temiscaming were relatively integrated into the Euro-Canadian wage economy, had a record of steady work in the mines and mills along the river, and knew how to defend themselves.

Deeper in the forest, however, were many who seemed to be deliberately resisting assimilation by staying as far away as they could from outsiders. We flew to a tiny community of Algonquins and Métis called Hunter's Point, on a piece of land jutting into Lake Kipawa. Mike had unsuccessfully tried to persuade these people to move closer to town, so they could find some work and would not need welfare to supplement their hunting and trapping. But even their village was too crowded for some of them; to meet two elders, Mr. and Mrs. Gabriel Paul, we had to travel by boat across to another point where they lived in a shack so simple its interior walls were made of cardboard.

Mrs. Paul had been one of the strongest voices against moving. "We are trying to do something for the Indian," Mike said to the old lady. "We need to stick together. We need support. We need members. Do you think you support it?"

Mrs. Paul nodded amiably, and said that her son, the local chief, had told her about it. "He told me, 'Mike wants me to help him,' that's what he said." In her terms, this was an enthusiastic endorsement.

We stopped at another spit of land to round up Michel Constant, a seventy-four-year-old who also preferred to live alone in a small shack at a distance from the village. "You coming to the meeting?" asked Mike.

"Well, I don't know," said the old man.

Back in the village, seven people gathered in the school to hear what Mike had to say. Twenty minutes after the meeting started, Michel Constant came in and listened quietly from the back of the room. They had no particular issues that were bothering them. Mike asked them to pay one dollar a year to the association. "You hate to even mention money to them," he said, as we climbed into the plane.

The next day we drove north up the Ottawa Valley, then headed east along a rough gravel road to a small town called Winneway. Like hundreds of native communities across the country, it was not to be found on Canadian maps. In Winneway the meeting was rather more lively. Here the people were wondering when they would get a sewage system. "I've moved my backhouse so many times I don't know where I'm going to move it next," said Wilbert Polson, to gales of laughter.

Mike held up a map and pointed to a huge area marked "Indian territory", which he said was recognized in 1763 as belonging to the Indians. "There has been no agreement made about that. It is all Indian land, all of that," he said, with a rare flourish.

"I still don't have room to move my backhouse," said Polson, breaking up the meeting.

Polson had been out hunting with a man called Regis Mathias, handicapped with a damaged leg, unable to work and trying to sustain his family of eleven on $42 a week in welfare payments. Mathias needed the meat to feed his family, but when they returned to where they had cached a moose carcass, a game warden had seized it and had written in the snow, "You dirty bitch, we will catch you yet."

Now Polson and Mathias were puzzling over a notice they'd received, written in French, which they could not understand, notifying them they had been charged with shooting a moose out of season and must appear in court. This was happening all over the province. The Minister had agreed verbally that Indians could hunt and fish at all times, but the game wardens continued to harass them, seizing food from their tables. Mike said the association would defend the case.

We drove further north along logging roads, ever deeper into the wilderness, to a small Hydro-Quebec dam and generating plant known as Rapid Seven, where nine Algonquin families were living. As at Hunter's Point, we had to take a short boat ride to meet most of the residents. Everywhere I went, I seemed to be meeting small groups of Algonquins living in the loveliest places, always just around the corner from the nearest settlement (however small that might be).

These people came out of their two log cabins to greet us. But it was evident they would never go to a meeting, so Mike did his stuff as we all stood around in their beautiful forest clearing. Everyone said the best person for Mike to talk to would be Roseanne Kudjick, because a month before she'd been on a course in Montreal until she'd got homesick and returned to the log cabin. They sent for her, and she came out of the cabin, a shy, beautiful young woman, smartly dressed in the new clothes and suede pumps she had bought in Montreal, slowly brushing and braiding her long black hair. Mike said he would write to keep her abreast of what was happening. She said almost nothing, but her body language at least did not indicate refusal.

I was new enough at meeting native people to be amazed at the ambiance in these small communities. Many of the Algonquins appeared to have little visible means of support. Apart from a few elderly people, none of those we met spoke Algonquin, and as a collectivity they seemed to be barely hanging on to the material world by their fingernails. I was more impressed by the exotic nature of their condition than by any hope for its amelioration. I thought, quite erroneously, that they were a colourful, historical hangover.

A pivotal role in history
I lost touch with the Algonquins during the next two decades. In 1977 I went to live in Ottawa, and it didn't particularly bother me

that the city was built on Algonquin land. I was typical of most inhabitants of the city: I seldom thought about what had happened to the people who had first lived there.

It was only when I started reading the history of native-European contact that I realized how important Algonquin control of the Ottawa River had once been. For decades during the seventeenth century, the Algonquins decided who would move deeper into Canada, and who wouldn't. From an island in the river opposite the modern town of Pembroke, they maintained a kind of tollgate from which they controlled access to the Canadian interior.

In 1613, the Algonquins denied the French access to the interior, stopping Samuel de Champlain for so long that he finally returned in disgust to Lachine.[1] Since he had arrived in Canada in 1603, Champlain, an employee of a French trading company, had wanted desperately to penetrate the interior by way of either the Saguenay or Ottawa rivers. He had heard about a northern sea, but for ten years various aboriginal chiefs anxious to protect their role as middlemen in the fur trade had dissuaded him from going further inland.

The Hurons, who lived beyond the Ottawa in the country between Georgian Bay and Lake Simcoe, were the great traders of eastern Canada. They were able to move freely because of their alliances with Algonquins, Montagnais, Crees, Nipissing and others. When the Hurons came down to Quebec from the interior bearing huge loads of furs, Champlain quickly realized that these were the people he should befriend. To prove his friendship, in 1609 he went to war at their side, along with the Algonquins, against the Iroquois. The Iroquois controlled the St. Lawrence, the Algonquins the Ottawa. When Champlain shot one of their chiefs, it was the first time the Iroquois had seen firearms. Henceforth, the enmity of the Iroquois towards the French made the Ottawa the only safe route into the interior for Champlain.

Champlain further cemented relations with the Algonquins by sending a number of young men to winter over among them. These men had orders to learn the languages and find out what they could about the rumoured northern seas and the route to the east. The Kichesipirini (Algonquin) chief, Tessouat, took one of these young men, Nicholas de Vignau, to his territory straddling the Ottawa River. When Vignau returned to Quebec City in 1612, he told Champlain he had travelled further west to the territory of the

Nipissing, and had then journeyed north with them to a body of salt water. Champlain returned to France, but was so excited at the prospect of finding the northern sea that he hastened back to Canada in 1613, determined to follow the route Vignau had described.

During his journey into the interior, Champlain was met along the way by various Algonquin parties, who showed him how to avoid the many enormous rapids on the river. They finally directed him to the summer camp of Tessouat on Allumette Island, carefully chosen because the surrounding rapids made it possible to control the passage of strangers. Tessouat and Champlain feasted, and Champlain asked for four canoes to take him upriver to the Nipissing, whom he said he wanted to engage as allies in war. Tessouat agreed, but warned Champlain against trusting the Nipissing. He then announced that his council had decided they would be better able to ensure Champlain's safety if he postponed his visit until the next year. Obviously, neither party was levelling with the other: the French really wanted to explore and make trading contacts, but said they were seeking an ally; the Algonquins really wanted to prevent the French from trading directly with the interior tribes.

When Champlain angrily told them that Vignau had been among the Nipissing and had not found them so unfriendly, the fat was in the fire: it turned out that Vignau had never been upriver to Nipissing country, had never visited the northern sea, and had, in fact, stayed the whole winter with Tessouat and his people. When Vignau finally admitted he had lied, Champlain had to prevent the Algonquins from killing him. But the *contretemps* forced Champlain to abandon his voyage to the interior. Instead, he invited the Algonquins to go downriver and trade with him at Lachine. On June 10, fourteen days after heading inland, he turned back towards Lachine, accompanied by forty Kichesipirini canoes loaded with furs.

Two years later, the Hurons took Champlain inland because he had promised to help them in their war against the Iroquois. This time the Algonquins, allies of the Hurons, allowed him to pass. Champlain visited the Huron villages and then travelled with an Algonquin-Huron war party into the Iroquois heartland in what is now northern New York state, where he took part in an inconclusive battle. Whatever he may have thought, among these people Champlain was by no means in control of his own destiny. After the battle his allies refused to deliver him back to Quebec, but insisted he return with them to the Huron country, where he passed the winter.

The Indian alliances were rather fragile. During the winter a serious quarrel broke out between the Algonquins and the Hurons over treatment of a captured Iroquois, and Champlain gained some credit by mediating the quarrel. Because he had helped them in their dispute with the Hurons, the Algonquins now allowed him to contact their trading partners, the Nipissing. Even so, he never made it to the northern sea. After promising to take him there, the Nipissing made excuses not to do so. The Indian stalling tactics were remarkably successful: no European made it overland to that northern sea for more than half a century.

A changing view of aboriginals

Clearly the Algonquins, when first contacted by Europeans, were an accomplished people, with a viable economy based on hunting and trade, skilful in diplomacy with their neighbours, capable of defending themselves by arms, and effectively in command of an important area of central Canada. This is very different from the traditional Canadian view of aboriginals as passive, bewildered onlookers and victims, who played no constructive role in the creation of the modern state. The history of the Ottawa Valley has usually been presented as if it began with the settlement of Perth by discharged soldiers in 1816, or, at the earliest, with the arrival from New England of Philomen Wright in 1800. Seldom has the valley been portrayed as the homeland of a self-confident aboriginal nation that played a key role in the development of trade.

Fortunately, this Eurocentric view has begun to give way. A new generation of ethno-historians now works from different assumptions. "My primary goal," writes the anthropologist and historian, Bruce Trigger, "has been to demonstrate that native behaviour was based on the rational pursuit of desired ends at least to the same extent as that of Europeans."[2] These historians have for the first time enabled us to transcend our absurd "we're civilized, you're savage" preconceptions.

But who, exactly, were the Algonquins? And how did they differ from other aboriginals living in eastern Canada? Here again, Eurocentric history has been an unreliable guide. When Europeans first arrived, eastern Canada was inhabited by many loosely related peoples with similar economies, beliefs and languages. Europeans invented their own names for these groups, and largely ignored the names used by the people themselves. Algonquin (sometimes spelled Algonkin) is a European-bestowed name derived from a corruption of the Maliseet word *Elakomkwik*, meaning relatives or allies. But the Algonquins had half a dozen different names for their various branches – Onontchataronon, Weskarini, Kichesiprini, Keinouche, Matou-weskarini, Otaguottouemin and others. The same was true of the Iroquois, the Hurons, and every other major group. All these nations called themselves by names that most Europeans had never heard until they were brought to our notice in recent years, pre-eminently by Trigger in his wonderful study of the Hurons, *The Children of Aataentsic*. Cree, Montagnais and Naskapi are all European-bestowed names for peoples who were broadly similar, but called themselves by such names as Innu (which, in its modern revival seems to include both Montagnais and Naskapi), Eeyouch, Eenouch (for different branches of the Cree), and so on.

Most of the people in central Canada called themselves Anishinaabe, a name that has also recently been revived by the aboriginals themselves. The Anishinaabe (sometimes spelled Anishnabai, or Anicenabe, or Anissinapek) include the Algonquins of the Ottawa Valley, the Ojibway of northwestern Ontario, the Ottawas or Odawas, Nipissing, and Mississaugas of central Ontario, and the Chippewa and Saulteaux (these being alternative names for Ojibway) who extend into Manitoba and Saskatchewan.

The boundaries in the forest among these different hunting groups were always fluid. Groups would shift with the animals, inhabiting one place for a few years, and then moving as their subsistence needs dictated. Consequently there was always intermarriage among the groups, especially on the edges of their territories: for example, between Algonquins and Crees, or Algonquins and Nipissing. It seems that the people of the eastern Canadian forests were differentiated mostly by their dialects. The Anishinaabe had in common a dialect chain of the Ojibway language; people further north in the eastern sub-Arctic had a dialect chain of the Cree language. At the geographical extremities of these dialect chains, the languages could be as different as, say, Dutch is from English. Most of this nomenclature was invisible to the arriving Europeans, and officially Canada still maintains those same cultural blinkers: in a list of the cultural and linguistic affiliations of Indian bands published by the government of Canada in 1980, the names Anishinaabe, Nipissing, Saulteaux,

Chippewa and Mississauga are not even mentioned.

If education is supposed to teach children what actually happened in the past, the story of what Euro-Canadians did to the Algonquins of the Ottawa Valley should be taught to every Canadian schoolchild. First, the Crown in 1763 guaranteed that their lands would not be occupied or developed without their consent. Then their lands were occupied, and they were pushed aside. Then all their protests were ignored.

The Algonquins displaced from the lower Ottawa drifted to Montreal, and were among those taken by the Catholic priests to settle at Oka, north of Montreal, in 1717.[3] These Algonquins returned to hunt in their territories along the lower Ottawa every year, only to find them increasingly occupied by strangers. Within a year or two of the Royal Proclamation, the Algonquins advised the British government that they intended to clear their hunting grounds of anyone who had settled illegally.

The government urged them to be patient, but twenty years later the incursions were still occurring. The Algonquins claimed that "the animals have become distant, we find very little for our families to live on." In at least twenty-five similar petitions over the next hundred years, the Algonquins asked that settlers be stopped from invading their lands, or that those illegally there be removed, or at least that Algonquins receive compensation for the lands taken. From time to time, the colonial government admitted the justice of the Algonquin claims; once, in 1829, after nearly sixty years of such protests, the government promised to prosecute illegal settlers, and even threatened to evict them. No prosecutions or evictions were ever undertaken. As we have seen, exactly the same thing happened to the Mikmaqs in the Martitime provinces.

Gradually, the justice of the Algonquin claim was conveniently forgotten. The government, while refusing to protect the Algonquins' rights, threatened to punish them if they tried to protect those rights themselves. By 1836, the government decided that the Algonquin claims had been "fully settled and adjusted" (although this was demonstrably untrue), and a few years later began to describe the Algonquin claim as "perfectly novel".

The Church wanted all Algonquins to be under its control, and kept pressing the colonial government to set up reserves for them. The government liked the idea: it wanted to get Algonquins off the land, too. So in 1851 reserves were established at Temiscaming and River Desert (now Maniwaki) in Quebec, to which all Algonquins were expected to move. The Algonquins from Oka moved with the priests to Maniwaki, but those still living south of the river in Ontario stayed where they were, and most of the northern people never moved. Thereafter, the record shows that all Algonquins who remained outside the two big reserves were treated as squatters in their own land.

When I was again in contact with the Algonquins in the 1980s, I asked people in Barriere Lake, one of the northern communities, why their ancestors had never moved to Maniwaki. They said it was a long journey of several days by canoe, and some who made the trip in 1851 caught smallpox and died. Repeatedly, such experience of the outside world had convinced them that it was better to keep to themselves. Thus began a division among the various Algonquin communities, particularly those who moved and those who stayed put, which persists to this day.

This whole story is yet another cruel passage in our history, whose details remain virtually unknown to Euro-Canadians. Only recently have Algonquin researchers begun to assemble their version, with somewhat dramatic results. On the basis of that research, the only remaining Algonquin community in Ontario – Golden Lake, 100 kilometres west of Ottawa – filed a land claim in 1983 covering "all the lands in the province of Ontario which form part of the water-shed of the Ottawa River, below the Mattawa River, that are now in the possession of the Crown". This includes Algonquin Provincial Park, Parliament Hill, and all Crown lands east to the Quebec border. In Quebec, a document presented in 1988 by the Maniwaki reserve laid claim to 650,000 square kilometres of land stretching from the Eastern Townships to Lake Superior. The government has accepted this as a generic Algonquin claim, but four of the nine bands in Quebec have challenged its evidence.

As I discovered from the people of Barriere Lake, who live in the centre of LaVérendrye wildlife reserve, modern Algonquins still decide very much for themselves, just as they always did in the past, what actions they will take. We will see more of these distinctive and determined people in Chapters 11 and 13.

10

The fantastic world
of the Indian Act

We have seen how racial and cultural prejudices gradually evolved into the Indian Act. It is time to examine in more detail the extraordinary powers of control this law gave the government over the lives of aboriginal people.

Many Canadians who discover what has been done under the Indian Act can scarcely believe that such things happened in Canada: the all-embracing, totalitarian controls taken over every aspect of Indian life; the deliberate degradation of native cultures; the mean-spirited regulations that first reduced aboriginals to penury and then ensured that they stayed poor; the fascistic race-classification system, invented and administered by a race of faceless civil servants; the neglect of aboriginal education and health; the deliberate subjugation of all things Indian to the physical and psychological dominance of non-Indians. These historical cruelties are responsible for the collective misery and individual personal tragedies of much contemporary aboriginal life, to such an extent that each aboriginal nation described in this book is engaged in a gargantuan struggle to overcome the consequences of the 120 years they have been subject to the Act.

Parliament passed the Indian Act in 1876 with 100 sections, which nearly doubled in the next thirty years to 195. By that time a Canadian Indian could scarcely sneeze without permission of the Superintendent-General of Indian Affairs, a title given to the responsible cabinet minister.

Canada's first Prime Minister, Sir John A. Macdonald, was more than willing to interfere with Indian life on moral grounds. He wanted to pacify the Indians, turn them into Euro-Canadians, and in general get rid of them as a coherent social and political entity. But he didn't want trouble or rebellion from the natives, so he opposed their exploitation by merchants, settlers or speculators, and tried to stop people from selling them liquor, or taking their women into prostitution.

In general, the 1876 Act formalized the inferior status of Indians. It contained many prohibitions on their conduct and restrictions on their freedom, which were greatly expanded in the next few decades. For example, Indians were not only forbidden from selling, alienating or leasing their reserve land, but also prevented, unlike European immigrants, from acquiring a homestead in the western territories. This prompted one Member of Parliament to protest that because they were given an annuity of $5 a head, the Indians were "deprived of every right and privilege which a white man holds dear".[1] Indians who deserted their families or were imprisoned were no longer eligible for annuity payments. Another MP protested that he saw no reason why an Indian who left his family should lose his income when a white man did not.[2] Perhaps the most startling provision is that any Indian who qualified as a doctor, lawyer, solicitor, notary, minister or priest, or who attained any university degree, would, "*ipso facto*, become enfranchised...", that is, "deemed to be no longer an Indian". Never had it been so clearly stated that the purpose of Canadian policy was to turn Indians into white people.

Even in its current "modern" form (the last major revision was in 1951), the Indian Act resembles a system of apartheid created by a bumbling Anglican vicar, full of misdirected good intentions. The Canadian system was perhaps never as brutal as South Africa's apartheid system, and not as overtly imposed by force of arms, but it systematically isolated a minority people and undeniably set out to destroy their economy, culture, religion and institutions.

In 1874 Macdonald appointed Lawrence Vankoughnet to head the Indian branch of the Department of the Interior (which was elevated to the status of a department six years later), and left him to it. Vankoughnet ran the show for nineteen years, eventually dictating personally almost all major decisions taken by his department, and irrevocably setting Canadian policy on its restrictive and inhumane course. He had a poor view of Indian life and kept cutting the rations given to starving reserve Indians, while also cutting the aid that was designed to make them self-sufficient in agriculture.

"You should by every means in your power endeavour to persuade the Indians within your district to pursue industrial employment by cultivating the soil," Vankoughnet wrote to an Indian agent in 1880. "And no encouragement should be given by you to idleness by gratuitous aid being furnished to able-bodied Indians."

The patronizing attitude of the time was neatly summarized by Alexander Morris, Lieutenant-Governor of Manitoba and the Northwest Territories, who, in 1880, after negotiating for the government the major western treaties with the Indians, wrote:

> Let us have a wise and paternal government...doing its utmost to help and elevate the Indian population who have been cast upon our care, and we will have peace, progress and concord among them.... Instead of the Indian melting away as snow before the sun...we will see our Indian population, loyal subjects of the Crown, happy, prosperous, and self-sustaining....[3]

The reality was vastly different. Gradually the Indians retreated to the reserves set up for them, mostly far from the centres of population. For perhaps fifty years they were seldom seen by the Canadian people, and only occasionally heard from. During these years their population fell dramatically. They did not vote, had no political power, and no capacity to combat the small handful of officials who took control of Indian policy. From time to time word would filter into the press of desperate conditions on some of the reserves, but for most Canadians, Indians were simply those unfortunate people who reminded them that the benefits of their favoured land were not uniformly distributed to all.

So little attention was paid to Indians by the Canadian body politic that in 1880, total spending by the Indian Affairs Branch was only $700,000, including $232,000 paid in annuities in compensation for the surrender of land rights. Health and education spending together amounted to only $16,000. Although both of these expenditures increased in the following decades, by the 1930s total spending by the Department of Indian Affairs hovered under $5 million and had not reached $7 million by the end of the Second World War.[4]

Here is a list of some of the controls imposed on aboriginals in the fifty years following passage of the Indian Act in 1876:

Land:
Although most Indian land was in remote places, it was never far enough out of the way of advancing settlement to be beyond the covetous eyes

of Euro-Canadians. In principle, reserves were held in trust for Indians, and could never be sold, surrendered or leased without their agreement and that of the Crown. But as settlement moved across the country, there was constant pressure to get at even the small parcels of land that remained in aboriginal hands, and the principle was often violated.

Pressure on Indian lands was especially strong from the turn of the century to the First World War. In western Canada, in particular, Indian lands were often felt to stand in the way of new transportation facilities (such as railways), resource exploitation and growing urban centres. There was a general feeling among Canadians that Indians were impeding progress; the civil servants making the decisions usually shared these attitudes, and encouraged land surrenders.[5]

In 1910, Commissioner of Indian Affairs David Laird said the reserves in the west were "much in excess" of what Indians could ever work profitably, and recommended that "idle" lands should be surrendered, and the money used to improve Indian living conditions. In 1911, a new law allowed that any reserve adjoining a town of at least 8,000 people could be expropriated, even against Indian opposition. This was a complete rupture with the traditional trust relationship; but the Minister of the Interior, Frank Oliver, said the government should never allow Indian rights "to become a wrong to the white man".[6] Under this law, a judge (who should "have regard to the interest of the public and the Indian band") could order Indians to be removed from any part of a reserve, compensated for improvements made, and placed on some other reserve set aside for them.

In 1918, when wartime food production was a priority, the Superintendent-General of Indian Affairs was given power to lease all uncultivated land in a reserve without obtaining a surrender from the Indians. Whether the Indians liked it or not, the government could then send someone to cultivate their land and charge the cost of stock, machinery, material or labour against any funds held by the government on the band's behalf. Income from the leases may or may not have covered these costs. What was certain was that, by these measures, Indians lost control over their reserve lands.[7]

In all of these ways, some two million of the 7,500,000 acres of Indian lands were surrendered.

Community government:
Traditional chiefs were replaced with elected officials; power was

taken to depose chiefs or councillors who objected to any policy and declare them incompetent. The Indian Advancement Act of 1884 (later folded into the Indian Act) was designed in its own words "to confer certain privileges on the more advanced bands...with a view to training them for the exercise of municipal powers". Among these "privileges" was that the elected band council would have as chairman a government official, the Indian agent, with full power to control and regulate all matters of procedure and form, and to advise council. Any by-laws passed had to be approved by the Superintendent-General, so the agent was in a position of immense influence, given the huge powers at his employer's disposal.

Many aboriginal groups bitterly opposed this policy. The Mohawks of the Bay of Quinte advised the government that they had "renewed their Council Fire according to their rites, and have decided to do away with councilmen...and have hereditary chiefs take their place".[8] All the Mohawk reserves rejected the elected councils. In 1899 at Akwesasne (formerly known as St. Regis), 100 people seized the Indian agent and drove the police off the reserve. A few weeks later, police returned and in a scuffle shot and killed one of the unarmed chiefs, Jake Fire. Government officials are said to have then made fifteen Indians drunk, persuaded them to nominate each other for council, "and this is how the elective government under the Indian Act system was implemented at Akwesasne".[9]

Restrictions on movement, assembly and speech:

With the virtual extermination of the buffalo in the 1880s, conditions among Indians on the prairies were desperate. The government, nervous of an uprising by discontented Indians and Métis, introduced restrictions on assembly and movement, which are not unlike those later used by the apartheid system in South Africa.

In 1884, it was made an offence "to incite or stir up any three or more Indians, non-treaty Indians or half-breeds", or to make any request of a civil servant "in a riotous, routous, disorderly or threatening manner, or in a manner calculated to cause a breach of the peace".[10] Such a law left much to the interpretation, but appears to limit to two the size of any Indian political assembly. In those nervous times, the Vagrancy Act was often used to prevent Indians from "loitering" around towns near their reserve (in other words, Indians were often arrested and bundled out of town). With the Riel rebellion in 1885, this was considered inadequate, and a system of passes was instituted by which Indians in western Canada were forbidden from leaving their reserves for any purpose without a pass issued by the Indian agent. Although the system was admitted by police to be illegal and in violation of treaty guarantees, prairie Indians without passes were regularly arrested and returned to their reserves. There is evidence, remarks one historian, that this system was still being enforced in some places until 1936.[11]

At around the same time, it was forbidden to sell to Indians ammunition or cartridges (which once had been given by the government as presents) without written permission.[12]

Production:
In the 1880s, powers were taken to prohibit western Indians (who were said to be "wilder" and less competent than the Indians of Ontario and Quebec)[13] from selling any grains or root crops to anyone without the written permission of an Indian agent. If they did so, such a sale could be declared null and void. As we shall see in Chapter 15, the "west" at that time extended as far east as northwestern Ontario, where the small-scale efforts of the Ojibways to cultivate their lands were destroyed by this law. At the same time, no one was allowed to sell anything to an Indian without the written permission of the Superintendent-General.[14] Nor were Indians allowed to sell to anyone off the reserve anything that was given to them by the government in the form of a present or annuity payment. For example, if an Indian was given a cow, he could not sell its calves without permission, and if he did, the calves could be seized from whomever bought them. These laws were reaffirmed as late as 1933, and were in force until 1951.

The fact is that Indian efforts to create an agricultural economy (the ostensible aim of government policy when the treaties were signed) were deliberately thwarted by government regulation. Manitoba historian Sarah Carter has recently shown that restrictions on the sale of produce were but a small part of an overall government policy that resulted in the strangulation of Indian agriculture in the last decades of the nineteenth century. Much of this policy was introduced under the administration of the malevolent, Indian-hating Hayter Reed, who was appointed Indian Commissioner in 1888, and succeeded Vankoughnet as Deputy Superintendent-General in 1893.

At various times, Indian farmers were forbidden from using farm machinery, were required to make their own tools by hand, were limited to working forty acres when the minimum land that white farmers could make a living from was 160 acres, and were subjected to a lunatic policy designed to maintain them as "peasant farmers", working only for subsistence.[15]

Liquor:

From the first, the authorities took the power to interfere in what goes on inside Indian homes. The laws of the 1880s forbidding Indians from consuming or possessing liquor were gradually expanded, until anyone who was found to possess liquor, to be drunk, or to be gambling inside an Indian tent, house or wigwam could be ordered out by the Indian agent; if he refused to go, he could be arrested and become liable to imprisonment. It was a crime for anyone to give liquor to an Indian, and a criminal offence for an Indian not to tell the authorities where he or she had obtained liquor.

Furthermore, any Indian could be arrested for drunkenness without a warrant. Half of any penalty imposed for these liquor offences was paid to the informer, a system evidently designed to encourage spying within Indian reserves.[16] These laws were not changed until 1951.

Education:

In 1894, the government finally became interested in Indian education. Power was taken to secure compulsory attendance of all Indian children at school, but with the added provision for "the arrest and conveyance to school and detention there" of any children who might be prevented from attending by their parents or guardians (who, in such a case, would be liable to imprisonment).[17] At the same time, power was given to the government to establish industrial or boarding schools, or to declare any existing Indian school to be such, and to "commit" to such schools "by justices or Indian agents" Indian children under sixteen, who could be kept there until they were eighteen. To maintain such schools, the government could take any annuities or other moneys due to the children so committed. In these sections of the Act, the language used is akin to language dealing with criminals. And in fact, that is how the Act was sometimes used. In the early 1970s, I heard many Indians of the Mackenzie Valley describe how the priests would come downriver by barge, in each village seizing

Indian children to take to school, and how parents would send the children to hide in the bush. It is now widely acknowledged that the native schools established under these laws were among the most arbitrary and indefensible institutions ever created in Canada.

In 1947, Father J.O. Plourde, superintendent of Indian welfare and training for the Oblate Commission, a Roman Catholic order that ran many schools across Canada, testified to a joint parliamentary committee as to the enormous benefits that Indians obtained from the Order's residential schools. Indians, Father Plourde said, were gradually coming more and more to appreciate these schools, and "our reserve Indians...are now begging for" more such schools:

> We are of the opinion that the daily discipline in force in our residential schools, which calls for rising at a given hour, spiritual exercises also at a stated time, plus breakfast, dinner and supper, intermingled with hours of classwork and recreation, have in themselves more power to stabilize the nomadic habits of our Indian brethren than any other system of education.[18]

By 1991, the Order had changed its mind about the benefits the Indians obtained from their schools; the Reverend Doug Crosby, president of the Oblate Commission of Canada, in one of the most extraordinary and revealing statements ever made about Indian education in Canada, offered native people a fulsome apology for the very existence of the schools. Reverend Crosby said:

> We wish to apologize for the existence of the schools themselves, recognizing that the biggest abuse was...that the schools themselves happened...that the primal bond inherent within families was violated as a matter of policy, that children were usurped from their natural communities, and that, implicitly and explicitly, these schools operated out of the premise that European languages, traditions, and religious practices were superior to native languages, traditions and religious practices.[19]

Crosby also apologized for the physical and sexual abuse that he admitted had occurred in these schools. Far from helping Indians, he said, the schools had been part of the imperialist mentality with which the peoples of Europe first approached the aboriginal people. "We recognize that this mentality has, from the beginning, and ever since, continually threatened the cultural, linguistic and religious traditions of the native people."

The United, Anglican and Presbyterian Churches have also made apologies for various roles they have played historically in the native education system.

Health:
As with education, so with health: for the authorities, the problem was always how to detach aboriginal people from their own communities or families in their own interests. Usually a Canadian is free to decide whether to go to hospital or not, but when Indian agents had difficulty persuading Indians to go to a white hospital, more drastic measures were taken.

In 1914, the Superintendent-General was given power to make regulations for cleaning up unsanitary conditions on Indian reserves. To do this, his officials could enter any premises they considered unsanitary, alter or destroy any building they considered unfit for human habitation, limit the number of people living in premises they considered overcrowded, remove or keep under surveillance persons living in infected places, "and any other matter which, in the opinion of the Superintendent-General, the general health of the Indians of any locality may require". In case anyone in the Indian community should object to any of this, the new law laid down that the Superintendent-General's viewpoint should prevail over existing band regulations or rules.[20] These powers not only authorized a bureaucrat to do anything he felt like, but opened the way for generations of health and social workers to judge Indian homes and living conditions as unfit by the standards of middle-class white communities, with tragic results. Authority to fine and imprison anyone who did not comply with these measures was taken in 1918.[21]

Enfranchisement:
As the years passed, the Canadian authorities became more and more desperate over the unwillingness of Indians to enfranchise, that is, to abandon their Indian status and become fully-fledged Canadian citizens, so in 1920 they took the ultimate step. Henceforth, Indians would have no choice in the matter of whether they wished to continue to be Indians: an inquiry could be held into the fitness for enfranchisement of any Indian, whether he or she wished it or not. An Indian judged to be worthy of the honour of Canadian citizenship, could be compulsorily enfranchised within two years.[22] After an out-

burst of criticism, this compulsory provision was dropped in 1922; but it was reintroduced in 1933, and remained the law until 1951. Even then, the government made an effort to retain it, but retreated under pressure. Voluntary enfranchisement, however, remained government policy until 1985.

Inheritance:

Indians have never been free to decide for themselves what will happen to their goods and possessions after they die. In 1880, power was taken to allow the Superintendent-General "to decide all questions which may arise respecting the distribution...of the land and goods and chattels of a deceased Indian", and to remove the widow (or any other nominated person) from administration of her husband's estate.[23] Four years later, the law was changed to ensure that an Indian could not leave his land or goods to anyone further removed than second cousin, and that the widow, to be confirmed as her husband's beneficiary, must be "of good moral character" (in the opinion of the Superintendent-General) and have been living with her husband at the time of his death.[24]

In 1894, the Superintendent-General was given authority to disallow any part of any will. It was now written that he should be the "sole and final judge" of the moral character of the widow. The powers taken were now so involved and detailed that nine long clauses were needed to describe them.[25] Even after the revision of the Indian Act in 1951, the minister retained complete authority to reject or accept wills made by Indians.

Ceremonies, rituals, amusements:

As early as 1884, the Canadian government outlawed the Potlatch or Feast, the ceremony by which west-coast aboriginal nations maintained the balance of obligations on which their social order was based.

Explaining the importance of the Potlatch, Delgam Uukw, a Gitksan chief, wrote in 1987:

My power is carried in my House's histories, songs, dances and crests. It is recreated at the Feast when the histories are told, the songs and dances performed, and the crests displayed. With the wealth that comes from respectful use of the territory, the House feeds the name of the Chief in the Feast Hall. In this way, the law, the Chief, the territory and the Feast become one. The unity of the Chief's authority and his House's ownership of its territory are witnessed and thus affirmed by the other Chiefs at the Feast.[26]

Little of this was understood by the Europeans who first went among the west-coast nations. The newcomers watched in dismay as people whom they believed to be impoverished distributed their wealth among family and neighbours during a ceremony that could last as long as three months, each step carried out according to traditional ritual, with much feasting, singing and dancing. The missionaries who swarmed up and down the coast at that time considered the Potlatch barbarous and debauched, an obstacle to conversion to Christianity. The government considered the ceremony "pernicious".[27]

West-coast aboriginals never accepted the 1884 law, but continued to celebrate the Potlatch throughout the coming decades (as shown by the plaque in the Museum of Civilization, mentioned in the Prologue), often suffering imprisonment for it.

Also banned at the same time were the Sun Dances of the prairie nations, rituals of central importance to both the secular and religious realms (which were inseparable in aboriginal thinking.) The terms in which these rituals were forbidden under the Act reveal the Euro-Canadian mindset: the key element objected to in the Potlatch was "the giving away or paying or giving back of money, goods or articles of any sort" whether before, at or after the celebration; while the prairie ceremonies were described as "a celebration or dance of which the wounding or mutilation of the dead or living body of any human being or animal forms a part".[28]

These prohibitions were extended in 1914 to cover almost any performance that an aboriginal person might like to give or attend. A new section was added to the Indian Act forbidding Indians west and north of Manitoba from taking part in "any Indian dance" outside of their reserve, or in "any show, exhibition, performance, stampede or pageant in aboriginal costume" without the consent of an Indian agent. Anyone who induced or employed an Indian to perform such things, could be imprisoned for a month and fined, even if the performance never took place.[29]

In 1930, the government went virtually crazy for passing prohibitions on Indians. If an Indian who came before a court was judged to be "misspending or wasting" his time by frequenting a poolroom, the owner of the poolroom could be required to forbid him entry, in violation of which both the Indian and the owner could be sent to jail for up to thirty days.[30] By that time, aboriginal people, forbidden from drinking, gambling, dancing or playing pool, attending or taking part in performances, or celebrating traditional rituals, might have been forgiven for wondering just what they were expected to do in their spare time.

The end of the Indian Act?

A few years ago, I wrote a magazine article outlining these controls imposed on Indian life in the last hundred years; and from time to time I have spoken to college and university classes on the subject. Invariably, young people are amazed that their country should have been guilty of such repression. Their education has not covered it; their textbooks are almost silent on the matter.

The proposal in the 1992 Charlottetown constitutional accord to recognize the aboriginal right of self-government would have spelled the end of this appalling Indian Act. The 1992 referendum campaign increased public awareness of the inadequacies of the present legal structure governing aboriginals. And although the defeat of the accord may have postponed this change, it now seems likely that, at long last, the days of the Indian Act are numbered.

Off to school

For several generations of Indians, the schooling provided under the provisions of the Indian Act caused a devastating break in the normal course of their lives. Decades later, thousands of aboriginal people across the country are trying to recover from the effects of these experiences.

In 1973, a Cree friend of mine, Buckley Petawabano, of Mistissini reserve in northern Quebec, described to me with irrepressible humour his experience of going off to school:

"Indian Affairs used to threaten people that if they didn't send their kids to school, they wouldn't get any welfare. Personally, as far as I can remember, I was sort of anxious to get to school, to see what was going on. But when I got there it was a different story. I just couldn't relate. I couldn't speak any English for two years, but what helped me was that there were a lot of other Indian kids there from Rupert House, Fort George, Nemaska and other places. We were sent to Moose Factory in Ontario because we were Anglicans, and the Anglicans had residences for Indian kids only from Ontario to B.C.

"I spent six or seven years there and then we were shipped down to Sault Ste. Marie. After grade seven or eight they shipped us out of the residential school and put us in private homes. Now there's a different trip altogether. When I entered the private home my land-lord, he was a really great guy, the first night he says to me, 'Buckley, I want to talk to you' . Somehow I felt at ease with this guy. The first thing he talked about was segregation. I had never heard anything about that in my life before.... He said, 'You know, never worry about what other people say to you, you should just worry about how you feel.... You know what segregation is all about, eh?' I am pretending to know, because I am trying to be nice. He said to me, 'Don't ever think you're a bad guy, like those guys in the movies'. He was serious, you know. I think that's how he was trying to relate to us.

"The landlady was really nice, too, but the rules we were given in a pamphlet for each boarding student were totally white. Like, you can't kiss your girlfriend, but you can have a date with her. Like, an Indian chick, she lives five blocks away, you can go pick her up, take her to a movie, have a coffee with her, bring her back before ten-thirty, all these rules. What really embarrassed me a lot was that I'd go downtown and my friends are down there laughing at me, 'Here's a guy that's got a date.'

"An anthropologist from McGill came into town and we were so glad to hear from him because we were hoping he'd have news from home. We went to see him, then for a whole week – holy shit, the whole thing was questioning, bang, bang, bang. I kept saying, 'Yeah, great school, I learned a lot, I got 80 per cent in history,' all these facts, a totally different way of looking at the education thing.

"My concept of white people was that they were very superior in a lot of ways and my duty was to accomplish what the white man can do.... Like be an electronic engineer, a pilot, just as good or even better. That was my concept. I guess they laid that on us in a really slick way, history books, movies, just showing Indians in a bad sense. Mostly...well, for one thing, there was fear, when you're in an environment different from the one you're used to, speaking for myself, 90 per cent of the time I would act out of fear.

"When the principal made this speech to us, saying, 'We're here to teach you English and anyone caught talking any other language will be punished' . That's a pretty heavy statement, but you can't re-ally protest, because when you're in the bush you respect who's looking after you, and you have to respect who's looking after you wherever you are. Otherwise you get thrown out. Your parents are in the bush, so where are you gonna go? Survival is survival. When you're a kid you depend on an older person for your survival, and we'd always been taught to respect the person we survived on, and I guess we took it from there, we respected all older people.

"I finished high school, grade twelve, and left at about nineteen."

11

Barriere Lake: People of the Stone Weir

In the fall of 1988, nearly twenty years after my trip up the Ottawa Valley with Mike McKenzie, I read in the newspaper one day that a group of Algonquins had come to Ottawa in the hope of seeing the Prime Minister. They had pitched their tents on Victoria Island in the middle of the Ottawa River within a stone's throw of Parliament Hill. I was in the habit of cycling past the island every day, so I decided to drop in on them, just to provide a friendly face in what I supposed would be a tense situation for them. I could tell from the way they looked – their dark skins, long black hair, rough working clothes, shy withdrawn manner, and their hesitancy in English – that they came from some remote place, had not intermarried much with whites, and were still following the traditional life of the bush.

These Algonquins were protesting that the forest in which they had always lived was being destroyed by logging companies that were literally hacking their way of life to pieces day by day. The Algonquins wanted to stop this destruction, but no one in authority would listen to them, and they'd become so desperate that they'd decided to go to the top man. If they didn't get any satisfaction today, they said, they intended to camp on Parliament Hill until they did. After all, they had a perfect right to camp there, because it was still unsurrendered Algonquin territory, as was the whole valley of the Ottawa River.

Prime Minister Mulroney refused to see them, so they returned a week later to carry out their threat. On September 28, 1988 – an epic day for the Algonquin people – they pitched their tents on Parliament Hill, and some sixteen of them were arrested and charged with "committing a nuisance on a public work". This act of defiance occurred just 375 years after the Algonquin chief Tessouat stopped the French from passing upriver.

When this happened, I was working on a book about the economic and environmental problems of the globe. My head was full of facts about the brutal impact of our industrial culture on the biosphere, and the many solutions proposed by the Brundtland commission, which had examined this problem for the United Nations General Assembly. The commission had concluded that the Earth is in serious danger, and that a new, environmentally sustainable form of development is needed. Among other things, the commission praised the knowledge and wisdom accumulated by the world's indigenous peoples, recommending that they be given "a decisive voice" in all decisions being made about development of their traditional lands.

Politicians everywhere rushed to embrace this idea of sustainable development. Canada's provincial and federal governments quickly endorsed it and pledged to rebuild our economy along sustainable lines. Businesspeople jumped on the bandwagon: the biggest polluters were transformed almost overnight into vociferous supporters of environmental virtue.

The Algonquins had now decided to put this new-found concern to the test. Metaphorically waving the Brundtland report, they appeared on the doorstep of a Prime Minister noted for his brave words about the need for environmental change, and told him the time had come to put up or shut up. His government had endorsed the Brundtland concept, they said; now they wanted it to be applied in their hunting territories. The government response was to arrest the Algonquins and charge them with committing a nuisance.

The Algonquins asked if I would be interested in making a film about what they were doing. I managed to persuade the National Film Board to put up enough money to allow me to do some research, and in December 1988 I set out for Barriere Lake, in the middle of Quebec's LaVérendrye Park, 250 kilometres north of Ottawa, where the people lived who had been arrested on Parliament Hill.

At home among the headwaters

The people of Barriere Lake have always called themselves Mitchikanibikongink – People of the Stone Weir.[1] The rolling, forested wilderness around the headwaters of the Ottawa and Gatineau rivers is their ancient homeland. Their name comes from a natural stone bridge over which the waters of the two rivers would flow at certain times of the year, moving from one watershed to the other. Fish would feed and spawn in the shallows around the stone weir, and it became the central gathering place for the Algonquins. Then, suddenly, in 1871, it was all flooded, buried deep in a reservoir behind a dam, and the fish, animals and people had to move elsewhere.

Euro-Canadian settlement spread into the Ottawa Valley early in the nineteenth century, displacing the Algonquins from the lower Ottawa. Those who lived among the headwaters of the river, many miles to the north, were more fortunate. They were bypassed by settlement, industry, Church and State, until timber merchants arrived among them, chopping logs in the last decades of the nineteenth century. Even then, the northern Algonquins were able to survive: the logging technology was simple, the forest vast, and the early intruders did not create roads or settlements. The People of the Stone Weir rode out the interruptions and maintained their way of life.

Today, Barriere Lake (the reserve is called Rapid Lake) cannot be found on most ordinary Canadian maps. Yet the Algonquins remain the only permanent population in a very large area of country. The nearest substantial settlements are Maniwaki and Mont Laurier to the south, and Val d'Or to the north, each roughly 90 miles away. Due east and west, however, there is no settlement across an enormous stretch of country from the Ottawa River to La Tuque. For 300 miles, the forest is criss-crossed by logging roads, but the only signs of non-native habitation are temporary logging camps, and some tourist outfitters spotted around the lakes. Otherwise, the Algonquins have the territory to themselves.

Two months after I met the Algonquins on Victoria Island, I was driven north through a heavy December snowstorm on my first visit to Rapid Lake. Normally a three-hour drive, the trip took more than five hours, for the road was slippery and visibility almost nil.

From the gate of LaVérendrye Park we drove fifty or sixty lonely miles, past the sole government service centre, and then bumped the last five miles along an icy gravel road to the village of Rapid Lake. It was quickly arranged that I would stay with J.B., as everyone called him, and I was taken to his house.

J.B. – Jean-Baptiste Wawatie – turned out to be a taciturn character who moved slowly and spoke hardly at all. But he greeted me warmly and prepared some food for me. I soon realized I was in

Indian country, because people kept coming in without knocking, usually to borrow or buy a packet of cigarettes, which they all expected J.B. to have. Rapid Lake is not one of those modern Indian towns with a smart, high-priced motel and a well-stocked village store. In fact, Rapid Lake is a reserve with very little in the way of material goods. It has no store, taxi, restaurant or barber shop, or any of the other normal services of a Canadian village. Virtually all of the $4 million of income that comes into the reserve every year is taken to Maniwaki and spent there.

Not long after I arrived, J.B.'s sister-in-law, Irene Jerome, burst into the house, settled herself at the kitchen table, and with a harsh acerbic wit began to regale me with one tale after another of the inequities inflicted on the Algonquins by an unsympathetic Quebec government.

"Long time ago," Irene said (a phrase that recurred in her conversation like a chorus), before the government had interfered, there had been no such thing as a trapline. Everyone had their territory, people did not fight among themselves, money was not a consideration. But since the government had insisted that traplines be registered, people had to make a map every year showing where they had caught animals, and had to send the map to the government with a cheque for $12. If you didn't have $12, you could lose your trapline. Irene told me of people who had returned to their traplines to find their cabins burned and their rights pre-empted in favour of strangers. Still, her people tended to ignore the government, as they had always done. They still used their own lands, even after they had been robbed of them. They trapped on them when the new owners were not there.

As casually as if she were describing a walk down the main street, Irene told of walking nine hours home after her truck had broken down on a forest road. She talked for a long time about her five sons and her daughter – aged thirty-four to twenty-one – who had all been to school, one as far as university, and whom she was now instructing in the ways of the bush. She talked about the medicines she could find in certain places at certain times of the year – always under the guidance of her mother, Lena Nattaway, the matriarch of the community, whom I met later – and where to find the bark she needed to make baskets, and how she tanned moose hides for dresses, coats and blankets. I was to find later that within the native world, Irene Jerome is famous throughout the northeast of the continent for her deep knowledge of all these traditions.

To support her large family Irene had worked for fourteen years in the United States; she'd been a cook in Maniwaki; she'd worked for outfitters in their camps; but she'd finally tired of all that and decided to come home and live like an Algonquin. Now she spent most of her time, summer and winter, twenty-five miles to the north, not far from the original Stone Weir, where her mother has her bush camp and lives surrounded by her vast collection of children, grandchildren and great-grandchildren, eighty-five in all.

"I keep the things I make," said Irene, "the baskets, and clothes and blankets, because I want the young people to see them." Thus she never has enough income or work stamps to qualify for unemployment benefits, and in times of need, she had sometimes thought about going on welfare. But "too many people go on welfare," she said. "I don't like the way Indian people have been treated. They are getting lazy. These days, people are dying before they're sixty. Long time ago, people used to work hard and live longer. Today people sit around too long. Their veins shrink. Long time ago, people had good veins. Their blood was working real good."

I gathered from what Irene told me that the reserve was divided politically. The chief and council were on one side, wrestling with the problems of modern life, while others, particularly those grouped around Lena Nattaway's huge family, put their faith in Algonquin traditions. Therefore, there was bound to be some suspicion of the film I was setting out to make at the request of the council, and no doubt that was why Irene was so quick to find out what I was doing. It was good of her to introduce me to this potential minefield. Over the next few months, I acted as if these divisions were none of my business. And when the community was in crisis twelve months later, everyone did pull together around a heroic effort to stop the clearcut logging. The divisions within the community turned out to be, as it were, skin-deep. Whatever the political differences, Lena Nattaway was the heart and soul of the community, deeply revered by everyone.

I came to have a great respect for this talkative, aggressive and sometimes ferocious Irene. Deeply knowledgeable about her culture, she is full of laughter and jokes, and an enormous amount of fun to be with. She will deliver a harangue about how she doesn't like or trust white men, while serving you, at a moment's notice, a huge plate of moose meat or fish. I once asked her if she had any old photographs she could lend me. She dove into her cabin, hauled out one cardboard box after another, and in her harshest tone delivered a tirade about how she couldn't trust me with any of her pictures, all the while handing over to me a fascinating photographic record of the past of her people. Irene, in short, is one of a kind: once met, never to be forgotten.

She ended that first visit by telling me an extraordinary story that put her mocking, anti-white outbursts into perspective, and conveyed a sense of the heroic dimensions of life in this wilderness. Not long ago on the highway Irene and her family had picked up a solitary white man who seemed to be in distress. He told them he had run out of gas seventy-five miles from the nearest gas station. For some reason, he had thrown away his keys and his money, had taken his Bible from the car and had started to walk. He had walked ten miles when they picked him up.

"We talked to him," said Irene. "We changed his clothes, and we persuaded him to phone his mother.

"He was a French-Canadian who owned a jewellery store that went bankrupt. He felt that no one cared. We told him his mother would always love him, whatever happened."

Getting to know them

The next morning, I walked in on the four members of the band council, who were having a meeting in their office basement, surrounded by maps of their territory. Dark-complexioned, stocky and strong of build, guarded in manner, careless of appearance, these four men reminded me of the first native hunters I had ever seen, twenty years before, when a group of Ojibway had climbed into a train that was taking me across northern Ontario, and I'd known immediately that I was in the presence of a different sort of people. These band councillors – Jean-Paul Ratt, Jules Papatie, Michel Thusky, and chief Jean-Maurice Matchewan – were typical northern Algonquins. In spite of the pressures to assimilate, they'd kept their Algonquin family names; but because of the strong Catholic influence in the reserve in the 1950s, they had been given French Christian names, although of the four, only Michel spoke French. I discovered that for years the Barriere Lake people had been shuffled around the province for schooling like so many bags of potatoes, sometimes to French schools in Amos or Val d'Or, at other times to English schools in the south, always in response to some completely arbitrary decision made

The inscription celebrating Chief Clelaman's Potlatch

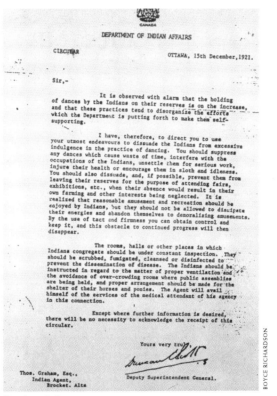

CANADA

DEPARTMENT OF INDIAN AFFAIRS

CIRCULAR

OTTAWA, 15th December, 1921.

Sir,-

It is observed with alarm that the holding of dances by the Indians on their reserves is on the increase, and that these practices tend to disorganize the efforts which the Department is putting forth to make them self-supporting.

I have, therefore, to direct you to use your utmost endeavours to dissuade the Indians from excessive indulgence in the practice of dancing. You should suppress any dances which cause waste of time, interfere with the occupations of the Indians, unsettle them for serious work, injure their health or encourage them in sloth and idleness. You should also dissuade, and, if possible, prevent them from leaving their reserves for the purpose of attending fairs, exhibitions, etc., when their absence would result in their own farming and other interests being neglected. It is realized that reasonable amusement and recreation should be enjoyed by Indians, but they should not be allowed to dissipate their energies and abandon themselves to demoralizing amusements. By the use of tact and firmness you can obtain control and keep it, and this obstacle to continued progress will then disappear.

The rooms, halls or other places in which Indians congregate should be under constant inspection. They should be scrubbed, fumigated, cleansed or disinfected to prevent the dissemination of disease. The Indians should be instructed in regard to the matter of proper ventilation and the avoidance of over-crowding rooms where public assemblies are being held, and proper arrangement should be made for the shelter of their horses and ponies. The Agent will avail himself of the services of the medical attendant of his agency in this connection.

Except where further information is desired, there will be no necessity to acknowledge the receipt of this circular.

Yours very truly,

Duncan C. Scott

Deputy Superintendent General.

Thos. Graham, Esq.,
Indian Agent,
Brocket, Alta

Circular to Indian agents

From the beginning, Euro-Canadians abhorred traditional aboriginal ceremonies. The Potlatch held by Chief Clelaman in 1892 was illegal under Canadian law when the sign, above, first stood outside this house in Bella Coola, British Columbia. But with the recent revival of interest in native observances, the sign has been transferred to the Canadian Museum of Civilization in the nation's capital, where it is proudly exhibited as proof of an enduring aboriginal culture. Below: Official tolerance of native customs is relatively recent, as attested by this 1921 circular ordering Indian agents to suppress Indian dancing, signed by the Deputy Superintendent-General of Indian Affairs (and well-known poet), Duncan Campbell Scott.

NOVA SCOTIA MUSEUM

Chief Gabriel Sylliboy

OWEN FITZGERALD

Alex Denny

The Mikmaqs of Nova Scotia have never ceased to consider themselves a nation whose treaties with the Crown override all subsequent legislation. Two great defenders of this tradition have been, top, Chief Gabriel Sylliboy, who led the Mikmaqs from 1926 until his death in 1964, and one of their current leaders, Alex Denny, appointed to the lifetime job of Grand Captain in 1968 when he was only 28.

Sakej Henderson

Marie Battiste

This married couple has played a key role in the Mikmaq cultural and political revival of the last two decades. Top: Sakej Henderson, legal adviser to the Mikmaq Grand Council, a graduate of Harvard, watched at work by his daughter Anne. Below: Marie Battiste, curriculum adviser to the Eskasoni Education Board, and a graduate of Stanford University.

Ojibway family mends canoe

Savant Lake community, 1992

The nomadic, productive life of the Ojibway was supposed to have been assured by Treaty 3, signed in 1873, a year after this family (top) was pictured mending its birchbark canoe beside one of the great Ojibway waterways in northwestern Ontario. But the treaty did not protect them: within a few decades, Ojibway people were pushed out of their reserve near the town of Ignace, and were reduced to spending half a century wandering as squatters on Crown land. This battered community, now centred in Savant Lake, is pictured in 1992: Chief Ed Machimity leans against the tree, his father Albert in the white cap on the steps.

The Ojibway, however, are struggling to revive. Joe Pitchenesse, of Wabigoon (top, facing page), pictured with his brother Bill examining a *manomin* (wild rice) lake, is leading an increasingly successful drive to develop traditional economies. Below, their sister Mary Rose (right) watches as Linda Williams works a *manomin* roasting oven at Wabigoon in 1992.

ANDREW CHAPESKIE

Joe Pitchenesse

MAGGIE BRADY

Manomin roasting oven, Wabigoon

Lena Nattaway

Barriere Lake road blockade

The Barriere Lake Algonquins of Quebec, both young and old, have rallied to the defence of their way of life against destructive logging of their homeland. Above: Lena Nattaway, born in 1913, a veritable encyclopedia of Algonquin knowledge and experience, brings two of her many great-grandchildren to her fishing camp on the shores of Cabonga reservoir in 1991. Two years earlier, virtually the whole community courted arrest as they blockaded a logging road, below.

Lena's daughter, Irene Jerome, (top, facing page) is celebrated for her handicrafts and other traditional skills; below, her sons Eddie Wawatie (centre) and Joe (right), bring in a load of fish from their nets on the reservoir. In 1987 Eddie surprised a *Toronto Star* reporter with his lyrical description of Barriere Lake life.

Irene Jerome

Eddie and Joe Wawatie

Lawrence Vankoughnet

Hayter Reed

Duncan Campbell Scott

For the first 65 years of Confederation, a succession of deputy ministers ran the Department of Indian Affairs as almost a personal satrapy. Lawrence Vankoughnet, top bureaucrat from 1874 to 1893, set the tone. His wing collar, muttonchop whiskers, and jaunty fur hat cut a rakish figure among Canadian civil servants of the Victorian era. He was followed by Hayter Reed (1893-97) who, although he had a poor opinion of Indians, liked to dress up as one, as he did for this costume ball in Ottawa in 1896. Renowned poet Duncan Campbell Scott had a free hand for nearly two decades, from 1913 to 1932. These men presided over one of the great disasters of Canadian history: the decline of previously vigorous aboriginal communities into extreme poverty and psychological disorder.

by distant bureaucrats. Out of this educational mish-mash, most of them have emerged with English as their second language, but 40 per cent also know French. Few of them spoke English or French until the 1960s, and most of those over thirty are still not especially fluent in either language, which could account for their shy, wary manner.

To my surprise, the band councillors did not have much information to offer for the film. I had the impression they were still getting used to the idea, although they had asked me to make it. They spoke of their dismay that, during the summer, some of their people who'd been camping out in the forest had been sickened by chemical spraying. For them, this was like a visitation from hell, threatening their very survival. They complained of the gradual loss of traplines, the impact of clearcut logging, the effect of the government's movement to privatize much of the park, and of widespread poaching by whites. They told me the community was still 85 to 90 per cent dependent on country food that they caught themselves, although there were fewer animals, birds and fish than only a few years ago. Moose, their major source of food, were disappearing.

"Twenty years ago," said the dark, burly chief, Jean-Maurice Matchewan, "when you called moose, a whole bunch would come. Now they don't." His people had once held winter community hunts when moose gathered on small islands in the reservoir; as many as ten hunters would surround the islands while others drove the moose out. Now, there weren't enough animals to make such a hunt worthwhile.

I left the councillors to continue their meeting and wandered around the village, down past the tiny Catholic church, now visited only occasionally by a priest and more or less abandoned by the younger people, and on to a tourist lodge standing on a point just outside the borders of the reserve. This had once been the Hudson's Bay store, but had been closed many years before, and sold to a Maniwaki businessman who now runs American and Quebec tourists through there for a few days' fishing during the summer: a business that the Algonquins, given the chance, could be doing for themselves. So right here, on the edge of the reserve, were what remained of the traders and the Church, the two great forces that had for so long dominated the community.

As I walked past the large primary school, I was surprised to hear the children using the Algonquin language while playing together. In many parts of Canada, aboriginal children cannot be persuaded to speak their own language, even if they understand it, a sure sign that a culture is on the slide.

When I returned to J.B.'s house he unexpectedly produced some documents from a drawer, which he thought might be of interest to me. As I pored over them, I began to learn the agonizing story of how Barriere Lake had been gradually overrun by the advance of Euro-Canadian civilization. The 1871 dam that had flooded the Stone Weir was built to store water for floating logs down the Gatineau. Railway lines constructed through Algonquin territory by 1912 introduced outside competition for the animals, and afterwards the Barriere Lake people lived through many bitter decades. They sought refuge by keeping to themselves, but that only reinforced the tendency of governments to treat them as if they were not there, or at least had no rights. For more than forty years, from at least 1919, the Quebec government repeatedly refused to confirm their owner-ship of their land, arguing that it was under timber licence and within a fish and game reserve. In contrast, land grants were given to the Hudson's Bay Company and the Church as soon as they asked for them. Finally, in the late 1950s, at the urging of the Church, Quebec offered the Algonquins the use (but not the ownership) of fifty-nine acres of sand on the shores of the Cabonga reservoir. The people themselves were not consulted. So the reserve was estab-lished by an order-in-council of September 7, 1961. It referred to the Algonquins as "les sauvages", a term that has long since lost its benign meaning, even in French. This is not remote history: the man who signed the order-in-council was Jean-Jacques Bertrand, who was Pre-mier of Quebec just before the first term of Robert Bourassa.

A study of Barriere Lake made a couple of years before my visit in-dicated massive unemployment, an extensive dependence on alcohol, and a complete absence of the management skills needed if they were to gain control over their own affairs. Thirty per cent of the people were under sixteen, and the population was expected to double to more than 900 in the coming fifteen years. Yet there was no room for more houses. I began to understand why the Algonquins had op-posed the building of a hydro line into the reserve: they did not want to be confined forever to these fifty-nine acres, but hoped – a desperate hope, given the attitude of the Quebec government – that in the fu-ture they could confirm their rights to the 6,000 square miles of their traditional lands, and eventually establish a viable, prosperous village, somewhere other than on the eroding shoreline of the reservoir.

The reports I read at J.B's included a sad story of an abortive effort by the people to acquire some skills through a self-help initiative. In April 1987, Barriere Lake produced a plan to employ ten welfare recipients to build three houses, and in the process get on-the-job training in construction, planning and management. It was supported by the Quebec regional office of the Department of Indian Affairs, and officials of the Canadian Employment and Immigration Commission called it the best plan of its type they had seen. An employment consultant was lined up to help the trainees to tender for work outside the community after the project was finished.

But these same supportive bureaucracies imposed so many delays that authority to spend money was given only in the following February, after the summer building season had passed. The houses were built by a determined band council, but the band was stuck with a $24,000 debt for extra winter construction costs. In the end, the scheme failed so totally to reach its social objectives that the report described it as "a nightmare".

A genuine matriarch

Later I dropped into the little house occupied by Lena Nattaway. Irene must have prepared her mother for my visit, for Lena settled down to talk to me willingly enough. It is not surprising, I suppose, that in a community still so strong in its traditions, so firmly attached to the forest and the hunt, there should be a genuine matriarch, a veritable repository of the wisdom and knowledge of the tribe, and that is Lena.

A tiny, lively woman, born in 1913, Lena Nattaway has the worn face and hands of someone who has worked hard outside all her life. She has a sharp-eyed, kindly expression under the bandana that she always wears, and a quick, combative style of talking. I had watched her drive up on her snowmobile a few minutes before we met, for she was still in the habit of going out alone on the twenty-five mile trip to her camp near Barriere Lake. A couple of months before, she had been one of the protesters who had invaded Parliament Hill. When a special court hearing was held to demand the return of the Algonquin tents seized by the RCMP, Lena's testimony about how vitally she needed her tent had been the most powerful influence in persuading the judge to order the release of all the tents.

Lena told me that, until she was married at the age of eighteen, she had lived with her grandparents. Her grandmother had lived to ninety-seven, and therefore must have been born in 1854. Lena's great-grandmother, born in the early years of the nineteenth century, lived to 110. To talk to Lena is to be carried back to an age when the Algonquin hunters were still little affected by the white civilization beginning to encircle them. She remembers when there was no such thing as store food, only the moose, rabbit and fish caught by the people, and the blueberries and other wild food that they picked.

"Long time ago we didn't have any cabins," she told me. "We lived in wigwams made of bark. In the winter it was no problem to sleep in the bush. We had rabbit fur clothing, you could not freeze or get cold with it. It wasn't necessary to have a fire. We used spruce boughs for bedding, and we wouldn't get wet. I didn't even have a tent, even after I got married. Everybody lived all over the place. We had half-way houses, built like teepees so anybody could sleep in them on their way from one place to another."

Lena remembers when there was no money. "If you wanted something you would trade moccasins, or tools, or whatever you had." The Algonquins made their clothes from moose hide, their coats and blankets from rabbit skins. Her grandmother made beautiful dresses from marten fur, and the first cloth Lena could remember was sacking, from which they made dresses.

"Long time ago, we had no place to sell furs, we only trapped when we needed fur for ourselves. We would hunt so we had enough food to last for a week or two.... In the summer no one stayed in one place for long. We scattered in small groups, gathered our own foods, fish, ducks, blueberries.... We had to keep moving all the time.... Long time ago, we had no money for guns, so we used bow and arrow, and slingshots. There used to be so many ducks and geese we could get close to them. If we wanted potatoes or onions, we found them growing wild in the bush, we could find them winter or summer.... We made our own pipes, and got wild tobacco from the bush," said Lena, obviously enjoying my astonishment at her tale. "There's none of it here, but I know where there is some."

They used rawhide strings as fishing lines, and made hooks from the penis bones of otter or fisher, honing them down to a sharp edge. They made needles from animal bones. When white men came they tried to make farmers out of the Indians. At Jerome's Point (near

Barriere Lake), where Lena was raised in a large extended family, the people began to grow their own food in a large garden.

"Long time ago, before the white man came, it was better. Nobody ever got sick. But after the white man came, and put the logs in the water, by and by everything was spoiled. Even the taste of the water, even the medicine in the bush. Then many people began to get sick. It wasn't us, it was them, they spoiled everything. Long time ago, before the white man came, we never had any shortage of food. Only after the white man came was there shortage."

Lena has had three husbands and fifteen children, and while she talked to me some of her forty-three grandchildren, still living with her in the house and being brought up by her, were coming and going. What she was telling me was a history of Canada, a Canada well within living memory, but one that has never appeared in history books. I was astonished to find this veritable encyclopedia of neglected knowledge hidden away in this tiny village, amazed that I had never heard of Lena before.

Three years later, when the Algonquin lawyers applied for an injunction to stop the logging, they entered as evidence an affidavit by Lena in which she described her youthful wanderings as a member of hunting parties to places throughout the territory that for her still bear Algonquin names: Kanameksakak, Kaokokagamak, Kamajegamak, Nishcuttea, Chochocoane, Wigwasekak and so on, original Canadian names that were replaced by people who came later.[2]

After her first marriage, Lena lived at Grand Lake Victoria for a time, and later travelled east to the Obedjiwan people. All these people are different, she says. "Kitcisagik, Winneway, Obedjiwan, by the way they speak, you know the difference, you know where they are from. Even at Kitcisagik [Lake Simon, a few miles to the north], they're a little different. They make things different. Maniwaki people don't sew the baskets the way we sew here. They sew with a long stitch. They finish it faster but it breaks faster. When we saw the baskets hanging in the spring and fall we could tell which people made them.... Same thing with the canoes they make."

Lena described how the Algonquins used to gather for feasts, when the chief would assign people to their different territories for the coming season. Their old chief, David Makokos, when he first saw the white people with their crosscut saws, had warned about what would happen.

"Every word the chief said about what's going to happen is happening today," said Lena in her affidavit. "The people tried to stop it, but they couldn't communicate with the white people.... They took too many white men's words. They didn't know what they were being told. There were promises made to the Indians, as long as the water streams, as long as the grass grows, as long as the sun shines, the Indians will always be respected. Today they say there is a different law now. Our people should be free to hunt, to trap, to use the bush, that's what the people were promised.

"We don't want timber cutting. It is killing all the herb medicines, the animals and medicine that the animals eat. They shouldn't hurt the trees that the animals eat. They're going to hurt the plants growing on the ground from the machines they use now. This is worse, it's just like bringing a monster over here to ruin everything.... They are cutting all kinds of trees now. When they used a bucksaw long time ago, they didn't hurt the other trees. They just took the ones they wanted, the animals had something to eat. And there's no job for the people. The machine is doing all the work.

"That's why we can't find any good birch bark: the trees have been hurt. We have to go to the big island to look for it. It's so hard to find. We use it for canoes, feast basket, basket for tapping the maple, the *skitenagon*, the *kukukunagon, atoban, wigwemot*, all kinds of names for baskets.

"Long time ago they tried to stop us from hunting beaver, muskrat, otter. The game wardens used to wait for us in the portage. They would know where we trap...they were going to search us. They were going to take everything we got. If we were caught carrying a gun across the highway they'd take it away from us. I don't know why they did that. We never did understand them. Every time we'd get caught like that, my husband would give me the gun because I'd give the game warden a hard time, I'd even ask for a piece of paper for why he'd take the gun. The first time I stayed here at Nanoatnak, the game warden came and told me I had to go back to Kitcisagik because moose season was opening. I told him it was my trapline. The big boss came and told me I had to go back. I might be hit. I told him I wouldn't move."

Bypassed by history

The recent history of Barriere Lake is a case study in the arrogant indifference to aboriginal life that has characterized Canada in this century.[3] Between the late 1920s and the early '80s, Quebec passed nearly a hundred orders-in-council that had to do with traditional Barriere Lake lands, setting boundaries for parks and reserves, establishing regulations for hunting, fishing, tourism and so on. At first, these regulations did betray some recognition that Algonquins were living out there in the wilderness, subsisting on the animals in the traditional way. In 1928, when pressure on the forest was reducing the natives to desperate conditions, a Quebec order-in-council set up the Grand Lake Victoria Indian game reserve of 6,300 square miles, for the use and benefit of Indian people. The regulation recognized that Indians had previously occupied these lands exclusively; and the stated purpose of the reserve was to end conflicts between them and non-native hunters, whose penetration of the territory had already caused severe game shortages. Sadly, from that promising moment of concern, it has been all downhill.

Only a year later, in 1929, Gatineau Power, a subsidiary of Canadian International Paper (CIP), decided to use the Gatineau River to generate power for its mill on the Ottawa, and built the Cabonga dam, creating a reservoir in the very heart of the Barriere Lake lands. The dam was built with cavalier indifference to the affect on the Barriere Lake subsistence life. No compensation was paid for the many square miles of hunting lands put under water. In fact, the Algonquins were never told how much land was to be flooded. Documents from the time show that a rise of fifteen feet in the water level on Cabonga Lake would have flooded eighty square miles; but today the level is admitted to be twenty-two feet above the natural level, so the flooded area must have been more like a hundred square miles.

Of course, it would not be true to say that aboriginal interests were totally ignored. CIP in its generosity was prepared to compensate the thirteen or fourteen people who still lived at the original Barriere Lake site, across the lake from the flooded Stone Weir. It was figured that they would be adequately looked after if given $30 each to buy lumber, paper, doors, windows, and nails to build a sixteen-foot-by-sixteen-foot cabin. So the company paid $525 in total compensation, and the Hudson's Bay Company wrote to the government to praise CIP's generosity. The Dozois reservoir was created twenty years later, flooding another seventy-seven square miles, much of it Barriere Lake hunting territory.

No study was ever made of the impact of all this flooding on the

Barriere Lake hunters. In fact, until the late 1980s, they were never advised when to expect a change in the water levels, which simply rose and fell, winter and summer, according to the needs of the power stations. The Algonquins have always used the reservoir for travelling on, so the collapse of the ice in winter resulting from changing water levels has been dangerous for them, and devastating for beaver, marten and other small animals.

Quebec soon reneged on the commitment that a large area should be set aside for exclusive Indian hunting and fishing. After 1928, the province made no serious effort to enforce the aboriginal right, and in 1936 revoked it, opening the hunting of big game in the Grand Lake Victoria reserve to non-natives.

In 1939, without bothering to consult the Algonquins, the province built a major road north to the Abitibi region directly through the Indian game reserve, and declared ten miles on either side of the highway to be the "Mont Laurier-Senneterre Highway Fish and Game Reserve". Forget any Indian rights that may have been established in 1928: everyone, Algonquins included, was now forbidden to hunt or fish inside the new reserve, whose purpose was declared to be "to protect game and fish against abuses, so that this region may permanently answer to the requirements of the tourist trade". The order-in-council setting up this new reserve withdrew the land from the Grand Lake Victoria reserve and specifically stated that this ended all "privileges" for Indians in the withdrawn lands.

In 1948, Quebec renamed what was left of the Grand Lake Victoria Indian hunting reserve as a beaver reserve, and reduced the exclusive Indian right only to trapping. By all of these measures, traditional native uses of the forest were gradually restricted without any pretence of consultation or consideration of native needs. In 1953, a large area was set aside as a moose reserve within which it was forbidden to take this animal, so central to the Algonquin way of life. In 1945, 1950 and again in 1953, the highway reserve that had been chopped out of the Indian hunting park was much enlarged and renamed LaVérendrye Wildlife Reserve (commonly called Park), with the objective of promoting tourism. All hunting was forbidden within the park. The Barriere Lake people ignored these regulations, and thus began an era of running battles with the game wardens, who regularly seized the equipment and meat with which the Algonquins tried to feed their families. At the same time, a large tourist establishment owned by Euro-Canadians was built along the highway, and its owners were given exclusive hunting rights in the area.

This catalogue of indifference to the Algonquin interest has continued unabated to the present day. Not only has LaVérendrye Park grown larger, but in all of the regulations governing its use there is only one mention of Indians: namely, that with its establishment they lost all their privileges. Until recently, tourism has been accorded first priority in the park, although even tourism now takes second place to logging. Wildlife protection has received the occasional nod, but Indians have been ignored. For example, in 1965 the government decided to open up LaVérendrye Park for a one-year controlled moose hunt. The hunt has been renewed every year since. Originally, the regulations required that hunting parties must use guides. Barriere Lake people did get considerable work as guides as a result of this regulation. Someone must have found out, because in 1980 this requirement was dropped, and the Barriere Lake people have had virtually no guiding work since.

In 1978, the Parti Québécois government of René Lévesque created a brand-new people's movement, a province-wide system of ZECs (Zone d'exploitation controllée), which gave citizen organizations authority to manage areas requiring protection for wild animal populations. The rationale was to abolish the many exclusive hunting and fishing rights held by private clubs on public lands. "Equitable access" was supposed to be the key principle of the new system. The ZECs are self-financing, raising money from fees, access charges to the areas in question, and sale of their services. Two ZECs fall completely within Barriere Lake's traditional lands, three overlap them, and two border their territories. The legislation makes no mention of Indian rights, or Indian hunting or trapping, nor are there any provisions to involve Indian communities in management of the ZECs.

Twelve tourist outfitters have been given exclusive hunting rights for their customers in lands still used by Barriere Lake people. Six of these outfitters operate within what is left of the beaver preserve, where two outfitters even have exclusive rights to trapping, although trapping within the reserve is supposed to be restricted to natives only.

The Barriere Lake lands today are subject to administration by at least four Quebec government ministries (each ministry having two regional offices with something to say); two forest management units; two regional municipalities; and a Crown corporation known as SEPAQ (Société des Etablissements de Plein Air du Québec), set up to manage recreational activites within wildlife reserves, and required to make as much money as possible. None of these organizations in any way takes native interests into account: for example, land planning is done both by ministries and municipalities without any reference to the fact that the Algonquins use the land. The only explanation for such omissions, so consistent over so many years, and covering so many organizations and functions, is that racist assumptions about the inferiority of native people are still the norm.

Searching for the aboriginal essence

After talking to Lena Nattaway, I went to see her grandson, Jacob. I had already been told by one of the few non-Indians in the reserve that Jacob was a little unusual, and perhaps he is, to a non-Indian. His mother, Irene, had told me how he was now concentrating on living a completely Indian life, to the extent of going into the bush in winter carrying only minimal staples such as salt, pepper, grease and bannock, challenging himself to live off whatever he can catch.

Jacob is a stocky, physically powerful man in his early thirties, with a direct gaze and an enigmatic manner, friendly enough but with a slight air of indifference, as if anything I might say would inevitably be meaningless to him. He showed me many small artworks he had assembled from stuff picked up in the bush, with which he had covered his walls. He said he did this to show his children that use can be made of everything. He'd returned to the reserve twelve years before, and had been working ever since "to get to the point where I do not really need anything".

Jacob had quit grade eight in a French school, had taken a high school diploma course in the United States, and a night course in linguistics in Chicoutimi. Now he was trying to find the essence of being an Indian.

"I get lonesome in the city. A week in the bush and nothing bothers me.... The things we have here in the village, we don't need these things. Here, to make a living, you have to find a job, you need a car and so on. So you need money. Money becomes your priority, the first need of existence. If you live out there, you don't need anything of that, but you can still live out there, it costs you nothing. You can get fish, animals, fruits, medicines, but we have forgotten that.

"If they ever try to define what is an Indian, what is it? Is it the colour of our skin, is it because we are trappers? For each nation there is a body of self-sufficiency. There are doctors, professionals, lawyers, carpenters, judges, and so on. That's what a nation is. But a long time ago each individual Indian was all of those things. You could say that what it takes to make a white nation, it takes to make one Indian.

"There are two types of freedom: one is learning everything; the other is being what you want to be. How I am trying to be free is to get my blood flowing again. I am curing myself. I have always thought it was medicine to be outside. Right now I do not use any machines at all. I use a four-foot bucksaw to strengthen my arm.

"I tried preaching for a while, but it didn't work out. A priest preaches religion, but it stops at the church. What is he aiming for? What is he doing within the government system? Is it only to confuse people with the religion of self-esteem? The role of the priest is to make you believe in a superior being, unreachable unless you pray. And you never get an answer. From what I have learned, when I pray to Mother Nature, she gives me an answer, a different way of understanding existence, because we know we come from Mother Nature."

Two years ago, government officials had taken away Jacob's father's trapline, because they said he was taking only ten or fifteen beavers a year, mostly for food, far short of the annual quota of forty-five. Now they'd given the trapline to some French-speaking trappers who went there for two weeks, cleaned out the forty-five beavers, and took off. When the white trappers weren't there, the family still used their traditional land.

The return of Jacob, and others like him, to this tiny, overcrowded, impoverished place, a mere fifty-nine acres whose sandy soil is being washed away by the waters of the reservoir, is a phenomenon that requires some explanation. Four hundred of the 440 band members live on the reserve, and most of the rest are at Maniwaki, Hull or Val d'Or getting an education. Many, like Jacob, have spent several years living elsewhere. For over fifty years, the Barriere Lake people have carried on a tradition of working at a mink farm near Rochester, New York, and many went to school there.

Conditions in the reserve are rough. At the time of my visit, only sixteen people had salaried employment; most were on welfare. Many families were doubled up, with as many as eleven people to a house, and there was no space for more houses. In many parts of Canada, reserves like this have lost up to 60 per cent of their band members as people drift to the cities to escape the pervasive hope-lessness. What has drawn the Barriere Lake people back home?

An eloquent answer was given to a reporter by Jacob's twenty-year-old brother, Eddie, who had just returned to the reserve from school. In 1987, when the Manitoba chief Louis Stevenson invited the South African ambassador to visit his Peguis reserve, *The Toronto Star* had the idea of comparing a typical Canadian reserve to a typical settlement in South Africa. *The Star* sent its reporter, for some reason, to Rapid Lake. Just outside the village, the reporter ran across Eddie walking along, and asked him about life in Rapid Lake.

"We're a very privileged people," said Eddie. "I'm not sure a lot of other people will understand that. But I've been in the city. You look up into the sky at night and you can't see anything. But here, in the bush, you can see everything. You have everything. It's just all there....

"Most people worry so much about living that they neglect their freedom. We don't ever forget that. That's what I have in the bush. It's where I choose to live, where I want to live."

Eddie was far from starry-eyed about living conditions on the re-serve. In fact, he was so worried about those conditions that he said he was not sure it made sense for a young person to start a family. Still, he had chosen his path in life. He was one of the six children whom Irene was instructing in traditional ways; and he was learning still more by sitting at the feet of his remarkable grandmother, Lena.

Fighting the modern moloch

The dominant organization in the Barriere Lake lands is the Quebec Ministry of Energy and Resources. The ministry's mission in life is to set the rules for all extractive resource industries in the province. When the Algonquins examined how the wildlife reserve is adminis-tered, they discovered that Energy and Resources controls habitat, while the Ministry of Recreation, Hunting and Fishing is responsible for wildlife. Somehow it has not occurred to the Quebec govern-ment that there is a connection between wildlife protection and the habitat on which the wildlife depends.

Because the Energy and Resources ministry calls the shots, the whole of LaVérendrye wildlife reserve was designated an area of pri-ority forest production in the late '80s, with only minimal acknowl-edgment of the needs of wildlife, and none at all of aboriginal use of the forest. The central instruments in the new provincial system of forest management were to be the so-called CAAF agreements (*Contrat d'approvisionnement et d'aménagement forestier*). These give private logging companies the right to manage the forests for twenty-five years, renewable indefinitely thereafter for five years at a time. When the Algonquins examined the guidelines, they realized that, bad though their situation had become, the worst was yet ahead: their way of life would not survive unless they could stop the signing of the CAAF agreements, or at least modify the rules to take account of aboriginal needs.

Research done for the Algonquins by Rebecca Aird of Ottawa reveals the extent to which they have lost ground over the years. By the 1890s, all of the forests they used were already subject to timber leases; the first logging roads were built in the 1920s, when CIP emerged as the big leaseholder. The timber concessions were granted by the provincial government at the giveaway price of $8 per square mile. By the 1950s, most trapping areas had become accessible by road, but the resulting damage to the traplines was mitigated somewhat by the work that Barriere Lake people obtained in the forest operations. This work ended when mechanical methods of clearcutting were introduced in the 1960s. By the '80s, forest roads through the Algonquin lands were being subsidized by government by up to 50 per cent of their cost, and both the main operators in the Barriere Lake lands, E.B. Eddy and CIP, were receiving substantial government subsidies.

The two forest management units in the Barriere Lake lands now provide wood for thirty-two pulp and paper plants and four lumber mills. Nearly half of LaVérendrye Park has already been clearcut. Under the government's plan, slightly increased production would be allowed, so the fate of the Algonquins would be in the hands of the same companies that had already hacked their forest to pieces – and the aboriginals were not to be given a chance to influence their decisions in any way.

The same research shows how disadvantaged the Algonquins have become even in their access to wildlife within their traditional lands: government figures indicate that by 1987, 68,000 fishermen were taking 250,000 fish out of the lakes and rivers in the Barriere Lake lands. Comparative figures for moose kills were difficult to find, but in 1978, 215 moose were taken by sports hunters, and only 125 by Algonquins for subsistence. In twenty years, the average age of moose killed fell from 7.3 years to 4.5, the density of moose per square kilometre from 2.5 to 0.26, and successful hunting parties fell from 80 per cent to below 40 per cent. These figures confirm what the Algonquins already know – their animals have been handed over to outsiders, who are wiping them out.

Estimates of revenue taken by the government from these recreational activities reach $2 million a year, with private outfitters taking in another $2.5 million from 6,000 visitors, and ZECs $400,000 from 43,000 visitors. Some of these figures do not cover exactly the areas of land in contention, but they certainly indicate that great sums of money have been taken off the Barriere Lake lands. While all this was happening, the original owners of this rich and productive territory were living in one of the most rudimentary villages in all of Canada, overcrowded, unemployed, and deprived of almost every municipal service.

A crazy case

The court case in which the federal government charged sixteen Algonquins with causing a nuisance on Parliament Hill began late in 1988, and staggered through the courts for more than four years. The federal government adamantly refused to drop the charges. The sixteen, including five women, were charged under the Public Works Nuisances Regulations. When the case came to Ontario provincial court, the Algonquins' lawyer, David Nahwegahbow, tried to get his clients off on a number of technicalities. When that strategy failed, Nahwegahbow said he had no alternative but to enter aboriginal title as a defence, since the Algonquins have never ceded title to the Ottawa Valley, and his clients therefore have a perfect right to camp on Parliament Hill. The federal lawyer shot to his feet to argue, first, that the court had no jurisdiction over aboriginal rights, and second, that in this case the question was not who had legal title to Parliament Hill, but *de facto* control, management, charge or direction.

Nahwegahbow quoted a number of recent Supreme Court cases in which it was recognized that aboriginal title could not be derogated from by the Crown's utilization of land, unless the Indians agreed.

Judge Brian Lennox said that in considering whether this argument was relevant to the charge, "I have to proceed on the assumption that you have established aboriginal title.... And I have come to the conclusion that, assuming there is an ascertainable aboriginal title, it is not irrelevant to public works, and I propose to permit Mr. Nahwegahbow to submit his evidence."

Nahwegahbow said he would need at least eighteen days to lead his evidence-in-chief, without counting cross-examination. To the dismay of the Crown, this modest local court, which was already jammed with a backlog of cases, seemed to have set itself up for a marathon case simply to hear a nuisance charge. Incredibly, the federal Justice Department immediately put a team to work to research the case against the Algonquins. But whenever the case came back into court, the government was not ready to proceed. This went on for almost three years before the case was stayed in 1992. The uncertainty created by the government's persistence amounted to harassment of one of the most defenceless groups of aboriginals in the country, and threw a strange light on the mindset of the Department of Indian Affairs, and its minister, Tom Siddon – the supposed protectors of the aboriginal people.

A rube in the bush

Before I left Barriere Lake on that first visit, J.B. said I could go with him on his snowmobile around the reservoir to look for animal tracks. It was an extremely cold December day. I dressed in everything I could find, but J.B. didn't spare me: I had to cling behind him as tightly as I could while he gleefully zipped across the ice at top speed, bumping crazily round the narrows, where you can never trust the ice because of the constant changes in water level.

J.B. was having a great time. But to be honest, I've never been much for this kind of adventure. Soon I felt as if I were freezing to death, although I couldn't admit it. It reminded me of a time, years before, when someone had taken me by dog team out on Great Slave Lake from Yellowknife to the nearby Dene village. It was something I'll never forget, but I'm not knocking myself out to repeat it. I marvel at these people who travel behind dogs for miles across the tundra, or canoe the rivers of the boreal forest for week after week, or barrel through the wilderness on roaring snowmobiles, but I'm not one of them. This is not a book about wilderness adventure.

We didn't see any animal tracks, and that evening my eye started to ache from a touch of frostbite that bothered me for weeks.

12

The harvest of a failed policy

I have seen enough aboriginal communities, and learned enough of their history, to know that the onslaught against them has not been perpetrated only by federal legislation. Aboriginal people have been taken advantage of by their neighbours, by municipal and provincial governments, by people who operate and work for business enterprises, and even by many of those who have come among them promising to help, such as missionaries, teachers and officials (and journalists, of course). The attacks on aboriginal people, the efforts to destroy their economy, undermine their religions and beliefs, and eliminate their languages, have been a communal enterprise, entered into with varying degrees of vigour and enthusiasm by most Euro-Canadians who have dealt with them.

I am aware that this is a harsh indictment, and many Canadians will refuse to accept it. Yet I believe that, although officially colonialism lies far in our past, in daily practice we continue to apply colonial policies within our hinterland where most aboriginals live. The indigenous people of Canada still live in enclaves as distinct minorities dominated by larger populations, who continually assert that their needs have priority over those of the minority. Policies for developing these areas of the country serve only the interests of the larger population, whose laws stand ready to impose those policies whenever the indigenous people object. In many parts of Canada, the effort to win some modification of those policies has forced the aboriginals into a series of desperate and usually losing battles.

As we saw in Chapter 10, the formal instrument for this crude politics of oppression has always been the Indian Act, whose implemen-

tation has impoverished Indian people, reducing them to a dangerous state of social alienation and psychological dependency. This objective appears to have been pursued with, as they say in the criminal
courts, deliberate intent – at least by the bureaucracy. For decades
the aboriginal people were at the mercy of the Department of Indian
Affairs, which became almost a law unto itself, administering the
subject nation of aboriginals as if the department were a Canadian
version of a Persian satrapy.

For forty-two of the sixty years after the passing of the Indian Act,
three senior bureaucrats, Lawrence Vankoughnet, Hayter Reed and
Duncan Campbell Scott, were the satraps. Their official title was
Deputy Superintendent-General, and successively they were given
virtually a free hand in Indian policy. They all appear to have taken a
dim view – even a contemptuous view – of Indian life. Their main
aims were to save money and get rid of the Indian problem by getting rid of the Indians through assimilation. As Scott confessed in a
much-quoted statement to a House of Commons committee in 1920:

> I want to get rid of the Indian problem.... I do not want to pass into the
> citizens' class people who are paupers...when they are able to take their
> position as British citizens or Canadian citizens, to support themselves,
> and stand alone. That has been the whole purpose of Indian education and
> advancement since the earliest times.... Our object is to continue until there
> is not a single Indian in Canada that has not been absorbed into the body
> politic, and there is no Indian question, and no Indian department.[1]

During these sixty years, the appalling living conditions of the
aboriginals seldom came to public attention. The efforts of the aboriginal people themselves to bring their plight to public notice
through Parliament were rebuffed. A few individuals raised a fuss
from time to time. The Roman Catholic Bishop Gabriel Breynat cam-
paigned for several years to have some help extended to the Indian
people of the north. Playing the traditional role of the missionary as
the advance man for colonialism, he had persuaded the Indians of
the Northwest Territories to sign Treaty 11 in 1921, because the government had promised they would be able to hunt, trap and fish free
from white competition. After a few years Breynat realized those
promises were not going to be kept.

By that time, many northern Indians had become so debilitated by
malnutrition that they couldn't resist influenza. "Pathetic almost to

the point of tragedy was the helpless native under the grip of this disease," wrote one Inspector of Indian Agencies in 1928.[2] A doctor visiting the Northwest Territories in 1934 reported that after examining Indians for a month, he had not found a single physically sound individual.[3] In 1936, Breynat sent a memorandum to the government about the condition of Indians in the Northwest Territories:

> ...Since treaty was made...their physical condition has gradually deteriorated until at the present time it is quite alarming. Whole families die off, bands containing many families have been wiped out, infant mortality is so high that it is difficult to believe. One often meets old people who have had from ten to fifteen children, of which none is surviving.... In every camp widows may be found, more or less derelicted, and often the condition of orphans, if made known in the press, would bring nothing but discredit to the government....[4]

Breynat wrote an article in the press entitled "Canada's Blackest Blot". "The Indians...are the most wretched people in Canada," he wrote. "It is estimated that [their] per capita income during 1935-36 was $110.... Compared with them the most miserable relief recipient elsewhere in Canada lives like a king."[5] The government's response to Breynat was to reduce spending on Indian health services.

Thousands of aboriginal servicemen returned from the Second World War to find themselves confronted by the same awful conditions of life, the same discriminatory and hostile attitudes, as before they went to fight for Canada's freedom. They were still not allowed to vote, own land, sell their produce freely, or even enter beer parlours, and in some places were refused admission to restaurants, hotels and cinemas. *The Native Voice*, the newspaper of the Native Brotherhood of British Columbia, declared that Indians were prisoners in their own country, forced into the position of

> the poor man mentioned in the Gospel who lived off the crumbs that fell from the rich man's table.... This is particularly galling to us, as the table and what is on it was at one time exclusively our own, and we intend to, and do, demand our rightful position on terms of equality with our fellow Canadians.[6]

The parliamentary committee of 1946-47
The gross injustices revealed by such complaints forced the House of Commons and Senate to appoint a special joint committee to examine

and consider the Indian Act. The committee's hearings began in 1946, and resulted in the 1951 revision of the Act. For the first time since the Indian Act had been passed seventy years earlier, the Canadian public through these hearings was presented with the appalling evidence from the reserves.

The proceedings began with a symbolic breaching of the bureaucratic castle by two stalwart aboriginal leaders from British Columbia, Reverend Peter Kelly and Andrew Paull. These were the same men who had managed to get aboriginal rights discussed by Parliament in 1927, only to be told that their claims were "more or less fictitious". When they read that the 1946 joint committee intended to hear only officials of the Indian Affairs Department during its first session, Kelly and Paull travelled to Ottawa and demanded to be heard immediately. "I stand before you this morning," said Andrew Paull defiantly, when they let him in, "not as a suppliant. I stand before you [as] your equal.... Let us get that understood before we go any further...." [7] Rev. Kelly said:

> The Indian is a minor in the eyes of the law. As far as being heard is concerned he is in a stage of non-age. But for purposes of raising revenue he is taxed. When it comes to defence of his country his services were accepted and were generously offered....Yet he is denied any voice in the affairs of the land.

Over the next two years, a parade of aboriginals, missionaries, officials, schoolteachers, doctors, social workers and scientists appeared before the joint committee, bringing facts, figures and eye-witness descriptions that revealed just how far aboriginals had fallen behind all other groups in Canada in living standards, health, education and prosperity.

The joint committee was told that by 1946, Indians had only 5,580,000 acres of reserve land left, an average of forty-three acres per head. This was less than a third of the standard of 640 acres for a family of five that had been laid down in most of the treaties. Only the Saskatchewan and Alberta Indians had more land than this national average, while everywhere east of Ontario, aboriginals commanded only about a tenth of what they had on the prairies.[8] Half of these Indian lands were forested, and only 184,000 acres were under cultivation, proof of the success of Hayter Reed and his officials in strangling Indian agriculture.

Some officials, such as J.P.B. Ostrander, the Inspector of Indian Agencies in Saskatchewan, spoke up warmly for the Indians, claiming that too much land had been sold, and too little money spent. He said:

> We in the field who have lived with them for many years have seen unpleasant things which few of you know anything about and which the Indians have not had a chance to bring before the people of Canada. This is the first opportunity they have had.[9]

Ostrander said that much more money would be needed to do what was necessary. "During the twenty years that I was an Indian agent, the people of Canada and Parliament were not always generous with the Indians, rather the reverse."

Indian income, in total, had increased to $126 per capita, only a fraction of the Canadian average. Of the $16 million that Indians earned, $5.5 million came from wages, $4.5 million from hunting, fishing and trapping, and $3.5 million from sale of farm products.[10] Relative priorities for the reserves were shown by a table that counted 430 churches, 266 schools and only thirty-six sawmills on all the reserves in Canada.[11]

The total federal budget for Indians had reached $6 million by 1930, then dropped away sharply in the next five years, and did not reach its former level until 1945.[12]

Appalling health standards

When the Second World War ended, it was more than thirty years since the Indian Act had armed government with enormous powers to enforce higher health standards on Indian reserves; yet Indians were still dying in huge numbers from diseases that had long since ceased to threaten non-native Canadians. The aboriginal death rate from measles was forty-six times greater than among non-Indians, from whooping cough thirty times greater, influenza twelve times, tuberculosis seventeen times, and pneumonia eight times.[13] These are diseases caused by malnutrition and poor sanitation, and appear to reflect the meagre aboriginal land-base and extremely low aboriginal incomes.

These many years of neglect had especially affected those Indians who depended on the forest economy. A team of doctors who studied the health of "bush Indians", as they were called, in northern

Manitoba in the early 1940s, were appalled:

> They were not sick according to lay opinion, but when we examined them carefully from the medical standpoint, they had so many obvious evidences of malnutrition that if you or I were in the same condition, we would demand hospitalization at once.... We were struck with the inertia...the lack of initiative, the indolence of these people. Physically, they shuffled about, they moved slowly.... It was obvious their mental processes were going at a very slow rate.... We found in one particular band the TB death rate was fifty times the rate among the white population of Manitoba.... Infant mortality among one band was forty times the rate of a well-regulated white district in Canada.[14]

The doctors blamed the lack of decent food. They said that a hunter who forty years before would have started off his season in the bush with 100 pounds of flour, was now taking 600 pounds, because of the diminishing availability of game. The doctors calculated that some 85 per cent of the calories consumed by these Manitoba "bush Indians" came from white flour, sugar and lard, a diet extremely deficient in protein. As a result they were receiving only 100 milligrams of calcium, compared with 900 needed for minimum good health; only one-third of a milligram of thiamin, instead of one-and-a-half milligrams; only 235 units of vitamin A, compared with 5,000 needed; only ten units of vitamin C, instead of seventy-five. Not surprisingly, these people were said to be smaller than forty years before. One doctor said:

> The Indians live during the winter months in small one-roomed shacks. Frequently the conditions are almost unbelieveable, as many as ten to twelve people living in a shack twelve feet square.... Sometimes there may be one broken down single bed, but the majority sleep on the floor.

The Canadian Welfare Council and the Canadian Association of Social Workers implied in their brief that the government had shown greater concern about the diet of prisoners in federal penitentiaries than that of the Indians, "who are equally the wards of the government, but who have not been convicted of crimes against society". The Council remarked acerbically that Indian housing was so appalling that they had become "a race of slum-dwellers".[15]

An Indian agent testified that when members of the Mistissini band in northern Quebec were examined in 1941, 60 per cent of them were found to be "exhausted".[16] A Quebec MP said that Algonquins in the Maniwaki reserve, living from part-time lumbering, tourist guiding and some trapping, had to carry their water a quarter of a mile, had no electricity for their school, and no school places for many of their children.[17] A northern Ontario MP reported after a tour of half-a-dozen remote reserves:

> Indians living on these poorer reserves are providing nothing for the future, but what money is earned is spent from day to day. Their children are poorly clothed and greatly undernourished. Unless something is done by the department to teach and encourage these Indians to do something to help themselves, I can see no future for them but to remain wards of the government for all time to come.[18]

The MP read a lettter from a teacher complaining that no one on these reserves was receiving any training that would fit them to make a decent living, although the Indians were capable of, and eager for, such training.

The Indians of the Fort à la Corne reserve in Saskatchewan sent an eloquent brief, arguing that provincial controls on trapping and hunting had plunged them into destitution. Without the flour ration, they said, there would have been starvation in the reserve, and they added:

> The Indian is not himself, the way he used to be. He was strong, with great endurance and could go without food for days, but now one or two meals missed in a day will nearly knock him over. We are in want of the food we were accustomed to. We are in a dormant or torpid state, undernourished, weak, without energy and of low vitality. The people say Indians are lazy, but we can have no ambition in the state we are now. We lack the vitamins that will help us to become a strong and healthy people.[19]

The effects of "progress" on aboriginal lands
Evidence brought to the joint committee explained how in many places aboriginals had suffered from the fallout of Euro-Canadian economic developments, which had been undertaken without thought for their effects on aboriginals. For example, Hugh Conn, an official of the Department of Indian Affairs, described how the aboriginal economy of northern Manitoba had been destroyed by sediment deposits resulting from land clearances.[20] These had altered the

water level in the Saskatchewan River delta and had almost wiped out the muskrats, on which the aboriginal economy was based. In northern Quebec, the collapse of the beaver had brought many Cree trappers to the edge of starvation, (something that is still vivid in the minds of older Crees, as I found in the early 1970s). The cause of this collapse was the building of the railway across the north around 1930. White trappers moved north on this train, and quickly wiped out the beaver population.

In both these places, exceptional measures had to be undertaken by the federal and provincial governments and the Hudson's Bay Company to restore the animal populations. In Manitoba, the creeks that fed and drained the delta were dammed to raise water levels; in Quebec, all beaver trapping was suspended for several years to allow the animals to revive, both through natural means and through trans-plantation from other areas. Eventually in Manitoba, the ameliorative measures were extended to cover some 300,000 acres of land; and in Quebec and Ontario, beaver preserves were established covering most of the northern forests. For a change, aboriginals were involved in both schemes. In Quebec, once white trappers were excluded, tra-ditional Indian methods were sufficient to restore the animals to the levels that had existed for centuries. The Quebec system was admin-istered largely by the natives themselves.

The grim experience of the Stoney Indians of Alberta, as described to the joint committee, revealed something of the hostility towards aboriginal needs shown by the Euro-Canadians who settled the prairies. Calgary MP Douglas Harkness said that the Stoney reserve – "steep gravelly hills and extremely sparse grass" – was so inhos-pitable to cultivation that in twenty years, vegetables and potatoes had come to maturity only twice. [21] From the beginning, the govern-ment had known the Stoney reserve was inadequate to meet the needs of the people forced to live there. In 1884 Prime Minister Sir John A. Macdonald admitted as much, and added that "After a trial of several years, it was concluded last spring to give up the attempt to cultivate land there and to withdraw the farming instructor".[22]

The poor treatment given them under the Indian Act was not the Stoneys' only problem. Even after the reserve was established, they continued to hunt in their traditional lands in the Rocky Mountains: it was the only way they could survive. But when the Canadian Pacific Railway was pushed through in the early 1880s, the game quickly diminished. The new Banff National Park took more of the Stoney hunting grounds in 1885, and thereafter the government reluctantly had to provide rations even for this resourceful and proud people.[23] Bureaucrats, led by Vankoughnet and Hayter Reed, constantly tried to restrict these rations to the barest minimum. At the same time, incoming settlers from Europe and eastern Canada objected to the Stoneys' hunting outside their reserve. The message from Euro-Canadian society could not have been clearer: the Stoneys were unacceptable to the growing prairie society, whether they were on the reserve, or off it. They quickly became, in the words of the *Calgary Herald* of that time, "the pariahs of the civilization which has surrounded them". [24]

In the two decades before the First World War, the Stoneys petitioned the government year after year for more land in their traditional hunting territory in the foothills of the Rockies. In 1909, they claimed land they had always regarded as their own on the Bighorn-Kootenay plains in the headwaters of the Saskatchewan River.[25] The response was that they would first have to surrender land in their reserve as compensation, but in any case, remarked one official testily when the Stoney request came to his desk, "The department is averse to making these almost continuous changes".

Eventually Indian Affairs agreed with the proposal, and in 1910 recommended it to the Department of the Interior. Just as Algonquin claims had first been accepted by governments and later denounced as "completely novel", so the Stoney claim was accepted, then ignored. The matter was taken no further. Competing claims always took precedence over Indian hunting. Railways, mines, timber rights, forest reserves, gas fields, pipelines – everything was more important than Indian needs. Desperate to make a living, about a third of the Stoneys took to wandering through the foothills, supporting themselves by doing odd jobs for ranchers. "This is at best a precarious existence," remarked a petition of 1943 (forwarded to the parliamentary joint committee three years later). "Lodged in teepees or deserted shacks, they have little protection against winter weather. They are undernourished, underclothed and poorly housed. Yet even this is preferable to living on the reservation." The petition said that 780 Stoneys were supposed to subsist on reserve land which non-Indians familiar with its resources affirmed "would be incapable of sustaining more than seven white men".[26]

The poor record of the schools

The joint committee heard of a dismal record in education. While the Indian population had increased in the previous ten years, the number of Indian children in school had fallen.[27]

The government had left education in the hands of the Churches. Religious orders operated the government-owned residential schools, with damaging results that were not formally admitted until the comprehensive apologies issued by the Oblate Order and the United Church in the 1990s. By 1946, even the combined resources of Churches and governments were able to provide school places for only 18,000 of the 26,000 children of school age.

About half of the pupils attended the residential schools run by the four collaborating Churches – Anglican, Roman Catholic, United and Presbyterian – and the other half attended federal day schools on the reserves. Neither system was satisfactory. Attendance rates in the reserves averaged 70 per cent, but in some provinces were as low as 44 per cent, and the dropout rate was high.[28] In all of Canada only 113 Indian children were recorded as having reached the first year of high school in 1946, and none higher. Ninety-three children had been placed in schools with whites, even fewer than some years before.

Everyone who gave evidence was convinced that the future lay with education. "Education, gentlemen, is the answer to the Indian's problem," said Guy Williams, secretary of the Native Brotherhood of British Columbia. "It will lead him into professions; it will lead him into trades; it will lead to a situation where the Indian will be self-supporting." [29] The sympathetic Mr. Ostrander from Saskatchewan said:

> The whole future of the Indians depends on education and welfare services. That all costs money.... All the[se] deliberations will fail unless Parliament is going to see the need for supplying a great deal more money than we have had in the past.[30]

Parliament did not heed this advice until a quarter of a century later.

Not all reserves agreed on the type of education they wanted. A veterans' organization from Manitoulin Island said: "We love our religion...and are very much opposed to the public system of education being foisted upon us.... We wish to keep religion in our schools as we have always had it from the beginning."[31] But the people in

Caughnawaga (now known as Kahnawake) wanted religion out of the schools: "The only thing children learn is praying and singing and marching to church during school hours," they complained.[32]

One of the few Indians who had become enfranchised and had succeeded in the white world, Brigadier Oliver Martin, an Ontario magistrate, pleaded for an education that could "give Indians pride in their race". He said: "You can never make an Indian into a white man...but you can make an Indian a good Canadian, and it would not take very long if the task were undertaken with sympathy and understanding."[33] Martin listed two dozen successful Indian physicians, engineers, clergymen, teachers, soldiers and businessmen whom he knew personally. He added that Indians would "gradually assimilate" through educational and economic advancement.

Assimilation rejected

Brigadier Martin's version of assimilation did not include the idea that Indians should, or even could, lose their heritage, but the joint committee heard from many Indians who rejected any suggestion of assimilation whatsoever. The representatives of Kahnawake wrote:

> We base our arguments on the merits of our aboriginal heritage, as we never imparted or ceded any of our rights to any government or nation. We do not want enfranchisement in any form whatsoever. We do not desire to be governed, or to be considered eligible to vote for any dominion or provincial elections.... We have no interest and never will be interested in a vote for any other form of government except our own Six Nations government. [34]

The veterans of Manitoulin said: "It is our considered opinion that all Indians should have the right to vote in federal elections, but on no account should they be forced to surrender any of their present rights and privileges in order to be able to vote."[35] The band at Fort à la Corne, Saskatchewan, said: "Forget about enfranchisement. You can't make a white man out of an Indian overnight. We don't want the vote, it will be the first step towards taxation." [36]

The Mohawks of St. Regis, Ontario (now known as Akwesasne) testified:

> With one accord the chiefs and members of our tribe want the Indian Act taken away from our reservation! This Act for the compulsory en-

franchisement of the Indians not only violates our sacred agreements and treaties, but while it stands there is no security of the Indian home! [They added they had been told by Indian agents that they must forfeit their homes and lands if they wanted to qualify for relief.] Officials of your government have violated our treaties, have entered our reserve for the purpose of drilling wells and making roads, have sent men to survey our lands...all done without permission from our head men. We have given up every fertile field, forest and stream. All that we have left is our small reservation, yet now by laws that we know nothing of and had no say in making we may lose what little land we possess.... We ask but life and liberty and freedom to run our own little country without outside interference.... Are we to be exiles in our own country? We think it better to remain a good Indian than a poor imitation of a white man![37]

Many white "experts" offered contrary views to the joint committee: Bishop H.J. Renison, after a lifetime spent among the James Bay Crees, said, "The time is inevitably coming when they will be absorbed.... In a hundred years this whole problem will be solved.... They should be gradually absorbed into the stream of Canadian life."[38]

The noted anthropologist Diamond Jenness said that the policy of isolating Indians in reserves, although it had kept them from starving, had turned them into pariahs and outcasts who had developed the warped mentality of displaced persons. He produced a detailed plan for the "liquidation of Canada's Indian problem in twenty-five years", through abolition of all separate Indian schools and reserves, and the enfranchisement of all Indians as full citizens who would enjoy the normal rights and privileges of Canadian life.[39]

His ideas were favourably received by the Committee.

The slow pace of change

The parliamentary hearings of 1946-47 demonstrated that government policy towards the Indians during the previous seventy years had been a disastrous failure. But by the time Parliament had worked through the report of the joint committee, leading to draft legislation in 1950, then a consultation with nineteen Indian leaders, and finally a second draft in 1951, the new version of the Indian Act that emerged was not much different from the policies that had wrought this failure.

Compared to its predecessors, the 1951 Indian Act was tightened up somewhat. Some of its more onerous provisions – particularly in respect to liquor and voting, the prohibition of certain ceremonies and dances, the compulsory enfranchisement of Indians, and the freedom to sell agricultural produce – were eliminated. In what was probably the major change, the Act allowed children to be directed away from the Church-run residential schools and sent to ordinary public schools.

But the general lines of federal policy continued. The paternalistic atttude that "the minister knows best" was retained. More than half of the sections remained at the minister's or cabinet's discretion, although now the minister's intervention in band or personal matters required approval by the Indians. The new Act had 125 sections, down from 195 in 1906, but still more than the original Act of 1876.

From this convoluted process, it was clear that the people in power were not ready to embrace Indians as equal and valued partners in the adventure of building a nation, and were not, in fact, overly concerned about the appalling conditions on the reserves. Thus the administration of Indian policy subsided into another period of somnolence for almost two decades.

Nevertheless, the 1946-47 joint committee did mark the first effort ever made by a Canadian government to survey opinion on Indian policy. The hearings started the process that gave rise in the late 1960s to government funding of native political organizations – a measure that transformed the politics of native issues in Canada, leading eventually to the guaranteeing of aboriginal and treaty rights in the 1982 Constitution.

Impoverishing Cowessess

In 1991 Mrs. Theresa Stevenson, a livewire in the aboriginal community of Regina, Saskatchewan, told me the story of her life. Mrs.
Stevenson is one of those people who can move mountains. She
has, among other things, organized a meal programme for aboriginal schoolchildren who otherwise would have little to eat during
the day. She told me she and her family had spent sixteen years in
the United States, and when I asked why they had left Canada she
replied: "Should I tell you the truth? All right: we were starved out
of Canada in 1955."

Mrs. Stevenson was brought up in the Cowessess reserve, not far
from Regina. In the decade following the 1946 hearings of the parliamentary joint committee, described in the last chapter, conditions
were so terrible on the reserve that she and her husband felt they
had no option but to get out. "There was such a feeling of hopelessness," she told me. "I felt I was surrounded by four walls and
would never get beyond them."

An aunt in Montana sent them $30. They arrived in Montana
with only a few nickels in their pockets, but for the next sixteen
years were able to keep working at jobs such as housekeeper, gas
jockey, or whatever they could find to keep body and soul together
and maintain their children in school.

Eventually the Stevensons returned to Canada to take advantage
of free university education for Indians. Now one of their children
is an ordained minister, another is the property manager for the
City of Regina, and a third also works for the city. The escape from
Cowessess worked out, as they had hoped, in better opportunities
for the children.

S T O R Y

As Mrs. Stevenson described for me the desperate poverty in the Cowessess of the 1950s, I realized that she was describing a community I had heard about before, whose economy had been systematically destroyed by the application of the government's Indian agricultural policy (already mentioned in Chapter 10). In the 1880s, this same Cowessess reserve had been in the economic vanguard of Canadian Indian life, as prairie Indians adjusted to the destruction of their traditional economy by becoming agriculturalists.

The story, as told by Sarah Carter in her remarkable book, *Lost Harvests*, is this:

When the Saulteaux and Crees of southern Saskatchewan negotiated Treaty 4 in 1874, they tried hard to get government help to establish themselves in agriculture, in order to replace their economy that had been based on the disappearing buffalo. The people who followed Chief Cowessess tried to maintain their hunting life in the Cypress Hills as long as they could, but eventually their headman, Louis O'Soup, led a group of them to the Qu'appelle Valley, east of Regina, where their reserve was surveyed in 1880. Although hampered by the poor equipment provided under treaty, O'Soup and a number of others turned out to be excellent farmers. Already by 1883 they had made enough money from hay sales to buy mowers and rakes. By 1884 they owned eighteen oxen, had eighty-six acres under cultivation, and were doing so well that the Hudson's Bay Company opened a store on the reserve. Visitors commented on their fine individual farms and the superior quality of their housing. In 1888 O'Soup won prizes for his cows and steers in open competition at the Broadview fair.

An agency report for 1890 shows that Cowessess had more land under cultivation than any other reserve in southern Saskatchewan. The reserve's farmers had fenced 740 acres, broken 580 acres, were producing nearly 5,000 bushels of wheat, oats, rye and root crops, and owned more than seventy oxen and horses.

After 1885 they became subject to government policies designed to constrict Indian farming. They had no grist mill, and were not permitted to travel any distance to have their cereals ground – a disadvantage so damaging that Chief Poundmaker, who lived in a neighbouring reserve, complained that his people were starving while sitting among huge piles of grain. In 1890 a policy was introduced to break up the reserves by subdividing them. A few years

144

later came the decision to turn Indians into peasant farmers, forced to subsist on forty acres.

The aboriginal farmers were forbidden from using machinery, and were required to make their tools by hand, using no nails and screws. An Indian farmer was not allowed to sell his own produce or cattle, or even to buy anything without a permit, and could not visit a friend or a market town without permission of the Indian agent. If these regulations were designed to ensure that Indian farmers would not compete with their white neighbours, they succeeded; reserve farming, naturally, began to seize up.

Disgusted, Louis O'Soup gave up farming in 1898 and left Cowsessess for Manitoba, where he made his living by hunting. In 1907 more than half the reserve was "surrendered", and sold to buyers who lived as far away as eastern Canada, Chicago and Iowa. During the First World War, under the threat of compulsory purchase, "greater production farms", as they were called, were established on Indian reserves. The one on the Cowessess reserve, managed by the Department of Indian Affairs, was a failure. The government then adopted a policy of leasing reserve lands to non-Indians.

Thereafter, non-native visitors to the reserves often expressed shock at the sight of Indians living in poverty, while their lands were worked by outsiders. By 1928 Cowessess had only 29,000 of its original 50,000 acres left.

"Government policies made it virtually impossible for reserve agriculture to succeed," comments Sarah Carter. "In the early years of the twentieth century...[aboriginal farmers] fell further behind and became increasingly isolated."

And by the 1950s, reserve conditions had become so desperate that Mrs. Stevenson and her family were literally "starved out of Canada".

13

Barriere Lake:
taking on everybody

In September 1989, nearly a year after my first visit to Barriere Lake, the Algonquins took physical action to resist the continuing destruction of their forest. They blocked six logging roads to deny access to companies intending to open up whole new areas of Algonquin hunting territory to clearcut logging. In the century-and-a-half since Euro-Canadians had arrived among them, it was the first time that the Barriere Lake people had been forced into active resistance to defend their way of life.

My being on the spot at the time, to make a film, enables me to describe in some detail a struggle that is typical of many such protests now occurring across the country. For the Barriere Lake people, it has proven to be a long and frustrating experience. Eventually they succeeded in forcing the federal and Quebec governments to work with them in establishing a co-operative conservation strategy for their hunting territories. But, as we shall see, they have found it even more difficult to have the governments implement that agreement than to have them sign it. At time of writing, more than four years after the people pitched their tents on Parliament Hill, their future is far from assured. They have spent hundreds of hours in meetings with government representatives, but are under constant threat of renewed logging, and still have to hold themselves ready to reestablish their road blockades at any time, knowing that they run the risk of arrest, conviction and possibly imprisonment. For a people who for generations minded their own business in the forest, and have always chosen to defend their way of life by keeping to themselves, these are traumatic experiences.

A controlled sort of chaos

I made two filming visits to Barriere Lake in 1989. The first was in February, to film Algonquin trapping and hunting in winter. This proved to be difficult, because clearcutting had already so devastated the territories around the village that the hunters had to travel long distances even to set up a beaver trap. This meant our film crew had to haul our hundreds of pounds of equipment by snowmobile, making it difficult to keep the equipment warm enough to do the job. While we were filming, dozens of huge trucks were racing across the Algonquin lands, carrying logs that were being cut at a rate of thousands a day.

The Algonquins decided to take us out to a place not too far away, where we could at least film them setting their traps in the wilderness. I will never forget that expedition. The band councillors had promised enough snowmobiles for our whole party, including drivers, and we arranged for a nine o'clock takeoff. It was at least twenty-five degrees below zero that day. No one arrived at nine o'clock, nor at ten, and when I decided to investigate, I was told that Michel Thusky, the main organizer, was 150 kilometres away in Maniwaki, and there seemed to be only one snowmobile available. I returned to tell the crew this alarming news. But about half an hour later Michel materialized as if from nowhere, and a flotilla of machines – far more than we needed – were gunning their motors outside the house. I should have known, because I'd experienced it plenty of times before: Indian organization has the appearance of a controlled sort of chaos that seems headed for disaster, until it all comes together as if by magic at the last minute.

We wrapped our batteries around our waists and set off behind Archie Ratt, a grizzled and delightful middle-aged hunter who was going to do the work for our cameras. Not the least of Archie's attractions was his dog, a mongrel he'd been hunting with for fifteen years, which responds with a lunatic enthusiasm to Archie's every whisper and grunt. A few miles along the road, the expedition ground to a halt, and after a lot of palaver someone headed back to the village. When I asked what was up, Archie said he was going to set a marten trap, but he'd forgotten the bait.

Soon I began to realize that this place said to be not so far away was also not so close. We travelled about twenty-five miles, bumping and scraping over flooded shorelines strewn with dead logs hidden under the snow, easing through the narrows past broken ice, and occasionally toppling into the snow as we negotiated steep slopes and sharp bends. We travelled through large areas laid waste by clearcutting, and came eventually to a small lake with a beaver lodge on its far shore. We pulled up short of it to agree on a plan of attack. We did not want the pristine snow in our movie to have been crossed by a dozen snowmobiles; but then, after some more palaver, there was another unexplained delay. Someone headed off back in the direction we'd come from, and with a great deal of laughter, they told me that we would have to wait a while. "Archie's dog has eaten the bait," they said, and someone had gone all the way back to the village to get more.

For a long time that afternoon, we tramped around in four feet of snow, filming Archie and his dog and his friend, George Thusky, setting a number of traps and gathering medicine from trees in the forest. Our batteries froze several times, causing the camera to run slowly, but I found that the snowmobile suit loaned me by the chief was just the ticket for those conditions; to my astonishment I felt warm and comfortable throughout the day.

Next day Michel took us far to the east along logging roads to a place called Lake Ottawa, where Canadian International Paper (CIP) had a logging camp. Not far from the camp, he had secured the use of a cabin big enough for us all to sleep in. We had come this far mainly to film an elderly lady who had lived alone in the area for many years. Her name was Caroline Maranda, a wonderful old lady whose little cabin was almost buried in snow at the top of a steep slope above a lake. She made an extraordinary picture as she sat at her table expertly rolling cigarettes as she talked. But she was nervous of our camera and lights, and since we did not understand her language, we had no way of ensuring that she was telling us the stories and giving us the insights we needed to bring our film to life. In the event, sadly, we were unable to use her in the film.

We wanted to see the clearcutting, and Michel drove us for miles along increasingly narrow roads. At one point a huge truck laden with hundreds of logs suddenly appeared around a corner, barrelling down the centre of the road and forcing us into the snowbank as if we were not there. "I think we had better go back," Michel said.

Next morning we drove in a snowstorm to one of the places where CIP was gathering logs and piling them for flotation down the Gatineau River when the ice broke in April. If anything on our week-long shoot had been worth the effort, this certainly was. As we drove down the hill to the assembly-point, we were confronted by the biggest pile of logs I have ever seen, or can imagine seeing – tens of thousands of them trucked in hourly from all over the Algonquin lands. It had taken only ten days to assemble this pile, which was one of six such assemblies the company was making along the river.

For the first time I really understood what was at stake. For here was the power of money, big money, mobilized by big business. And this money has a logic of its own. It doesn't care about niceties such as wildlife preservation, about land classifications such as wildlife reserves, about concepts such as aboriginal rights or Indian title, or even about such ludicrously lightweight ideas as justice and equity. What likelihood was there, I wondered, that the interests and rights of 440 impoverished Algonquins could ever outweigh the power of this money?

Escalation of the conflict

When my crew and I returned to finish the filming in September, the Algonquins were all fired up, and had taken to the barricades.

Ever since they had decided to act in their own defence eighteen months before, the Algonquins had taken an extremely reasonable approach. They did not think it worth formally entering a claim to land. Some claims had already been fifteen years in negotiation, so if they followed that route, their forest would be completely gone and their way of life with it, long before they got a settlement. Instead, they decided to appeal to the Quebec and federal governments to work with them in establishing a long-term conservation strategy for their traditional lands, with the purpose of building an economy that would make a place for logging, sports hunting, tourism and Algonquin traditional life. They had put this proposal to the governments more than a year before, at the same time asking for an eight-month moratorium "on activities which impact negatively on our way of life". They had received general approval for the idea, but in very vague terms, and so far had failed to persuade the Quebec Minister of Mines and Native Affairs, Raymond Savoie, to meet them.

On August 28, eleven months after their arrest on Parliament Hill, came the spark that lit the Algonquin bomb. One of their people was told by workers from the Quebec Ministry of Energy and Resources that he had to move out of his home because they were about to spray the forest with a chemical called glyphosate. This recalled the upsetting events of the previous summer, when some Algonquins had become violently ill after eating berries that, unknown to them, had been sprayed.

As a matter of urgency, the Algonquins tried to set up a meeting with the ministry's regional director in Hull, but were refused. "We rely heavily on the fruits of this land for our subsistence," stated Chief Matchewan, in a letter to Minister Savoie on August 28, "and we hold unextinguished aboriginal title to the area. Your government knows this, yet nobody asks us if it is alright to spray there.

"Having been denied what we feel is a reasonable request, we have no choice but to take the matter into our own hands. This will advise that we have set up a blockade to stop [ministry] workers from carrying out chemical spraying within our traditional lands."

This blockade brought out most of the community in enthusiastic protest, and they won their point: the government reluctantly agreed to postpone further spraying until the following year. Pressing their advantage, the Algonquins tried to set up further meetings to discuss their proposed moratorium, and to ask for a delay in the signing of the CAAF agreements with the logging companies, but they got nowhere. They began to realize that the spraying was merely a symptom of the whole problem, which was the determination of government and industry to press on with clearcut logging in defiance of the Algonquins' clearly expressed opposition.

We arrived in Rapid Lake on the Tuesday evening following Labour Day to find the village almost deserted. Most people were out along the main road, blocking access to some new logging roads. We hurriedly assembled our equipment and set out to film the action. We found that the Algonquins had set up a small tent village on a logging road under construction, and were unconcernedly cooking an evening meal. It was a typical aboriginal protest, with as many women and children on the barricades as men, and with a beguiling air of normalcy, as if this were just another day at a bush camp.

These blockades had been erected after Michel Thusky, who has a remarkable ability to get along with everyone he meets, had obtained from some loggers maps of company plans for wholesale logging in the only nearby areas that had been left uncut. This was the first the Algonquins had heard of such plans, which amounted to a direct slap in the face after their long efforts to enter a dialogue with the governments. Almost on the spur of the moment, they decided to block access to the half-dozen new roads being cut into the areas proposed for logging. Although no logging was yet being done, machinery was already at work preparing for it. The Algonquins drew up a paper that they handed to all the workers, telling them of the blockade in defence of their rights, and requesting that they stop work. Everyone stopped.

The Algonquins really didn't have enough people or resources to man six separate blockades. But having brought work to a halt along all six roads, they concentrated their action at a site twenty-five miles south of their community, not far from the government-owned tourist centre of Le Domaine. All we could do was wait around and see what happened.

A dialogue of the deaf
From their central blockade the Algonquins sent people out to check that no one had resumed work. But early the next morning word came that machines were at work again along one of the roads, and the chief advised us that he and his people were going to bring this work to a halt.

This was another amazing example of aboriginal organization. We were ready to leave at ten o'clock, but could not do so because Michel had gone on an errand and was expected back soon. At eleven o'clock we were about to leave, but someone was checking out one of the other roads and would be back soon. After lunch the chief told us we should go ahead: he would be along soon, he said, but I figured it better to wait for him. At three o'clock he sent us ahead with one other car, and we bumped along a logging road for more than twenty-five miles until we were deep in the wilderness. Our guides told us the machines were working a few miles ahead, but we should wait for the chief. We waited for half an hour or so before the chief drove up in his car. He got out and said, "You guys go ahead, I'll be with you soon," climbed into his car and headed back along the lonely, deserted track. I had begun to despair that anything would ever come of this expedition that had already taken up a whole day of our precious time, but we moved slowly forward until we spotted two bulldozers at work in the distance.

We got out of our van and were ready to film the machines when, out of the blue, the chief's car came around the corner, followed by another, then another, and finally ten or twelve cars that pulled up in a line and disgorged at least fifty men and women. As if it had been orchestrated by a Hollywood director, at that moment a pickup truck drove slowly down the hill from the opposite direction, driven by the contractor doing the work, a good-looking young business-man who got out of his truck and asked in French, "What's going on?" He approached the chief, who does not speak French, and said in halting English, "Can I explain to you what we're doing?"

"I know what you're doing," said the chief. The dialogue that en-sued between them lasted for ten or fifteen minutes, and symbolized the incomprehension that has characterized the Euro-aboriginal rela-tionship ever since we arrived on this continent.

We are not cutting the forest, said the young man. We are prepar-ing the ground for planting, and next year we will return to plant two million trees.

"I know what this leads to," said the chief, waving at the forest. "You are going to take down all these trees, anything you don't want."

But, said the young man, as if they had failed to hear him, we are doing only planting. I am an environmentalist, just as you are. I am not cutting the forest but improving it, reviving it, and he added, in a remark I will never forget: "I am here to tell you about the forest." Since the Algonquins have lived in this same forest for thousands of years, the sheer effrontery of his statement was breathtaking.

"I know what you're doing," said the chief. "You will plant only one species, and then you'll spray to control other vegetation." This would not create a forest that would be good for wildlife, which was the issue that the Algonquins were concerned about.

The more the young man insisted, the more the chief stuck to his guns, pointing out from time to time a few remaining trees of a species that would inevitably be cleared out when the new, improved forest was planted. The young businessman agreed with him: of course, trees that were no good would be removed, he said, seeming not to realize the damaging nature of this admission. Gradually it became clear, as the chief continued his polite but relentless criticism, that the young planter was not an environmentalist after all, but just an entrepreneur who was in the process of creating a commercial forest.

Finally the contractor said he would have to get in touch with the authorities. "You can tell them," said the chief, "that we will be down there blocking off this road. No one will be allowed in."

"No one?" said the young businessman, beginning to realize that the chief was serious.

"No one," said the chief.

"Well, it's not up to me any more," said the young man. "I am a simple businessman trying to make a living. It's up to the government now."

"Thanks for your co-operation," said the chief, shaking hands. "No hard feelings." The young man climbed into his truck and with a rather sickly smile negotiated his way past the Algonquin car fleet.

Police and business together

The next day, the police arrived, and the standoff began in earnest. The loggers and their employers (mostly small local businessmen who had been contracted to do the cutting by CIP, the major lease-holder) milled around uneasily on the west side of the main road, wondering when they were going to get to work to feed their families; while on the other side, more and more Algonquin tents went up along the first hundred yards of the logging road. These tents were discreetly hidden in the bush, their wood stoves giving off plumes of smoke that curled lazily into the air, creating a scene of tranquillity quite at odds with the tension felt by everyone.

From the moment they arrived, the police automatically assumed the law was on the side of the companies. They were nervous and irritable to find us there, shoving our microphone in their faces every time they tried to talk to someone.

A sergeant from the Maniwaki detachment marched self-importantly up to Pancho (as everyone called Chief Matchewan) and asked if he could have a word. "Go ahead," said Pancho gruffly. On the surface the chief was a plain, ordinary fellow, certainly no spellbinder in English, his second language: but in this crisis one could feel him taking on the mantle of leadership and expanding to fill it.

"I want to know your intentions for today," said the sergeant.

"Just to be around here. Don't let these guys start."

"And what is your right concerning that?" asked the sergeant. "About this territory here in LaVérendrye Park?"

"A right to live," said Pancho belligerently, "to have food on the table."

"You have some paper about that?"

"We are not talking about dealing with rights to the land," said Pancho, launching into a speech. "We are talking about food on the table, and protecting the natural habitat, the wildlife. We are just trying to bring to Canadian attention that this is a wildlife reserve they are raping."

"Do you have some document to prove you have the right to live here, something like that?"

"We've been around here for thousands of years. That gives us the right to live off this land," replied Pancho.

When we included this remarkable dialogue in the film we eventually made, the sergeant's bewildered insistence on seeing a document to prove an occupation that everybody knew pre-dated documents, laws, and even the presence of Europeans, never failed to get a big laugh from the audience. This was yet another exchange exemplifying the gulf between the two cultures.

The police were obviously itching to get the Indians out of the way, so that they could enforce the cutting permits that the loggers were waving at them. The officers kept rushing back and forth in their cars, seeking advice. They had a real problem. To open the logging road, they would have to arrest a lot of people; what would they do with them? They were 150 kilometres from the nearest town, and did not exactly have a fleet of Black Marias at their disposal. They might have got away with a couple of symbolic arrests if they'd been confronted only by the Indians; but a Toronto television crew had arrived, we were there with our cameras, and in the afternoon the two Algonquin lawyers, David Nahwegahbow and Gérard Guay, turned up. The lawyers announced loudly that this was not a police or criminal issue, but a civil matter, that the road being blocked was not a formal road, just a cutting in the forest, and that what was at stake was an argument between two competing rights – the cutting rights of the loggers, and the ancestral rights of the Algonquins.

The police were frustrated. When I asked the sergeant if he was thinking of calling for reinforcements, he said he would summon as many officers as he needed. What did that mean? I asked. "We have 4,000 officers in our force," he said. "If we need them, they will all be here." This was foolishness, of course, but revealing of the police mindset.

At the end of a day of impotence for the police, the sergeant angrily told the Algonquins he would be checking up on them. Later that night, they found out what he meant. He sent a detachment five miles north on the main road to set up a roadblock. There they waved through every vehicle driven by a European – I can vouch for that, because our van was waved through – and pulled over every vehicle driven by Indians. They were given tickets for minor traffic offences: broken windshield, broken wipers, tail-light not working, children riding illegally in the back of a pickup, and so on. Next morning it was discovered that forty-eight summonses had been handed out to Algonquins, and the lawyers announced they would be entering a complaint to the Quebec Human Rights Commission against this racist application of the law.

The loggers agreed informally that they would not try to restart work over the weekend. So the Barriere Lake people, who were already beginning to feel the strain, went home to go fishing in an attempt to recharge their emotional batteries and restock their food supplies for the coming week's challenge.

We took advantage of the break to go to Lena's camp, where we hoped to shoot the many traditional activities that were always underway there. The camp is a little paradise, a collection of about a dozen cabins where the whole family, four generations of them, drift in and out all the time with moose and fish and small game. I had asked the band council to notify Lena that we would be visiting, but somehow the message hadn't got through, and when I asked her if we could come back and film on Sunday, Lena's daughter Irene, in her abrasive way, said they would not be there; they were going out into the bush, far off, to collect medicine. How about Monday? Monday they would not be back. What time were they leaving on Sunday? Early, very early. We could film you leaving, I insisted; we will be here.

On Sunday morning we arrived before the family was even awake. They turned out sleepily, grumpily, but I could sense in Irene a certain grudging respect that we cared enough to be there. She and Louise, her daughter, set about making us a massive breakfast. But we had caught the old lady on a bad day; Lena was fed up with being filmed. A young man had filmed her with a videocamera the previous summer, and when he had returned later he didn't show her the results, and she was offended. When we asked if we could film her setting her nets, she refused.

This was a dismaying prospect: a film on Barriere Lake without Lena was unthinkable. We had filmed a compelling interview with her during the winter, and needed footage of her at work to complement her words. Fortunately, Irene understood. She disappeared into her mother's cabin and persuaded her to go down to the lake and climb into the canoe with her. Lena was grumpy all the way through the filming, snapping at Irene in Algonquin as they eased the nets overboard. When it was over and we all stood together on the shore, I asked Irene to thank her mother. Lena heard her out, gazed at me with distaste and growled, "White man!"

By the time we were through filming, they had strapped their canoe on top of their van and were ready to leave on a trip that would take them many miles into the interior of their territory – first along the logging roads, then by canoe through the waterways, until they came to the place where they knew they could find the medicines they needed, and that were available only at that time of year. Lena had quickly recovered her good humour: she shook hands with us cordially as they left, and I felt we had fulfilled her requirements for honest effort.

The law weighs in for the companies

When the blockade resumed the following Tuesday, the situation was tenser than ever. The scene had an eerie beauty: in a heavy, early-morning fog, the loggers lined up beside their trucks along the road, and directly opposite them all of Barriere Lake's children stretched for almost a hundred yards, carrying painted placards and signs that they'd prepared over the weekend, denouncing the government for its 200-year failure to talk to them. Chief Matchewan had managed to mobilize most of the community. At least 300 people had come out, from old women in wheelchairs to young mothers with babies wrapped cosily in the traditional *tikanagan*.

Before the weekend the companies had said they would seek a court injunction against the picketing, and the Algonquin lawyers had been preparing their case. But now they discovered that an *ex parte* injunction proceeding (that is, one in which the second party is not present) was under way without them in a Hull courtroom. For a time it appeared from their lawyers' telephone discussions with the judge that they were going to win the case, but then news of the verdict came through: without being represented in court, the Algonquins had been ordered to end all protests, demonstrations and pickets of any kind, to permit all cutting, and to allow the companies to remove logs and equipment. The Algonquin lawyers felt they'd been double-crossed.

The chief said there was no question of their obeying such an injunction. In an act of defiance, the Algonquins moved eighteen tents overnight from the shelter of the surrounding forest into the middle of the logging road. The people had decided not to surrender meekly; anyone who wanted to open the logging road would have to move them physically. That was not going to be a pretty sight.

By noon, the text of le injunction against the blockade was pinned to a tree: it had been taken out in the name of Canadian Pacific Forest Products Ltd., the owner of CIP, and part of the huge Canadian Pacific corporate empire. The balance of forces could not have been more one-sided: one of the biggest companies in the land was setting out to crush a small group of poor people who were getting in the way of production and profits. Effortlessly, these big battalions had been able to line up the law and the police on their side.

Under closer examination, however, the injunction was found to contain a hilarious mistake. A map had been drawn up of the area under injunction, evidently by someone who didn't know the country, enclosing only the proposed cutting areas on the other side of the main road, and omitting the area of the main blockade. By late afternoon, the police still hadn't arrived.

Next morning, members of the Comité de Vigilance Environnemental Régional (CVER), an environmental group from Senneterre, arrived in a large bus equipped with a mobile kitchen from which they handed out food to people on the blockade. They also brought two fax machines, with which they began to pepper the province with information about the Algonquin action, transmitted from the nearby government tourist centre. Many of these environmentalists were militants of the Parti Québecois. Their president, Jake Roulo, was an old-timer for whom activism was in the blood: he'd been contesting the status quo as a member of Quebec's tiny Communist Party as long ago as the 1930s, and the whiff of defiance from the Algonquin barricades had flushed him into action. CVER announced that, since the injunction had been taken out against the Algonquins, their members were prepared to stand in front of the Algonquins when the police arrived, and defy them to get another injunction. This was a welcome act of courage and commitment, for it showed that even Quebec nationalists could find reasons to support the aboriginal cause.

Next morning, down at Le Domaine, a dozen police turned up in several large vehicles, and it seemed that a confrontation was imminent. But it was still unclear how even a dozen police were going to handle a whole community camped in the bush, without terrible scenes of intimidation and violence that would immediately become national news. So it was not surprising that the office of Mines and Native Affairs Minister Raymond Savoie quickly sent word that the companies were not keen to enforce their injunction, although another injunction was being sought by a different group of contractors. The Algonquin lawyers pressed Savoie for a meeting, as they'd been doing unsuccessfully for more than a year. This time he agreed, but wanted to fly four of the leaders out to his office. The Algonquins insisted he visit the community, to experience for himself the anger of the people, but he refused.

There was another brief, comic incident when two policemen showed up at the blockade to issue a summons against Algonquins alleged to have manhandled some workers earlier that morning. The policemen didn't know the names of the people to whom they wanted to issue the summons, and they could not specify the offence; so, as the people around them began to mutter angrily, they turned and left, summonses still in hand.

No more was seen of the police reinforcements; they had apparently thought better of their intention to clear out the Algonquins. But that afternoon, presumably at the urging of CVER, André Pelletier, the mayor of Val d'Or, arrived. Well-known for his environmental interests, Pelletier was contesting the provincial election against Savoie, and he spoke briefly but with great feeling in support of the Algonquins.

Next day – the blockade had now lasted almost two weeks – electoral politics worked an unexpected magic: less than twenty-four hours after his opponent had appeared, Savoie himself, elusive for more than a year, turned up in a helicopter, ready to give the community an hour of his time. The people sat him down, fed him some moose meat, and began to harangue him. When they let him go five hours later, Savoie had accepted in principle their request for a moratorium on logging in areas critical to wildlife, and had agreed to meet with the Algonquins and the federal government to discuss the community's proposal for a conservation strategy. A few days later, the companies agreed to suspend their injunctions, the Algonquins let them remove their equipment, and a brief moratorium on logging was put in place pending the promised meeting on September 28 – a year to the day after the Barriere Lake people were arrested on Parliament Hill.

We ended our filming with the Minister's visit, thinking (and hoping) that the film was going to have a happy ending.

A long, slow haul

Such hopes were premature. At the promised meeting on September 28, the Algonquins had not even finished making their case before the Quebec Minister of Forests, Albert Côté (a former logging company president), stormed out of the meeting, refusing even to listen to their request that the logging moratorium be extended for ninety days, and that the issuing of the CAAF agreements be delayed. Only the day before, CP Forest Products had agreed in principle with both requests. Under the law, Côté did not have to issue the CAAF agreements formally for another six months, but, almost spitefully, he delivered them only a week later, thereby setting in train a process that required the agreements to be signed within ninety days of being received. To put it mildly, this was shocking arrogance and bad-faith bargaining. Less than a month after their meeting with Savoie, the Algonquins felt they had no option but to return to the barricades.

Almost immediately the police moved into the forest to force entry for a logging crew. They pushed and hit out at the men, women and children blocking their way, forced Chief Matchewan to the ground, handcuffed him and took him away to jail in Mont Laurier. They threatened they were going to keep him for months, but had to release him when the Algonquin lawyers turned up later that same day. Georges Erasmus, National Chief of the Assembly of First Nations at the time, denounced the Quebec government's "stormtrooper tactics" and asked Prime Minister Mulroney to intervene to protect native communities in Quebec from the police. Quebec regional chief Konrad Sioui wrote to Premier Robert Bourassa that such tactics were gaining Quebec an image of "hardness and abuse of power". He added (prophetically, in view of the Oka crisis that erupted a few months later): "These police invasions towards our First Nations citizens are absolutely not the solution to maintain harmonious and sincere relations."

In desperation, the Algonquins wrote to all the companies and unions concerned in the logging, in fact, to everyone with any interest in their forest, asking for understanding of their dilemma. In a letter to all directors of CP Forest Products Ltd. they asked the company to disengage voluntarily from the CAAF approval process, now ticking away inexorably.

In spite of everything, the threatened logging did not begin. On October 20, 1989, only three days after the arrest of the chief, the Algonquins held an information seminar in a large tent erected on that same logging road that had been at the centre of their blockade. In the modern world of electronic communications, it makes little sense to hold an information meeting 250 kilometres from the nearest city. But this seminar showed that what makes sense to Euro-Canadians is not always sensible. Native leaders from across the country – Mikmaqs, Mohawks, prairie Crees, Quebec Crees and Six Nations – gathered to express support for the Barriere Lake people. There was something about that meeting – the cosy warmth of the tent, the fragrant country stews and bannock served to everyone, the undemonstrative but genuine welcome given to strangers, who were assumed to be there to support the Algonquin struggle: whatever it was, the meeting had a special aura. I'd been to hundreds of press conferences in my life as a reporter, but never one like this. Somehow or other, the unusual ambience of this seminar made its way into the reports of even the most detached and indifferent journalists, who, like me, found it hard to resist the charm of the Algonquins when they met them on their own ground.

Algonquin hopes were again raised when John Ciaccia, who had negotiated the James Bay Agreement for the Quebec government in the '70s, replaced Raymond Savoie as Mines and Native Affairs Minister. Ciaccia understood aboriginal issues. On December 12, he agreed that the CAAFs should not be signed until April, that they would contain clauses necessary to protect the Algonquin interest, and that the wording of these clauses would be worked out with the Algonquins.

Could the Algonquins be getting somewhere at last?

More years of broken promises

As it turned out, they were not getting anywhere.

Space does not permit a recitation of all the details of this story, which is, I am sorry to say, being repeated across the country almost every day in dealings between natives and governments. The Algonquins soon discovered that, in spite of John Ciaccia's promise, the wording of the CAAF clauses covering their needs was settled between the government and the companies, without Algonquin involvement. More fruitless meetings followed, until, with the April signing date looming up, the Algonquins applied to Quebec Superior Court for an injunction to stop the signing of the CAAFs.

Outaouais judge Orville Frenette of Quebec Superior Court, who has been consistently unsympathetic to aboriginals, scarcely had to pause before finding that the Algonquins had not established any right to their territory, or any evident threat to their way of life. Frenette produced an astonishing argument to prove that there are no aboriginal rights in Quebec. He said the French Crown had never recognized native rights because the Crown had believed "that America was populated by infidels who had to be conquered and evangelized, and that the territories were too sparsely populated to recognize the rights of these people."

As Chief Matchewan pointed out to a House of Commons committee a month later, a judgment in our day that invokes the idea that Indians were infidels (dictionary definition: pagans, or disbelievers in religion), as a justification for denying aboriginal rights, is not only bigoted and racist, but equivalent to denying women their rights on the grounds that they were formerly declared to be non-persons.

Having failed to delay the CAAF signing, the Algonquins now had to watch helplessly as the agreements put the management of their forest in the hands of logging companies for twenty-five years. This was done before there was any agreement on the special provisions needed to meet Algonquin concerns. The Algonquins continued to block logging roads, incurring the ire especially of a Gatineau logging contractor, Claude Bérard, who kept insisting on his right to cut the forest. By August 20 1990, with the pressure against them mounting, the Algonquins decided on another courageous but desperate measure. Overnight they pushed a huge mound of sand across the main road that connects the Abitibi region with southern Canada, completely shutting off all traffic, and announced that they would leave it there until Minister Ciaccia agreed to meet them. In the middle of the night, apparently, there were tense and dramatic scenes, with infuriated truckers on their knees at the foot of the sand pile scrabbling to push it out of the way. Ciaccia immediately flew north by helicopter to meet the Algonquins, and they agreed to lift the blockade at seven o'clock the next morning.

The blockade of the main road was a dangerous move, but it seemed to get results. On the spot Ciaccia agreed in principle to the conservation proposal that the Algonquins had been pressing for more than two years, and said he would place it before the Quebec cabinet. Two days later, he announced the cabinet had adopted the plan in principle. By the beginning of September (a year after we had finished our filming), a tentative agreement was reached. The National Chief of the Assembly of First Nations hailed the proposed agreement as possibly ushering in a new era of co-operation between First Nations and governments throughout the country.

But now began a long battle over how much of the forest would be covered by the proposed agreement. Every time the Algonquins felt they had an agreed draft, the Quebec government would at the last minute change the wording (for example, from "sustainable development" to "sustained yield" – a totally different concept). This process took almost a year.

When finally settled on August 22 1991, the Trilateral Agreement (involving Canada, Quebec and the Algonquins) provided for a four-year study and inventory of all natural resources over a large area covering most of the traditional Barriere Lake lands, and laid down a formal process and timetable for the parties to work together towards identifying "sensitive zones" of the forest, essential to wildlife. The work was to be done through special representatives nominated by each party (the Algonquins chose Clifford Lincoln, former Quebec Minister of the Environment), who had first to draw up a set of "provisional measures" for protecting these sensitive areas of forest, and then work towards an agreed management plan that would become the object of a negotiation between Quebec and the Algonquins in the autumn of 1994.

For the Algonquins, the agreement had a glaring weakness. In spite of all their pleas to the contrary, the CAAF agreements were allowed to stand, guaranteeing Bérard, the Gatineau businessman, and others, continued access to the trees in La Vérendrye wildlife reserve. Almost from the beginning, the work of identifying the sensitive areas of forest was stymied, essentially because the Quebec Ministry of Forests acted as if the right to cut trees overrode all other rights. And they had the CAAF agreements on which to base their argument.

What happened over Christmas of 1991 indicates the hostile climate in which the Algonquins found themselves negotiating: they were promised that some "sensitive areas" of forest would be left alone by loggers, but they returned after the holiday to find that four hectares of wildlife-sensitive forest had been completely removed in a clearcutting operation. When they protested to their federal and provincial partners in the Trilateral Agreement, shoulders were shrugged: what could be done about it now?

Thereafter, the agreed process of negotiation went so badly that it had effectively broken down by the following April. In August 1992, the parties agreed to the appointment of a mediator, Mr. Justice Réjean Paul, who had had long experience of aboriginal issues as a member of the Cree-Naskapi Commission established under the James Bay and Northern Quebec Agreement of 1975.

Judge Paul's report is worth describing in some detail, because it throws light on the entrenched Euro-Canadian attitudes that aboriginal people have to deal with as they struggle to re-establish the economic and social viability of their communities. Although he phrased his judgment in conciliatory and moderate language, the mediator blamed the Quebec Ministry of Forests for the breakdown. He said the CAAF agreement signed by the ministry with Claude Bérard's company covering the Algonquin lands "does not respect the Trilateral Agreement, either in the spirit, or the letter of the Agreement". A clause included in the CAAF agreement referring to the study of the Algonquin lands was so vague and ambiguous as to be virtually meaningless. (This is why the Algonquins insisted for so long – and were promised – that they should be involved in the wording of this clause. Of course, they never were.)

Judge Paul said the clause referred only to "the territory containing traplines held by the Algonquins", a definition nowhere mentioned in the Trilateral Agreement, and therefore left wide open to interpretation by the companies. Given this wording, said the mediator, "It becomes evident to even the least knowledgeable observer, that there were problems on the horizon, and in fact problems did arise."

Furthermore, the CAAF agreement said that when the Trilateral study is completed, the Quebec Ministry of Forests "will determine the extent of the forest management unit" and the volume of lumber "that can be attributed" to the logging company – thus apparently usurping the function of the proposed management plan that would emerge from the Trilateral Agreement.

The mediator also said the Ministry of Forests submitted to the special representatives a work plan that was not called for in the Trilateral Agreement, suggesting that the Ministry simply had no patience with the whole process. "The Quebec view is that the technical work is under their sole jurisdiction pursuant to the laws and regulations of Quebec, whereas the Algonquin view is that the Trilateral Agreement requires a technical team coordinated by and responsible to the Special Representatives."

This same arrogance evidently was carried by the governments into the area of funding. The mediator wrote: "For this agreement to function, funding is essential. If one wants it to die, one only has to shut the funding tap. Since April, the funding tap, both provincial and federal, has been shut."

He said that when the government funds were shut off, the Algonquins had used funds from their band budget, "to the detriment of their other programmes", to carry out anthropological studies and produce "maps of excellent quality indicating...their sensitive zones and sacred territories." His conclusion was that "It is David, and not Goliath, who is attempting to sustain the agreement."

Judge Paul suggested that the Trilateral Agreement might even have the status of a treaty, since it fulfills all three criteria for recognition as a treaty that were laid down by the Supreme Court of Canada in 1990 in the *Sioui* case. If the courts were to characterize the agreement as a treaty, it would take precedence over provincial laws. But "even if it is not a treaty...it is a solemn agreement which...must always be omnipresent when the CAAFs are granted by the Ministry of Forests to private entrepreneurs."

This is an important ruling for all native people in Canada, because it deals with an issue likely to become more and more common in the coming years. The Crees of Waswanipi in James Bay had already had a similar experience with the Quebec Ministry of Forests, even before the Algonquins rose in their own defence. The Waswanipi trappers, also under threat from clearcut logging, carefully identified all areas of their traplines essential to wildlife and to their own lives in the bush. They provided maps to the Ministry of Forests, whose officials replied that it would cost the logging companies too much to respect the areas essential to Cree life.

This dilemma is certain to be faced by other native groups across the country. More often than not, scientists employed by governments refuse to accept that aboriginal knowledge is really scientific, and will not take it into account in policymaking.

"The Ministry wants, by way of logging, to assist the economic development of a disadvantaged region, hard hit by unemployment (35 per cent of the workforce in August 1992)," wrote Judge Paul. He left no doubt that in his opinion this is a worthy objective. "But this logging must not be done to the detriment...of the First Nations. [They] must be clearly associated in this in order to also derive a certain benefit." He wrote that Quebec's special representative, Dr. André Lafond, agreed with him that the Trilateral Agreement is "a marvellous tool for the intelligent management of a forest. Why then," he asked, "are we at a point where we can almost see such a beautiful project collapsing?"

I do not think the answer is difficult to discern. History has called upon our generation to rewrite the terms on which our forebears took over this country. If we are to do this with equity and justice, and with respect for the insights that aboriginal people can bring us, we will have to insist that our bureaucracies and institutions make the necessary accommodations to native interests. Unfortunately, provincial governments have been slow to get this message. In February 1993, Quebec sullenly withdrew from the Trilateral Agreement, accusing the Algonquins of being "unreasonable". It was later shamed into resuming its co-operation.

Sadly, one has to conclude that although the Barriere Lake people have been eminently reasonable in their requests, they have encountered only implacable hostility from our institutions, bad-faith bargaining from our bureaucracies, and racist arrogance from many individuals.

Undoubtedly the nadir of their struggle was reached – at least in the psychological sense – in August 1992. The logging contractor Claude Bérard, in an interview with a Gatineau radio station, called the Algonquins *"griboux"*, which he described as a bug that lives in outhouse excrement and attacks genitals. In Rapid Lake, the people were shocked. What had they ever done to deserve such contempt?

Their lawyer, Gérard Guay, spoke for them: "The effect of these insults on the community," he said, "has been devastating."

14

Our wealth, taken from their lands

Industrial development, promoted by government, has borne heavily not only on the Crees and Algonquins of Quebec, as already described, but on native communities almost everywhere in Canada. Aboriginals have mounted resistance against many forms of development: in Ontario and the British Columbia interior, it is primarily against logging or pulpwood harvesting on traditional lands; on the Pacific coast, aboriginal fishing grounds have been invaded; in Alberta, the oil companies ride roughshod over anyone who stands in their way; in northern Manitoba, a relatively self-sufficient aboriginal way of life has been almost ruined by hydroelectric projects that the provincial government of the 1970s promised would greatly improve aboriginal fortunes.

There is now a growing public recognition that natives have been given a raw deal, and something must be done about it. This is the most positive result of the 1990 Oka crisis. The Canadian people have finally discovered something we should always have known: billions of dollars in wealth have been siphoned from lands still occupied and claimed by aboriginals, whose economies have been shattered and whose people have been reduced to poverty.

Now that it has penetrated the public consciousness, this reality will never disappear again. It can no longer be swept under the carpet of Canadian politics. For reasons of equity, justice and practicality, Canada is going to have to deal with this issue throughout the coming decades.

In response to changing public opinion, efforts are being made in some places to redress the injustices of the past. In the early 1990s,

166

the New Democratic Party government of Ontario has broken with traditional attitudes by returning to native people some authority within their traditional lands. The province has permitted Algonquins to hunt within Algonquin Park; and in northwestern Ontario it has established the Whitedog Area Resources Committee to give the Ojibway people of the Wabaseemong First Nation (also known as the Islington, or Whitedog, band) a say about natural resources, land use and economic issues in their traditional territory of 900,000 acres, or 1,400 square miles. This, for a community whose formal land holding has been restricted for many years to its reserve of 24,000 acres, is a considerable advance.

Because of the high priority given to traditional aboriginal fishing in the Sparrow decision of the Supreme Court of Canada (dealt with in more detail in Chapter 20), the federal government has also had to move to restore aboriginal access to west-coast salmon fisheries. In both provinces there has been a strong negative reaction from hunters and fishermen, who do not appear to realize (or, if they realize, to care) that these resources were stripped from the aboriginal people either illegally, or through shoddy, dishonest negotiations.

So far, these measures are rather exceptional. More commonly, aboriginal people have had to take to the barricades in defiance of corporations, police forces, judges and governments, in hazardous and usually unsuccessful actions to ward off industrial development that threatens to devour them.

Three aboriginal strategies

Aboriginals have followed three methods to assert their land rights: political negotiation, legal action, and direct action. Unlike Americans, Canadians have always favoured political negotiation over legal action, which (as I show in more detail in Chapter 20) has never figured much in the thinking of aboriginal people in Canada, until the last two decades. The attitudes of the courts are extremely variable, and there is no doubt that a better solution is a political agreement freely entered into between native people and the democratic representatives of mainstream Canadian society. Movement in this direction is always underway somewhere in the country, centred around the land-claims process, through which the federal government is negotiating new treaties.

But the land-claims process, begun in 1973, has been so slow, and so subject to dishonest bureaucratic procrastination, that by 1987 many natives had lost faith in it, and the Assembly of First Nations formally decided that the time had come for direct action.[1] In James Bay, the Ottawa Valley, northwestern Ontario, the Queen Charlotte Islands off the west coast, and throughout the Northwest Territories, natives have learned that it is one thing to get governments to make agreements, and something else again to force them to honour those agreements. Hence, they have had little choice but to adopt the third strategy – direct action.

So far direct action – blockades, defiance of injunctions, sit-ins, armed resistance – has certainly increased public awareness of aboriginal concerns. But it has been met with sometimes draconian force, and has seldom yielded practical results in the form of improved policies more sensitive to native needs. In addition, direct action has caused a great deal of hardship and suffering for those who have engaged in it.

Some of these native struggles against the industrial machine – for example, that of the Lubicon Crees of northern Alberta – have been highly publicized not only throughout Canada, but in Europe and elsewhere. Others, like that of the Haida attempt in British Columbia to exert management authority over their traditional salmon fishery, remain virtually unknown outside their own province. Media interest is arbitrary and ethnocentric. Coverage of these issues is erratic and fitful, and often appears to depend on whether the events are sensational enough to catch the headlines (which are always dominated by negative news). If anyone is killed, as at Oka, the issue automatically becomes news; a native person has only to take gun in hand to leap onto the front pages. As disadvantaged blacks in the United States discovered long ago, the quickest way to arouse media interest is to start shooting.

Early in 1993, the media flocked in droves to Davis Inlet in Labrador after six children tried to commit suicide, in a mass gasoline-sniffing incident. Throughout Canada, editorials and commentators deplored the conditions of extreme poverty to which the Davis Inlet people had been consigned, and people of goodwill asked themselves how such a thing could happen. The answer to their question had been given only the year before in a remarkable book, *Nitassinan*, by Newfoundland author Marie Wadden; but the media had paid little attention to her chillingly documented description of the colonial

168

policies imposed by Canada on the Innu people for many decades, and the terrible suffering that ensued.

Joining with their friends

In 1990, native people joined forces with a coalition of 100 environ-mental groups (representing a million people, it was claimed) to form Canada's Future Forests Alliance: an organization that set out to stop the giveaway of the boreal forest to multinational companies by provincial governments, and to improve forest management. The coalition discovered that more than $13 billion of investment was planned by pulp-and-paper and logging companies throughout the country. Almost everywhere, aboriginal people are living in the areas slated for these investments.

The companies form a veritable roll-call of multinational giants — Boise Cascade, Bowater, Canadian Pacific, Abitibi-Price, Daishowa and Oji Paper of Japan, Domtar, Fletcher Challenge of New Zealand, Kruger, Louisiana-Pacific, Noranda, New York Times, Procter and Gamble, Scott Paper, Stone-Consolidated, Stora of Sweden, Weyerhaeuser. Among them they announced plans to upgrade sixty-four mills, to increase production in thirty-one mills, and to build some twenty-five new ones.[2] The government responded loyally: Parliament's Standing Committee on Forestry threw caution to the winds and recommended that the forest cut in Canada, already at an unsus-tainable level, should be increased by 100 per cent by the year 2050. The plans were so enormous in scope that Canada's Future Forests Alliance described them as "the biggest giveaway in Canada's history".[3]

In Alberta alone, one-third of the entire provincial land-mass was involved in forest leases to Daishowa and other companies. The lands occupied by a half-dozen isolated Cree communities in north-ern Alberta, who had been trying to assert a land claim since the 1970s, were included in this massive giveaway.

A member of the alliance, Greenpeace, used its international con-nections to mount a campaign in Europe against British Columbia's irresponsible logging and harvesting methods. In response, the forest-products industry threw its money and weight behind the Share movement, a right-wing free-enterprise group based in the United States. Suddenly, for every environmental campaign, there was a cor-responding Share counterattack by supposedly grassroots organiza-tions bearing names such as Northern Community Advocates for

Resource Equity, Northshare, Share the Temagami, Share the Forest, Share our Resources, Share the Stein, Share the Carmanah, Share the Clayoquot.[4] The main organizer of these was an American, Ron Arnold, who said the environmental movement was a threat to industrial civilization and was being used by the Soviet Union to cripple the economy of the free world.

The Future Forests Alliance recognizes that native people stand in the front lines against this onslaught on the forest. In a submission to a Ministry of Forests hearing, the Valhalla Society, of British Columbia, wrote:

> Native people are going through the agonizing experience of seeing the precious resources hauled off their land before they can get their land claims recognized. The big corporations haul the wood away to mills in other areas while Indian people languish in poverty. This injustice has reached a point which can no longer be borne by the native people, and they have increasingly resorted to land blockades.[5]

For the 3,000 members of the Bigstone Cree, wrote Greenpeace in a position paper,

> ...corporate logging means that five to ten thousand square kilometres of their land base and 35 to 40 per cent of their income will have been removed from their sustainable economy. Forest management agreements spell the end of the bush economy for indigenous peoples and begin a cycle which concludes with the disintegration and destruction of a way of life.... Caught up in an abstract world, removed from the place where the impacts of their actions are felt, decision-makers are not forced to live with the consequences of their decisions.[6]

Having watched these multinationals at work in many parts of the country, and elsewhere in the world, I am not optimistic about the outcome of this struggle. The corporate belief that the forest is a place to mine trees has behind it such overwhelming force of money and influence that so far the struggle for social justice and environmental commonsense has made scarcely a dent.

Towards a sustainable economy

A remarkable aspect of the native response to the rape of their lands has been their effort to point Canadians in the direction of the future sustainable economy, as recommended by the Brundtland Commission,[7] and endorsed (although only in words) by every level of Canadian government. The Barriere Lake Algonquins have not been alone in this: in fact, the detailed proposals for sustainable development put forward by (to mention a few examples) the Teme-Augama Anishnabai of northern Ontario, the Haida of the Queen Charlotte Islands, and the Lheit Lit'en and the Chilcotin Ulkatcho Kluskus Nations of the British Columbia interior, give practical expression to the aboriginal concern for the well-being of Mother Earth.

The proposal of the Teme-Augama Anishnabai, a Nipissing people who live between the Crees and the Ojibway in northern Ontario, is typical. In 1988 they suggested that their land dispute with the Ontario government be resolved by creation of a joint stewardship council to manage the disputed forest. The council's objectives would be to maintain the health of the land, and to become financially self-supporting by harvesting the timber in a way that would ensure the continuance of the forest into future generations.

These objectives fly in the face of current practices in Canadian forestry. The Anishnabai definition of sustainability is very different from what happens now. Sustained life, they say, requires that the life of the Earth, air and water must be protected and maintained, so as to create an interdependent home for all biological life-forms: "Designated trees and/or forest areas must be allowed to die, fall to the Earth, decay and return to Earth, thus giving life to Earth which can then support the growth of a new forest for future generations, forever."

They interpret sustained development to mean, first, a political system for effective citizen participation in decisions; second, an economic system able to generate surpluses and technical knowledge on the basis of self-reliance; third, a social system able to solve tensions arising from disharmonious development; fourth, a production system that preserves the ecological base for development; fifth, a technological system that can search continuously for new solutions; and sixth, a flexible administrative system with the capacity for self-correction.

To ecologically aware people, this Anishnabai proposal seems no more than common sense. But it fell on barren ground. The Ontario government (Liberal at the time) was not particularly interested, preferring to think in the traditional terms of buying out the native interest, to free land for use by private business.

The Temagami struggle

The Teme-Augama began their struggle to defend their land in 1973. Over a twenty-year period they have followed all three routes – political negotiation, legal action and direct action, without (at the time of writing) achieving the solution they seek. Their land claim is based on their belief that they didn't sign the Robinson-Huron Treaty of 1850, and therefore never ceded their rights in land around Lake Temagami, north of North Bay, Ontario, which they regard as their ancestral home. When they took the issue to court, the Ontario government argued that someone had signed on their behalf, and they therefore had no further claim on the land.

The Robinson Treaty over which this argument has raged so fiercely was the forerunner of the numbered treaties later signed by Canada with the western tribes. This was the first treaty in which aboriginal people were granted reserves in return for the surrender of all their rights in the land. In what later became the typical pattern, the treaty was not made until minerals had been discovered in the Ojibway lands near Sault Ste. Marie, and businessmen wanted to exploit them.

The treaty negotiator, W.B. Robinson, told the Ojibways that their land was pretty well worthless to whites, and was unlikely to be settled by them, so they would be free to hunt everywhere, except in those few small places that became occupied. Given these assurances, the Indians agreed to sign the treaty on payment of 96 cents per head per year (later increased to $4).

The Indians assumed, wrongly, that they were not really giving up anything by signing the treaty. They thought they would be free to use all the land just as they always had, and would, in addition, receive the proceeds from mining. In the circumstances, one would have to conclude that this was a duplicitous negotiation.

Reported Robinson to the Governor: "I trust His Excellency will approve of my having concluded the Treaty on the basis of a small annuity and the immediate and final settlement of the matter, rather than paying the Indians the full amount of all moneys on hand, *and a promise of accounting to them for future sales*" (my emphasis).

If, indeed, the Indians had obtained a piece of all future sales, as they had asked, they would have become rich. But of course, the Indians did not prosper. Their main band was confined to a new reserve at Garden River, where, thirteen years later, a priest complained in a letter to *The Globe*, Toronto, that the people were starving.[8]

The trickery continues

It is almost 150 years since Robinson signed his two treaties with the Ojibway. But the day of the loaded and misleading negotiation is by no means over. Canada today is a patchwork quilt of vast industrial schemes built on aboriginal hunting lands, schemes that are usually presented as if they will bring immense benefits to the aboriginals, but almost always turn out to destroy the very basis of their lives.

Native groups in almost every province have been forced to defend their lands from the depredations of those who have been given permission by governments to extract timber, oil, gas, electricity, fish, animals or whatever other wealth the aboriginal lands may hold. For example, the Crees of Lubicon Lake in Alberta were living in relative peace and prosperity until their lands were wanted for oil exploration in the 1970s. Just as the Robinson Treaty of 1850 was the problem for the Teme-Augama, so Treaty 8, signed in 1899, was the problem for the Lubicon Crees. After fifteen years of fruitless legal wrangling, they were pushed into taking the desperate measure of declaring themselves a nation, establishing road blockades, and setting up their own system of permits for oil companies. Their nation lasted only five days before the blockades were demolished by the RCMP. At time of writing, five years later, they have still not achieved the settlement they have been seeking, but their people have been reduced to almost total dependence on welfare.

In the 1960s and '70s the coherence of aboriginal life throughout northern Manitoba was destroyed by the damming of rivers and lakes for hydroelectric development. Everybody in the province was in favour of this except the people whose lands were to be flooded, who had used the waterways for centuries to sustain their way of life.[9] First, in the early '60s, Crees were moved from Chemawawin on Cedar Lake to Easterville, to make way for the Grand Rapids hydro project. Their new location proved to be a poor place for hunting and trapping, and the fish were soon contaminated with mercury. People who had always been self-sufficient soon became dependent on welfare, and prey to manifold social problems.

In the '70s an even larger scheme, the diversion of the Churchill River into the Nelson, was imposed on even more people. First, the NDP provincial government of the day claimed it had the legal right to flood Indian lands without consent; then it claimed that no Indian lands would be flooded. Such evasive rationalizations are typical of governments that have decided to impose schemes on aboriginal people, who, they believe, will not be capable of fighting back.

Crees who had depended on the productive fishery in South Indian Lake soon found their food chain, too, contaminated with mercury. Fishing became difficult because of floating debris in the lake. The whitefish declined in quality to the lowest grade, and the Crees' once self-sufficient community became not only heavily dependent on social assistance, but wracked with levels of violent crime far greater than the Canadian average.

The Crees at Cross Lake were assured that their lake would fall no more than a pencil-length, and that hydro power would cost them only a few dollars a year. In fact, the lake fell three feet, their fishery was severely damaged, their moose and waterfowl harvest disrupted, and their hydro charges now amount to more than $1,000 a year. In an effort to obtain the benefits promised them, these communities have been pursuing court actions ever since the projects were built.

One resident at a 1973 meeting said:

> We want to be left alone. We can make our own living. I've been here for fifty-one years. I never had any electric light in my house.... I can get along without electric power for the rest of my life, if I have to. Why do they want to destroy our fishing and our trapping, which they will? They don't talk that way but we know they will.

And they did.

A brutal action

That Manitoba Crees of 1973 could have been speaking for the Cheslatta Indians of British Columbia, who were removed from their homes in 1952 to make way for ALCAN's Kitimat aluminum complex, in one of the most brutal actions ever taken in Canada involving displacement of aboriginal people. Like the Manitoba Crees, the Carriers of Cheslatta had for centuries been making their own living by fishing and trapping, getting along without electricity or other modern conveniences, and wanted simply to be left alone.

Their innocence was, however, rudely shattered one day in early April, when they were suddenly told that the lake around which they lived was being flooded, and they would have to abandon their villages within ten days. To make matters worse, it was the time of year when the ice was breaking up and movement was at its most difficult.

The Cheslatta people lived in inaccessible lake country a few miles south of the town of Burns Lake on the main east-west road between Prince George and Prince Rupert. They were a completely self-sufficient people who kept extensive traplines over a wide stretch of country, hunted for meat and fur, harvested berries and plants, fished for a seemingly endless supply of trout, char, kokanee and whitefish from their lakes, owned herds of cattle, horses and other livestock, and kept large gardens for household use. They had an annual visit from a priest, but otherwise saw few white people, and had little contact with the outside world.

When officials from ALCAN and the Department of Indian Affairs arrived at their reserve on April 3, 1952, only fifteen of the Cheslatta people, most of whom knew no English, were able to get to the meeting. Their hereditary chief had died the previous year, and they had no leader, so for the first time ever "a government chief" was hurriedly elected at the urging of the officials.[10]

This is what the officials told the band: to build the hydro plant for their new aluminum smelter, ALCAN had completely blocked the Nechako River. To sustain the millions of salmon that migrated up the Nechako every year, a small temporary reservoir was being created on Murray Lake, around which the Cheslatta people lived in several villages. The dam would be completed and closed on April 8, and the waters would start to rise. Consequently the people had to get out of there. The officials explained that the Indians had no say in the matter, and it would be in their best interest to co-operate and surrender their land peacefully, since they could not stand in the way of such a large development project. They said they would be back to accept the surrender of the land on April 16.

This whole process was completely illegal. First, the licence to build the dam was not issued until July 26. Second, Indian land was being flooded without obtaining the consent of the Indians, usually obtained through an instrument of formal surrender. Third, the process violated all Indian Act guidelines covering surrender meetings, which provide for third-party advisors, time for reflection, and the option of refusal. In the typical spirit of the time, all this happened without any public awareness, and, in fact, the action did not come to public notice until thirty years later.

The officials arrived back on April 20 with official surrender documents for the people to sign. By this time the band had formulated some demands. Through their interpreter, Abel Peters (who had only eight years before been wounded in the battle for Normandy), they asked that new land and buildings be purchased before they moved, and requested a monthly pension for each band member for life, compensation for traplines, and new roads to unsurrendered reserves. The officals said these demands were "fantastic, unreasonable, exorbitant, and definitely out of the question".[11] They said if the people refused to surrender their land, they would still have to move, and would receive no compensation. Although the waters were not rising as quickly as expected, and there was no real hurry, the departmental officials said they wanted to get it done now, for the Indians could become even harder to deal with if given more time. The officials of both government and company began to pressure individual Indians, offering them $150 a head, but their resistance was strong. "The interpreter, Abel Peters, son of the Chief and a veteran of the Second World War, was very difficult to deal with, being against any sort of compromise.... He did most of the talking and appears to be able to sway the majority of the members to his way of thinking," wrote W.J. McGregor, the Indian Affairs regional supervisor, to Ottawa.[12]

Eventually, under pressure, the band members voted (unanimously, according to departmental records) to surrender 2,600 acres in ten reserves for $130,000 "provided that this amount is sufficient to reestablish our Band elsewhere to our satisfaction on a comparable basis. The total cost of our moving and reestablishment to be borne by the Aluminum Company of Canada." The surrender documents were signed on April 21. The band now says these documents were forged.

"It was most frustrating attempting to negotiate with these Indians," wrote McGregor. "They are a backward group, have had little supervision and consequently little knowledge of the Indian Act or departmental policies. They had little knowledge of values, hence we were unable to establish a basis for negotiations."

"Everything was crooked," said Abel Peters, in 1991. "Crooked all the way! The DIA and ALCAN together.... The DIA never stick with us. Against us all the way!"[13]

The people had a terrible time after they moved. They were scattered far and wide; many had to live in tents through the following winter, and children died of tuberculosis. Before most people had a chance to return to their villages and collect their possessions,

ALCAN moved in and burned every building to the ground, although the people had been assured that everything would be safe. Although ALCAN had promised to pay all moving and re-establishment costs, they were "never heard from again....The Cheslatta people were camped in tents at Grassy Plains. Living conditions were inhuman. The people were sick, mad and broken-hearted." [14]

Said Abel Peters in 1982: "I lived in a tent for seven months and had to buy everything to start over. I was lucky because I had a pension from when I was hurt in the war.... Lots of people died after they moved.... The houses were all in terrible shape and there wasn't enough time or money to fix them up before winter. [My] house was only half-finished when we moved in. We had to put a new well and pump in because the water was unfit to drink.... The road was very, very bad and we spent lots of money to try to fix it, but it never was any good."[15]

In the mid-'80s I interviewed Abel Peters for my NFB film *Supercompanies*, about the international aluminum industry. By now an impressive but somewhat embittered elder, he said almost half the band members had died as a result of their hardships when they were cut off from their hunting, trapping and fishing territories. Drugs, alcohol and suicide were now constant problems. Most people lived on social assistance; unemployment stood at a chronic 85 per cent. His interview perhaps explained why ALCAN detested the film and tried to have a television screening of it cancelled.

Since 1984 the Cheslatta people have been pursuing a specific claim for compensation for their suffering. The federal departments of Justice and Indian Affairs, who are both judge and jury in these cases, rejected all their claims except for the purchase price of the relocation land. The Cheslatta people have had to go to court, at immense cost, to insist on their rights.

On April 21, 1992, the Cheslatta people commemorated the fortieth anniversary of their relocation. With a supreme sense of irony, they presented a document to federal officials written entirely in Carrier syllabics, and offered it to them for their signatures. When the officials declined to sign, Chief Marvin Charlie took the pen from their hands, wrote an X opposite their names, and declared it "official", just like the 1952 document of surrender.[16] Symbolically, at least, the tables had been turned.

Haidas in direct action

In the mid-1980s, the Haida people of the Queen Charlotte Islands (which they call Haida Gwai) moved into their irreplaceable rainforest for a series of direct actions in defence of their land. They blocked roads, encircled trees, stopped the ever-advancing loggers in their tracks, and defied the police to arrest them, which the police did in great numbers. The Haida's actions were decisive in forcing a reluctant provincial government to negotiate with the federal government for a new national park, which was established contingent on settling the Haida claim to the whole area.

This was only one of many actions taken by the Haida to protect their right to harvest the resources they have traditionally used. For several years they have been struggling to exert control over the salmon fishery. Here again they have used the methods of political negotiation and direct action, where necessary; and again they have found the law ranged against them, this time in defence of a private entrepreneur who has simply chosen to flout the wishes of the Haida and all other users of the resource.

The point of conflict has been Henslung Cove at Langara Island, on the north tip of the Queen Charlottes, a traditional Haida fishing place for chinook salmon. In 1981 the Haida named the cove Duu Guusd and declared it a tribal park. In 1985 chinook harvesting levels were reduced by international agreement in an effort to rebuild the stock. Haida, commercial and sports fishermen all agreed to reduce their harvest.

While this agreement was being negotiated, the controlling agency, the federal Department of Fisheries and Oceans, permitted establishment of a new type of commercial sports fishing – large floating lodges from which tourists sally out in small boats to catch their quota. The lodges are based on Langara Island, and their share of the harvest rose rapidly from 2,000 fish in 1987 to 6,000 in 1988. That year the Council of the Haida Nation declared a moratorium on development in their tribal park. By then six floating lodges were using the area, and by 1989 their catch within the tribal park was estimated at 10,000 fish.

Over the winter of 1990, the Haida held a commission of inquiry, and introduced a management plan that required all charter operators to register with them, and pay a fee for the resource they were using. The plan limited the number of guests at the lodges, and halved the daily limit established by the federal government. Commercial fishermen working in the area supported the Haida plan.

Seventy-five per cent of the sports fishing operators agreed to register and follow the Haida rules. But one major company, Oak Bay Marine Group, of Vancouver, refused. They flew in tourists in defiance of the plan, and when a Haida war canoe tried to blockade the cove on July 5, 1990, there was a collision with a small plane.[17] The next day the Oak Bay company was granted an injunction by the British Columbia Supreme Court restraining the Haida from interfering with the company's operation.

The response was immediate: the Haida met incoming tourists and tried to persuade them to go home; those who refused were met at Sandspit airport in the Queen Charlottes with a similar request. Five tourists agreed to return to Vancouver. By this time about seventy non-native trollers had responded to the Haida call for help. They converged on the Oak Bay lodge and prevented float planes from landing in the cove. The company had to bring in its tourists by helicopter.[18]

A few days later, a huge flotilla of 200 fishing boats, most of them non-native, blockaded the fishing lodge.[19] Some seventy people spread out along a neighbouring beach to prevent helicopters from landing. Early in August, Ernie Collison, vice-president of the Haida Council, was arrested and flown to a Supreme Court hearing in Vancouver for allegedly violating the terms of the injunction.[20] Although he had to give an undertaking to keep the peace and be of good behaviour, Collison said: "I don't feel like I've committed any criminal activity. We're standing up for our rights as native people."

The stand-off continued in 1991. By that time the Haida had extended their management plan to cover all of the Queen Charlottes. The Haida canoes returned to the cove and twelve Haida faced criminal charges for violating the court injunction.[21] The Haida charged Bob Wright, the owner of Oak Bay, with having a "buffalo mentality" – that is, of being ready to wipe out the chinook salmon, in much the same way as the buffalo was eliminated from the prairies in the 1880s.

This dispute is one of the most significant that natives have undertaken in Canada in recent years. Aboriginal leaders now realize that if they are to establish control over the resources to which they have a right, they will have to act in such a way that non-natives will agree to place themselves under native jurisdiction. This is proving to be doubly difficult, because in most places the natives have been able to assert their rights only by adopting confrontational tactics. To move from confrontation to conciliation and agreement with suspicious neighbours is a long process; many excellent plans, and many good intentions, have foundered under the strain.

For example, in the 1980s the Gitksan-Wet'suwet'en people, who live along the Skeena River in northern British Columbia, passed a set of bylaws that gave them power over the fishery in their reserves.[22] The bylaws were not disallowed by the federal government, so they became law. But the 25,000 non-natives in the area, especially those downstream from the reserves in question, felt they were affected. An alliance of sports and commercial fishermen and the provincial government, supported by the federal Department of Fisheries and Oceans, sought and won an injunction that placed the Gitksan bylaws in abeyance.

Such incidents have repeatedly demonstrated that Euro-Canadian law is designed above all to protect private property. We shall examine the law's efficacy as an instrument for defence of the aboriginal community in Chapter 20.

15

Ojibway: being watchful was not enough

In 1991 I visited Kenora, a small town in northwestern Ontario surrounded by about a dozen Ojibway reserves. I had lived there briefly in the mid-1950s not long after arriving in Canada as an immigrant. My wife had taught at the Rabbit Lake school, just outside the town, and every day we had passed the Cecilia Jaffray Indian Residential School, a grim-looking structure whose aura suggested a reform institution.

Although I did not meet any Indians at that time, we happened to rent a house from a man who kept a trading post, accessible only by water, out on an Ojibway reserve at Shoal Lake. He was a binge drinker when he came to town (I remember his family having to go out searching for him after a few days), but he would take a bottle of liquor with him when he went back up the lake, and would never touch a drop for months at a time. Years later I knew a number of aboriginal hunters who behaved in exactly the same way.

Every day my wife and I walked around the uncluttered shore of the Lake of the Woods (where a luxury hotel now stands) to get to the bus station. It was so cold in January and February that we usually finished our walk with icicles hanging from our nostrils and our cheeks covered in frost – quite an exotic experience for a couple fresh from New Zealand.

Even then, Kenora was not friendly to aboriginals. Later I discovered that our landlord's family, at any rate, was free of racism, for they intermarried with native people and his family name became quite prominent among band lists of status Indians.

Kenora is one of a number of small Canadian towns that have a reputation for unsympathetic and even hostile attitudes towards the native people on their streets. In 1946 an Ojibway called Tom Roy, from the Whitefish reserve south of Kenora, described a racial situation not unlike the American south, when he testified before the parliamentary joint committee described in Chapter 12. "The Indians are not allowed to occupy rooms in any of the hotels. I cannot even get a room myself," Roy said. The police had told him that discrimination against Indians was outside their jurisdiction, and they could do nothing about it:

> The information I got from the police was that the Indians are filthy and some would get a room and would raise some trouble drinking. But why should I get blamed just because my fellow-Indian did something wrong? I have seen white lumberjacks filthy and raising a lot of trouble in rooms, more than I ever do or ever will do. So filthiness is not the reason. It's because we are Indians. Some of the restaurants would not serve Indians for the same reason. I was told once to get out. They told me that, being an Indian, they would not serve me.... At the Palace theatre, the Indians are given the farthest section of the theatre to watch the show. We are not allowed to sit with the white people or pick out our own seats. At the Bijou theatre we are not allowed to go in at all. Now, our money is just as good as yours. This has been practised too long and I ask you that you put a stop to it.[1]

Forty-five years after Tom Roy made his complaint, I heard it repeated when I dropped into the Neechee Friendship Centre on Kenora's Main Street in 1991. I ran into Pete Seymour, whom I had first met in the early '70s on one of my trips through Kenora-area communities. Pete was one of the Canadian Indians who returned from the Second World War to discover they were still treated as second-class citizens, excluded from restaurants, hotels, cinemas and bars, disallowed from voting in elections, and in many small towns regularly hauled off the streets and bundled out of town on the slightest excuse.

"I came out of the army on December 22, 1945," Pete told me. "I was still wearing my uniform when I went to the movies with my sister right after Christmas, we used to call it old Joe Derry's theatre, and as we entered they sent us up to the balcony, they said, 'That's where the Indians go.' I got mad as hell right there. I asked for my money back, and we walked out."

182

Tom Roy suggested in 1946 that Indians be allowed to enter bars and liquor stores, because as the law then stood, it was illegal for them to be in possession of liquor, and they tended to drink it down as fast as possible for fear of getting caught. They would then wander away from town, fall asleep on a railway track, get run over, or maybe go off in a canoe and capsize. "That has happened time and time again.... In the town of Kenora alone last year the Indian fines on liquor were $1,500, which all went to the federal government." He said the town was asking for some of this money, "which will make conditions worse for the poor Indians, because the local police will be after them more".

Although Tom Roy protested vehemently to the joint committee, nothing happened. Indians were given the right to enter bars in the 1960s, but were still not allowed to take liquor onto the reserves, and were arrested in huge numbers for drinking on the streets. When they did get the right to take liquor to the reserves, that didn't improve matters, either: in fact, many aboriginal people think it was the worst thing that ever happened to them, and numerous reserves across Canada have banned liquor from their territory.

In the 1960s, the Ojibway around Kenora made national news by marching on the town in protest against the terrible conditions they had to put up with. But again, change was minimal. When I first returned to Kenora in the early '70s, the town had become well-known for the severe alcoholism among its native people, and also for the fact that it was almost impossible for native people to get work there. I remember visiting the addiction treatment centre, and buying for a few dollars a painting on brown wrapping paper by a young Indian working in one of the centre's back rooms, using art as therapy. He later became famous as the painter Carl Ray, but he died at an early age, a victim of the pathologies that were raging in the reserves of that region (as, in fact, they still are).

By the '70s the Cecilia Jaffray school had been turned into a residence for Indian children who came in from the reserves to attend public schools. The residence was now a warm and welcoming place, under the firm but tolerant direction of a Saskatchewan Saulteaux, Colin Wasacase. The Ojibway in the region continued to be restive as they watched their communities decline, and in 1974 they returned to the charge, again pouring into Kenora from the reserves, this time to occupy a park that the city was creating on Indian land.

That protest, Joe Seymour of the Neechee Friendship Centre told me, "lit a fire under governments".

The fire was not hot enough. By the late '70s there were so many violent Indian deaths in and around Kenora as a result of alcohol, so many beatings, so much fighting, so many drunks passed out on the town's back streets, that the Friendship Centre started a street patrol. It has been effective, but in the '90s the street patrol must still work the town every night between four p.m. and eight a.m. They take the people they pick up to a thirty-bed detoxification centre run by Randy Councillor (who told the story of his life in Chapter 3). In the month before I visited in 1991, the centre had taken in 264 people, of whom only thirteen were first-time users. So the problem drinkers are now limited to a small group who hang around town, supplemented by transients stopping off in Kenora for a few days on their way from Thunder Bay to Winnipeg.

On my return to Kenora in 1991 I found that the town has been slow to change. Indians are seldom hired by local businesses, even if they are qualified, and they are usually refused loans by the banks.

I was able to visit three reserves in the region. Each is still suffering from the prejudices of the past. There is a sense in each of them that a revival is underway, yet all three communities are held back by the reluctance of their Euro-Canadian neighbours to make room for them in the local economy.

The fact is, the colonial mentality is alive and well in the Canadian hinterland. Largely shut out of local economies, the aboriginals are confined to impoverished reserves whose economies are minuscule, and many of whose people are so severely damaged that they can barely function.

Savant Lake: overwhelmed by outsiders

To reach the Saugeen Nation band, I had to drive some 350 kilometres northeast of Kenora, past the milling town of Dryden, and beyond Sioux Lookout into wilderness country. The deeper you penetrate it, the more remote this country feels; but even this backwater has not escaped the attention of our industrial machine. I drove through large areas of clearcut forest before arriving at a place called Savant Lake, a collection of a few houses where a small group of poor Ojibway live. They are squatters on Crown land in an area where once they were the only inhabitants.

Savant Lake is actually two communities, bisected by CN's main railway line: whites on one side of the line with a school, stores, hotel, motel and services, Indians on the other with virtually nothing. The nondescript Ojibway houses are scattered along a small bush road. There are thirty-nine families, 160 people in all, living in twenty-one little houses, many of them tarpaper shacks. Chief Ed Machimity and his wife Violet have four bedrooms, but twelve people sleep in them. This is more or less the norm.

By Canadian standards, the living conditions at Savant Lake are poor. The people have no indoor toilets; and they have to drive twenty-five kilometres in their pickups for drinkable water, since the lake from which they used to take water is now polluted. The Ontario Ministry of Natural Resources (MNR) claims that it gave them a water-storage system a few years ago and they don't use it. All around them logging companies clearcut huge areas of the land that they themselves once harvested for animals. But if they wish to fell a few trees to build a house, the Ojibway need a permit from MNR. They've been living hand-to-mouth like this for many years.

Ed Machimity is a large, amiable, plain man, but there is nothing amiable about the fight that he and Violet have waged, with the support of their community, to assert the hunting and fishing rights that they believe were confirmed in the treaties. In March 1990 the chief wrote an anguished letter to Indian Affairs Minister Tom Siddon:

> We know that we were wrongfully dispossessed from our common site decades ago. We believe we have a legal claim in this matter. But we have no resources to fight it.... Until recently we were left in relative peace and quiet. But the loggers have come. The miners have come. The hydro-electric people have come. The tourist operations have come. The bureaucrats have come. All of them tell us that they have the right to regulate us in our own land. What a situation is this!

Many years ago, these people had a reserve somewhere near the town of Ignace, 130 kilometres to the south. Somehow or other they were pushed out of that reserve, driven off the land, as their elders recall, when loggers and settlers arrived. Their members were dispersed across this vast wilderness, and subjected to persistent regulation by this cold, remote and distant entity, MNR.

At first things were not too bad. People like Ed's dad, Albert, simply moved into the wilderness and carried on their lives as trappers, living in the bush all year round, following the movement of animals, and the changing seasons, as their people had always done. Later, when the industries arrived, the Saugeen people found themselves hemmed in by a myriad of regulations, until one day they were told they were squatters, and must pay MNR to lease the land that they had always thought was theirs.

Everything changed for these people when Ontario introduced trapping licences in 1946. The licences were presented as a means to protect their trapping grounds from encroachment by outsiders. So when non-native hunters appeared among them, they felt they had been betrayed by the authorities. Hunting and fishing lodges were built without their permission, causing, as the elders recall, steep declines in game and fish populations.

Ed Machimity has been carrying on his people's fight to reclaim their rights at two levels: first, to get a recognized reserve in which they can build a proper community; and second, to insist, against all the entrenched power of MNR, on recognition of their right to harvest and manage the area's wildlife. The Saugeen have been successful in the first of these objectives. They were promised a reserve in 1985. They chose the land a few miles north of Savant Lake, but nothing happened. For several years Ontario refused to hand over land for the reserve unless compensated. Finally the NDP government waived this demand, and in December 1991, the federal and provincial governments signed an agreement with Saugeen and five other remote communities further north, to provide them with a total of 610 square kilometres of reserve land, and $60.5 million for new houses, sewers, water and electricity supplies, to be built over the next seven years.

Certainly, this was progress, although $60 million does seem little enough money to build six communities for 1,200 people who, as acknowledged even by the federal minister, have been living in Third World conditions.

Chief Machimity took me from house to house to meet some of the elders. They all revealed their regret over the decline in their lives since outsiders moved in and took over their resources; discussed their cautious hope that things could get better; and admitted their anxiety about the future of their children and their culture.

"My dad was a good hunter," said one. "There were no game wardens, we could eat what we caught. We lived a happy life, a free life.

There was no liquor, no welfare."

"When we used to travel these areas, we were the government," said another. "We had freedom, nothing to fear. Now we have government guys trying to prevent us from travelling in certain areas. The government has tried to rob us of the whole land. They never go out, they stay in their offices. That's where they sit to steal."

The chief's brother, Gilbert Machimity, said: "All those years I lived in the bush, there were no taxes, just freedom. We lived on dried fish and moose meat. We picked wild rice. We picked berries and sold them to the stores."

Ed's father, Albert, born in 1915, lived with his wife in a small crowded cabin on a hill overlooking the lake. The living room was crowded with clothes, sewing machines, pots, tubs, ancient furniture and a wood stove surrounded by logs. Although in their seventies, they were still bringing up a grandchild, a baby not yet walking. Albert said: "I remember when the law started on Indian people. We began to see that something was wrong. Around 1940 we began to notice Americans coming in. I was involved in guiding them, but as more came, we felt the laws become more restrictive. They wanted everything for sports hunting. They were more concerned with their economy than with our survival." (Albert died the year after my visit.)

Everyone at Savant Lake was worried about the children. Only three from Savant Lake had made it through high school in the last ten years. They all hope that traditional values can be strengthened once they get their reserve, and their own community school, but somehow it seems to have been beyond the powers of the parents to insist that their children learn the Ojibway language. Most of the children are returning from school without skills, and settling into a life on welfare.

Throughout these visits, I kept hearing a strange story that seems to remain in the memory of the Savant Lake people as an example of the callous indifference with which they have always been treated. An Ojibway man returning from the First World War got off the train at Ignace and walked many miles back to his home. On the way he infected everyone he met with influenza. So many people died that one day a doctor, who appeared mysteriously from somewhere (no one knows where: there was no doctor at the time in Ignace, but there was one in Sioux Lookout), gathered everyone in a building said to be on Pine Island in Savant Lake, and set fire to it. One version has it that not everyone was dead when the fire was set; another

that only the dead bodies were burned; another that two men escaped from the building to tell the tale, and the son of one of those
men had died only two years before my visit. The older people had
often heard the story from that man.

Wabigoon: spirit confronts the machine

On the reserve of Wabigoon Lake, in the forests east of Lake of the
Woods, the Anishinaabe (as increasing numbers of Ojibway now call
themselves) are struggling to co-exist with the modern world while
trying to maintain their own most cherished values. There, a determined former alcoholic called Joe Pitchenesse has been working for
some years to restore traditional methods of wild rice harvesting. At
Wabigoon they now claim that their product, Kagiwiosa Manomin,
is the best wild rice in the world. They are selling it to organic-food
distributors in Europe and Japan, but their insistence on reasserting
the spiritual importance of the plant, on doing everything in the traditional way – supervising its growth, and organizing the harvest,
picking and processing according to methods handed down from the
elders, with all the necessary ceremonies and celebrations – has brought
them up against government officials and businessmen who believe that
mechanized, chemical methods are needed to maximize production.

For Joe Pitchenesse wild rice, *manomin*, is not just a product but a
natural element alive with spiritual power. He believes his people develop their sense of self-worth through the ritual and community involvement during the *manomin* harvest. In 1990, Pitchenesse wrote in
a paper delivered to a wild rice committee:

> *Manomin* carries the memories and experience of our people.... When the
> Anishinaabe people treat the *manomin* with proper respect, then *manomin*
> responds by giving itself up for the sustenance and livelihood of the
> people.... Anishinaabe people are bound to respect the spirituality of
> *manomin* and their relationship to the plant.[2]

This is a similar ethic to that governing the relationship between
an aboriginal hunter and the animals he hunts: provided the hunter
behaves with proper respect, the animal gives itself to the hunter for
the sustenance of his family.

The Anishinaabe believe the *manomin* lakes must be held in communal ownership. The *manomin* responds to the specific body of
water in which it grows. Thus some grains will naturally be larger

than others, some areas more or less productive, depending on the ecological dynamic of each area. Every *manomin* lake cannot always produce to the maximum, as industrial growers would wish. "This is what our spirituality teaches us to respect. It results in the maintenance of biotic diversity.... When chemicals were added to one of our most important rice lakes, no white man can imagine the turmoil and pain this caused in our community, especially to our elders."

Joe Pitchenesse learned about wild rice by paddling for his grandmother, Maggie Chief, who lived until she was 102. Later, his father, Paul, was a rice boss, one of those who organized and oversaw the rice harvest.

The bosses were, and still are, chosen at meetings of the heads of families. They have to know how the rice is growing, so that the required feasts and rituals can be held. They decide when the grain is ready for harvesting, and assign areas to different families to assure an equitable harvest for all. They maintain order and ensure that enough is always left for the animals and birds.

As a child Joe was hidden by his parents when the priests came to take the children to the residential schools. Eventually he attended an Indian Affairs school built on the reserve, and afterwards took a mechanics course at Thunder Bay. Then he became a logger, and, like so many young Indians of his time, a drinker. As drinkers, they didn't fool around: he remembers one weekend when just three of them finished off twenty-seven cases of beer.

When he returned to the reserve in 1978, Joe found the rice harvest in decline. The people were being threatened that their rice lakes would be given to white competitors. So Joe quit drinking and became a rice boss like his father before him.

Now the community co-op, Kagiwiosa Manomin Inc., is producing for a commercial market – using computers in the office, but strictly organic methods of production. In the old days, native pickers would get seven cents a pound for rice that retailed at up to $20. Today the co-op pays the pickers $1 a pound, twice the rate paid by non-native companies. They cure their *manomin* in a row of seven "parchers", poplar-burning ovens developed with the help of the Mennonite Central Committee; the parchers get rid of the moisture, harden the grain and bring out the flavour. Joe's sister, Mary-Rose, knows the secret, which she really can't explain to anybody, of when it is done just right. "You can tell by how it feels and smells," she says. "I learned it from Mum." Her mother, May, always knew by feel, smell and sound exactly when the rice was toasted to perfection. The kernel was then detached from the hull by being trampled by mocassin-clad feet. Today's custom-built parching ovens have been designed to duplicate May's expertise. The mark of excellence is that the processed rice sold in the shops takes only fifteen minutes to cook, compared with perhaps an hour or more for rice prepared by more commercial methods. But the big difference, according to Mary-Rose, is that the commercial producers lay the rice out and allow it to ferment before processing it, resulting in a harder, more brittle grain whose shiny black appearance is designed to appeal to the consumer. Certainly, you can tell the difference in flavour, as I discovered when I ate the Wabigoon rice, the best I have ever tasted. A Canadian supermarket chain offered to buy all the Wabigoon production, but the mass-marketing approach of such chains does not fit Joe's idea of proper human relationships, and he refused.

Wabigoon provides a prime example of how native perceptions about land-use so often clash with the ideas of white administrators. A 1978 moratorium restricted harvesting in northwest Ontario to natives. Government then tightened its control by issuing block licences, so that for the first time the Anishinaabe had to seek a licence to harvest *manomin*. Even within this system, some lakes whose *manomin* stands had been tended by Wabigoon people for generations were given by government to white entrepreneurs. In recent years these entrepreneurs have joined with government officials to press for a review of the moratorium, and for elimination of the native block licenses. They say that production has fallen behind the commercial methods used in other provinces. Pitchenesse is determined that his people will lose no more of their lakes.

"[To allow] individual licensing of lakes with no regard to...the centuries of aboriginal seeding, harvesting and caring for *manomin* stands, would not only be a mistake, but an out-and-out crime," wrote Joe Pitchenesse to a Thunder Bay newspaper.

He accused government officials of:

> ...constantly attacking our very fragile existence. It is hard, as a native, not to be totally cynical due to past experience. Just look at the trapping industry as an example. How is it that bureaucrats always come in with big plans, and we land up on the sidelines looking on as spectators?

Over-production develops...when too many greenhorns have too many get-rich-quick solutions.... Then the complaints start about negative return on investment.... Blame again is imminent and seemingly never ending. So it is with wild rice.[3]

Shoal Lake: "No acknowledgement that we live here"

The people of Shoal Lake reserve number 39, sixty miles west of Kenora, near the Manitoba border, have suffered enormously from the destruction of their economy to serve the needs of Euro-Canadians. The reserve's economic lifeblood was drained when Winnipeg tapped into Shoal Lake for its water supply in 1918. The changed water levels wiped out wild rice from many bays that had always been loaded with rice. Wild rice was as central to the reserve's culture as it is in Wabigoon Lake, and the people never recovered, although they could have, if given half a chance.

Some years later they developed a successful walleye fishery, but cottagers and tourist lodges began to compete for the fish, and the Ojibway fishery was closed by the government, supposedly for five years. Fifteen years later, it is still closed. There was no consultation or compensation. "There was never any acknowledgement that we live here," says Chief Eli Mandamin. With nothing to do but sit around and wait for the next welfare cheque, people who had been prosperous, self-sufficient and independent fishermen started to drink. Many eventually became so desperate they would sell off their furniture to get a bottle.

Still only in his early thirties, Chief Mandamin grew up in the tragic social circumstances of a degenerating community. He became a full-time drinker at the age of nine, and kept at it for fourteen years. "I grew up with a sense of not being anything. Drinking was an alternative to suicide." He got into serious trouble dealing drugs, and emerged from a long prison sentence with, at last, a knowledge of "what alcohol really is". When he returned to the reserve, he was ordered by his peers to join a sacred circle, whose members told him he must give everything away. Following these instructions, he gave away all his worldly possessions. "When you give everything away, it is surprising how things drift back in your direction." Eight years after he quit drinking, he was elected chief at the age of thirty-one, a notable act of forgiveness and tolerance, which I wonder if we could match in our society.

Eli and his Uncle Steve, a band councillor, opened the band office on a Sunday afternoon to meet with me. Eli said that normally, before meeting me, he would have had me meet with an elder "to create an atmosphere of openness and understanding". But since no elder was available "I have left my drum open at home, so that understanding can be achieved".

Steve is also a recovered alcoholic. Now in his forties, with a family of three, he believes he is still marked by his childhood experience at the Cecilia Jaffray school at Rabbit Lake, where "we always had a pair of eyes looking over our shoulders. We weren't free. About half the teachers were religious, half laymen. Sometimes I wish I could forget them. The skills they taught us were not the skills of survival."

Steve believes such experiences explain why it is still hard to motivate people in the reserve. "Whatever we do, they feel they are not part of it," he said.

The Shoal Lake people believe that government policies and regulations cannot help but undermine their economy and way of life because government assumes that natural resources are state assets to be allocated to users on a competitive basis. A whole change in attitude is needed, Chief Mandamin said, if Ontario practice is to be brought into line with the Brundtland recommendation that indigenous people should have "a decisive voice in the management of resources in their traditional lands".

"It is very scary what the white man is doing," the chief said. "But perhaps the whites are going to exhaust themselves. Eventually they will get their senses back." He gave a mysterious, confident smile. "You know, we are not going anywhere, and I believe we are here for a purpose."

He took me for a drive around the lovely reserve lands, which meander across the hills and around the bays of the lake. Because of the lack of work, only about 270 of the band's 400 members live in the reserve. Their big problem is that all development in the region is for Euro-Canadians, who not only press their schemes regardless of their effect on the aboriginals, but oppose projects that could possibly lift the reserves out of stagnation.

For example, there are already 800 cottages around the shoreline of Falcon Lake, which is in the same watershed as Shoal Lake. As the aboriginals see it, these cottagers "bring everything from Winnipeg and contribute nothing to our economy.... Their pollution drifts down in our direction, and we end up with it all." The cottagers resent any scheme that they feel might damage their vacation environment. Here is the rub for the aboriginals. At the time of my visit, the cottagers were strongly opposing a proposal that gold mines should be reopened in an area to which the band controls access. "We are trying to channel all the transportation for the mine through here," said the chief. "That will require that we build a motel, laundromat, and so on." The mining company had agreed to train band members and employ them up to executive level. The Ojibways wonder why their Euro-Canadian neighbours should be trying to prevent them from creating an economy to replace the one already destroyed by non-Indians.

As we entered a round house that they have built for ceremonies, Eli ran tobacco down each of the central posts and placed it on the ground, in offering to the Earth. There has been a revival in the reserve of Ojibway customs, including that of the Mediwewin society, the Anishinaabe religion whose four doorways extend west into Manitoba, east as far as Toronto, and down into the United States, part of the religious revival that is strengthening the confidence of aboriginal people as they move to change their relationship with Euro-Canadians.

The deal, as they see it

"We have researched the conditions at the time that we signed our treaty in 1873," said Charles Wagamase, an activist and official with Treaty 3 Grand Council, based in Kenora.

"Our people were well aware of what the treaty was, and were perfectly content with how they were living. It was not a life of drudgery and suffering. There were a lot of beautiful songs and ceremonies. There is a lot of evidence people were living a good life here which they did not want to change."

We were lunching in the dining room of a tall modern hotel in Kenora, on that same lakeshore road along which my wife and I used to walk to the bus in the 1950s. Charles is a tall, lean man of about forty. The deep copper tone of his skin and the jet-black hair falling around his shoulders suggest a family whose Ojibway blood has been not much diluted through intermarriage. His manner is polite and conciliatory. He speaks softly, but with an intensity that is reflected in his challenging gaze.

"Nobody gives up everything for a welfare cheque. So what we are after now is the same thing as our ancestors offered these people in

1873, and what they offered us."

And what was that deal? I asked. He told me in story form.

"My uncles and I were out hunting back then. We met a guy with a white face and a beard, in a clearing. There were five of us and one of him, and we could not talk, we had no common language. We had to try to find out what this guy was doing here. Our way is to be kind first of all, and strong, as a second approach.

"We find out he needs a place to live, to raise his kids. He says, 'I want to come and live with you people.' He wants to share this beautiful country with us, every square foot of which we use. Every little pond, somebody travels it and knows it.

"We take it back and think about it. We know what is going on. There is active trading all over North America. We have made deals in the past with the Sioux and Mohawks. We are well aware of the Indian wars. We can use violence and eject him, or come to some kind of arrangement. That's what we did."

He looks around the room at all the diners, most of them Euro-Canadians, apparently on business. "I am a treaty person," he says. "So is every non-native person here. The only reason they are here is because of the treaty. We made arrangements on minerals, hunting and fishing, economic development, and in exchange we agreed to share 55,000 square miles of rich, rich country."

A confident, prosperous people

In September 1873, treaty commissioner Alexander Morris, representing the Canadian government, had to wait at the northwest angle of the Lake of the Woods for almost a week before the 800 Ojibway who had gathered – the forebears of the Machimitys, the Mandamins, Joe Pitchenesse and Charles Wagamase – were ready to talk to him. Four years before at a general council, the Ojibway had decided on the terms they would present to Morris. Their main concern was their continuing ownership of the land, and their need to preserve the right to hunt and fish in their traditional areas. In addition, they wanted help to improve their cultivation of the soil. They had already created nearly 200 acres of gardens and farms, most of them scattered across the many islands in Lake of the Woods, where soils and climate were most favourable to agriculture. They had watched more and more strangers coming into and across their country, and they realized agriculture would be important to their future.

194

The people who now confronted Morris were confident, productive, ingenious, prosperous and warlike. Three times already they had turned back emissaries sent by the Canadian government to make a treaty, each time insisting that northwestern Ontario was their land, and they wanted proper compensation for their co-operation in allowing others to use it.

Until about 1850, most of the Europeans they had encountered were simply travellers on the way to somewhere else, people like LaVérendrye in 1731, and Alexander Mackenzie in the 1790s, who wrote glowing accounts of the Ojibway country – its lakes teeming with fish, its forests and game, its independent people so skilful in tapping the resources of the land. [4]

The Europeans established trading posts, and the Ojibway sold them fish and other supplies. The aboriginals had developed a diversified economy using all the resources of the land – fur, fish, wild rice, corn, potatoes and other vegetables, large and small game, maple sugar, and manufactured items like pitch, twines and canoes.[5] This economy was so strong that in the half-century following the 1820s, the aboriginal population of the area grew from fewer than 500 to more than 2,500.

Hudson's Bay Company records from the first years of the nineteenth century speak eloquently of the size of the Ojibway sturgeon fishery, one of the most productive in North America. The Ojibway would gather in their hundreds at the rapids on their many surging rivers and take huge numbers of the fish with hooks and lines, spears, harpoons, weirs and nets. A popular method was to spear the fish from wooden platforms built out over the rapids. The Ojibway used every part of the fish, curing and storing much for later use, and making a special pemmican from the pounded flesh and oil. Sturgeon oil was used as a condiment. The roe (or caviar) was eaten. A profitable trade was done in a substance known as isinglass, manufactured by the Ojibway from gelatin obtained from the air bladder of the fish. Each sturgeon yielded about an ounce of isinglass; its preparation was a long process of cleaning, washing, scraping, drying, pressing and packaging. The substance was in high demand in European industrial centres during the fur trade period, especially for making glue, and as a clarifying agent for wine and beer.

"The glue the natives saves out of the sturgeon is very strong and good," remarked James Isham, a Hudson's Bay Company trader, in

1743. "They use itt in mixing with the paint, and itt fixes the Colours so they never Rub out."[6]

For more than sixty years, the Ojibway of this area sold 1,000 pounds of isinglass every year, and usually earned more from it than from beaver. [7]

No one who rubbed up against the Ojibway was left in any doubt that they considered themselves in complete control of their land. They frequently went to war with the Sioux. As late as 1857, the explorer Harry Youle Hind met forty-six warriors on an island in Lake of the Woods "who had just returned" from an expedition against their enemies.[8] Hind had helped himself to vegetables from Ojibway gardens; he was reprimanded by Ojibway leaders and was ordered not to stray off the regular travel route approved by them. Their chief told him:

> We do not want the white man; when the white man comes, he brings disease and sickness, and our people perish; we do not want to die. Many white men would bring death to us, and our people would pass away; we wish to live and to hold the land our fathers won, and the Great Spirit has given us. [9]

The Ojibway were described by explorer Sir John Richardson in 1849 as

> ...saucy, and independent of the Hudson's Bay Company, from the fact that they have abundance of sturgeon and great quantities of wild rice.... They are certainly of an independent, and I should say, unmanageable disposition; and their natural ferocity is not lessened by their constant wars with the Sioux.[10]

A reluctance to sign

But Europeans were coming, whether the Ojibway liked it or not. In 1857 the Royal Geographical Society sent an expedition under John Palliser overland to the Red River (now Winnipeg). Palliser met Indians all along the way who were "anxious to know what the Queen intended to do with the country when it was taken from the Hudson's Bay Company" (as it was thirteen years later). Palliser promised them that the white man would never take their land by force.[11]

The following year, a surveyor who later became a Member of Parliament, Simon J. Dawson, made an exploratory trip through the Lake of the Woods area to Red River. He held "a grand council" with the Indians on Lake of the Woods. "They made no opposition to his passage after he had provided them with the usual presents of tobacco and tea, but they appear to desire to have it clearly understood that the country is theirs, and they do not abandon any of their rights by permitting the government surveyors to pass."[12]

Dawson came to know the Ojibway better than any other European, and in 1868 he wrote:

> They are very intelligent, and are extremely jealous as to their right of soil and authority over the country which they occupy.... They are shrewd and sufficiently awake to their own interests...and they neither reply to a proposition, nor make one themselves, until it is fully discussed and deliberated upon in Council of all the chiefs.... At these gatherings it is a necessity to observe extreme caution in what is said, as, although they have no means of writing, there are always those present who are charged to keep every word in mind.[13]

In 1868 the Ontario government began to build a road, the so-called Dawson route, from Lake of the Woods towards Red River, without waiting for legal formalities. Steamers began to operate on the lake,[14] which did not improve the attitude of the Ojibway chiefs. By 1869 the Canadian government's need for an agreement with the Ojibway had become urgent, not to say desperate. In that year, William McDougall was appointed Lieutenant-Governor of the whole territory to the west. McDougall did not have a sure touch with native issues: he had bungled the surrender of aboriginal land on Manitoulin Island in 1860, and he had no more luck on this occasion. On his way to take up his appointment, he travelled through the United States, but was stopped from entering Red River by the Métis, led by Louis Riel.

The result of that confrontation was that Manitoba joined Canada in 1870. More than ever, the Canadian government needed to obtain safe passage through Ojibway country. Emissaries were again sent out, and the Ojibway repeated what they had told Dawson more than a decade before: they were not going to give away their land for nothing, and they wanted a comprehensive treaty. They remained so recalcitrant that the treaty commissioners moved into Manitoba where they signed Treaties 1 and 2, while the forest Indians continued to stall.

In 1871 a commissioner was sent to Fort Frances, authorized to negotiate right-of-way through the Ojibway territory. For a second

time the Ojibway refused to sign, although they agreed not to interfere with travellers. The commissioners returned in 1872 with more
concrete proposals, but for a third time the Ojibway refused. The
commissioners reported:

> ...[the Ojibway] are well informed as to the discovery of gold and silver
> to the west of the watershed, and have not been slow to give us their
> views as to the value of that discovery. "You offer us," said they, "three
> dollars per head, and you have only to pick up gold and silver from our
> rocks to pay it many times over." The chief of the section where the dis-
> coveries had taken place was emphatic in expressing his determination
> to keep miners from his country until he had been paid for his land.[15]

Next came Alexander Morris. Morris wanted access for Canadians
into and through the 55,000 square miles of the Ojibway country.
He had already decided he would offer an annuity of $5 a head, pre-
sents of $10 a head, and reserve lands amounting to one square mile
(640 acres) for every family of five.

But the chiefs wanted more: $10 a head annuity, a $15 present, $50
a year for each chief, and other amounts totalling $125,000 a year. If
these demands were satisfied, they said, they would talk about the land.

"This is what we think," said the leading Indian spokesman,
Mawodopenais, "that the Great Spirit has planted us on this ground
where we are, as you were where you came from. We think where we
are is our property."[16] Another chief said: "The sound of the rustling
of gold is under my feet where I stand. We have a rich country. It is
the Great Spirit who gave us this. Where we stand upon is the
Indians' property and belongs to them."[17] Yet another said: "...It is
our chiefs, our young men, our children and great-grandchildren and
those that are to be born that I represent here.... The white man has
robbed us of our riches, and we don't wish to give them up again
without getting something in their place."[18]

This feeling that they had been robbed came from their unhappiness with the Dawson route. The Ojibway believed they should have
been paid for the wood used to build and operate the lake steamers,
and for the use of the route itself. They wanted to talk about that before discussing anything else. Dawson had paid the Ojibway three
dollars a head in the first year the Dawson route was used, but they
had received nothing since. Dawson was part of Morris's negotiating
team, and he now told the chiefs that he had paid them for cutting

wood, but had always asserted "a common right to the use of wood and the water way".

Morris decided to brazen it out, asserting that the land was owned by the Crown, and the wood was free to those who cut it. "Wood and water," he said grandly, "were the gift of the Great Spirit, and were made alike for the good of both the white man and red man."

"What you say about the trees and rivers is quite true," responded a chief, "but it is the Indian's country, not the white man's." The Indian feeling was so strong, Morris wrote later, that if he had failed to make the treaty, within a year the government would have been compelled to send an armed force to defend the water route.

The chiefs also produced a formidable list of demands for agricultural support. They asked for substantial quantities of stock, seed and implements: cattle ("ten cows and one bull") oxen, teams of horses, lambs, pigs, ploughs, harrows, garden tools, and thirty bushels of seed wheat, twenty bushels of peas, and various kinds of garden seed.[19] They asked that each chief should receive these materials every four to eight years. These demands reveal a serious commitment to continue with the diversification of their economy. One chief in particular, who lived near the English River south of Lac Seul, said he already had 200 barrels of potatoes, but insisted that he wanted oats, turnip and barley seed for the next year's planting.[20]

Modern researchers have estimated that at around the time of the treaty, the Lake of the Woods Ojibway were already growing enough corn, potatoes and wild rice to sustain all of them for 193 days out of the year. This was about half of what they needed for basic sustenance; they caught enough sturgeon every year to provide the other half.[21]

All these demands had been worked out over the previous four years, but Morris refused even to discuss them. Then one chief came forward representing 400 people from Lac Seul. He said his people wished a treaty. They wished a schoolteacher to teach their children the knowledge of the white man. They wished for some grain and seeds, implements and cattle. This was the break in the Indian front that Morris had been hoping for. He had always known, he said, that the chiefs were not of one mind. They should go and talk it over again.

When negotiations resumed, another five hours of hard bargaining over details ensued. The chiefs wanted, and were refused, free passes on the Canadian Pacific Railway. They wanted, and won, a

prohibition on liquor in their reserves, and freedom from being con-
scripted to fight in the white man's wars. They asked if the mines
would be theirs, or if an Indian who found a mineral would be paid
for it. "I told them," reported Morris, "that he could sell his information if he could find a purchaser, like any other person." This left the
impression that they would profit from future mines, but no mention
was made of this in the treaty.

Finally, ten days after the two sides had gathered, twenty-four
chiefs signed, accepting $4 a head annuity, $12 a head as presents, a
sum of $1,500 for ammunition, $25 a year to each chief, and some
clothes, flags and medals. They did not obtain anything like the agricultural help they had asked for, but were given an extensive inventory of tools and implements, as well as oxen, wheat, barley, potatoes
and oats. The chiefs undertook to maintain peace with the whites, and
not to trouble those who took up residence among them, or who travelled through the territory. They were promised reserves covering
their main locations, where the government agreed to maintain schools.

For many years the Ojibway had used maple groves, fishing stations, berry patches, garden sites and wild rice beds, so when they
came to select their reserves they had many places to protect. The
government agreed they should have "farming reserves" (essentially,
the islands on which they had most of their gardens), as well as "wild
land reserves".[22]

An Ojibway priority was to protect the sturgeon fishery. This had
been promised even in the order-in-council of 1871 setting up the
negotiating commission, and when the treaty was written it said that
"the Indians shall have the right to pursue their avocations of hunting
and fishing throughout the tract surrendered....subject to such regulations as may from time to time be made" by the government, and
"saving and excepting" any lands that might in future be needed for
settlement, mining, lumbering or other purposes.[23]

Two of the major fishing sites, at Manitou Rapids and Long Sault
on Rainy River, were set aside in circumstances that appeared to confirm the uninterrupted Indian right to fish there. The government
added a rider that if locks or other public works were needed at those
sites, and if these destroyed the fishery, the Indians must be "fairly
dealt with in consequence".[24] It appears that both government and
the aboriginals assumed the country would continue to be populated
mainly by Indians for the indefinite future, and it was therefore

unnecessary to go into detail about the exact meaning of the fishing right. Morris told the Indians: "It may be a long time before the other lands [that is, lands other than Indian reserves] are wanted, and in the meantime you will be permitted to fish and hunt over them."[25] Taken in conjunction with the promise of protection for their fishing sites, Morris's statement offered the Ojibway more than later Canadian administrators were ready to grant.

In return for all these concessions and promises, the Ojibway ceded their rights in 35 million acres. The terms of the treaty were more generous than those of the two treaties signed in Manitoba,[26] but the wording is portentous:

> The Saulteaux tribe of the Ojibbeway Indians, and all other the Indians inhabiting the district hereinafter described and defined, do hereby cede, release, surrender, and yield up to the government of the Dominion of Canada, for Her Majesty the Queen and her successors forever, all their rights, titles and privileges whatsoever to the lands included within the following limits....[27]

The concluding ceremonies were solemn, and, in light of what has happened since, poignant. Mawodopenais said:

> I take off my glove and in giving you my hand I deliver over my birthright and lands; and in taking your hand, I hold fast all the promises you have made, and I hope they will last as long as the sun goes round and the water flows.[28]

A sense of betrayal

"People do not make a treaty to become poor, to have their children suffer, to go from being respected to being assaulted and humiliated," Charles Wagamase told me. "A hundred and twenty years later your people are saying, 'We are here, we are now established and rich, we don't think we have a deal anymore.' " He looked at me as if hoping that somehow I could explain this. "We gave them our hand. We signed these treaties. And people now say, to hell with you Indians. You're just a bunch of welfare cases, alcoholics. We are tired of supporting you."

He gazed around the hotel dining room reflectively, as if trying to look into the minds of everyone there. There was a long silence. Then he looked back at me and asked, "How did they come to that mind?"

The Ojibway believe, he said, that the treaty provided for education and economic development, but they had never been given the opportunity to develop equally with the whites. "As Indian people we recognize that the land has rights, we have to be responsible to the land and ourselves. There are ways to do that so everyone would benefit. Clearcutting a forest is an assault, a destruction of life, turning land into a desert. That's no way to take care of this place. If we had been allowed to involve ourselves over the last 150 years we would be setting forestry policies, we'd be running companies, and income would be coming into our communities.

"I think the people of Canada have to look in the mirror and ask themselves why they don't keep their deals. Where it gets tough is that our reasonable solutions are always rejected.

"I deal with government people every day. I try to move these issues forward. Sometimes I get, not angry any more.... I look across the table at these people, and I say to myself, these guys, their job is to keep our people poor. We have to try to trick them into giving our people a decent opportunity in life."

Working to create poverty

The Euro-Canadians who moved into the area in the years following the treaty assumed, like Dawson and Morris during the negotiations, that the land was now theirs, Crown land, and the Indians had no further rights in it, except in the small areas set aside for reserves. The fact that Indians continued to use all the land in accordance with the promise made in the treaty was regarded as a temporary irrelevance.

For ten years or so, events unfolded rather as the Ojibway had hoped. They put enormous work into clearing land on their reserves, and did so while also hunting and fishing. Unlike Indians who went into reserves in western Canada, the Ojibway did not have to be provided with government rations. They were self-sufficient, and even prosperous, as many accounts of the time attest.

They worked against great odds, however. The agricultural equipment they were given was so shoddy that the Indian Commissioner in Winnipeg, J.A.N. Provencher (who had helped Morris negotiate the treaty), was found guilty by a departmental inquiry of "defrauding the Indians" by deliberately supplying them with inferior equipment and stock.[29]

Nor did the government keep its educational promise: the chiefs believed education should include training in farming and building, but the government refused this type of help and did not appoint a farming agent until the 1890s.

In spite of all difficulties, by 1882 the Ojibway had 214 acres under cultivation, and two years later Ebenezer McColl, who succeeded Provencher, reported from Rainy River:

> The industry and perseverance of these Indians are most remarkable. The appearance of their magnificent gardens would excite the admiration of the most advanced agriculturalists. Their request for five bushels of seed wheat, a cradle, and a breaking plough, is deserving of favourable consideration.[30]

The Ojibway did not realize that, even while the treaty was being negotiated, the government was establishing regulations for fishing, land use and commerce which rendered meaningless the promises given in the treaty. The policies that rapidly reduced the Ojibway to penury have been meticulously researched for the Ojibway by Tim Holzkamm and Leo Waisberg. Here are some of them:

The destruction of the sturgeon fishery:

A federal Fisheries Act passed in 1868, five years before the signing of the treaty, prohibited fishing for trout and whitefish between certain dates, banned net fishing on Sundays, banned spear fishing (except for Indians with permits from the minister) and provided for a closed season by regulation, thus creating the conditions in which the Indian fishery could be handed over to others.

Within a decade, commercial fish companies selling into the United States were permitted to operate on Lake of the Woods, and began a devastation of the sturgeon population that must rank as one of the worst ecological disasters in our history. For many decades the Ojibway had maintained the harvest of sturgeon at between 250,000 and 400,000 pounds a year. In the first half of the 1880s, the commercial companies more than doubled the take to an average 864,000 pounds a year, and in the last part of that decade to 1,250,000 pounds. Naturally, the Ojibway fishery began to collapse. In 1894 Manitou and Long Sault, the essential centres of the Ojibway economy, reported "no fish", while great scarcity was reported from every other place invaded by the commercial fishermen. In contrast, the lakes where Ojibway remained in control – Wabuskang, Lac Seul, Wabigoon, Shoal Lake, Whitefish Bay – continued to report large catches.[31]

The fishery could not sustain such depredations. Within five years the average yearly catch had dropped to 137,000 pounds. In 1907 pollution from a new pulp and paper mill in Fort Frances further degraded the sturgeon spawning grounds. The decline continued until by 1925 not even 2,000 pounds were being shipped. It has remained at that level ever since.

In the House of Commons Simon Dawson raised the question of the Ojibway treaty right to fish, but was coldly told by Sir John A. Macdonald that the right was not exclusive. Dawson wrote to the Deputy Minister of Indian Affairs:

> As an inducement to the Indians to sign the treaty, the commissioners pointed out to them that...they would forever have the use of their fisheries. This point was strongly insisted on and it had great weight with the Indians, who for some years previously had persistently refused to enter into any treaty. Now, if in breach of this, the white man is about to sweep the waters of every living thing down to a minnow, what becomes of the stipulation in the treaty?[32]

Thanks to Dawson's campaign over many years, fishing was eventually made exclusive to the Ojibway on Lake of the Woods. The British government was asked to intervene with the Americans to stop commercial fishing on their side of the lake, but this was never done. After the turn of the century, the Ontario government stepped in, overriding the lethargic Indian Affairs department with policies frankly hostile to Indian rights. With the destruction of the sturgeon fishery, the first nail had been driven into the coffin of the Ojibway economy.

The destruction of Ojibway agriculture:

Poor equipment, seed and cattle, some seasons of early frost and drought, plagues of flies and grasshoppers – all these played a role in the rapid decline of the promising Ojibway effort in agriculture. But more important was an amendment to the Indian Act in 1881 empowering the government to prohibit the "sale, barter, exchange or gift of any grain or root crops or other produce grown upon any Indian reserve."[33] The prohibition was really designed for western Canada, but the Lake of the Woods region was not declared part of Ontario until 1899, so the restrictions were applied there too. Chiefs were warned that they could be deposed if they sold food without permission, and purchasers were discouraged by the prospect of a large fine if they were caught buying Indian produce. Chiefs immediately began to complain about having their produce rot. It became impossible to persuade their young men to practise farming when they were not allowed to sell their surpluses. This ridiculous policy strangled Ojibway agriculture.

Land under cultivation began to decline after 1890, as younger men took work in the bush and on the steamers, and returned to hunting and fishing for subsistence. The government increased, rather than reduced its controls: for example, by using surplus hay to support government-owned cattle, and deferring payments.[34] All such measures added to the economic pressures on the Ojibway.

Construction in 1887 of a dam to improve navigation at the outlet of Lake of the Woods flooded many low-lying hay fields, gardens and precious wild rice fields. The Grand Council pleaded for some protection, but the building of dams was just beginning. Six years later, a hydroelectric dam was built on Lake of the Woods, raising the water level by more than six feet. Later, dams built at Lake Wabigoon, Rainy Lake, Lac Seul, and on the Winnipeg and English rivers destroyed more gardens, meadows and wild rice beds, affected muskrat and other animal habitats, killed shoreline timber, and flooded reserve lands, villages and cemeteries.[35]

The imposition of Euro-Canadian game laws:

The Ojibway customarily sold surplus fur, meat, leather and other animal products to supplement their incomes until the last years of the nineteenth century. But as soon as Ontario took control in 1899, the provincial government stepped in to restrict the hunting rights granted under the treaty, just as they were doing with the fishing rights. "Many instances of absolute persecution of Indians on the part of officious game wardens have been reported," wrote H.J. Bury, federal supervisor of Indian Timber Lands, in 1929.[36] He mentioned that one warden had recently confiscated all the deer meat the Islington band had killed for food, and also the skins they needed for moccasins. The province's attitude, unvarying over the decades, was summed up by the statement of a deputy minister of game and fisheries in 1939, to the effect that the Indians were not going to be allowed to live on the province's moose, deer and fish, and some other way should be devised for them to make a living. The province manipulated its regulations to open reserved Indian fishing spots to all comers, thus brutally violating the Indian fishing right. Then it began prosecuting those who exercised their game rights, a policy that has continued right into our own times.

No chance of employment:

When the mining and forestry industries first moved into the area, the Ojibway were the only source of available labour; they worked in gold mines, on steamboats, on railway construction, in lumber camps, and in helping settlers to clear fields. "I have much satisfaction in saying that they are among the best and steadiest labourers we have had," remarked Simon Dawson, reporting in 1871 on Ojibway working on the transportation route.[37] But as more whites moved into the area, employers, "unwilling to tolerate cultural differences in the logging camps", ceased to give them jobs.[38] Shut out of the broader forest industry, the Ojibway were also prevented by the government from cutting the small forests on their own reserves. Instead, permits were given to outsiders to cut reserve forests, and the proceeds were placed in trust for the bands. As early as 1883, a departmental report from the Assabaskasing agency complained that the department had allowed the Indians to be "defrauded of their most valuable inheritance" by unscrupulous lumbermen who were allowed to violate the law and go unpunished.[39]

Similarly, the informal treaty promises about mines were ignored. As more whites moved into the area, not only were the Ojibway no longer offered work in the mines, but, with the encouragement of the Ontario government, year after year thousands of acres of Indian reserve lands were appropriated for non-Indian use. At least one mine was developed right on Rat Portage reserve (Kenora), and the Indians received nothing from it.[40]

In the decades following the treaty, the major transportation routes linking east and west were driven through land every inch of which, as Charles Wagamase said, was known and used by native hunters. In 1925 new gold mines made Red Lake into the busiest freight airport in the world. Huge paper mills were built at Kenora, Fort Frances, Dryden and Thunder Bay, fed by widespread logging throughout the territory. The whole area became dotted with hydro dams, power stations, reservoirs and transmission lines. Finally, the lakes were handed over to tourist lodges and weekend cottages for city people.

All this development took place on land that the Indians had been told, years before, whites would not be interested in. When the federal government transferred land to the provinces, the Ontario government began to call the shots about how it would be used. As I discovered during my visit in 1991, over the years the initials MNR – the provincial Ministry of Natural Resources – have attained a sinister connotation for the Indians. No wonder: usually, MNR land-use regulations were drawn up on the assumption that the Indians were not there.

Pushed to the margins

The Ojibway lived in such a way that their work, culture, language, religion and values all arose from their activities on the land. When their wild rice harvesting, fishing, hunting and trapping were undercut, not only were they impoverished economically, but in spirit also. Wrote H.J. Bury, in his indignant 1929 memorandum to the Deputy Minister of Indian Affairs:

> The Lake of the Woods Indians are physically suffering from the wrongful treatment meted out to them by the province, patiently awaiting the time when their wrongs will be redressed and their rights vindicated.... [They] are possibly facing today the worst conditions of living that they have ever experienced. Prevented from hunting for food, restricted from commercial fishing, failing to secure a blueberry crop, they will assuredly need all the help and assistance that it is possible to give them to tide them over the winters.[41]

Bury urged that the Ojibway be given the right to take game and fish for food at any time, be assigned exclusive trapping areas, and given priority in commercial fishing. Nothing was done. Their decline continued.

In 1946, Tom Roy, speaking for Grand Council Treaty 3, told the parliamentary joint committee described in Chapter 10:

> We contend that the terms of [our] treaty were violated or abrogated by the federal government on or about April 16, 1894 when, without notifying the Indians, the federal government transferred the natural resources to the provinces, with whose laws we have to comply since then. The Indians have tried to protest against this; they have made trips here to Ottawa asking the Indian department for protection. The answer has been: "This comes entirely under the provincial governments, and there is no authority whatever vested in our department to change their laws."[42]

Roy said that in 1944 he interpreted in court for two members of the Whitefish Bay band who set their nets outside the reserve and were charged with violations of Ontario's game laws. He said thirty-six heads of family from the reserve were given the same commercial fishing licence as was given to one white man outside the reserve. The lake was overcrowded, and Roy said:

> According to the terms of our treaty, they claimed it was their right to fish anywhere outside the reserve, as promised in the avocation guaran tee.... The magistrate found the boys guilty under violation of the Game and Fisheries Act, and that the treaty no longer existed, or was recognized by provincial authorities.... Several of our nets have been confiscated time and again by the provincial game wardens.... This is just to let the committee know and ask that some protection be given to these Indians of their aboriginal rights which were guaranteed to them by Her Majesty the Queen.

It would be good to be able to report that things have changed for the Ojibway in the half-century since Tom Roy made his complaint to the joint committee. But as I found in 1991 during my visits to the reserves, the attitudes and policies that have undermined the Ojibway persist to this day. Northwestern Ontario is still in the grip of MNR; treaty hunting and fishing rights are still being regularly violated; government bureaucracies still hinder Ojibway economic activities such as wild rice harvesting and commercial fishing. In all of this, the Ojibway have run up against assumptions that are deeply embedded in the Euro-Canadian psyche. When MNR makes regulations to permit logging, mining, sports hunting and fishing, or hydroelectric operations designed for Euro-Canadians, the Ministry sees itself as merely engaged in sound administration on our behalf. From the Anishinaabe point of view, these regulations are designed to take over, for the benefit of outsiders, land on which the Anishinaabe have always been capable of living a good life. To them, our sound administration looks remarkably like theft.

How much time is left?
"I think there are some things that give us hope," said Charles Wagamase. "But at other times I question this hope. We cannot allow all of this to become anger and bitterness. We have to try to figure out some solution.

"The last twenty years of welfare have been very, very destructive. We have to find working opportunities for our people. The scariest part is that very little hope is being offered to the people under twenty-five. Right now their violence is directed inward, but as we educate them about the treaties, and why their lives are the way they are, I can feel a backlash growing. These young people are not going to sit across the table and play word games, as we have been doing. They are going to take that table and turn it over. It is crucial for us, and for non-natives, to show that solutions can be achieved by talking.

"I am very fearful for my son, who is fourteen. In ten years, if he hears me saying the same thing he is going to tell me, 'You have been saying that for twenty years, and we still have people giving up their kids because they cannot afford to feed them.' I know what the depth of their anger is.... Yet it doesn't have to be this way at all. It is too hard to contemplate what might happen.... We keep coming forward with these reasonable solutions, and keep being rejected. Clearly, that has to stop. One of my biggest fears is that we are not going to get what we want until there is a major change in the social order.

"The way I see my involvement is this: I am Anishinaabe. I am walking the land as my ancestors did. We will always be here, still walking this land. Now, whether these things you see around you – [he waved towards the city, the roads, the jetties and homes along the lakeshore] – will always be here, nobody knows that. But there are sure some big cracks in it all.

"The meter is running on this great civilization."

16

"Without land our people
will be nothing"

When I arrived in Winnipeg and told a friend I had been visiting reserves, she suggested I should fly up to Pukatawagen – a small Cree reserve that, on the map, looks lost in the depths of northern Manitoba. What was happening there, my friend said, was well worth looking into, and would add a dimension to what I had found in northwestern Ontario and further east. I had only a couple of days available, but decided to take her advice. Long experience of travelling the remote parts of Canada has taught me this kind of tip is usually worth following. Extraordinary things are happening out there. Great stories are lying around waiting to be written. All you need is the energy, time and money to get you there. I supplied the first two; *Reader's Digest* the third.

I soon found myself flying over huge lakes and meandering rivers. One moment, the landscape looked like tundra; the next it was the familiar black and white of the snow-covered spruce forest. This land has always been inhabited by Cree Indians, but was opened up to outside settlement twenty-five years before with the creation of the mining town of Thompson. Of course, since the 1790s there had been traders and Catholic missionaries, but the aboriginals had been able to absorb what those visitors brought without too much disruption of their way of life. I was soon to find that the changes brought by the modern world are on a far different scale.

From the air I caught a glimpse of what looked like the world's loneliest road – snaking through the wilderness among huge areas of frozen water, linking two tiny mining towns, with nothing in between. Looking at this desolate and endless landscape, I found it hard to realize that we had not even reached what most people think of as the Canadian north.

We landed just before dark at a strip about 160 kilometres east of Thompson. I had not seen any sign of a village as we came in. I hoped it was not too far away; although the chief had told me by phone that he would have someone meet me, no one appeared. The airport shed was locked, and the temperature was about thirty-five degrees below zero. This was no place to hang around; when a van turned up and disgorged a number of young people for the next flight, I asked the elderly driver if he could take me to the village.

The driver, Hyacinth Colomb, turned out to be the village taxidriver, among other things, and he dropped me off at the motel in the community centre, where I thought a room had been booked for me. They'd never heard of me at the motel and all rooms were occupied. But a consultant who was visiting the village from the Maritimes immediately said I could share his room.

I had less than twenty-four hours to spend in the reserve, but the chief was busy that evening, and I had to wait until the morning to see him. With so little time available, I was reluctant to sit around all evening. I knew there must be plenty of people worth talking to, but had no idea who they might be, and, since the offices were closed, no way of finding out. It occurred to me that Hyacinth Colomb, the taxi-driver, was interesting. I've always enjoyed talking to Indian elders, who usually love to tell you about their past. So I asked directions to his house and went calling. It turned out to be a lucky impulse.

History according to Hyacinth

Hyacinth lived in a spiffy new six-bedroom house, and was looking after his two four-year-old grandchildren for the evening. The house was part of the rebuilding of the village, now almost completed, carried out under the businesslike and aggressive leadership of a young chief. The old man told me he'd been born in 1916, and brought up eating mostly moose meat. "That's why I'm so healthy.... I ate lots of moose blood soup. When we cut a moose open, the blood would come running out from where the heart is. We'd save that and make soup of it. Well, when we'd boil meat, we'd take a little chunk of moose blood and put it in flour — we'd eat lots of that. We lived on beaver, muskrat, ducks, we had plenty to eat."

When he was a child, Hyacinth said, people didn't have formal traplines, but would trap all over: wherever there was good fishing, they'd spend the winter there, trapping and fishing. At the age of ten, he was sent out to a Catholic boarding school at Sturgeon Landing, midway between Flin Flon and The Pas. It was a long journey south by canoe that took about a week and a half. "They would send six men to take the kids out to school, with eight kids in a canoe. When we left Puk every little kid had his own paddle; we had to work our way."

When I asked him what the school was like, he said, "Well..." – as he did at the beginning of virtually every sentence he spoke – "Well – I guess it was good enough in those days.... Well" – reconsidering – "it was like ten months in jail. We went in August, and came back in July. We had a little playground where we had to play day after day, but some Sundays we were allowed to go for a walk, three miles out.... Well – it wasn't bad at all. I learned English mostly after I came out from school. I hardly ever talk English. I talk good Cree – of course, that's my language. It's funny: when I went to school, the government sent us out to learn English. The chiefs wanted us to come back and talk Cree. Now the government wants people to talk Cree again.... Well – that's something you can't understand.

"My kids talk Cree, but their kids.... Well – what's going to happen to these kids?" he said, gesturing at his grandchildren (who were playing noisily in English). "If I was to talk to these kids in Cree, they wouldn't know what I am talking about. That's one thing that's bad.... All the Cree language will be forgotten. More than half of it is forgotten now."

His schooling lasted only five years, until 1931. By 1935, when he was nearly twenty, people began to stay in one place, and settled down with registered traplines. They still had dogteams until the snowmobiles came in 1950. You could have either four or six dogs: to feed six, you really needed a lot of fish; four was better. They also had their own little gardens in those days. Now people no longer have gardens, but buy potatoes from the store. They used to have the geese in spring and fall, but the geese don't stop any more at Pukatawagen. They still fly over, but since Manitoba Hydro dammed the Missinippi, the Crees' river (known to us as the Churchill), and diverted the water south into the Nelson, the waterfowl don't come down any more.

After leaving school, Hyacinth worked in mines and sawmills, and each fall went back to his own trapline north of Lynn Lake. In 1952 he went to work for the game guardian branch of the provincial Department of Natural Resources. He was supposed to stay two years, but lasted nearly thirty, retiring in 1980.

When he started as a warden, trapping and hunting were open all year round. Restrictions came in during the early '60s. People were told they couldn't kill moose out of season, but nobody stopped them, he said. By the '70s, the muskrat began to disappear. Years ago a trapper could take 200 to 400 skins in a season. Between them the local trappers took 6,000 pelts. Nowadays, "Well – you're only able to get ten or fifteen."

The main reason for the decline has been the Island Falls dam, built in Saskatchewan sixty kilometres upstream from Pukatawagen. The first three turbines were opened in 1930, and the seventh in 1959. "On account of that dam," said Hyacinth, "sometimes the water goes high, but mostly it stays down. It's no wonder the muskrat disappeared...when it dries out, all their food is on dry ground. The trapping is just about dead out. Well – what's the use for us to trap? There's very few beaver. If there was a beaver house on the river in the fall, and you caught the beaver in the spring, all its fur would be gone.... When they let the water out on top of the ice, the animals even freeze out in their houses."

So far, Hyacinth said, they don't have too many outsiders coming in for moose in the fall. "We don't have much to worry about up to now, but when the highway comes in" – as currently planned – "there will be all kinds of people coming." This story sounded familiar, a rerun of the Barriere Lake experience. Even remote hunting economies cannot avoid the pressure of people and change in the modern world.

"Well – people are spoiled," said Hyacinth, although it didn't sound like it from what he was telling me. "I'm not the only one saying that. The young people today, they don't want to work. In the old days there was no such thing as welfare. Well – that's why the older people stay in a job when they can get one, they are used to work. The young people work five days and quit – too much trouble." Hyacinth himself seems never to be idle, even at seventy-five. In 1965 he started to run a truck, as a sideline, then he went into the taxi business. At the same time, he was a garbage man, looked after the school bus, was the mailman for thirteen years, and chief of the band for four years.

I left him in his neat little house as the grandchildren were running out of steam and had to be put to bed – but not before he had given

me an earful about the impossible economics of these new houses.
"They asked me if I would like a new house. I said yes. Okay, they
said they would build me one. Then I went down to the office and
they gave me a bill for $516. Well – we all kicked like hell, and
they're going to put the rent down to $400. I told them I am not
going to starve myself to pay for my house. There was nothing
wrong with my old one. There's one guy here, he's only got the old
age pension. He's paying the same as me. Well – he's supposed to
move out this month back into his old house."

Hyacinth and his wife had always lived in the log cabin only a few
yards from his new house, and had never had to pay rent. They'd
been well-off there. With their old age pensions and his pension
from the job, they were taking in $1,716 a month. In their log cabin,
their monthly costs for their wood stove, water barrel, hydro and
telephone were only $400. But in this new house their total costs
were $1,240 a month.

Everyone was finding these new charges tough to handle,
Hyacinth said. Living costs are now so high that wives and husbands
both have to work, and there are only five employers – the nursing
station, the school, the band office, the store, and (from March to
December) construction work on the new houses. He shook his head
gravely: "I don't know what's going to happen in the future."

I had certainly heard this story before, too. An industrialized economy is now structured so that at least two incomes are needed in the
average family just to pay mortgages, taxes and utilities, and to buy
the food and clothing that few people can produce any longer themselves. This type of economy is driven more by the needs of the financial system than of the family. What is surprising is to travel
hundreds of miles into the wilderness and to find that even so far
from the centres of urban life, self-sufficiency is on the way out.

A good story by any standards
I had been told that Pascall Bighetty, the young chief I had travelled
so far to meet, was one of a kind. He had made money on his own
account in real estate, and was also a leader who had reversed a disastrous situation in his reserve.

I didn't really know what to expect, and when he arrived for our
morning appointment, I was surprised to find that Bighetty looked
more like a young trapper than a businessman. A tall, heavily built,

awkward man, with a hesitant walk, very dark-skinned, and with his long hair in a pony tail, he was dressed like almost everyone else in cowboy boots and jeans. Everyone wanted to talk to him while he was having his morning coffee in the restaurant. He had a rather distracted air, and I was afraid he might be anxious to get rid of me. But I needn't have worried. When we went upstairs to his office, he shut the door behind us and gave me his whole attention, as if I was the only person in the world he was interested in.

Pascal Bighetty's story is amazing by any standards. The village of Pukatawagan was heavily under the influence of the Catholic Church for generations, but by the early '70s had degenerated into a lawless, hopeless place. Living conditions were grim. Everyone lived in small log cabins without electricity or running water, and alcoholism was so pervasive that the *New York Times* (in an article no one has ever found) is reputed to have said that the village had the highest per-capita homicide rate in North America.

People, dead drunk, stumbled back and forth through the village, brandishing guns to such effect that on one day alone nine accident-victims were buried from the band office. The situation became so bad that the nursing station was closed, all the teachers fled, and the reserve was left without a school. There was no RCMP presence, and members of the council were usually drunk, including Bighetty, the new twenty-three-year-old chief.

Bighetty had become a drinker early in life. He had been thrown out of grade eleven in St. Boniface, a suburb of Winnipeg, for drinking. But when he was elected chief, he began to realize he would have to stop drinking if he was to be a real leader. It wasn't easy; but by 1976 he had stopped. He then realized he needed management skills in this job, so he went back to university to study management. In 1982, when he was thirty-three, he returned to the reserve and again became chief, taking over from Hyacinth Colomb.

Bighetty had a strong motivation to lift his reserve from its poverty. He had been brought up in a family of sixteen children, of whom only eight had survived. There was no floor in their house, and they could see the stars through their roof, so there was little heat, and their drum of water would be frozen every morning.

"We had this mentality, to accept to be poor," he said. "It still makes me mad when I think about it. The government allowed it, and the churches brainwashed our grandparents and parents to believe that if they were poor on earth they would go straight to heaven."

On his return to the reserve, Bighetty immediately began negotiating with Manitoba Hydro for the village to be connected to the provincial power grid. "And that's the point from which it all took off." The band borrowed almost $2 million from various federal and provincial government programmes and built the new community centre, including restaurant, motel and shops. Gradually they bulldozed most of the old village, and brought in CMHC housing, financed under a programme for low-income people.

Once the dependency on alcohol had been beaten, the council sobered, the village rebuilt, the band set up Pukatawagan Development Corporation and began to borrow money to make outside investments. They now own three rental buildings in Winnipeg, three in Flin Flon, and twenty in Lynn Lake, always full. They own an airline working out of The Pas. They have a joint-venture fishery with a government agency. They make a million dollars a year out of the hotel and shops in the community centre.

The band dealt with the violence in a unique way. "We passed a bylaw, upheld by the courts, that all firearms should be kept by the council in one place."

The school reopened in 1976, with classes up to grade ten; so not only are the teachers back, but the band is now negotiating for a new school up to grade twelve, hoping they can reduce the high dropout rate. Cree is taught for one forty-minute period every day, and the school keeps a trapline where students are taught traditional ways.

Pascall Bighetty is not the type to sit around agonizing about the future. He knows that a small group of marginalized people living far from the centres of power in a remote wilderness, with few obvious economic resources, are not well placed to prosper in the modern economy. But Bighetty has great faith in business as the solution to Pukatawagan's future problems. He is strongly opposed to socialism, which he says keeps people poor, and is an active member of the Liberal Party. With a non-native partner, he started an off-reserve business a few years ago, and admits to having made a lot of money personally in real estate in Flin Flon and The Pas. He is reputed to be a millionaire. He wrote to his band members in 1986:

The trapline days are over.... I will never see the caravan of canoes leaving for their annual hunts.... Education holds the key to the future....

The beaver, muskrat, fish and moose will become extinct if the government have it their way.... If [they] are not successful in taking away Indian rights, [then] lumbering, mining, tourist, highway and hydro development will kill off the animals.... Land speculators will come in by the hundreds to buy the best lands around the community. Big firms...will take over development.... We cannot stop progress. We can only do the best we can to become part of development. However, we cannot become part of development if we do not have educated people. We can beat the system if we can manipulate the second coming of the white man. We need to train our own managers, teachers, lawyers, engineers, doctors, economists, nurses and even politicians. We must become the conqueror, rather than the conquered.[1]

To carry out this dream, Bighetty has deliberately made a wide range of contacts among decision-makers. His economic development plan, prepared in 1986, was vigorously implemented, and most of its aims were achieved by 1991. When I visited the reserve, they were preparing to start a trucking business, a band-owned maintenance garage, and were in the process of buying a commercial tourist lodge on the Churchill River fifty kilometres northwest of the village. The year after my visit Bighetty took a position as special consultant to the Manitoba regional director of the Department of Indian Affairs, but working out of the office of the Assembly of Manitoba Chiefs.

Bighetty is one chief who leans towards the establishment. Yet, as I have found so often, aboriginal people are hard to categorize: although a conservative in his economic approach, Bighetty has his radical, anti-authoritarian side. This was evident three years before, as he wrestled to get control of the village's justice system. The village leaders were dissatisfied with the way the travelling court operated. Sentences were too lenient, they felt, and people were being remanded until charges were dismissed. "We set up our own justice committee, but to the judge it was a joke." So they told the judge he would be arrested and jailed if he came back to the village. He stayed away for almost a year. "Two years ago they agreed to listen to us." Bighetty used his high-placed contacts: working with the Chief Justice of Manitoba and the Ministry of Justice, the band established a process under which the judge is obliged to consult the village justice committee before sentencing anyone. "We know the people here. We have our own table in court while cases are being heard.

Quite a few sentences have been modified as a result of our suggestions: some sentences have been higher, some lower."

After an hour or so, the chief had other business to do, and left me with a promise that we would meet again later in the day.

It's cold up there

I went down into the restaurant, which I have to confess is not one of the great restaurants of Canada, limiting itself, as most Indian reserve restaurants do, to chips, steak, hamburger, spaghetti and coffee. Aboriginals are not supposed to buy and sell delicacies such as moose, caribou, bear or beaver meat, so even in aboriginal communities where natural foods are abundant and delicious, the restaurants are usually of the greasy-spoon or, at best, fast-food type. Since they are usually the only game in town, it's impossible for a visitor to avoid them.

I chatted for a while with Chris Gagnon, a Québecois from Chicoutimi who had settled in The Pas, and had a contract to maintain Pukatawagan's heavy equipment. He had just driven his huge maintenance truck four hours north over the winter road, and it was ticking over noisily outside as we talked. He said the temperature was usually so cold in Pukatawagan that he never turned his engine off while there: left off overnight, the engine would take hours to start again. I soon saw what he meant.

Glen Lawson, the consultant who'd shared his room with me, was supposed to leave that morning for Sherridon, a former mining village two hours south across the winter road. Lawson was a specialist in environmental remediation, and had been called to Sherridon because acids were leeching from the tailings of an abandoned mine into a fishing lake. But by mid-morning he hadn't left, because the van had been left outside for two days and was like a block of ice. They'd tried everything to get it started; the only solution was to push the van into the nursing-station garage. Half a dozen of us were mobilized to do the job. There was just the suggestion of a breeze off the lake; and that was all you needed to freeze your cheeks and feet. The temperature was at least thirty-five degrees below zero, even in the late morning. We heaved the van up a slight hill to the nursing-station. There it warmed up in the next couple of hours, and Lawson finally left by about three in the afternoon. This didn't faze him; people in the north are not greatly wedded to time.

I visited the school, which had eleven teachers from the Maritimes, and then Matt Sinclair, the band's executive director, told me how the Island Falls dam has almost eliminated the successful sturgeon fishery once operated by the Crees. Up to 1968 they had been able to take out a million pounds of fish a year (at $2 a pound), but the fluctuations in water levels had become greater in recent years, and "This year there was absolutely nothing.... I started full-time as a commercial fisherman in 1979," he said. "I got the nets and the boats, and since then the only year I've been able to make some money was 1983, about $2,000. Every other year I have either broken even or lost about $1,000."

He said the dam has been operating without a licence since 1982 (although obliged by law to renew every four years), and four native communities are suing for compensation. Pukatawagen is asking for $15 million a year for as long as the plant operates. Sinclair grimaced across the table at me. "The government say that we don't depend on country food. They are full of shit. You can quote me in your book.... These wildlife activists are killing us. I was invited to a panel discussion with them once.... I told them they should try lynx chops in the middle of February – it beats pork chops any time." He gave a sardonic laugh.

Throughout the north there is resentment at the campaign run by animal-rights groups against the trapping of fur-bearing animals. In Puk they believe their trapping methods, which always maintained a balanced, healthy population of animals, are less cruel than the water fluctuations of the Saskatchewan Water Power Corporation, against which the animal-rights campaigners have never uttered a word. These fluctuations regularly drown animals in mid-winter or isolate them from their food supply. "Sometimes in the late fall, when there are changes in water levels, we often see the animals sitting on the ice just waiting to die," Chief Bighetty told me.

Pukatawagan's official history, written by the chief's wife, Marie Adele Bighetty, says:

> During the spring trapping season, trappers go to the inland lakes to harvest muskrat and beaver because they know that the animals along the river are all decomposed. This is one of the reasons why the local trappers like to harvest as many animals as possible before Christmas. It is for humanitarian reasons and not cruelty, that trappers harvest animals

around Pukatawagan, contrary to what animal-rights groups say.[2]

In their chapter of the same book, the village elders write:

The great river that flowed freely for centuries has been blocked, but to a quiet stream. The river along Pukatawagan has receded over twenty feet. One wonders where the migratory birds all went. Our forefathers told us that migratory birds once darkened the skies. At one time huge flocks of crows, blackbirds, and geese would be mistaken for rain clouds.[3]

And Julian Bighetty, who was born "in a makeshift lean-to" in 1881, said in his story:

Pukatawagan was rich in wild food. I recall many times when I could not sleep because the water fowl made so much noise. They played and splashed in the water all night long. Ducks, geese, swan, and other small birds filled the air with noise. My grandfather and myself used to spear sturgeon at Bloodstone falls, known as Kamihkwapiskak. [The falls] were always blood red with sturgeon blood. I remember the thousands and thousands of waterfowl arriving from the south. The people were so happy to hear the annual returning of the summer birds.[4]

Struggle to confirm their land

Matt Sinclair has been handling the efforts made by the band members to fulfil their land entitlement under Treaty 6, signed in 1876. They were entitled to 44,000 acres, but received only half of it, and have been negotiating for the rest since 1978.

They have claimed another 20,000 acres in sixteen places of traditional use, mostly along the Churchill River. But Manitoba Hydro, having built the immense South Indian Lake diversion from the Churchill into the Nelson River in the 1970s (with the devastating effects on the Cree communities described in Chapter 14), has grandiose plans for continuing to dam the waters of this region. Manitoba Hydro now claims that most of the land chosen by Pukatawagan is within its power reserves, and lies in the forebays of proposed new hydro stations.

"But we were here first," said Sinclair, exasperatedly. He rattled off details of the sixteen areas the Crees have claimed, and the reasons the government has given for rejecting them. He said that in 1978 the province established nine guidelines for land selection. One of them was that selections should be ninety-nine feet above high-water mark. "We told them to go to hell. But they are still maintaining that priority, saying the land isn't available. We've tried to be reasonable. If they would agree to compensate us for any building we might do that would be flooded later, we would go along with that. But they just won't. We've run into a brick wall."

To give a specific example, Pukatawagan has made a land selection at Bloodstone Falls, remembered by Julian Bighetty as a central location for spearing sturgeon. But Manitoba Hydro says this is a proposed site for a generating station, and the paper company REPAP, of The Pas, has identified the same land as a potential site for timber harvesting, and as a land-access corridor.

"We have chosen some land on an island there, but REPAP says it is marked for clearcutting," Sinclair told me. "I told them, we have interests in that land and can't agree to their five-year cutting plans until they deal with our claims." Some of the land is also said to be subject to mining claims.

This is another story I've heard before; in fact, it is common across the country. As was the case for the Stoneys a century ago, every competing use still appears to have priority over the needs of the people who were here first. Although many Canadians are ready to agree to an equitable sharing of resources with aboriginal peoples, when it comes to the details, Euro-Canadian institutions simply dig in their heels and refuse to negotiate.

A relentless improver

I met Chief Bighetty again later in the afternoon. He was feeling more comfortable with me by that time, and took me on an extended tour of the reserve, pointing out the many improvements made under his leadership. I had a healthy respect for him by this time: he was a man who had done what he said he would do. I was struck, however, as we drove around, by his somewhat ruthless attitude to every evidence of a past that he seemed determined to bury. Here, a log cabin would have to go; there, a storeroom was no good; here, an outmoded house would be replaced by four units, next year, or the year after, or sometime. When I suggested that there must be people who couldn't pay the higher costs, he said there was no problem. Everyone paid rent according to income; those in difficulty had their rents subsidized.

The chief took me to his own home, spotlessly clean, positively shining. The walls were covered with ornate pictures and emblems, a

certificate from Brandon University, a feather and inscription com-
memorating Bighetty's work in helping to stop the Meech Lake
Accord. Two wolf skins hung in the windows, and there were the
skins of one cross fox and a red fox.

This time, he did not talk business, but culture. In spite of having
succeeded in urban real estate, he hates the cities, and would never
be able to live there, he said. It was still the very breath of life for
him to get out onto the land whenever he could, every day if possible. "When I finish work I like just to pull up my canoe and go out to
see the wildlife, the ducks, lift up the net."

The chief was almost scared sometimes, he said, that the people
could go back to the sorrowful years of the '70s. "At that time, you
know, we almost lost our language. My wife, who now teaches Cree,
didn't know how to speak it. Even old folks wouldn't speak to you in
Cree. The nuns always told us to speak English. We were taught to
be ashamed of our culture. When I went to school in Winnipeg I was
ashamed to go to a restaurant, the white people would look at me, I
just did not feel right, I was not proud of myself. Now everybody is
proud to be Missinippi Cree."

An old man, Solomon Colomb, had died at the age of 102 only a
month before my visit. He had remembered when Pukatawagan
was just a summer meeting place, and there were no houses. He had
been chief for twenty-six years, from 1933, and when the impatient
Bighetty was seizing control of affairs, Solomon had told him, "Do not
take too big a bite or you will choke. Learn to sweep the floor first."

That was wise advice, said Bighetty. "When I started I wanted to
do everything right away. But I can see now, I would never have succeeded. I would probably have quit in disgust already if I'd tried
that." Their council of elders, all in their seventies, had been the key
people in the move to take over the justice system, the most radical
action they'd taken. "They told me, 'Unless you take control, no one
will respect you, or the council.' "

Surprisingly, for a man with his business interests, Bighetty has become convinced that money is not the solution to his people's problems. "I don't envy the ones who have money. We already know that
rich bands lose lives. I would sooner have control of our fish,
our sturgeon, our migratory birds, our resources here. This is the
essence of self-government."

He said they are now arguing for licensing jurisdiction over all local tourism, trapping, fishing and hunting, and at least joint control over wildlife management, covering an area of 21,000 square kilometres. To create a self-sustaining economy, they are now negotiating for a tribal government district under their control. "I am not advocating only for native people, but everyone must get involved, white, Métis, or Indian," he said.

The chief spoke with pride of having taken control of band medical services – the first band in Canada to be funded directly by the federal Treasury Board, bypassing the provincial bureaucracy. His people are also taking over forest-fire protection, and have obtained a guarantee of first priority on employment in new gold and nickel mines. For the moment, Pukatawagan still depends on government transfers, with income of about $10 million a year from social services, old-age pensions and family allowances, and another $1.2 million in the form of welfare. But, "For true self-government, we should refuse these income tax dollars."

In the hope of doing just that Bighetty is advocating an ingenious scheme for recovering some of the dollar value of the nine million square kilometres of land the Indians have given away. "In 1985 that was equal to $285 billion of gross national product," he said. "If we could get two or three per cent of that in lieu of what we have lost, I think average Canadians would not object. Then we could organize our third level of government. Then we would not take money from tax dollars, and the $4 billion in transfer payments every year could be used for other things. Anyway, half of that goes for bureaucracy, and only half reaches our people."

Chief Bighetty has travelled all over the world looking at how aboriginal people handle their lands. In many places it is sad, very sad, he said. Only the Maori people in New Zealand appear to be ahead; yet they, too, are going to be assimilated.

"Without a land base, our people will be nothing," Bighetty stated flatly.

We finished our coffee, and he dropped me off at the hotel. Hyacinth had promised to pick me up at 5:15 p.m. to take me to the plane. By 6:35 p.m. I was getting anxious, but he turned up and said cheerfully, "Did you think I'd forgotten you?"

When he dropped me off at the airport, Hyacinth charged me $10, twice as much as he'd charged to bring me in. Just a little something to remember him by.

Off to the city

All over the country, aboriginals have been leaving reserves like those described in the last two chapters, to seek opportunity in the cities. In 1973, my friend Buckley Petawabano from Mistissini, who had a brief but exciting career as a teenage heartthrob in a television adventure series (he was particularly popular with German teenage girls, who wrote him hundreds of letters that he couldn't read), entertained me with this account of his first visit to Toronto:

"I was accepted for this course in Waterloo, Ontario, but first I went back to Mistissini, and my father and I were painting the house when some guys came in from the bush and brought in about twenty cases of beer. They told my old man and me, 'Hey, quit actin' so serious, come down and have a few drinks.' So we put our paint brushes away, and we drank for a whole week. We never got that job done. To this day [years later] my old man's house is still painted up to about three feet from the top all the way round.

"In July I got down to Montreal.... Finally on a Friday night I went to Toronto. When I got there I had only twenty cents. I didn't know anybody. It was Saturday morning when I arrived, with drunks all over the place. I was tryin' to figure out what I could do with twenty cents. My first time in Toronto ever, at a bus terminal, what was I gonna do? I finally thought of this guy Mike I'd met in Chibougamau. He told me his last name, and said to call his parents in Toronto when I got there, he might be there. So I phoned them, and they said call him at this other number. But when I hung up I forgot the number, so I had ten cents left. I tried their number again, but I got the wrong number.

"I started to walk with this old couple, and we passed a place and they told me, 'You can go and get soup in there if you go and pray.' I could see all these Indian guys in there, prayin', it's called the Fred-something mission. I asked the guy who was in charge would he lend me a dime. He says 'No, I can't.' I said, why not? He says, 'Go in there and pray and you'll get your soup and crackers.' I walked out and ran into these bums in suits, and I asked, 'Can you guys give me a dime?' And they said, 'Look at you, a strong, healthy young lad like you, you should be out working.'

"I went into this bar and the guy gave me a dime to make a phone call. So I dialled the number, and Mike's mother answered again and this time I wrote the number down. But next time I dialled the wrong number by mistake. My last dime: holy shit, I thought. I was really fed up. While I was on the phone my bag got stolen. I chased the guy through the crowd, but I lost him. I went back to the restaurant at the bus terminal, and the guy gave me a dime. I got the right number this time, and Mike tells me to stay right there, have a cup of coffee, he'll come and pick me up. I sit down, and the waitress comes and says, 'What do you want?' I said, 'Water.'

"Mike picks me up. He drives me to his father's house. Now I am in a really nice place. Swimming pool. Maids. Mike said to go in that room and grab a bathing suit. I go in, there's a whole line of bathing suits. I put one on, grab a towel, walk into the other room, and this maid says to me, 'Sir, can I take off your shoes, I'll give you a pair of sandals.'

"So I am swimming in this pool, no money at all, having a great time. Mike's mother calls me over and says, 'Here, young man, what do you want to drink?' I say I don't know, anything. She gives me a highball. I would swim around a bit, take a few dives and come back, and have a few sips. I had a great time from about one o'clock in the afternoon till about six. We went to a party that night and when I told Mike I didn't have any money at all, he took out a cash box and gave me some money, and the next morning drove me down to the bus terminal so I could get to Waterloo. That was my first time in Toronto.

"At Waterloo there were some guys from Red Power, and they were really knocking every white man in sight. I never saw that before, and I ended up being really great friends with those five guys, and for a couple of months I was so militant I would get drunk and say, fuck the white man. But I figured if you're going to be forceful and militant, you have to be physically with it, instead of all just talk. So I said, 'Listen you guys, do you want to take me on?' But none of them wanted to take me on.

"One of the heaviest pressures I've ever had was being told that I was not Indian. In one way I really didn't give a shit because I figured, what is an Indian, anyway? I am Buckley, my father raised me, Philip is my friend, all these guys are my friends and they never talk to me about Indians. But I go right across the country, and they say, 'Buckley, you're a sellout. You're working with the CBC and the NFB, and you're white.' I say, yeah, okay, I agree with you on every point.

"Political people tell me I'm not Indian any more. I never say anything to them, because what can I say? The way I look at it now is that every man is equal to me. I can do just as well as everyone else....

"When you're living in the city it's a matter of trying to maintain your sanity. You really have nobody to look up to, like a father or uncle. You're on your own. But who's to say who is sane or insane, anyway? Most of us have gone through all that bullshit, drinking and smoking to maintain our sanity, but it really puts a lot of heavy pressure on you as an individual."

A few years later Buckley returned to Mistissini, where he works as a communications consultant for the band council. Like many other people who tell stories in this book, he, too, is an ex-drinker.

17

The aboriginal city

About a third of aboriginal people in Canada now live in cities. Erma Bird knows from experience that many native people move there with unrealistic hopes of finding a job, an education, a decent life. They leave their reserves because they've run into a dead-end.

"Here is my personal theory," said Erma Bird, a sharply intelligent young woman, who knows whereof she speaks. She left Mistawasis reserve near Prince Albert, Saskatchewan, when she was eighteen, and when I met her in 1991 she was working in Regina. She's lived the urban Indian experience from every angle.

"Being born Indian or native, your chances of becoming successful according to white middle-class standards are very slim. The first thing you would be introduced to is education. If you do not go to a band-controlled school, you have to go to an integrated school. There you are in a minority, you are confronted with racism and discrimination, and a learning environment based on white middle-class values.

"A lot of the native children are poor, even hungry. They are exposed to the contempt of classmates, and even of some teachers. The number of native teachers is one per cent, but the native kids can be 25 to 40 per cent of a class. When you are almost right at the bottom, it's very difficult to survive. Such things as wearing the wrong clothing, that winter jacket you have to keep wearing, when you're the one who can't have that $200 jacket, it does something to your confidence.

"Then when there's so much said about Indians as savages, scalping, squaws, papoose – all the key words – it's very demeaning, and as you go higher in secondary school, you become maybe the only native student. In a high school like that, 94 per cent of native students

227

drop out before grade twelve. Only one out of every twelve native students graduates! Something is definitely wrong with the school system.

"The parents and grandparents of many of these students have themselves been through the cycle of no education, no jobs, and no hope. Many grow up knowing only family violence, alcohol, suicide. It's hard to break out of that. When you drop out, if you do not have a support system at home, you are going to fall through the cracks. That's how a lot of people get into drugs, alcohol, and petty crime. That's why 65 per cent of the men in our jails are native.

"The average native person who comes to the city with a grade seven education is going to be very intimidated, even to go to a restaurant to look for a dishwashing job. Even there they are going to ask for grade ten or twelve. But let's say they get through this, they get an education and qualifications, as more and more are doing. You still have to prove yourself. You still have to work twice as hard as a non-native person. You have to show your employer you can put out 110 per cent rather than 90 per cent. You are always under the microscope. They are always trying to find fault.

"If you even get the opportunity to enter the workforce, you are walking a very fine line, and they are just waiting for you to cross it. You are faced with discrimination and racism on a day-to-day basis."

Erma Bird is not a discontented radical, smouldering about injustice. At the time of our meeting she was a civilian officer of the Regina Police, engaged to sensitize other police officers to the reality of native people and minorities, and to build bridges among them all. And although Erma worked for the police, she was no hard-nosed conservative. She didn't think that because she had made it in the city, all native people should shape up or ship out. On the contrary, she knew what they were going through, she'd been through it herself, and she wanted to help.

Erma never expected to be doing this kind of work. When she left the reserve, she went to Regina with her brother to finish grade twelve, but then had no idea what to do. She worked as a waitress and a chambermaid, did telephone marketing, served pizza, then went to Calgary to baby-sit for a cousin. When she was still only nineteen, she got into life insurance and real estate for a year, but then moved to Edmonton and became a mother. That led to a native life-skills programme, and a receptionist's job for a programme run by three native women to prepare others to enter the work force.

"That built my confidence and self-esteem," she said.

With her five-month-old son, she moved to Saskatoon and enrolled in a social-work course with the Saskatchewan Indian Federated College, intending to stay only two years to earn her certificate. The course included much about Indian culture and values. Erma became so interested that she stayed four years and took a degree. As part of the course, she had to spend four months in the workplace. The Saskatchewan Human Rights Commission did not really want a social worker, but she persuaded them to let her work there, and began to learn about affirmative action and other programmes.

The Commission obviously knew a promising worker when they saw one: they offered Erma a job as an education officer in Regina. She would have to speak to audiences of up to 200, and thought she couldn't do it. She refused the job. They asked her three times; eventually she accepted. She discovered she could speak in public after all, and in the next five years became accustomed to making presentations on human rights, sexual harassment, racism and affirmative action. She worked so successfully that the police asked her to join them as a cultural-relations officer. The position had been established in 1983 following an inquiry into the use of police dogs against Indian and native people in Regina.

"It's slow work," Erma told me, "but we have made progress in the past year."

She reported directly to the chief of police, who supported her liaison work and her cross-cultural training programmes for his officers. When I talked to her, she had recently been seconded to develop an employment-equity programme, to try to hire more native and minority police officers.

She had developed one programme that she seemed to take particular pride in. Twice she had taken a group of twenty-four police officers to the Piapot reserve north of Regina, where they had been dumped at the band office without being told what was going to happen. "We gave the reserve the ownership of the officers for a day. I wanted them to experience what it is like to be a minority, to feel like our people do when we come into the city. Nothing is explained to them. It starts off with a pipe ceremony. They are expected to smoke the pipe and pray with the elders. At first the policemen all stay together, in their own group.

"They are then told about life on the reserves, about the residential schools, land entitlement, the problems people feel when they go to the surrounding cities. Then there's a lunch of bannock and soup. We try to create an open dialogue between the community and the policemen, and by the end of the day we see the police officers mixing with everyone. In the evening we give them the opportunity, if they want, to take part in a sweat lodge conducted by the chief. About 50 per cent of them took part. The evaluation later was positive on both sides."

Among other things, the job with the police convinced Erma that she still had things to learn, and much to contribute. A year or so later she left the police and enrolled in law school – probably, I would think, the only ex-chambermaid in the course.

Three lifers tell their story

Seven weeks before I met Erma Bird, I had sat for two hours in a Winnipeg coffee shop with three aboriginal men who did not work for the police, but had always had a lot to do with them. The three had collectively passed 115 years on this earth, of which they had spent fifty-nine in jail. They had been brought to meet me by Eric Robinson, president of the Aboriginal Council of Winnipeg, who, by talking to them and opening doors for them, had been trying to ease their painful realization that with their release from jail perhaps the worst part of their sentences was just beginning.

The story these men told me could practically stand as a symbol of what has happened to their people over the centuries. All three felt that they had been given negative labels from their youngest days, targetted for retribution by an unfriendly society, traumatized by the hostility of others, and then – classified as the lowest of the low – had never been, and never would be, given a chance to rise from the depths into which they had been cast. Their view of society was not just black: it was totally without hope.

All three had served their longest sentences for various degrees of alcohol-related homicide. Norm, the senior of the three, did most of the talking, as if according to some hierarchy. He was consumed with bitterness that non-natives resent native people for supposedly getting too many government benefits. Norm knew – as a fact of life – that "we are less fortunate than anybody else. In Winnipeg we are 10 per cent, right? In the jails in Manitoba we are 60 per cent."

Vimy, from a reserve near Kamsack, north of Yorkton, Saskatchewan, said he had been denied parole for twelve years because he refused to admit he was an alcoholic. As far as the system was concerned, he said, you are an alcoholic if you are an Indian.

Calvin, at thirty the youngest of the three, was sixteen when he went to prison. He said he had tried to stop a guy from killing another guy, and ended up arrested and charged. "I had a legal-aid lawyer. He didn't want to see me. I never discussed the case with him before I appeared in court. They gave me life." There was alcohol involved, he admitted. Everybody of his age experimented with alcohol. After that, he too was labelled an alcoholic. "I went through years in the prison system trying to fight that label. It's all racism. There's so much of it in jail, not so much among the prisoners, but the administration."

Norm had already served ten years in various institutions before he received his long sentence. He was charged with non-capital murder for which, he said, there was only circumstantial evidence. "But in this country, every trial of a native person is a grave miscarriage of justice. They assume you are ignorant – no great loss. I had a legal-aid lawyer, and I made a mistake: I went to see him three times. Before the case came on, everybody knew how long I was going to get. The opening statement by the Crown said, 'This man has a propensity to commit violence.' When they've heard that, they make negative reports on you when you're inside. They make a big thing of everything – if you're caught gambling, or you tell the guards to fuck off, that comes out as a propensity to violence.

"I saw my lawyer and the native court communicators once," said Vimy bitterly. "They said, 'Let's make a deal for ten years.' I said, 'Go for it.' Ninety days after the trial I had this letter from the Crown saying they were appealing the sentence. Right from the start I was...." His sentence collapsed in a gesture of bitterness and hopelessness.

Norm said: "Why are there so many natives in prison? First, we have a bunch of racist people in this country. We can't do away with that. It will always exist. Almost anybody can be convicted of any crime. Outside, we are not really part of the political system. It's a political thing; we are political prisoners. The Canadian correctional system is a big organization. They need to fill their institutions at all times in order to justify their work. They give more parole, hire more probation officers at $45,000 a year, and they do nothing."

Vimy said: "It all goes back to the treaties. A lot of our people tried to follow spiritual ways. The government tried to stop them. That's where it all started. Going back in history, any spiritual people on the reserves had to get a permit to leave."

"There's been an attempt at native genocide by the white supremacists in Canada," said Norm.

Eric Robinson said: "Stony Mountain Penitentiary was built originally to hold our forefathers, Poundmaker and Big Bear, who were against signing the treaties. So we are institutionalized from the time we are born, even to this day. From residential school, to reform school, to prison. Believe me, there are not a lot of aboriginal people who haven't been in conflict with the law in one form or another."

We were joined by Cecil Cooke, a young man from Elphinstone, Manitoba, working as a reporter for a native news service. He said he had been adopted into a non-native home when he was three. At fourteen he got into trouble, and at fifteen or sixteen, "I went crazy...I was always running away". He began to do a lot of drinking, and in the end he spent nine years in and out of jails.

Cecil said: "It boils down to an economic problem. When there are no opportunities it's hard for people to make it on the street. They start petty crime, and it becomes a necessity. But the guys who have been in there say a change has to be made. In my last four years in Stony Mountain, the older guys were advising that we should make a gradual change to a better economic system, try to get some training."

Norm said that when they leave prison, they need an opportunity to get a fresh start in life. They need a shop where they could upgrade their skills, equipping them with references so they could get a job. "As it is now, we have absolutely nothing. I roamed round here for two months when I first came out. I was expecting there'd be some programme for us, something simple, not a big outfit. But the unions lay down conditions against us."

Last year when he'd first got out, he managed to get an apartment and a job. One day he was picked up. Someone had phoned and said he had threatened them.

"It's like a great big dictatorship," Norm said, with resignation. "We have constitutional rights, but we have no money to contest anything. In the United States, even with a criminal record you can join the police force...the Bill of Rights applies to everyone. But in Canada, when you're an Indian, forget it."

Eric Robinson told me: "What it boils down to is: Indian people are a big economy. We keep the jails and the welfare system going. The aboriginal political leadership doesn't know what to do for guys like these." He paused and echoed something the guys had touched on bitterly a few times during the conversation. "You know, during a week I spent in a welfare office, there was only one immigrant came in."

Vimy said: "If we could only have what they have."

The officials agree with Norm and Vimy

Six weeks after I talked to the three lifers, someone in Edmonton gave me a provincial task force report that had recently been issued on the treatment of aboriginal people in the police stations, courts and prisons of Alberta.

Most Canadians have heard of the inquiries into the unjust, eleven-year imprisonment of Donald Marshall in Nova Scotia, the killing of J.J. Harper in Manitoba, and the fifteen-year coverup of the murder of Helen Betty Osborne in The Pas, Manitoba. Each of these inquiries investigated a particularly scandalous incident involving aboriginal people, and the racism against native people that they revealed within the Nova Scotia and Manitoba justice systems received national publicity.

The Alberta inquiry has received less attention, but in some ways is even more significant: it deals with the routine, day-to-day experiences that send 11,000 aboriginal people into provincial and federal jails in Alberta every year.[1] As I read the report, I realized that Erma Bird, Norm, Vimy and the others had not been exaggerating, but merely describing, from both sides of the prison wall, the same grim facts of life.

Many Canadians have become inured to the shocking statistics of aboriginal deprivation everywhere in Canada. The Alberta report contains plenty of them: although they make up only 5 per cent of the provincial population, aboriginals comprise 30 per cent of those admitted to jail; 48 per cent of women in jail are aboriginals; 43 per cent of children in public care, and 47 per cent of those in permanent guardianship, are aboriginal. An extraordinary fact – which may seem scarcely believeable to the average Canadian – is that one of every four aboriginals between the ages of nineteen and twenty-four were admitted to jail in Alberta in 1989.

The report is loaded with admissions of "drastic socio-economic deprivation" among aboriginals at every level, and "dysfunctional families and broken homes"; of infant mortality four times higher than among non-natives; child life expectancy ten years shorter; of a native being thirteen times more likely to live in a crowded home; ten times more likely to have tuberculosis; five times more likely than a non-native to commit suicide; three times more likely to be committed to a youth reform centre, or to die of accident, violence or poisoning; of having one chance in three of being unemployed for most of his or her life, or of being an alcoholic; one chance in four of becoming a drug addict. Here is the continuing legacy of the Indian Act, unchanged, it seems, since the report to Parliament by the 1946-47 joint committee – more than forty years ago.

Even this Alberta task force (including aboriginals, civil servants, a judge and a senior police officer), had to admit that aboriginals are not treated justly when they step into a police station, a courtroom or a prison. As I read the report, Norm's statement that every trial of a native person in Canada is a grave miscarriage of justice began to sound like only a slight exaggeration.

Evidence from hundreds of people across the province revealed a terrible situation: the aboriginal witnesses said, and the task force could not deny, that proportionately to their numbers, more native than non-native people are placed under surveillance by the police; of those placed under surveillance, more are arrested; of those arrested, more are charged; of those charged, more are convicted; those convicted receive longer sentences; those sentenced receive fewer paroles.

Dozens of people told the task force of this selective treatment, and of coming before courts staffed by lawyers, judges and officials who are totally insensitive to their cultural background, beliefs and languages. The task force discovered that a typical judge has no contact of any kind with native people except those who come into the courtroom as accused persons. Trial lawyers were so indifferent to the harsh criticism made by native witnesses of the legal-aid system that they refused to submit a brief to the task force, or have anything to do with it. They said the matter had been dealt with in an earlier report made twelve years before!

No wonder that in Alberta, fewer than 300 aboriginals are employed among the 15,500 police and prison officers, lawyers and judges who see them safely on their way to jail in such huge numbers.

Just as Erma Bird said, just as Norm and Vimy said, racism and discrimination are a pervasive fact of everyday life for native people in

Canada. "The task force concludes that racism is prevalent in our society," said the Alberta report. "...Aboriginal people are exposed daily to racism.... This racism exists in the criminal justice system as it does in the larger society. Ignorance of aboriginal people and the issues and problems they face appear to be a large part of the problem of racism."

That these attitudes continue into the 1990s is a terrible indictment of a country that has been moving steadily, at least since the 1940s, to make discrimination illegal on the grounds of race, colour, nationality, sex, age or disability.

Urban Indians, a volatile force

A couple of days after we met with the former convicts, Eric Robinson was locked in a meeting with federal Energy Minister Jake Epp, two ministers of the Manitoba government, and the Mayor of Winnipeg. No one who knew Eric in the 1970s would have expected to find him dealing in the corridors of power like that, but times change, and people change with them. In the '70s he was a member of the Red Power movement, a firebrand radical, and as recently as the mid-'80s he had written a book attacking the native leadership in scathing terms for selling out aboriginal rights during the debates on repatriation of the Constitution. Now he was lobbying all three levels of government to get a fairer deal for urban natives.

Robinson and I met over lunch in the coffee shop of the St. Regis Hotel, a busy, crowded fast-food cafe so popular with Indians that they all call it "the reservation". If you are having difficulty getting appointments with busy aboriginal leaders, your best bet is to hang around "the rez". Sooner or later everyone who is anyone drifts through to snatch a bite of food between their endless meetings. The choice of a coffee shop as the place to hang out is significant: the old days when people hung around in bars are long gone.

When I expressed mild surprise that Robinson was supping with Jake Epp, a Conservative, he took it in stride. "Red Power was a movement to create awareness," he said, "it was about identity."

"We've mellowed out now," said Vic Pierre, from Roseau River, who had happened into "the rez", and joined us. "In the seventies we were really hard-core. But we've learned from our elders. They told us it's not going to help to take up arms."

The Aboriginal Council of Winnipeg had been formed only a year before, in response to the baffling problem of how best to represent

235

the interests of urbanized aboriginals. It accepted all aboriginal people as members, regardless of status, a recognition of the reality of native life in the city. Because of Canada's rigid system of classifying aboriginals, urban Indians have posed a problem both for governments and for native organizations. The federal government accepts responsibility for the health, education and welfare only of Indians on reserves. Status Indians who move from the reserves to the cities become the responsibility of the provinces and municipalities (although they continue to hold membership in their band, and are still eligible for education grants). The line of authority of the Assembly of First Nations runs from the chiefs and councils of the nearly 600 bands in the reserves, so naturally the Assembly as an organization is concerned mainly with those from whom it derives its authority. In the west the provincial Métis organizations have until recently concentrated more on their locals in small communities than on Métis people in the cities. A third organization, the Native Council of Canada, claims to represent the many non-status Indians who have fallen between the cracks of the aboriginal classification system (as well as many status Indians living off-reserve). This incoherent system has meant that the needs of urban natives have not been properly met by anyone.

A year or so later there was a further reshuffling in this confusing setup. Eric Robinson quit the Aboriginal Council and formed the Treaty Council of Winnipeg, allied to the status-bound Assembly of Manitoba Chiefs. It was the first such "urban reserve" (as it might be called) recognized by a status-Indian body; but Robinson quickly had a letter from the Minister of Indian Affairs, Tom Siddon, refusing to meet him, and maintaining the traditional position that urban Indians are no longer a federal responsibility. It should be added that other Winnipeg aboriginals, who had put great hope in the Aboriginal Council's comprehensive nature, were disappointed that Robinson made this change, by which he appeared to validate the many government-created divisions among aboriginal people.

Robinson told me Winnipeg has 60,000 native residents, but others put the number at closer to 40,000, and some even as low as 20,000. The exact figure is vague because no accurate count of aboriginals has ever been taken in the city, but it is probably almost 10 per cent of the city's population. Robinson estimated there are 10,000 native students in the school system.

The Alberta task force estimated that 43 per cent, nearly 60,000, of the province's native people were living in cities in 1990, about 40,000 of those in Calgary and Edmonton alone. Erma Bird told me that in Regina natives already number between 25 and 35 per cent of the city's population (that is, from 40,000 to 60,000 people). The federal government says that one-third of status Indians are living in urban centres (that is, 170,000, plus about the same number of Métis and non-status Indians.) So in Canada today, aboriginals are no longer out of sight and out of mind as they were when given the legal status of minors in the last century. Their urban presence is going to grow rather than diminish.

The demands of urban natives are very similar to those of other disadvantaged citizens – jobs, housing and education. Robinson's brief to the three levels of government stated boldly that the social and economic system has no place for the aboriginal person living in an urban environment. "He is upbraided for being a tax burden on the average Canadian. He is a refugee in his own homeland, denied any control over his life, and yet conditioned to reject his aboriginal birthright." This has created a volatile situation, the brief said. Only the payment of welfare and "other sterile exchanges of money" is preventing the anger of urban Indians from making itself felt against the larger society. Meantime, the violence is directed inwards. The need is for governments to work with aboriginal people at community level to develop skills, resources and opportunities, rather than to impose solutions on them from above.

Later that week, I sat in on the latest instalment of a government promise to help native people develop their skills. For almost two years a Labour Force Development Strategy had been in the works. The federal government was promising to spend $1 billion over five years to upgrade the skills and training of native workers. A National Aboriginal Management Board had been set up, and the government had agreed to five principles that the natives had insisted on. Now, representatives of Winnipeg's sixty native organizations were meeting under Robinson's chairmanship to figure out exactly how they could get their hands on the money and make sure it was effectively spent. By the end of the evening, it seemed that yet more meetings would be needed: would another two years whistle by like this?

To show that he was good for more than coffee-shop sympathy, Robinson took Norm and Vimy along to this meeting. They are exactly the kind of people who desperately need the help that such programmes might offer. The meeting, however, basically involved multiple bureaucracies, native and government, manoeuvring for position as they planned to divvy up the money that would be available. I couldn't help wondering what it could possibly have meant to the two disillusioned lifers.

The central role of women

Women have played a central role in creating the sixty organizations built by native people in Winnipeg. Some of these women have been committed social activists, like Louise Champagne, Winnipeg-born, but with roots in the French Métis communities between Lakes Manitoba and Winnipeg (known as the Interlake region). Louise has poured her impressive idealism and optimism into setting up a child-welfare coalition, a co-operative food store, a native-owned apartment building, and a number of women's organizations. The central organization from which all these have derived is called Winnipeg Native Family Economic Development (WNEFD), whose purpose is to improve the quality of native life in Winnipeg. "People development," is what Louise Champagne calls it.

Others, like Marion Ironquil Meadmore, have gone into business for themselves, trying in the process to change negative images of aboriginals. Some, like Myra Laramie, have embraced native spirituality. She transmits its values to troubled native students in the city's schools. She knows what they are going through because she grew up in a middle-class suburb of Winnipeg, and remembers the isolation and pain of always being different.

In a busy backstreet office in an old house in north Winnipeg, Kathie Mallett and Sandie Funk of the Original Women's Network bring native women together, provide them with information, contacts and training, establish networks for them, and teach them how to get access to the media. They began this work to combat the determination of mainstream society to keep aboriginal women in their place, and they work on a shoestring budget.

"My family migrated to the city in the 1950s, when there were hardly any native people here," said Kathie Mallett. "My father was Métis, he grew up in Minnedosa, served overseas, but when he came back he couldn't get a job, so he ended up doing labouring work. My mother worked at jobs like chambermaid and sewing." To this day, her family is divided by government-imposed status rules: "My father is Métis, my mother status, and I have brothers who are non-status. I notice that my cousins who live on the reserve like to segregate themselves."

Sandi Funk's family has been Métis for 200 years, since John Peter Pruden arrived in Canada from Edmonton, in England, and married a Cree woman. "The family goes back seven generations, but my parents never identified with the aboriginal end of it. In school people would say, 'I am English, or German,' and I would say, 'I am Canadian.' It became important to me to find out what I was, and I started to identify with my aboriginal background. One professor I had said that only two Canadians are not Métis. But, you know, most racists aren't going to come and ask for your definition before discriminating against you. We are all Indians."

As aboriginal women in Winnipeg, Kathie and Sandi feel they are "doubly discriminated against." The mainstream organizations in the areas of education, child welfare, and justice have no aboriginals on their boards, and no aboriginal input into their programmes. "They decide what we need and tell us they've developed this programme for us. I'll give you an example. Just this week we got a letter from the Salvation Army home for unwed mothers. They said most of their clients were aboriginal women, and they'd been told that their programmes were not culturally appropriate. So they asked if we could provide them with some arts and crafts."

This kind of stereotyping is common. "The image is that we are all on welfare," Kathie Mallett said. "Only recently, a native woman who is going to university was buying some lottery tickets, and was told, 'So that's where all our welfare goes.' Our receptionist was recently asked to stand up in a bus by an elderly white man who said, 'You get bus tickets for nothing. I have to pay for my tickets.' Fortunately, there was a young white man there who didn't agree with him. He said, 'Don't you dare to stand up.' "

Sandi Funk said: "For us, self-government is to have control of our own services, for our own people, not to duplicate the services that already oppress us." She added with a wry laugh: "Women are usually the ones behind any worthwhile new initiative. Women usually develop the service that is needed, and once the work is done the men come and sit on the throne."

In another old house in another back street of north Winnipeg, Mary Richards and Ida Bear work to revive and support native languages. As every recent survey has shown, this is uphill work. Only three of Canada's fifty-two aboriginal languages are thought to be secure for the future – Ojibway, Cree and Inuktitut. Whereas the native language is "flourishing" or "enduring" in only some 30 per cent of aboriginal communities, it is either "declining", "endangered" or in "critical condition" in most reserves.[2] It is estimated that fewer than half of Canada's status Indians can speak their original languages; and about half of all aboriginal students receive no instruction in their own language. Nevertheless Mary Richards and Ida Bear, believing that "our languages are the cornerstone of who we are as a people," hold language courses all year round, and travel ceaselessly throughout the province to encourage people to adhere to the language they were born with. Only thus, they say, can aboriginal cultures survive.

The work of Winnipeg's many native organizations has begun to change the image of native people in the city. These days, the so-called native ghetto of north Winnipeg has far from the appearance of a slum. When you drive east from Portage Avenue and cross the Slaw Rebchuk Bridge over the railway tracks, you hit street after street where most of the residents are natives. The houses are small and old, and maybe could do with some sprucing up; but, except for the colour of the people wandering the streets, the area looks little different from your average inner-city neighbourhood. Here the schools have 80 to 90 per cent native enrolment; here is to be found the network of co-operatives and social organizations built over the years by these aboriginal activists.

"There are 3,000 aboriginal families living around here," says Louise Champagne. "It's the biggest Indian reserve in the country." WNEFD owns the assets of the retail cooperative, Neechi Foods. The store is struggling to break even, so that eventually it can turn profits back to WNEFD for investment in other kinds of projects. When the store opened a year before, Louise thought that political consciousness, and commitment to the aboriginal cause, would bring native people to the shop. "We have come a long way, to realize that the bottom line is prices," she said, with a slight world-weariness.

"The federal government is into developing a native middle-class, so they want us to sell shares." But at Neechi they are not interested in creating a capitalist enterprise. "The original native economies were communally based, with equality for women and children. But they were undermined by being attached to commerce and trade.

Now we have to build an economy that will encourage and support a culture based on sharing and social equality. If we can't do that, there is no such thing as self-government and self-determination. It all involves education. The real development work is sitting down in people's homes. It takes a lot of time and resources. We are centred on people development all the way."

Besides generating jobs and creating a neighbourhood economy, the shop aims to help native people find a market for their specialized production. Neechi Foods is a major outlet for the wild rice from the Wabigoon co-op, described in Chapter 15, and also the delicious blueberry and cranberry spreads made by the women of Wabuskang reserve near Kenora.

Louise Champagne is disappointed that the 200 native professionals who work at the schools, clinics and the child-welfare centre in the area do not shop at Neechi. She feels these people have bought into the values of middle-class Canadian society all the way. "They are all spending money on food. If they were spending it here they would be helping generate self-government and self-reliance," she said, but by spending their food money elsewhere, "they are underdeveloping this area as much as anyone else."

To businesswoman and lawyer Marion Ironquil Meadmore, the committed social ethic of Louise Champagne seems ill-directed. "A native food store will never make money, and they shouldn't be guilt-tripping people who don't shop there," she said matter-of-factly. "People will buy where they can get the best deal, and who can compete with the supermarkets?"

Ms. Meadmore owns one of several businesses that occupy a large native-owned office building in Winnipeg right opposite the St.Regis "rez". (A year later she moved her business into the country to the Roseau River reserve.) She produces directories listing native people from coast to coast, and has become an essential clearing-house for information. Nowadays, she thinks like a businesswoman. "I can't help it," she said, laughing. "I've become so mercenary. Whenever I meet someone, I think, can I get an ad from him?"

But Marion Meadmore, like Louise Champagne, has paid her dues. When she graduated as a lawyer in the early 1970s, she decided she didn't have time to sit around waiting for the government to be nice to her people and for several years she poured her considerable energy into setting up things for the community – urban associations, community college courses, police training programmes, and so on. Her crowning achievement was to found Kinew Housing. This happened when a friend of hers, a mother of two, could not rent a house in her last year in university, so Marion decided it was time to put in some sweat equity of her own. The native organizations at the time said urban Indians were not their problem. "They were jealously guarding their jurisdiction," she says now.

Canada Mortgage and Housing Corporation turned her away at first, but a week later found a clause in the legislation that enabled it to lend her money. Within six weeks she had bought her first house. That was the beginning of Kinew Housing, a native-owned, non-profit housing co-op. There was nothing like it in Canada at the time. Now most of the larger cities have similar corporations, run by and for native people. Kinew still exists, and now owns more than 350 houses scattered throughout Winnipeg.

Marion Meadmore knows almost everything that native people are doing across the country, and has become a walking encyclopedia of native success stories. She loves to recite lists of successful projects – tourist lodges in the Rockies, small airlines in the north, friendship centres that own apartments and hotels, band-operated convention centres and shopping malls that would knock your eye out. They all break the stereotype, proving that native people are as capable as anybody else. Canadians never hear much about these successes: Marion Meadmore knows why.

"The media are still awful. All those drunken Indians beating their wives! It is just not the case. If you look at this building, the lights are on all night, people are working so hard. When it comes to getting power, you can't get it by sitting in the woods with your arms folded. You get it by getting into the places of power, and to do that you need money."

Even now the media, although more sympathetic than they used to be, still tend to play up the problem people and places. One day while I was in Winnipeg, Marion was infuriated because *The Globe and Mail* described in graphic detail the drinking and justice problems in the Ontario reserve of Osnaburgh. The paper's intention may have been to reveal an injustice, a social wrong, but she did not see it that way.

"Why do they keep doing this to us? I spend my life trying to persuade people they can do business with us, and the media keeps knocking us back with these stereotypes.... They just go on and on.... That's the biggest problem we have, the media. Some day I am going to really take them on. And then, watch out!"

Her directories are crowded with the names of native professionals, people who operate hundreds of native-owned farms, retail stores, trucking companies, marinas, service stations, restaurants, airlines and outfitters. Eric Robinson's paper to the ministers quoted government figures indicating there are more than 5,000 native-run businesses in Canada, employing 31,000 people, with an annual payroll of $328 million. But, he said, other sources indicate there are now as many as 20,000 native-run businesses.

A less euphoric view

Stan Fulham, who now runs Kinew Housing, tempers the infectious optimism of these women activists. His office is in a neat, unobtrusive office building in one of these same north Winnipeg streets. Fulham is an older man with a Métis background from western Manitoba. He has lived in the city for many years and says that, for native people, the city isn't improving.

"When I was fifteen, sixteen, I worked for fifty cents a day. I rode the rods looking for work. I went through the war, prison camps. I raised four children. I was always optimistic about Canada. But that world doesn't exist any more. I'm not hopeful about the future. I see my children having one hell of a tough life."

Kinew buys its houses with money borrowed from private financial institutions, or from special federal and provincial programmes for native or low-income housing. When things are going well, Kinew can buy up to twelve houses every year. The co-op rents only to native people, and the demand far exceeds the supply. The tenants have to pay up to 25 per cent of their income, or whatever their housing entitlement is under welfare, but the financial viability of the tenants has decreased dramatically in the last fifteen years.

"If a single mother comes in with two children, she has a housing entitlement of $300 a month," Fulham told me. "That doesn't meet the mortgage payments, let alone our insurance, maintenance and administration. Her house will be costing us $800 a month, so we have to submit proof to CMHC of how much she can pay, and they subsidize the difference.

"For years and years the government didn't believe that this thing would work. After all, housing run by a bunch of Indians! After five years we were still on trial. They kept calling it the Kinew experiment." But it has worked. Marion Meadmore built well.

Stan Fulham said that most of the tenants arrive from the reserves with severe problems – destabilized families, education levels below urban standards, alcoholism, culture shock and money worries. Seventy per cent of his tenants are on social assistance, most of them single mothers with children, and only 30 per cent have jobs. When Fulham started in the job in the early '70s, the proportions were reversed. Seventy per cent of his tenants then were married, and working.

"I would say that what's happened in the past ten years is nothing to what is going to happen in the next ten years. Some of these reserves have as many as 2,500 kids in school, and absolutely nothing for them to do."

Fulham objects to use of the word "ghetto" to describe north Winnipeg. "What we have in Winnipeg is a large number of single, detached homes. We don't have these huge apartment buildings, it is not a ghetto like Chicago or Detroit. And the problems don't originate here so much as on the reserves. They bring their problems to the city, and as the social situation on the reserves deteriorates, so things get worse in the city.

"I've had a lot of older people tell me they ate better in the '30s and '40s than they can today. There were a lot of deer. They would fish and trap, they had small gardens. They would get jobs. You don't see that any more. Now there is so much drinking and abuse. There was a sharing amongst us then. That's destroyed. That's been one of our greatest losses. Government programmes like welfare helped to break that down."

When I asked him about the revival of spirit I have sensed among many native people, as they return to the sweat lodges and other ceremonies, he said it did not jibe with what he heard from the reserves. "What is this revival of the traditional ways that people talk about? I ask people. There's no buffalo any more. There are no teepees. They're not nomadic. They've been losing their languages for twenty years. They have television and satellite dishes. Their whole lives are permeated with the English language. I would like someone to tell me how to combat this. The young people don't want to talk these languages. Their parents can't talk to them. All the kids I meet talk to me in English."

Stan Fulham's alarm about the future of the native languages confirmed what I had learned in the reserves around Kenora: that even among people who feel that a spiritual revival is underway, the languages appear to be losing strength.

The problems are not confined to the reserves, said Fulham. He began to reel off the names of Métis communities scattered across the province. "In the Métis communities where I came from in western Manitoba, most of the people have intermarried with whites in the last twenty-five years. When you talk about Métis communities, their only resource really is welfare." That's why, said Fulham, about half of Kinew's tenants are Métis people who have drifted into the cities in search of work and education.

Sisters of hope

Against Stan Fulham's dark view of the prospects of urban natives, one can place the fervent optimism, missionary zeal and searing honesty of – again! – many women, who are working to help native children through the school system. At Argyll High School (which a year later was transformed into the first aboriginal high school in a Canadian public school system) I contacted Myra Laramie, mentioned earlier in this chapter, a counsellor for native students. I had already met Myra's mother, who told me that she had brought up her children not to speak Cree because she wanted to aid their integration into the city. I realized when I talked to the daughter that this protective measure had been a mixed blessing, for Myra has literally ached for her missing language, and as she has grown to womanhood has fervently embraced Indian spirituality with all her heart and soul. Raised in the city, Myra Laramie, now a mother of three, is reaching for every vestige of aboriginal identity that she can extract from memory, and is using it to touch the minds and hearts of her troubled students.

"When we would visit my grandfather and grandmother at Fisher River, where my mother came from, I would see my grandfather sitting with other people smoking the pipe. I used to think these things were dreams. I remember them sounding the little-boy water drum. They used to take me down to the river, and I would sit with all these old men. They would tell me, it is time for you to be quiet now, Grandpa has to do some work. When I heard from my uncle that my grandfather had a pipe, my memories became more vivid, of an incredible underground atmosphere, because he never had his pipe in the house, he had it buried in the bush.

"Our ancestors are talking to us now in our dreams, feasts and sweat lodges. The old people are coming through, and they are saying that we are doing things right, they are showing us how to go forward without making too many mistakes. Some of these are people who were prevented from doing their work when they were here; but now they are doing their work. I have found personally that it is just a matter of stopping long enough in this world to listen to the spirits.

"White people are amazed these things are alive and well. That tells me a lot about their attitudes of superiority. They believe they are so powerful they have killed things that have existed since time began."

It was touching to hear this young woman, deep in her struggle against her own deracination, say that "My first language is Cree, but I was robbed of that. I think in Ojibway, even though I cannot speak it. It's here in my head and my heart. The more the spirit of that language fills me, the harder it is for me to say what I want to say in English. The English language is the most inappropriate tool on God's green earth to speak from the heart."

As a description of the language of Shakespeare, that may be going a bit far; but one can see why she feels that way. "It's critical that we have a language to maintain the teachings. Even though I do not understand it, when I hear somebody speaking old Cree my heart gets really full. Something happens to me. I do not understand what it is.

"My traditional grandmother adopted me as a granddaughter. She lived at Roseau reserve. One of her greatest concerns, and mine, is about what happens when we open our doors to non-Anishinaabe people.... When I see non-Indian people with rattles and handdrums, things we hold very sacred, and they do not know how to take care of them, it makes me want to take my bundle and go into the bush and bury it so no one will know I have it."

This perfervid attitude is more akin to a proselytizing religion than to the calm and contemplative tone normally used by native teachers and healers. But Myra Laramie, for all that, is extremely down-to-earth.

"Our students here are in good heart, but ill health. These young people I work with have suffered things no human being should have to suffer, and have seen things no children should have to look at. And they have survived.... There is a strength in the aboriginal people that somehow transforms any form of oppression.... The spirit of these kids is strong. They just need some healthy structure, someone to guide them, not lead them by the nose, to provide opportunities so they can be who they are."

She said that aboriginal people have suffered five generations of abuse, and that has given them five generations of chemical dependency. "You have whole nations of people who do not know how to come out of it; it's the ultimate form of oppression, people oppressing themselves." And now, on top of everything that has happened in the past, they are being hit by AIDS. "I have been talked to by the spirits and they have told me it is part of my journey on this earth to work in the area of AIDS." She had just returned from a forum in Toronto which had established that aboriginals are contracting the disease from the heterosexual population at an alarming rate.

Many aboriginals believe, she said, that there are no gays in the aboriginal community, and therefore no AIDS. "We have to break these myths: there are aboriginal gays, but AIDS is not a gay disease; everyone can get it." While she was telling me this, the phone rang. She listened for a while and then said into the phone, "That's some serious shit. If you're bringing up blood, that means something inside is bleeding. We have to get you into a treatment programme as soon as possible." She put down the phone. It was a former student, she said. "No one ever really leaves Argyll."

She sighed deeply.

Learning to be proud

I told Myra Laramie I would like to meet some of her students. She said I should come back in a few days when they celebrated International Women's Day. She had arranged for a number of prominent native women to speak to the students. I expected a dry, scholarly seminar, but it quickly turned into something more like a confessional as one speaker after another told the students of her painful life.

The first speaker, a vice-principal in a Winnipeg school, praised her mother as her teacher and adviser, the great influence in her life. For the second, it was a stepfather who had held the family together. She had grown up in a small, isolated community, where whites, Indians and Métis lived in equality. "I did not know there was supposed to be distinction based on colour of skin. My stepfather spent a lot of time with me. He could pass in a white community, and warned me I could take the easy way out and leave my people behind. He instilled in me a sense of responsibility to my people, and since then, whenever I've been confronted with a choice, the choice for my people always comes through.

"My mother is an alcoholic," this woman said. "She has hit bottom so many times, there's no bottom left for her to hit. When I was ten she walked out, so I took over the responsibility of being the mother." A few years later, at sixteen, she became a mother herself, determined to give her children a better life than she had had. She had become an activist ten years before when she'd moved to Lynn Lake, a mining town in northern Manitoba. There she came in touch with people living in tents made of old plastic and garbage, who had been rejected even by their own, and were not even allowed to walk into the town's stores. She joined with other women, some of them non-native, and after years of discouragement, heartache and long hours of work, they had seen all of these people moved from tents into apartments or houses "and some even have jobs".

As the emotional level in the room rose, a woman who worked at Argyll told how, when she was seven, her mother had abandoned her eleven children. But her dad would always wake "us babies" in the mornings, even after a heavy night of drinking, "because we had to go to school". Sometimes they had nothing for lunch, but the father would "come to school and bring us bannock".

This woman said: "I am the only one in my family who feels strongly about my Indian-ness. There's just been something that has driven me. I was married when I was sixteen. Somehow I was able to keep on trying to improve myself. My husband couldn't keep up with me, so I took my children and worked for a better life for my kids. I didn't want to be poor, and I guess I had a big mouth too, because I used to get into all kinds of shit.

"I went to university when I was twenty-one. I went for two years. There was always something inside of me, driving me, I just felt I would not give up. Even now, in my work, I still tend to take on too much of the responsibility of the students; but I have realized that nobody can live your life for you."

It was hard to imagine a counsellor in a mainstream Canadian school revealing herself to a roomful of students in this way; but the confessions continued. A woman who works in a pre-employment programme, mother of four children herself, said she had never felt comfortable as a woman until the last two years, when she had managed to leave an abusive relationship she had been in for nine years. "I knew I was not living," she said. "I was dying slowly.... What keeps me going now, and doing what I have to do, is my children.... My oldest child is fifteen. He was a frightened little boy, and it has taken him all these years to become a nice, gentle boy.... I am finally at a point where I feel balanced, I feel whole."

The atmosphere in the room had become emotionally hyper-charged. And then a slightly older woman called Dorothy Betz, more Indian in appearance than the others, began to speak. "I was raised in an Indian residential school," she said. "I was orphaned. Nobody really wanted me. But coming out of there, having realized you are Indian.... I guess what I am trying to do is...."

She burst into tears. Friends hurried up to console her. Once under control, she struggled to her feet. Quietly she said to the students, "It took me a long time, and a lot of years, to say, 'I am Indian and I am proud of it.' I want you to stand up and repeat it with me." Nervously, the students stood up and repeated it without much conviction.

"No matter how long you take," she said, "you have to get it right out of your stomach, into the open. I used to visit institutions. It was really difficult to get the people in there enthusiastic about themselves.

"Do not be ashamed. Try standing before the mirror and say it to yourself. It is difficult when you first try it, but before you know where you are, you are proud of yourself. Say it with me: 'I am Indian, and I am proud of it.' "

After a few more tries, the students were yelling it to the rooftops.

Milton: born with a flair

Of the many young aboriginals who have led protests against the invasion of their lands by Euro-Canadian technology, none is more worth knowing (and few have become better known) than Milton Born With A Tooth. His protest took place on his home Peigan reserve in southern Alberta. It was an act in defence of aboriginal land.

Milton has received sensational coverage in the media as a root-and-branch radical; unexpectedly, I found him to be working closely with Euro-Canadians, and to be conciliatory, convinced that the environmental movement could become a key element in the defence of aboriginal lands. I saw why he so quickly became one of the best-known aboriginal people in the country: he has charisma, a vital ingredient for media success. Like many other native leaders, he had had a tragic childhood. He became an alcoholic when he was eight, following the example of his parents:

"We were raised by the bottle," he told me. "I remember the first time my parents went to town. They brought back cases, gallons of wine. A bunch of the older people sat around drinking it. They drank about a gallon and a half and then they all passed out, leaving us kids with the booze. We had the greatest party of our lives, and when they woke up they thought they'd drunk it all themselves, and went to town for some more."

Milton knows why this happened. "Back in the '40s and '50s our people still lived our culture in a way. But with the boarding schools came the suppression. Our people managed to maintain the singing part. Both my parents were fluent in the language. My father took me to some of the ceremonies. In my first eight years, all that was more important than anything. It was beautiful. Then the alcohol came, and that became more important than anything.

"I got to be raised by nuns for a while. They still had residential schools on the reserves. Then in 1967 they bussed us every day into the white town. When they first took us to the white school we got new clothes, glasses, even though we didn't need them. They checked our nails and hair and shipped us to school. The assimilation process was in full swing. But I never made it out of grade eight.

"Of my age group everybody said, 'This group of people are useless. They're not going to amount to anything. They won't listen. They've got no respect.' But they forgot one thing. I remembered that the first eight years had been good. It was something to hold on to. When I quit drinking, that was number one. I got tired of the cops. I thought, 'You do not know me. That's not what Indians are like.'

"My Mum was the greatest part of my quitting drinking. She was raised in the old life. She was one of the elders who knew the secrets. They were scared for us. But when I quit drinking, they opened that door to all the secrets. It was painful for her to bring it out, the government, the boarding schools, all that, but she did it for us. Why do white people want us to be so much like that? We would say, because of what we have in our blood. That's why I have not become so prejudiced. They want us for something. I know today we have this ability to be sincere without using makeup. I grew up within that, my first eight years. We still have a taste of it. Today I am glad, that's what I live on.

"Do Indians today put culture as their priority? Some put money, the justice system, having a nice house, clothes, very few people put culture as their priority. Few live it, breathe it, stand up for it, or are willing to die for it. It has to be considered an endangered species.

"When I run into trouble, I look to Nature. It will tell you things. Do you ever see a crow and a duck walking together? You never do, they respect the original way. We have to keep the originality, like bears, you never see a grizzly and a black walking the trail together. I hunt a lot. The elders say the bear uses Nature in a respectful way. If you want real strength, you live and breath with Nature. All that is what I put before our struggle."

In 1990 Milton became so famous that among Indians he is identifiable everywhere by that one name, Milton. When the Alberta government built a dam across the ancient river of his people, the Oldman, Milton and his followers hit on a response so novel that it captured the imagination of people everywhere. The federal court of appeals had ruled that the project should have undergone a full environmental assessment before construction started, but the province carried on building the dam, regardless.

So Milton revived the Peigan Lonefighters Society, and in August 1990, they began to remove a sixty-seven-year-old diversion dyke in order to reroute the river into its original bed. The effect of this would be to leave the new dam without water, and cut off the Lethbridge northern irrigation district, denying water to hundreds of farms and a number of towns. Although their diversion was being made on the Peigan reserve, local courts ruled that the province owned the river and the riverbed, and had a lease on the dyke and the land surrounding it.

"We used our culture to devise our plan. One of the elders told us we should talk to the caretaker of the river, the beaver. The authorities thought we could not move a river. The Solicitor-General said, 'Let the Indians play around with their Tonka toys.' They did not take us seriously. They were expecting us to take an awesome approach, science, measurement, all that, but here we came with a beaver's approach."

With a borrowed bulldozer, the Lonefighters also dug a two-mile ditch upstream from the dyke. To stop them, the police raided the reserve, but retreated when Milton fired a warning shot over their heads. He had decided that if they came in for him, only he would shoot it out with them. Only one sacrifice was needed, he said, and he was ready to die to protect the culture. The police backed off and put the Lonefighters under siege as they camped out on the river, praying and holding sweat lodges and ceremonies. The police later arrested Milton in the streets of Calgary. He was convicted on six firearms offences, sentenced to eighteen months, and jailed.

Heavy rains in November swelled the river and caused it to move through the Lonefighters' diversion channel. Late that month, a storm drove the Lonefighters from their camp. Seventy heavily armed police then moved in, with provincial earthmovers, bulldozers and construction crews, working feverishly to repair the breached dyke.

Any Indian who fires a shot anywhere in the direction of the police can expect to be demonized immediately in the press, and Milton was demonized. I expected to find in him a sort of reverse racism, railing against not only the system, but the whites who run it. Instead, I found a serene young man in his mid-thirties, dark-skinned, with a drooping moustache. His long black hair was pulled back into braids, and he wore a red shirt over a black un-dershirt – a man exuding authority, strong, vehement, but not bitter.

"Everything that Canadians oppose in apartheid is happening here," he said. "You put millions of dollars into helping South Africans, and yet, when I meet you on the street, you cannot stand the sight of me.... We have to get out of this bullshit, and tell peo-ple what the truth is.

"Environment – that is the word that gives us credibility to pro-tect our culture. They [governments] have a way of defining the sacred sites in their environmental world. We want them to put aboriginal rights at the head of the list as an environmental ques-tion, but they say they do not have a process for that. In our way, it is always one, the connection between the river, the roots, herbs, people, fish, the rocks we use for our sweat lodge. What is important is the uniqueness of our connection to it all. We still understand all that. We have not been assimilated that much into the system."

When they put him in jail, Milton Born With A Tooth spent a month in segregation in the hole. "The jail was full of native people, and they said I was going to cause a riot. But their segregation was nothing compared to what I grew up in. I told them they ought to get some nuns. They would show them how to discipline people. Before they would let me out they said I had to see a psychiatrist."

Milton appealed his conviction, on the grounds that the judge had refused to allow crucial evidence to be heard, and had been sarcastic and overbearing towards the defendant. Two years after the confrontation, the appeal court ordered a new trial, ruling that relevant evidence had been rejected by the trial judge.

During those two years, Milton travelled the nation, from one reserve to another, sleeping on the floors of Indian houses, sharing their bannock and their poverty, encouraging aboriginal people to do what they must to defend their territory. In the process he was probably causing a worse riot than the one the authorities feared – a riot within the minds of younger Indians who are looking for the best way forward.

18

Teaching, healing, learning

Almost everywhere I went within aboriginal communities, I was directed to the people who in a real sense are lighting the road towards aboriginal revival – the teachers and healers. Some of these have been formally educated, such as Dr. Oliver Brass, B.Th., B.A. Hons., M.A., Ph.D., a university president in Regina; or Ed Connors, a psychologist in Kenora. Others are self-taught inspirational teachers, like Alex Skead, who works out of the Sacred Circle, a Kenora healing agency, or the unclassifiable Charlie Nelson – social worker-healer-priest-confidant-teacher – who worked out of a small room in a native-run family-services agency in Winnipeg.

I have found when speaking to groups of Euro-Canadians a fairly entrenched belief that assimilation is the only viable way forward for native people. This is not so. To a considerable extent, even aboriginals who live in the cities have not embraced the values of the dominant society, but tend to find solutions to their personal problems by returning to the spiritual beliefs, ethical values, and cultural identity into which they were born.

The many programmes fighting addiction are merely the most visible manifestations of this revival. A group of anti-alcohol crusaders has spread across the country from Alkali Lake reserve, British Columbia, and implanted their now-famous Flying On Your Own healing programmes almost everywhere. The Anishinaabe people around Kenora have already created an extensive network of agencies that draw deeply on the Anishinaabe past, digging into the roots of ancient wisdoms, so that troubled young people can be reconnected with their heritage.

254

Colin Wasacase's Ojibway Tribal Family Services agency, one of many that native people are now running across the country, concentrates not only on the troubled child but on the child's distressed family. It works to revive the eroded, neglected values that were traditional to native communities and families. When Euro-Canadian social workers were running these affairs, the foster home, the group home full of apprehended children, the adoptive home, all of them off-reserve, were the norm. These have been largely replaced by the practice of placing a disturbed or neglected child with the extended family, or, when that is impossible, with another family within the reserve, or when that fails, within a neighbouring reserve. The aim is that children should never be detached from their roots among their own people.

The inhumanity of a system
In each of these agencies, one hears the same terrible stories about the many years of inhuman, bureaucratic behaviour by trained social workers who went into Indian reserves and applied the norms of white, middle-class Canada to their judgments about aboriginal life. In one place after another, these people would decide that a home was an unfit place for an Indian child to be raised in, and at the slightest excuse would whisk that child off into non-native foster homes or adoptive homes, a process graphically described by Wayne Christian in Chapter 3.

Sometimes the aboriginal parents were not told what was really happening. Initially, their children were taken away for six months. After that, many parents were told they were not yet ready to receive their children back home, so they would sign another six-month authorization. Many parents were not told that after twenty-four months in care, their child became a ward of the agency – ostensibly with the signed agreement of the parents – and could be put up for adoption. There are even stories about how children were sent from the north to hospitals in southern cities to be treated for illnesses, were later put out for adoption, so that the parents never heard of them again and had no idea where they were, or why they had lost them.[1]

The idea that native children might be better off with their grandparents, or uncles and aunts, apparently seldom occurred to social workers in these cases: a reflection of their generally negative view of aboriginal life. All this is gradually changing. For example, before the

Ojibway Tribal Family Services agency was established, around 300 native children were usually in care in northwestern Ontario. That figure has now been reduced to about ninety, most of them the children of a hardcore group of problem families whose parents are persistent drinkers.

"We've done everything we can to keep children out of the court system," Colin Wasacase told me. "Once they get involved in that, it is hard to get them out. There used to be about fifty court applications a month to apprehend our children, but we've got that down almost to zero, no more than one or two a month."

When the policy of apprehension was at its height, the number of native children placed in non-native homes ran into the tens of thousands across Canada. Many of these lost children have turned up at the Kenora agency from places as far away as Spokane and Quebec City, hoping to find their families. Colin Wasacase told me: "We reconnected one young man of twenty-three with his mother, but he kept asking her, 'How come you left me in a garbage can?' That was the story he was told by his adoption workers, but it was not true." Some of these failed adoptees have come back just long enough to find where their roots are, and are satisfied with that. But many who return cannot adjust, and drift away again.

The impetus for the Ojibway Tribal Family Services came from three chiefs who had themselves suffered from family breakdown, and in 1984 began to discuss ways to bring the current tragic system to an end. "We organized around counselling and prevention," said one of the originating chiefs, whom I met by chance in the agency's offices. "Now we have constant counselling going on among parents and children by very experienced, well-trained workers."

Ancient and modern knowledge
Sacred Circle is housed in a rustic cedar building overlooking Lake of the Woods in Rat Portage reserve, just east of Kenora. Here, Ed Connors, a Mohawk, and Alex Skead, an Ojibway, and their staff use history, tradition, ritual and the elders as instruments in their healing work.

The two men are a fascinating contrast. Connors is highly educated and grew up passing for white in Mississauga, Ontario, a suburb of Toronto. Alex Skead, the child of trappers and hunters, didn't get past grade five; he has been a carpenter, plumber, welder, truck driver, mechanic, guide and trapper, and is now one of the most respected and sought-after spiritual leaders in Canada. Skead is the elder who presented the pipe to the nation's political leaders and brought in the drums at the constitutional conferences of the mid-1980s.

The work that Connors and Skead do together is representative of the cultural rebirth of Canada's aboriginals: everything they do is marked by a reverence for Indian spiritual values – values that the two men have come to in quite different ways.

Connors is outgoing, enthusiastic and, I would think, inspiring for those who work with him. He has a European appearance and was brought up without any real knowledge of his native background. His grandmother's experiences at residential school persuaded her that the best way to protect her children was to keep them from identifying with their native heritage. Connors did not even know until he was eight or nine that his grandmother was fluent in Mohawk and owned property in Kahnawake, near Montreal. "I knew I had Mohawk blood, but in a very distant kind of way. I learned a lot non-verbally. People continue to pass on values based on traditions even though they do not identify them as such."

One day a school teacher asked him, "What are you going to do with your education to help your people?" Connors says: "It really clicked with me." But it would be some years before he lived in a native environment. After university, he first worked from Newfoundland to Regina as a clinical psychologist, specializing in infant mental health. As he began to reconnect with his native background, his work with aboriginal patients taught him about the healing properties of the family. He wrote his dissertation on that theme, and now says, "I have come to believe there are more benefits to the individual to be part of an extended family than there are drawbacks. The healthiest parenting styles are where a number of primary caregivers are able to support and involve themselves in the upbringing of a child. A lot of child and other abuse can be related to the breakdown of the family." Because they still include extended families, native communities have the potential to provide people with the healthiest social environment in the modern world, he believes. "A lot of social workers say conditions are not healthy if you have too many people living in one house, but we have to place our emphasis on values that may be very different from what is valued in society in general." He adds, in a statement that might seem shocking in modern Canada: "I have worked a lot with single parents. I am convinced the single parent was never meant to be."

By contrast, Alex Skead barely survived his few years of schooling. "I did not speak any English till I was ten. From that age I went to Catholic school for five years. I almost lost my culture, my identity. They shoved things in my mind that we were never supposed to learn. I would not say that I learned nothing. I learned how to put up with a hard life. But I was so brainwashed, I threw everything away that I had been taught about nature. Then I got into an accident. Maybe the Creator wanted me to sit down and think. I was in a chair for four months. I saw people drinking and ruining their lives. As soon as I could walk I got out on the street patrol."

Ed Connors asserts the myths, legends and prophecies of the aboriginal world as the key to healing the psychological and emotional wounds of the Ojibway people. "There is an ancient Hopi prophecy that North American natives will emerge from a period of midnight into a daylight that will see us once again become leaders in this land," he told me. The prophecy says this emergence would begin when the eagle landed on the moon. On July 20, 1969, the message was sent back to Earth by the astronauts from the moon, "The Eagle has landed"; that has been taken as the day on which the aboriginal revival began.

"The essence of this revival is the struggle to reconnect with the spirit of our people, their traditions, beliefs and values," Connors told me: something that is happening not only in North America, but everywhere there are aboriginal people. "Anyone who is connected with the healing pulse realizes it is not money, nor alcohol, nor housing conditions, nor anything material that is the essence: the essence is the spirit."

By way of illustration, Connors told me about a fifteen-year-old boy from Whitefish Bay reserve who had been brought to him four years before. He had been adopted as an infant and, although clearly a native, had been raised as a non-native, given no sense of his culture or identity, and only enough understanding of his real family to know he had been rejected. As a teenager his confusion led him to do frightening things: killing animals, hiding knives, setting fires and hiding his excreta all over the house. His adoptive parents could no longer handle him, came to consider him virtually crazy, and placed him in institutions.

"From the first time I met him I told him, 'You are not crazy. But you are living in a crazy world, where people don't have the ability to understand you.' I told him he had tremendous potential to be one of the healers. I thought it important to reconnect him as an Indian, so I placed him in a cultural education centre in Thunder Bay with an all-native staff, where they help young people rediscover the traditional values and beliefs." After eight months there, the boy's anti-social behaviour stopped. He chose to return to Kenora, got involved with a drum group, came to the Sacred Circle's sweat lodges, spent time talking with the elders about dreams, and learned to rely on his dreams as a way of understanding himself. He began to reconnect with his family – a difficult process – and returned to his reserve, where he was taken into the extended family, went back to school, and began to pursue his potential to become a healer, through being educated in both worlds.

The Sacred Circle started with a suicide prevention programme among youth. Skead advised Connors to begin the programme by going into the communities to talk with the elders.

"We did that," said Ed Connors. "It was incredible. The elders knew what their role should be. Their greatest frustration was that youth were beginning not to respect them, to place their emphasis on knowledge coming from books. The essence of a lot of our work is to recognize the power of healing – physical, emotional and spiritual – within that group of elders."

The Sacred Circle now holds gatherings where the elders share their stories and knowledge with troubled youth. Through these sessions Connors believes the young have begun to appreciate and understand the power of the ancient teachings. Alex Skead's sweat lodge is in such demand that it is working almost every night.

Similarly, when the Kenora detoxification centre and district hospital set up their programme for solvent abusers – sniffers of glue, paint and gasoline – they travelled all over North America looking for answers, only to be told by the elders: "We have the solutions right here among us." The elders now work with abusers in a wilderness camp, using sweat lodges and other rituals to put the patients in touch with the traditional spirits. The course ends with a shaking tent, that strange manifestation of shamanism, usually denounced by the Christian Churches as satanism, in which people are reputedly put in touch directly with the spirits, without the mediation of a healer. That such a healing method should be approved and run by a district hospital, and subsidized by the provincial government, indicates the radically different turn that healing programmes take when placed in native hands.

While working hard to revive native pride, languages and beliefs, most of the native leaders I have spoken to are also anxious to effect a reconciliation with their Euro-Canadian neighbours – but on a new basis of mutual respect. Alex Skead is one of those people. Tremendously in demand all over Ontario to give workshops on reserves, speak to young offenders, and teach imprisoned natives about their culture, he also sees himself as educating white people in the realities of aboriginal life: "When the constitutional conference in 1983 did not succeed, a lot of the chiefs cried, but I just laughed. I said this is my house, the House of Commons, but the government is not ready to learn. I told them it is going to take a long time. Every time they have a conference they close the door on us. They do not want to listen.

"I gave the Prime Minister a feather. That feather means I want a relationship that will respect my culture."

Healing and teaching in the city

Charlie Nelson and Oliver Brass may seem very different on the surface, but my impression is that they are engaged in essentially the same work. Both are working to heal the aboriginal trauma by restoring to its full meaning what Sakej Henderson, of Eskasoni, calls the spiritual realm of Indigena in North America. This is a work of importance to everyone who lives here.

When I met Charlie Nelson in Winnipeg, he was about to leave for the Whiteshell, that projection of the Canadian Shield on the Manitoba-Ontario border. Some rock formations – strange shapes, turtles and effigies of people – had been found there. The elders said it had always been a healing place. "Maybe we don't quite understand it yet," Charlie said. "It's been there for centuries. I have heard that people used to camp there when they came through for ricing from Kenora, and it was used by our Medewewin society."

For the next hour, this gentle and unpretentious man enveloped me in such a sense of warmth towards me personally and towards people in general (even those who have passed on), and towards the Earth, that I could have sat and listened to him for hours. As we talked, the idea that "maybe we don't know enough yet", a sense of knowledge evolving, kept creeping into his conversation. When I met him he was working out of the Ma ma wi chi itata (which means, We All Work Together to Help One Another) family-service agency in Winnipeg, but was seldom to be found there; he was always out talking to aboriginal people who might be in difficulty, telling them that they are not alone, connecting them to their ancient identities. Later he was elected councillor in the Roseau River reserve, which brought a change in his field of action.

Now forty-three, Charlie survived Catholic residential schooling in Winnipeg. "Then I tried to go to university, but instead I went travelling," he said. He went to Sun Dances, pow-wows and other celebrations, aboriginal gatherings for healing people. There, he listened when people spoke. He was looking for circles where he could find nurturing. He was searching for his own identity.

"I try to explain to people, you have got to have structure in your life, otherwise people make too many free choices. The Sun Dance, the pow-wow, the drum, the Medewewin, have structure."

Charlie is now a member of the Medewewin, an ancient Anishinaabe lodge whose influence appears to be replacing, to a large extent, that of the Christian Churches. The lodge has four doorways. The southern is in Wisconsin. The eastern is in Sudbury (although I have heard it said it now extends to Toronto). Winnipeg is the western doorway. The northern doorway extends towards the tree-line through the boreal forest within which Anishinaabe people live. "We are only a small number of people, maybe about a thousand. We have a healing place of peace and revival. It's hard to visualize. That place is not against anything. We come across so many life occurrences. We get angry. We have to heal some of that. We have to unload some of that stuff. We come back to the lodge for healing.

"I teach about what's on the centre of the Anishinaabe road. Each morning when we pray, we stand by the fire, offer that tobacco, look at the Earth where we came from.... If we are going to do something we have to make it sacred, clean, like the fire that burns in the centre of our lodge. We nurture that fire. We put only sacred things in it. I have heard it said that when you put this tobacco on the fire, there is a smoke comes from it that goes to the spirit world. I guess that's a way to give respect to the spirits.... Being human, we always want to renew ourselves. Having made some mistakes, we put tobacco down, and we ask for renewal again.

"The Anishinaabe values are kindness, truth, strength, sharing, but all of that within bounds. Sometimes we are too kind, eh? People take us for granted. We can be too strong, eh? We can begin to over- power somebody just by truth. You can really crush somebody if you aren't careful, eh? It's balance, eh? The old men talk about how giving we have been as a people, giving away all our land, until all we have left is truth and strength. We shared the land and the animals, and now we look at the problems our people have. I feel a lot of them have never had the opportunity to hear the Indian values.

"The cultural ways are coming back, but there's a long way to go. It's going to take a long time. There's a lot of things I have to learn, too. It's always been a few elders who have kept these things alive. They have a hard time with us, too, we try to modernize a lot of things. We test each other. The elders understand things by the old teachings. A lot of us have a hard time adjusting back to the way it was for our teachers."

I asked Charlie Nelson if he would describe himself as a healer. "Oh, yeah," he said. "Everybody can do it. If you spend time with somebody, you can heal them.... Some have more gifts, but everybody can do it. Especially if somebody has mental confusion. All you have to do is spend time with people and walk them through some stuff.

"I always go back to my own upbringing. My Mum really looked after us. She didn't have a Mum. My Dad provided. He hunted. He went out. He farmed for a while. He operated a dragline. He went to the Arctic. He used to sell wood. He was never on welfare." Now he wonders, Charlie said, what our children are going to learn (he has five of his own, from thirteen to two). What kind of jobs are they going to have in the future? Can we devise a work ethic that does not pollute the land, the water, the air?

He said the Anishinaabe impulse to fast comes from the urge "to visit with Mother Earth.... Anishinaabe people have this great desire to know more about Nature, to test a little bit of our fear, an inner re- solve to detach ourselves from our physical habits of eating and drinking, just to confine ourselves to natural things, to cleanse our body of all that physical stuff. It seems that our bodies become more pure, and that allows us to see things during that visit we have with Nature." He said that in this state, people can talk to the grandfa- thers who are gone, get from them their dreams and visions. "That's your identity, when you are contacted by the spirits." These were rit- uals of renewal which everyone should undergo at least once a year.

"I talk to a lot of people, nurses, teachers, I go to universities, I go to jails. I was telling some of these people, if we are any good we will be able to decrease the number of people in jails. If we can nurture ourselves as men and women, we do not have to fill up the jails. If we can come to terms with the road of peace and healing, there will be a lot fewer problems with alcohol, abuse and neglect."

Scholar from the reserves

Oliver Brass was a Saulteaux kid who, for some reason, just loved to learn. He was brought up on the Peepeekisis reserve, about forty kilometres northeast of Regina, and took his first eight years of schooling there. Once through elementary school, he and all the other native kids were shipped out to high schools off the reserve.

"It was notorious that nobody got through high school," he told me, when I met him in his book-lined university office. "However – I did." In the 1960s there were just a handful of aboriginal students in high schools, and the dropout rate before they reached grade twelve was almost 100 per cent. Almost, but not quite.

"I always loved to learn," he said, with an air of pleasurable reminiscence. "I don't know who taught me how, but I loved to read." Having zipped through high school, he pursued his interest in theology and philosophy. But none of these alone could contain his thirst for learning. He earned a degree in theology when he was only twenty-one. "I went and worked in the Church for three years, but my feet were still itchy and my mind still hungry." So he went back to university and took an M.A. This formal education did not detach him from his roots. He returned to the reserve in the mid-'70s, researched education for the band, and was elected to the band council. "But once again – I like to be around learning people. I went back to university."

He returned as a student to the University of Regina in 1977, just as they were setting up, in collaboration with the Federation of Saskatchewan Indian Nations, a unique educational institution – the Saskatchewan Indian Federated College. This is the college that ten years later would turn Erma Bird from a waitress and pizza slinger into a social worker. Brass began to teach there in 1979. The new college provided a focus for his continuing interest in Indian education issues, and he expanded his research into racism and Indian crime and incarceration. He earned his Ph.D. in psychology in 1984, and two years later – after only seven years as a teacher – became president of the college at the age of forty-two.

This college may well be the model for the aboriginal world of the future in Canada: its graduates are being educated in Western learning, but also being steeped in the traditions of their people. Eleven members of the board of governors are appointed by the chiefs of Saskatchewan, and seven represent Saskatchewan universities, the federal and provincial governments, and the students. The college calendar states: "Our mission is to enhance the quality of life, and to preserve, protect and interpret the history, language, culture and artistic heritage of the Indian people." The students, writes the Fine Arts department, "must learn to use the tools of modern society and have the heart of the past".

Day after day throughout the year, young Indians not only master Western philosophy, science, techniques and ideas, but study native languages and literature, the history of reserves, the nature of Indian cultures and personality, the Indian Act, the Hudson's Bay Company, the socialization of Indian children, the principles of Indian government, the role of plants in Indian art, and dozens of other subjects. Most of the young aboriginals who graduate from this college move into Canadian society equipped with the knowledge, talents and desire to transform the role of their people in Canadian life. In this college, at least, Indian history is not allowed to go by default.

"We started with nine students in 1977," Dr. Brass told me. "Fourteen years later, we have 1,200." The college draws students from every province and territory in Canada, and has seven international agreements with indigenous peoples' institutions in South and Central America and Asia. It has a campus in Saskatoon, offers classes in several Indian reserves, and has also delivered programmes in Manitoba, Alberta and British Columbia.

"We try to give students the feeling of being in a big family. We have five elders on staff, three men and two women, of whom four are very traditional, and one tends more towards Christianity."

The prospectus says: "The elders build an atmosphere of trust and respect. Sometimes students want traditional counselling in accordance with special needs. The elders will join with them in prayer, using sweetgrass and the stone pipe. Their psychology can restore student self-confidence and ease their minds."

Dr. Brass says that as they become educated, many aboriginal students discover a great interest in their heritage "especially in the spiritual aspects, getting back to feasts. It's just amazing. Ten years ago you would not see many students at Rain or Sun Dances. Now lots of them are there, trying to learn all they can."

Curiously enough, it is the people from the remoter areas of northern Saskatchewan who no longer have the pipe, the drums, the traditions. "They are very close to the land, they all speak the languages fluently, but they have been Christians for 150 years, and they do not have the ceremonial traditions. In the south of the province, only half the people still speak their languages. But they've always had the ceremonies, and one might say they have more Indian religious concepts about the world and how things work than do the people in the north. There's a lot of paganism in the southern half of the province. I use the word positively. To me it's a good word. Their belief system and practices are very much based on Nature – the quest for one's own vision, the use of various kinds of medicine. People here still fast for four days without water in the springtime, and do the shaking tent."

Typically, as he has done all his life, Dr. Brass has used his time as college president as much for learning as for teaching. "My own search and struggle has been one of rediscovery. We did not lose as much as some, but there's still a big gap between the knowledge of some of the oldest people, in their eighties, and my knowledge. I go and serve pipes to the old men, and take part in the Rain Dances. We have a lot of this in the summer. We are trying to get as much as we can from these older men and women. If we lose it now, it is something we will not get back, so we are lucky to have them."

Having watched for fifteen years over the development of a new, educated Indian elite, Dr. Brass is in a unique position to assess their character and their likely impact on the future. In 1990, the college graduated 600 students; in 1991, 700. "They are going out from the college with a lot of pride," he said. "Most of them are working in the Indian context. They are working at band level, they're working in cities, they're working everywhere."

And as Erma Bird had already shown me, these graduates are actively carrying the message to Indians everywhere of pride in their heritage. Even when representing a normally cautious organization such as the police, Erma Bird was outspoken and straightforward, full of confidence in her renewed faith in aboriginal values.

Higher education is already beginning to play a large role in

Indian political leadership. "In the days when an Indian was lucky to get through grade nine," said Dr. Brass, "we had semi-literate people going to Ottawa to argue with lawyers and engineers. They just were not able to contend with them. But now they are much better able to counter the arguments of the bureaucracy."

For most of this new leadership, self-government means taking control of their own finances, their own education, administration, and the planning and delivery of programmes "There are some people, such as the Mohawks, for whom self-government means sovereignty or semi-sovereignty. If you have a lot of your own money, that might have a chance of working. But if you are going to depend on the federal government, they can cut the rug out from under you pretty fast."

He said the Indians of Canada do not want to be independent of the federal government – in fact, are fighting against the off-loading of native services to the provinces: "And I agree with that myself." But another view is now taking hold: that aboriginal people have a right to a share of all natural resources in their province, and not just those on reserves. In Saskatchewan, where the Indians have never received the land they were entitled to under the treaties, opinion is now evolving towards the view that in future, money may be worth more than land. "It's hardly worth getting twenty new sections of land when there's nothing much to do with it," said Dr. Brass. "It may be better to get a few hundred million dollars and invest it."

He knows something about the government's lack of enthusiasm for funding things aboriginal. In 1990 he had to stand down as president of the Saskatchewan Indian Federated College to devote his full energies to raising money for a long-promised new building. The college has always been accommodated in the buildings of other institutions. Although the college represents the leading edge of the resurgence in aboriginal life, the federal government has given it only $5 million for the new building. Dr. Brass was trying to get $2 million from the province, and for the rest, "I get to go all over, begging for money." He hoped to raise $2.8 million from the corporate sector.

Right outside his office, a huge new institute for the French-language community (proportionately, a much smaller element in Saskatchewan society compared to aboriginal people) was going up, fully funded by the federal and provincial governments. "There's no fund-raising drive needed for that," he remarked.

As befits a scholar, Dr. Brass spoke pointedly, but without bitterness.

Gloria's baby: No chance

The social pathologies rampant in Indian reserves, so often mentioned in this book, are not just an abstract condition. In Kenora, I was given a wrenching reminder of the real suffering being undergone by real people in aboriginal communities when I visited Andrew Chapeskie and Doug Keshen, lawyers for the Ojibway Tribal Family Services agency. Chapeskie specializes in working to establish producer co-operatives based on indigenous values, while Keshen handles mostly legal work for bands in the region. When I walked into their office, Keshen was about to hold a meeting with some relatives of a woman whose baby had just been born in the town hospital and had been placed in the care of the Children's Aid Society. They had five days in which to arrange an alternative to the child's being taken away from the family, and placed in some situation off the reserve.

The bald language and grim detail of the affidavit signed by the social worker describe an appalling reality of reserve life:

On November 20, 1990 I spoke to Gloria [name changed], who was seven months pregnant. She had left the hospital where she had been kept overnight due to pains and bleeding. She said she left the hospital because she was bored. She decided to hitchhike (home).

On December 3 she again spoke to me and told me she had been drinking Javex and alcohol because she was angry at [man's name]. She was aware this was harmful to her baby.

On December 6 she spoke to me and informed me she had heartburn from the Javex and alcohol. She told me she had been sniffing the night before. She told me she considered suicide all the time, and her father had taken a gun away from her a few days before because of his concern that she would kill herself.

On Feb. 19, 1991 she was in the Lake of the Woods hospital where she was being treated for a hangover. She gave birth to a baby boy. The baby had an extra thumb, undescended testicles, wide-set eyes, low-set ears and a long space between the nose and lip.

These physical signs are often found in Fetal Alcohol Syndrome [FAS] children.

Dr. R. called Child and Family Services and informed us of the condition of the baby. She expressed concern about the baby's safety with Gloria.

Feb. 21. Dr. R. informed me...this child will have special needs.... She told me and I believe that physical signs of FAS usually indicate greater brain damage rather than less brain damage to the infant.

Feb. 21. I attended the maternity ward with a warrant to bring the child to a place of safety.... Gloria said she planned to take the baby home with her. I told Gloria I was apprehending the baby because I had concerns about the child's safety.

Gloria has had four previous children who were made Crown wards due to family violence, substance abuse, and unstable lifestyle in June 1989.

As a result of the meeting in Doug Keshen's office, a member of the extended family was found who was willing to care for the child.

19

Superbly mixed up:
the Métis

The many categories differentiating aboriginal peoples in Canada are confusing to non-natives. First, there are some fifty-three separate tribes or nations. Then, among individuals, some are recognized by the Canadian government as having Indian status, and some, known as non-status Indians, are not. As we have seen in Chapters 6 and 10, this particular division was invented by non-native bureaucrats and politicians. Then there are the Métis, who are different yet again. They are the offspring of European traders and aboriginal women; and in the middle of the nineteenth century, they formed their own remarkable nation on the prairies.

In November 1970 I sat in on a small meeting in Victoria, British Columbia, when a group of Métis and non-status Indian leaders decided to form the Native Council of Canada, their first national organization. I had been travelling around northern Alberta as a reporter, talking to native people, and when I had a free weekend in Edmonton, Stan Daniels, who was then president of the Métis Association of Alberta, suggested I should accompany him to Victoria and watch some history being made.

After generations as the most oppressed people in Canada, the Métis had decided to fight back. I wrote in a newspaper article at the time that if the treatment of status Indians, for whom the federal government acknowledged responsibility, was considered scandalous, "how can one describe the treatment of the other 250,000 Indians for whom almost no special programmes exist, and on whose welfare hardly a cent of government money is spent? If Indian poverty is bad, Métis poverty is worse. If Indian housing is inadequate, Métis housing is not fit for human beings. If Indian morale is low, their pride shattered in many communities, Métis morale has been even lower." [1]

"This is a very historic moment, a wonderful moment," said Dr. Howard Adams, the Métis professor from Saskatchewan, as the decision was taken to form a national body. "We are watching the rebirth of the half-breed nation that was shattered in 1885." Adams traces his roots back through French, Scottish and Indian parentage to the prairie Métis society that brought Manitoba into Confederation in 1870, and then was crushed in the Riel Rebellion of 1885. His great-grandfather was a trooper with the guerrilla leader, Gabriel Dumont, in the last stand of the Métis. Adams had a poetic vision of the glorious Métis past, and he was bitter. With justification, he considered the treatment of his people after 1885 to be "the most atrocious brutality that has ever taken place in Canada". One of his ancestors was a hero, yet "in our Métis community when we were growing up, we were so ashamed we never spoke of [him]. I was ashamed to be a half-breed. They taught me to be ashamed. They sent us to schools with their racist history and their teachers with white supremacist attitudes, who have deliberately worked to inferiorize us." [2]

I had first visited some Métis homes a couple of years before, when Willie John had taken me along the east shore of Lake Nipigon, in northern Ontario. We called in to a town called Macdiarmid, which at that time was divided between neat rows of Indian Affairs housing built for status Indians, and a jumble of appalling tarpaper and cardboard shacks inhabited by the neglected Métis. I had lived in India, had visited Ghana, Nigeria and other Third World countries, and had travelled among the poorest people in the world, but I confess that suddenly to find comparable conditions in the centre of rich, smug Ontario, whose people were constantly congratulating themselves on their good fortune, was something of a shock. I remember emerging from one of those dark and sombre shacks, blinking in the bright light of day above the sparkling lake, and having to shake my brain clear to remind myself that, yes, I was still in Canada.

My shock at that time explains why, when I began to look into Métis conditions in Alberta a couple of years later, I took an immediate liking to Stan Daniels, and conceived a great admiration for him. Stan is still remembered by native people throughout Canada as the guy who walked from Alberta to Ottawa with a sausage to dramatize the extraordinary food prices being charged to northern people. He was a rough son-of-a-gun, a former construction worker, who until the mid-'60s had never had a political thought in his head. Although he had always known he was Métis, for many years he hadn't been very interested in that side of his identity, until life, with its usual cruel irony, gave him a good reason.

In the years before he quit drinking, Stan and I talked throughout the night several times, moving from one bar to the next in Montreal or Edmonton and usually ending up scoffing food in some all-night restaurant. I always suspected that Stan didn't bother much about the niceties of democracy in the way he ran the Métis Association of Alberta. He ran the show, and that was that, and it is not surprising that he was eventually beaten in an election. But, whatever his limitations, Stan was a man who had stepped in where, for decades, angels had feared to tread.

The story of how Stan Daniels came to political awareness, told to me during one of our bar-crawls, was a real saga of native life in the mid-twentieth century. The story went something like this: a woman who was related to Stan in some way was charged with murder; in self-defence she had killed a man who had horribly abused her for a long time. Stan thought he had better take the day off work to see what was happening to her, and what he saw changed his life forever. His relative, a poor and defenceless Métis woman, received no serious defence, and was railroaded into a conviction and a long jail sentence.

Stan figured that, if this was how things were done in the name of justice, he had better do something about it. He had no idea where to start. He'd heard you should always go to the top, so he called on the Lieutenant-Governor of Alberta and asked him to correct this injustice. That dignitary said he couldn't help, but he handed Stan on to others. Stan went to them one by one, and in the end talked to dozens of people. Established lawyers were not interested in the case; they assumed there was nothing in it for them, and no chance of winning an appeal. Eventually, in desperation, Stan went to Edmonton's skid row, and asked people there if they knew of any lawyer who would help poor people, or drunks, or bums. He was told there was one lawyer who would take on a case, but he himself was a drinker. Somehow Stan found him, and persuaded him to take the case. To make a long story short, they got the appeal to court, and the woman's sentence was reduced. Stan realized that if this was how Métis people were being treated, there was plenty of work for him to do. Pretty soon he was president of the Métis Association, shaking things up on behalf of the most downtrodden people in the province.

I have never written about this story until now, and never verified any part of it. But I've always believed it, and now that Stan has gone, it reminds me of why I always liked him. The Métis Association was not exactly moribund when Stan breathed new vigour into it, but the people were in a downtrodden state, especially those living on the edges of small, rural communities; they were so poorly educated and trained that they had little prospect of making a decent living, were often cowed by the local establishment, and were subject to arbitrary police brutality as a fact of everyday life. Eighty per cent of them were on welfare. As far as the government was concerned, they were just ordinary Canadians who had fallen through the cracks. But Stan, and the many bright young Métis he gathered around him, soon found there was assistance available in government programmes designed for low-income people. His members qualified for this help, but never got it.

Since he didn't care too much about protocol, in his first years in office Stan simply drew up budgets to cover the Association's needs, and went ahead as if he had the money. By sheer determination, he obtained government grants of $185,000, at a time when he had only 485 members. There was so much to be done in the countryside where his members lived that in 1970, he hired extra field workers, for whom he budgetted $500,000. At the time he had only $183,000 coming in from various government departments. When other grants he asked for were refused, he fired the field workers, who marched in indignation on his office. Within a couple of days, Ottawa approved an extra $189,000.

That was the way Stan worked. He figured at the time there were a quarter of a million Métis and non-status people living an identifiable Indian style of life: "And," he added, with his blunt humour, "if we told them we had a thousand dollars to give each of them, the other two million would step forward."

I went with him once to a meeting of the Edmonton West Liberal Association. It was the period of Pierre Trudeau's flirtation with participatory democracy, so the Liberals had invited some non-members, including Stan. A resolution about the War Measures Act came to the floor. Stan leaped to his feet: "I would be really grateful if you could do something about this," he said. "The government beat us in 1885, and we've been living under the War Measures Act ever since." This was not exactly what the Liberals had had in mind when they'd asked him along.

The Native Council of Canada was formed originally from the three prairie Métis associations and the British Columbia Association of Non-Status Indians (BCANSI). At the time, native leaders were emphasizing the need for aboriginal people to unite, but the Native Council itself later split, and today represents non-status people, while the Métis have their own Métis National Council. (Both were represented, along with the Assembly of First Nations and the Inuit Tapirisat, in the constitutional talks of 1992.)

The impetus behind formation of the Council in 1970 was the knowledge that money was available to meet their needs, under social programmes then in place in Ottawa. "Things are moving fast in Ottawa," said Tony Belcourt, Stan's vice-president in the Alberta organization, at the Victoria meeting. "I have talked to these guys and they are waiting for us to organize. The money is there. I know it's there. But we are not getting it. That's why we need a national organization."

Tony Belcourt and Stan Daniels were different as chalk and cheese. Belcourt was a vigorous young businessman who had gone east determined to make the grade in non-native society, and, having done so, had returned to work among his people, "so that my Mum and Dad can get out of the goddammed shack they're living in." He became the first president of the Native Council of Canada, moved back to Ottawa, and played a key role in getting the Council firmly established and funnelling some of that federal money back to the provincial organizations. Later, as the Council began to founder between its two component groups, he went back into business as a communications specialist in Ottawa.

A people of constant surprises

From my first contacts with them, I have learned to expect surprises when meeting Métis people. They defy categories or stereotypes. They seem to include a high number of flavourful, interesting characters, and have a tendency to pop up in unexpected places, doing unexpected things. They have had perhaps the most romantic, tragic and surprising history of any group of people in Canada. When a

group of Métis appeared out of the west to attack Lord Selkirk's settlers in Manitoba in 1816, who could have expected that the leader
of these rough and rude people would be a twenty-three-year-old
who had already returned from a Scottish education and had lived
the life of a gentleman during most of his developing years? That
was Cuthbert Grant, who later became a magistrate, and was given
the title Warden of the Plains by the Hudson's Bay Company.[3]

There were already thousands of Métis across the prairies, offspring of Scottish and French traders and Indian women, and they
had developed a style of life so distinctive that many observers considered them already to be a people in search of a nation. They could
trade with the Indians in their own languages. They ran the communications routes for the Hudson's Bay and North West companies.
They were the most skilled people at handling the huge cargo canoes, and monopolized trade on the cumbersome cart routes that
criss-crossed the country. Most of all, they developed a great love of
the buffalo hunt, and the companies depended on them for meat,
skins, and that dried meat product known as pemmican, which was
the staple diet of the canoe-teams. The Métis organization of the annual buffalo hunt was so sophisticated that, in the words of one modern
historian, "When out on the plains they formed a sort of provisional
government."[4] These hunts were enormous affairs. In 1840, 1,600
persons took part, commanding 1,600 horses and oxen and 1,200
Red River carts. The hunt lasted all of June and July and brought in
more than a million pounds of meat and pemmican.[5] "They think of
themselves as the happiest people in existence," wrote Colin
Robinson, a leader of the Hudson's Bay Company, "and I believe they
are not far mistaken."[6] When the contemporary historian Alexander
Ross visited Grantown, their settlement near Winnipeg, he wrote
that the Métis "...cordially detest all the laws and restraints of civilized life, believing all men were born to be free. In their own estima-
tion they are all great men, and wonderfully wise.... Feeling their
own strength, from being constantly armed, and free from control,
they despise all others.... They cherish freedom as they cherish life."[7]

When the Hudson's Bay Company charter came under attack in
Britain in the 1850s, who should be there to lead the charge in the
House of Lords but a Métis, Alexander Isbister, already practising as
a lawyer in Britain – a prime example of the Métis tendency to be in
unexpected places at unexpected times. Inevitably, these proud and

Stoney camp in the Rockies

Stoney family "at home"

The Stoneys of Alberta (top) made a colourful picture as they wandered the foothills of the Rockies in 1902. The reality, however, was that their hunting grounds had been taken from them, and they were harassed by Euro-Canadians everywhere they went. Their impoverished condition is indicated by the lower picture of a Stoney family "at home" in 1906.

Woodland Crees,1884

Mistissini children, 1927

For many generations, aboriginal people have resisted all efforts to assimilate them to Euro-Canadian ways. These pictures of Crees in the James Bay region of Quebec, taken over a span of more than a century, indicate their adherence to a relatively unchanging way of life. By 1884 (top) traders and priests had already been among the Mistissini Crees for thirty years, but the people continued to move in family groups across their huge territory in search of the fish, game and birds on which they subsisted. Below: by 1927, these healthy-looking children were still being brought up in teepees. Half a century later, in 1972, Job and Mary Bearskin (top, facing page) prepare a fish for cooking in their teepee on the La Grande River. Below: although aluminum foil and paper towels are present in the goose camp of Norman Sam on James Bay in 1990, the essence of this hunting culture is unchanged: a child plucks a goose under the watchful eye of her grandmother.

GUY BORREMANS

Job and Mary Bearskin, 1972

BOYCE RICHARDSON

Norman Sam's goose camp, 1990

Young communicants at Pukatawagen on their knees

Pascall Bighetty, of Pukatawagen

Church and School: two Euro-Canadian social institutions that aboriginal people have had to contend with in various ways. Above, a familiar sight throughout aboriginal Canada: young communicants at Pukatawagen, Manitoba, on their knees as they are inducted into the rituals of Christianity by the Oblate fathers. Below: the village's young chief, Pascall Bighetty, speaking on May 9, 1978, marks the retirement of Father Emile Désormeaux after fifty-two years as the village priest. In 1991 the Oblates apologized for the existence of their aboriginal schools. Facing page, from top: Isaac Beaulieu helped wrest control of the reserve school in Sandy Bay, Manitoba, from the Oblates and the federal government; Myra Laramie counsels native high school students in Winnipeg; Oliver Brass heads the Saskatchewan Federated Indian College in Regina, an institution on the cutting edge of the aboriginal revival.

Isaac Beaulieu, Sandy Bay

Myra Laramie

Dr. Oliver Brass, of Regina.

BOYCE RICHARDSON

Jimmy Mianscum

EXPERT   RAPPORTEUR   CHAIRMAN RAPPORTEUR
                                    OF THE WORKING GROUP ON
                                    INDIGENOUS POPULATIONS

Ted Moses

Aboriginal resistance to assimilation is evident at every level. Top: in 1990 Jimmy Mianscum, a trapper whose family's land was taken for the town of Chibougamau, Quebec, decades earlier, is still protesting before the Quebec National Assembly. Below, a younger Cree, Ted Moses, works as a rapporteur during a meeting of the Working Group on Aboriginals in Geneva. At his left is Irene-Erica V. Daes, of Switzerland, chairperson of the Working Group. Facing page, top: Ovide Mercredi, National Chief of the Assembly of First Nations, and probably the best-known aboriginal leader in Canada, is painted by artist Glenna Matoush during a 1991 visit to Mistissini reserve, Quebec. Below, Peigan activist Milton Born With A Tooth of Alberta became celebrated among aboriginal people by touring ceaselessly with his message of resistance to developments imposed on Indian lands.

Ovide Mercredi, right, after having his portrait painted
by Mistassini artist, Glenna Matoush

Milton Born With A Tooth

Isaiah and Willie Awashish

Gilbert and Job on story rock

The link between elders and the young remains strong in most aboriginal communities. Above: a man who embodies the ancient wisdom of his people, Isaiah Awashish, listens with his son Willie (who later died in a tragic accident) at a 1974 political meeting. Below, in a scene from the author's 1972 film *Job's Garden*, hunter Job Bearskin mounts the famed story rock of the Fort George Crees to tell a tale to Gilbert Herodier, then in his twenties. The rock, which stood at the confluence of the La Grande and Kanaaupscow rivers, was later flooded under seventy feet of water by the LG2 reservoir.

independent people opposed in 1869 the Euro-Canadian drive to occupy the prairies. They opposed the invasion of their Red River settlement with force of arms, but also with diplomacy, and formed the government that brought Manitoba into Confederation. Their achievements to that time certainly justify the pride of a man like Howard Adams; the brutality with which they were subsequently treated justifies his bitterness.

That element of Métis surprise struck me when I first went to one of their Alberta colonies (as they were then called) in 1970. Although the settlement was among the poorest places in the country, the patriarch of the colony, Adrian Hope, with whom I spent the day, was a delightful and amusing man who spoke five languages, wrote poetry, had travelled everywhere, and was the son of an Indian woman and a professor from Edinburgh. He was intensely proud of being Métis. He had kept the flag flying during some really desperate years.

"I always say," he told me, "it was only the brave white men who left the old country, and of those who came here three out of four went home. They didn't have the courage to stay. Those who stayed chose the best Indian girls they could find. I figure if I am the progeny of the pick of both crops, I should hold my head up high in any company." And he did.

This same surprising quality was still in evidence when I went west twenty years later, to see how things were working out for the Métis people. Once again, I met a lot of flavourful characters.

The quintessential Canadian

Before taking my research trip west in 1991, I asked Tony Belcourt for some contacts, and he came to my house bearing three closely printed sheets of an enormous family tree. More than twenty years had passed since we had first met, and he was once again active in Métis politics, now as a member of an Ontario provincial organization.

Tony's family tree was an example of the remarkable pride of the Métis. A few months later, he gave the joint parliamentary committee on the Constitution a copy of the family tree to prove that Métis people are real Canadians. Tony's family originated in the Ste. Anne district of northern Alberta around 1780, when three Iroquois from Kahnawake – Ignace and Louis Kwarakwante, and Ignace Wanyante – went west with the North West Company, and stayed long enough to form families. Within half a century, the families formed by these three men numbered in the hundreds, and eventually they were among the Métis families who moved westwards to escape the Euro-Canadian settlers as they pushed ever further into the prairies. This dispersal fanned outwards from the Red River settlement, following the formation of the province of Manitoba and the betrayal by the Canadian political establishment of the promises made to Louis Riel. Riel himself went to Montana, but many others, such as Gabriel Dumont, moved on to Saskatchewan and Alberta. Once again they were dispersed following Riel's unsuccessful uprising in 1885.

In the course of this second dispersal, some of these families created small communities in the foothills along the British Columbia border – typical Métis communities, such as Kelly Lake, B.C., Tony said, where they had been trying to make a living in the traditional way ever since. He gave me a list of his relatives in Kelly Lake, but said I couldn't contact them in advance, because none of them had a telephone.

I was hoping to find Kelly Lake when I drove north on a magnificent April day through the snow-covered mountains of the Great Divide into the Peace River district of northern B.C. I didn't really know where Kelly Lake was, because I had been unable to find it on any map. But MP Frank Oberle's office had given me the name of Archie Calliou, and I thought I would start with him.

I found Archie, all right, a short, vigorous man of strong opinions, living in a comfortable bungalow in an ordinary street in the busy milling town of Fort St. John. Now retired after a lifetime of industry and activism throughout the Peace River district, he sat me firmly down in a chair at the kitchen table and set out to tell me the story of his life, as if he had been waiting for just this opportunity for years.

His name, he said, derived from two Iroquois brothers, Louis and Bernard Calihoo from the Six Nations reserve in Ontario, who came west for the Hudson's Bay Company in about 1825. They are said to have come by way of the Saskatchewan River from James Bay.[8] Archie said his grandfather had been born in 1854, had seen the Riel rebellion, and had told him about it; the grandfather had been "very proud to have worked for the Hudson's Bay Company for fifteen years as a clerk". At the time of the treaties, the family could have become status Indians, but "...my great-grandfather did not want it. He said we will make our own lives, so they divided up their land, each person had his own lot, they built their own houses, became self-supporting, and today some of them are professional people in

Edmonton." They founded the town of Calahoo, northwest of Edmonton, and that part of the world is still full of Callious and Callihoos and Calahoos, a proliferation that made sense when Archie told me his grandmother had been midwife to ninety-three of her own grandchildren.

Archie's grandfather moved in 1870 to Grande Prairie, Alberta, where he took up land close to the British Columbia border and lived mostly by trapping and hunting. He traded some of that land for a horse worth $50 ("Now that land is worth millions," Arch said) and gave some to Archie's father. This was good trapping country, and Archie as a youngster helped his dad trap, and learned how to handle horses. He absorbed from his father the lesson that "You should live with your head up, pay your taxes, and walk with your white brother.... I really took that to heart, to make a beautiful Canada, and I worked hard," he said. But as more settlers moved in, the trapping country was taken over by the oil fields.

When war broke out, "I lied my way into the army." Although the recruiting sergeant didn't believe he was old enough to enlist, Archie overcame this objection with a bottle of gin: the train was leaving for the east in an hour, and the sixteen-year-old patriot was on it. He was chosen – "handpicked," he says – to join the British paratroopers, and was wounded when dropped behind enemy lines in Germany. "When I came back I drank for about ten years, because I couldn't shake what I saw in Germany. I saw Belsen. I saw terrible things. I am still affected by it right now."

He worked as a heavy-equipment operator, then as a fur-buyer, and finally became a social worker and, when he stopped drinking, an addiction counsellor. Musical as a child – he remembers sitting on an old pot-bellied stove and singing songs every morning – he became an old-time fiddler, and his band, The Northern Echoes, have for years been well-known entertainers throughout the Peace River region.

Archie founded a friendship centre in Grande Prairie, but quarrelled with the directors because they wanted to call it a "native" friendship centre. "I wanted it to be for everyone," he said.

This whole story smacks of the charming, eclectic Métis attitude to life, but Archie has added a few twists of his own. Having absorbed the idea of independence as a child, he developed an intense distaste for becoming dependent on government help. His monologue was peppered with somewhat contemptuous references to native people who had taken the government dollar; he seemed reluctant to hand me on to any of them, because, he said, I would find only "a whole bunch of PMs – always crying poor me, poor me."

"You're not talking to a crying Indian," he proclaimed, "you're talking to a proud Canadian." He produced a newspaper clipping in which he had replied to the somewhat off-hand remark made by Bill Wilson, the British Columbia Indian leader, to the effect that perhaps natives would have been better off if they had killed the whites when they turned up on the shores of North America. "I wonder where Indians would be today without the white man," Archie told the newspaper.[9] He'd had his lung removed, he said, and added, "I'm thankful I didn't wake up to find myself in a teepee, or I wouldn't have survived. The comforts we enjoy today are because of the technology our white brothers and sisters brought to us...." He said he had a lot of favourable reaction from native people to this comment. He was sure very few Indians agreed with Wilson.

"I don't want to hear about Métis, native, Indian, Ukrainian, French, Scots, I am none of these," he told me. "I am a proud Canadian. I didn't go to fight for the white man or the natives, I fought for Canada." If he'd been at Oka, he said, he'd have dressed up in his medals and invited either side to shoot him. He was against Indian land claims, and described the Mohawks defending Oka as "a bunch of cry babies". He produced a long and amusing story about how the first real Canadian was a bastard of mixed blood – the first child born of Europeans and Indians – and said that his current battle, to create a Canada free of discrimination, was fifty times tougher than any battle he'd ever fought in the war. "Canada is falling apart because there is no love and understanding between us," he said.

By the end of the evening, although reluctant to go with me to Kelly Lake or Chetwynd, where Métis people abound, Arch thought it might be a good idea if we travelled 250 miles north to Fort Nelson, close to the Yukon border, where two of his children were living. So we took off the next morning, Arch entertaining me along the way with hilarious and alarming tales of his experiences as an addiction counsellor. I was glad I made the trip, which took us up the Alaska Highway through magnificent Rocky Mountain country.

In Fort Nelson, Archie attended Alcoholics Anonymous meetings, as he does wherever he goes. But I didn't get to meet any Métis people, except for Arch's son and daughter, both of whom have worked for years in the huge Fort Nelson sawmill. For them, their identity as Métis is no longer a major thing in their lives. If anything, while not denying their own heritage, they have inherited their father's jaundiced attitude towards other aboriginals. "I find Indians frustrating," said Arch's daughter, Vickie. "Sure, they're poor. But anyone's going to be poor unless they get off their butt.... You hear nothing but poor me, poor me...."

Where had I heard that before?

We arrived back in Fort St. John on a beautiful Sunday afternoon. I dropped Archie off and headed south to Dawson Creek, where I hoped to find my way to Kelly Lake. I checked into a motel at around five in the afternoon, and was again struck by how different these western towns are from those of eastern Canada. Dawson Creek has existed since 1912, but the housing, the main streets, the shops, garages and businesses feel as if they've just been built. So much seems new and temporary that one gets the impression that the town has time only for energetic stuff like building and moving things. Many of the hotels and restaurants feel relentlessly modern, as if insisting that they concede nothing in trendiness to longer-settled cities in the south. Dawson Creek is most proud of being Mile Zero on the Alaska Highway, but in the scale of civic pride the chopsticks mill, the waferboard plant, the oil and gas activity, the tax holidays for investors, seem to run Mile Zero close. In towns like this, Chambers of Commerce proudly trumpet their appeal for business, families, tourists, anything. "I came to visit my sister for a weekend and fell in love with Dawson Creek," someone writes in the Chamber's brochure. "The only way I would move would be if I could take with me the wonderful people I have met." This boosterish atmosphere has a sad side, for it emphasizes how irrelevant the aboriginal people have become to the concerns of the town builders.

The Dawson Creek desk clerk had a friend who said that Kelly Lake was about eighty kilometres south. I decided it was now or never, and headed south out of town, through the village of Pouce Coupe (where I had been told many Métis people still live) and off in the direction of the Alberta border. I soon found myself plunging deep into the bush on a lonely, rough road. After bumping nervously over sharp gravel for almost an hour, I came to a number of two-storey houses dotted among the trees around a small lake. I enquired of some young women who were walking by if anyone might know the history of this place. They directed me to a little house in a clearing.

I knocked, and a shout invited me to enter. Inside, an old couple were watching the hockey game on television. They cheerfully turned it off when I stated my business, and began to answer my questions about Kelly Lake with as little reticence as if I had been a life-long friend. While Ida Belcourt started to search through cupboards and drawers for books of local history, seventy-year-old Francis Belcourt, physically worn out from a lifetime as a trapper, remained propped up in his easy chair with his walker standing by in case he should want to move.

Francis's family had originated in Red River, and had been among those to move west after the first Riel Rebellion. Somehow, like many other Métis, they had never managed to move far enough to be free from incoming settlers. They moved on from Lac Ste. Anne, Alberta, in 1905, stopped for a few years in Grande Prairie, and arrived in Kelly Lake in 1915. Francis was the first child born there, in 1921, and had never lived anywhere else. This country is only a few miles west of where Archie Calliou trapped as a child with his father, across the border in Alberta.

At first, Kelly Lake was accessible only by toboggan trail. People came in the winter because the fur was always good, and returned to Grande Prairie for the summer. Eventually, some decided to stay. The first Kelly Lake squatters were Narcisse Belcourt and St. Pierre Gauthier, who settled in 1910. They were followed by others bearing well-known Métis names – Calliou, Gladu, L'Hirondelle, Letendre, and so on. "We trapped wolves, coyotes, foxes, lynx, marten, fisher, wolverine, squirrels, weasels, otter, beaver, muskrat," said Francis, reeling off the list with a gleam of pleasure in his eye. "The only animal we missed was mink. Lynx and beaver were the biggest. And we also had moose and deer, elk and caribou." The Métis fur trader, Gordon Belcourt, of Edmonton, for whom Archie Calliou worked for many years, had always bought a lot of fur in Kelly Lake.

With plenty of fur-bearing animals, and fish in the rivers, the trappers could make twice the average Depression-era wage of $150 a month. In those days everyone kept a garden, with cows, pigs and chickens. But in the last twenty years, Kelly Lake had been surrounded by new gas, oil and coal fields. The new service town of Tumbler Ridge was not far away. The new service roads had opened up Kelly Lake to the outside world, but had also frightened away the animals. Trapping had declined, and with the recent collapse of fur prices had now stopped almost entirely, Francis said.

I've never seen a place quite like Kelly Lake anywhere in Canada. It is still an unorganized community, whose only government institution is the school. There is no nursing station, no municipal council, no shops, and only one phone, in a public booth on the main street next to the school. "It's quiet here, away from the rat-race," said Francis with a smile. Twenty years ago, Kelly Lake had 350 people, but now it is down to 150. Young people who want work have to leave. Only one of the Belcourts' eleven children is still living at home; the others are scattered around the region in small towns, working in all sorts of ordinary Canadian jobs – on the oil rigs and seismic crews, in the logging camps. The younger people no longer speak Cree. "They know they are part-Indian, and that's about it," said Francis. "I don't think they realize where their ancestors came from." Like the family of Archie Calliou, this Métis community seems to be in the process of being assimilated. And throughout this territory, a colourful way of life is passing.

A vigorous social and political presence
Elsewhere in the country, however, the Métis are far from passing away. Five days later, I walked into the office of the Métis Association of Alberta in Edmonton, to find that Stan Daniels' fledgling organization had grown into a thriving enterprise full of entrepreneurial and political energy. The current president was Larry Desmeules. Short, plump and round, Desmeules was a Métis character, at one moment off-hand and flip, the next laughing and joshing with his employees; at one moment praising the Premier of the province, the next denouncing the iniquities of government policy. When I arrived to interview him, he acted so off-hand that I feared he wasn't going to talk to me at all, and was anxious to get rid of me as quickly as possible. But there was a picture of Stan Daniels on the wall behind him, and when I started to talk about Stan and the old days, Desmeules eased up and was soon proudly showing me through his establishment, taking me on a trip downtown, and offering to buy me lunch.

I was surprised to find that he was not an Alberta Métis at all, but was born in Macdiarmid, on Lake Nipigon in Ontario – that same depressed little town where, in 1968, I had first encountered the appalling conditions in which so many Métis were condemned to live in Canada. Desmeules still owned a house there, still had a sister and other family members in commercial fishing there. His mother, now seventy-four, has become a political organizer. But Larry himself left for the west twenty-two years earlier, because he'd been unable to support his four children. In Alberta he started his own floor-covering business, and later got involved in Métis politics. "I look white, I don't speak Cree, and I am from another part of the country," he said as we walked around the premises. "So when the election comes 'round, I have a hill to climb before I start." He laughed: the joke was on him.

He had found that "There is some sort of glue that holds the Métis people together.... Our people go where the work is," he said. "Nobody really knows where all our people are. We have tribal people and contemporary people and tribal-contemporary."

Unlike Archie Calliou, Desmeules liked being identified as Métis, but like Calliou he valued the freedom from dependency on government. Under his leadership the Association adopted the new name, Métis Nation of Alberta. "I am a hundred per cent Métis, I am not half of this or half of that. Our people are not all poor. We have people in our organization who are millionaires. A man walked into my office yesterday, he is drilling all over the world. We could become Indians, but we do not want to be wards of government. We don't want Indian Affairs interfering in our lives. We think they are doing a lousy job. We pay taxes like everyone else. We are not a special people, but we have special problems."

The main problem is lack of economic opportunity. To deal with it, Desmeules concentrated on creating work, improving education, and providing housing and financing for Métis people. The Association's housing corporation owns nearly 800 houses, and he set up a lending corporation that has helped 325 Métis businesses. "Only thirty-three of them have problems," Desmeules said proudly.

Because Métis people are often denied loans by banks, the Association started an institution that makes small loans of $3,000 or less – for example, to someone who might be in need of a crucial piece of machinery, such as a chain saw for a business selling firewood in Edmonton.

The Métis now control their own child-and-family-service organization. They put 75 per cent of their Association membership fees towards an education fund to help Métis children through college.

They produce a flourishing, unsubsidized newspaper, *Native Network News*, which gives detailed coverage of all native affairs in the province; it sells so much advertising that it was one of the few native newspapers in the country unaffected by the federal government's cuts in native communications grants in 1991.

These are all positive achievements, but the other side remains – many Métis are still living in grim conditions, dropping out of school, filling jails, lacking work. Although conditions have improved in the quarter-century since Stan Daniels began revealing to the public the facts of Métis life, there is still a long way to go. A flurry of investigations in the early '90s has shown that in small northern communities, Métis still tend to live on the fringes of town, are under-represented in the workforce, have lower education levels than other residents, and account for up to 50 per cent of the inmates in local correctional institutions. Eighty per cent levels of unemployment, said one report, result in "feelings of low self-esteem and despair", which lead to "a brewing hostility" among natives overwhelmed by industrial developments in which they play no part.

"Problems of family violence, suicides, school dropouts, medical and emotional disorders, rising numbers of teenage parents, are slowly destroying the families in these communities," said the report, a joint effort by government and the Métis Association. Many well-meaning programmes launched by federal and provincial governments have failed because they were always imposed from above, with little, if any, input from those they were designed to help. To avoid this type of problem, Desmeules negotiated a framework agreement with the province of Alberta, designed to involve Métis people in the decisions that affect their lives.

He was not dismayed by past failures. "Our kids in schools are suffering. It's not unusual for them to be called dirty Indians. Discrimination is there, it's alive, and it's against other ethnic people, too. But we don't bother about it. Education is going to clear it up.

"I have a lot of relatives who are in a poor state," he said. "The solution is not to throw money at them. The solution is to help them get their courage back, after they've been so badly beaten."

In March 1993, the Alberta Métis lost an effective leader when Larry Desmeules died suddenly.

The Métis settlements

Alberta remains the only province where Métis people have a land base in any way comparable to the Indian reserves. In the 1930s, Alberta established eight Métis settlements; it was at one of these, Kikino, that I had met Adrian Hope in 1970.

In those days the struggle to make these colonies work was heartbreaking; they had attracted only 2,700 of the 60,000 Métis people in Alberta. The main reason was the severe regulations imposed by the province on the people who tried to establish themselves in the Métis colonies. A settler applying to enter a colony had sixty days to choose his land, and a year to show some improvement on it. Usually he would build a log shack. The Kikino settlement board had managed to establish a small communal cattle herd, and a newcomer could rent four cows from the herd for five years if he was able to show he could feed them through the winter. To do that, he would have to leave his family behind in the log shack and find labouring work on the roads, because he would need money to buy a harness and team with which to gather wild hay for winter feed from the colony's sloughs. If the cows made it through the winter, they would calve in the spring. He would then pay one of his four calves back to the mother herd as rent. Thus he could laboriously build up his herd, a few at a time. And how successful was all this painstaking effort? "Well," Adrian Hope told me, "one guy recently sold thirty-six calves. At about $100 a head, he got $3,600. He's independent, so we don't have to worry about him any more. But some people, they've no capital, they couldn't make enough feed, and some have had to leave."

Similar conditions applied to the building of a house. The individual had to go into the bush, find the lumber, get it planed, and put it on the site. The community would then hire its own people to build the house. Total cost: $2,000. Adrian told me, "The housing that the province provides for people on the outside, the housing that is supposed to be available to everybody, you'd have to grow ulcers for twenty years to pay for it." In 1970 some people were able to afford an extra $400 to get the house wired for electricity, plus the $100 fee to connect it. But no one yet had any plumbing, or any prospect of it.

"When we have our own doggone home, we can tell the rest of the world to go to hell, and that's worth something," Adrian said. "When I moved into my own log house, I was king of the castle." The government believed the Métis colonies were a form of welfare; until 1980 they were administered by the Alberta Department of Social Services.

But at least the settlements did provide the Métis of Alberta with a land base (albeit not on good land), and today the residents of the settlements are relatively fortunate. Among them they have 1,250,000 acres of land, an area almost as big as Prince Edward Island, and their population is still fewer than 5,000. The 60,000 status Indians of Alberta have a land base not much bigger.

The old attitudes have finally given way to a more humane approach. In November 1990, Alberta established a unique form of democracy for these settlements. A Métis Settlements Council has been set up, and ownership of the settlement land vested in it. Elected councils now administer land transfers, development planning, finances, membership and all the other prerogatives of local government. All Alberta Métis have the right to locate on the settlements.

The government is providing $310 million over seventeen years to enable the settlements to reach self-sufficiency. For the first seven years, each settlement gets $3 million, tailing off thereafter, until, after seventeen years, they are on their own.

The hope now is to create employment in the settlements. The main problem may turn out to be that many young Métis people, even those who grew up in the settlements, may not want to return from whatever life they have established in the towns and cities of the west.

Revisiting Kikino

I decided to drive north to Kikino, the settlement I had visited twenty years earlier. The trip takes one through the well-ordered farmlands northeast of Edmonton, but as I moved further north, the neat farms gave way to bush. With the snow not long off the ground, I passed a number of Métis farmers burning off scrub in preparation for the new season.

I found Kikino much changed. In an administration office bustling with activity, Roger Littlechild, the twenty-eight-year-old administrator, told me the new government arrangements were unlocking provincial resources the Métis had never had access to before.

One of the biggest changes has been in education. There had been no school twenty years earlier, but I had described in a newspaper article how a programme called Newstart was trying to upgrade the skills of some adults "in nine or ten beautifully equipped trailers".[10] At that time the adult students were accepted as couples. The men were taught trades, the women home economics. Their children were looked after in a trailer nursery while the parents learned to read and write. Now Roger told me that his parents had been one of those couples. His mother's painful struggle through grade six, his father's through grade five, had started an upgrading process in the family that had continued ever since. "My older brothers, who are now in their thirties, got through grade nine," Roger said, "and the rest of us – there are nine in our family – have made it through grade twelve." Such educational upgrading appears to be typical of the whole community.

About half the people now support themselves by farming and ranching. Many work away from the settlement in neighbouring towns, with which, Littlechild said, relations are now good. With plenty of land available, most breadwinners have more than one job. Roger raises Arabian horses, a brother races thoroughbreds. As I drove around the settlement I came across Jack Lynis, a stepson of Adrian Hope, who had returned to Kikino with his wife Donna eight years earlier, after working five years for Syncrude on the oilpatch at Fort McMurray. Jack now supports his family by building log houses, but also has 220 acres, of which he keeps half in cultivation.

"Actually, our land is not good," he said. "I will have to work it for twenty years before it is as good as the first white farm outside the settlement. Their land was the same as ours, but they've been working theirs year after year."

From a drawer somewhere in their charming log house, Donna found a poem of Adrian's that is now taught to English classes in the new Kikino school, and has been turned into a song:

Have you ever been to Kikino
When spring is in the air?
With birds' gay songs afloating
And the sun shines everywhere?
As the Lone Pine Creek goes roaring by
Beneath the big blue sky,
Oh! I'm glad I live in Kikino,
When spring is in the air.

Evidently, Adrian's unquenchable spirit is still alive in the settlement. He would be glad to know he is still contributing, years after his death.

For years when the Kikino children were bussed every day to schools in the town of Lac LaBiche, the other kids called them welfare bums and similar insults, and there was a high dropout rate. Since the settlement school has opened, going up to grade six, the children no longer face this discouraging experience, or the wearying twelve-hour days, including the long bus ride to town and back. The settlement school has begun to teach Cree. For the first time in thirty years, a Kikino person has made it to university, and is intending to return to work in the settlement. There is now a store, a hall, a community centre, and a wildlife ranch, with a herd built up over eight years to more than 100 tuberculosis-free buffalo. Settlement housing is slowly being rebuilt under an Alberta rural-housing project, providing the Kikino people with the opportunity to upgrade their skills as they do the work. Down by Whitefish Lake, the Adrian Hope Resort has two beach fronts, ninety camping spots, and four rental cabins.

Not everything is perfect, of course. "We used to have 500 moose on our land: now we have about twenty," said Jack Lynis. There are seventeen gas wells on the settlement, and though the Métis receive rent for the surface rights, they receive nothing for the gas itself. "They've been piping gas out of here for twenty years. They came in, raped us, and left the pipeline in the ground, making money – for them," Jack said.

But he certainly didn't regret having returned to the settlement, and felt it offered a good future for his child. Working at Syncrude, Jack felt he was never discriminated against. "In Canada today we are a melting pot," he said. "I worked with Newfoundlanders, Chinese, Jamaicans, people from all over, and got along with everybody."

Compared with twenty years ago, Kikino is stepping into the modern world. And so, it seems, are the Métis people of Canada.

20

The Law:
a doubtful ally

In their efforts to defend their way of life, aboriginal nations have pursued both political negotiations and legal actions. Both have proved to be slow, cumbersome means of working out a new deal with Euro-Canadian society. The problem is that the rules of the game have been set by Canadian institutions, and these rules, by and large, are designed to protect the political and legal status quo.

The law has proven to be a doubtful ally for aboriginal nations. When they have been forced into direct action in last-ditch defence of their lands, the law has always been there, a pliable instrument with which to beat them into submission. And it is not just in punishing direct action that the law can be depended upon to flay aboriginals; many nations have also found that federal and provincial governments use the law to avoid having to observe legislation that they themselves have passed. In fact, some court judgments of the late 1980s and early '90s have been almost feudal in the contempt they have shown for aboriginal life and rights.

It is true that other judgments have been more friendly. Some courts, notably the Supreme Court of Canada, have begun to respond to the aboriginals' argument that they have always had rights, even under Euro-Canadian law, and that historically these rights have been persistently denied in an effort to impoverish and marginalize aboriginal people. Taken all in all, however, one has to admit that from the aboriginal point of view the law has shown itself capricious – its view of aboriginal reality dependent to a remarkable extent on the preconceptions of individual judges.

Until the last twenty years, aboriginal people in Canada seldom looked seriously to the law for relief from the injustices and disadvantages imposed on them. A few cases dealt with aboriginal lands, or aboriginal title, between 1880 and 1920, but these were mostly argued between various Euro-Canadian jurisdictions; their impact on aboriginals was usually a side issue. From 1927 until 1951, Parliament made it illegal to raise money for defence of an aboriginal claim – a measure that not only brought political action on their behalf to an end, but also obviated the court cases they might otherwise have pursued. Only since the 1960s have aboriginals resorted to the law with any great frequency.

Since then the law has not shown itself to be much use to them. It embodies completely European assumptions about land and government, and its precedents arise from completely European events. There is little room for such anomalies as the aboriginal assumption that no one can own land (but that the land is nevertheless theirs by right of their long occupancy and use of it); or for the loosely-structured, consensual forms of government conducted by aboriginal communities, which do not fit our neat Euro-Canadian political categories; or for the extremely practical, communal measures by which aboriginals have always managed the wildlife that they depend on. In fact, ever since the law was first applied to relations between aboriginal people and Europeans occupying their lands, its assumptions could be summarized by the catch-phrases: "We're civilized, you're savage," and "We've arrived, now you move over."

Given that we are all brought up with the idea of the law as a majestic presence in our national life, of the law's even-handedness towards all citizens, it is almost painful to track its blatant hypocrisies, dishonest leaps of logic, and (when forced to the wall) its barefaced reliance on unproven *obiter dicta*, whenever it has been forced to consider the rights of the people who were here before the law arrived.

It is typical of the law's relationship with aboriginal people that when one particular case was argued which has cast a shadow over all legal judgments about aboriginal land since 1888, the Indians were not even present in court, much less represented in any way. In fact, that case had nothing to do directly with Indians and the land. It arose from a quarrel between the federal and Ontario governments about which of them had the authority to issue a permit to the St. Catherine's Milling and Lumber Company to cut a million feet of lumber from land that had been ceded and surrendered by the Ojibway fifteen years earlier. Both governments argued that ownership of the land had passed to them with the signing of Treaty 3 in 1873. This required a judgment on the nature of the rights the Indians had ceded. The dispute went for settlement to the Privy Council in London, and those gentlemen, who had never set foot in North America and knew nothing about indigenous land-use traditions, came to the conclusion (very conveniently) that any rights the Indians may have were granted to them by the Royal Proclamation of 1763; and that these rights exist "subject to the goodwill of the Sovereign" (in other words, that they can be abolished if the Sovereign feels like abolishing them). Roland Penner, Dean of Law at the University of Manitoba, remarked sardonically at a 1991 symposium: "Pleasure of the Crown? If it pleases me, you've got them, if it doesn't please me, you don't have them?" [1]

In short, the St Catherine's Milling judgment legitimized the law's assumption that simply by arriving here, Europeans legally became owners of the lands of Canada. Right up to the present day, the law has leaned on that judgment. When Indians enter Euro-Canadian courts to argue land issues, they are not, to use the current catchphrase, on a level playing field. One side is assumed from the beginning to have simply taken ownership of the land of the other side, and the law interprets everything in light of that assumption.

Even when the Supreme Court of Canada began to lean towards accepting aboriginal rights in 1973, it still embraced the underlying assumptions of the Privy Council judgment of 1888. The Supreme Court added only that before deciding to extinguish Indian title, the Crown must make its intention "clear and plain". ("That's all?" asked Roland Penner. "As long as the intention is clear? Choose your words carefully and say, 'It is my intention to extinguish your rights.' Game over. They're extinguished.") [2]

A more sympathetic tone

During the 1980s, under the influence of Chief Justice Brian Dickson, the Supreme Court of Canada became more sympathetic to aboriginal claims. For example, Dickson held in a 1983 judgment that "Indian treaties should be given a large and liberal construction in favour of the Indians, and...doubtful expressions [should be] resolved in [their] favour." [3]

Further support was given by the same court when Ronald Sparrow of the Musqueum band in British Columbia appealed a prosecution for fishing with a net larger than allowed by a licence issued under the federal Fisheries Act.[4] This was the first case in which the Supreme Court was called on to interpret what the 1982 Constitution Act meant when it recognized and affirmed "existing aboriginal and treaty rights". In overturning Sparrow's conviction, the Supreme Court said that any proposed legislation must take account of its effect on aboriginal rights, in such a way as to "uphold the honour of the Crown, and must be in keeping with the unique contemporary relationship, grounded in history and policy", between the Crown and the aboriginals. The Court called this "a special trust relationship" and said this must be the government's "first consideration" in determining whether any legislation can be justified.

The Sparrow case dealt not with land rights, but with fishing rights; and the Supreme Court held that in the allocation of a resource to which aboriginal people have traditional rights, the only interest that ranks higher than the aboriginal right to fish for food is conservation and management of the resource.

Chief Justice Dickson was also responsible for two other opinions, delivered in judgment on the Guerin case in 1984, that strengthened the hand of aboriginals wanting to defend their rights. This case concerned the lease by the Musqueum band in 1952 of 162 acres of its reserve land to a golf club.[5] In the fashion of the time the entire transaction had been handled by federal officials. Years later, the band suspected improper dealings, and in 1975 sued the federal government for breach of trust. They won a $10-million settlement from the Federal Court, but the Federal Court of Appeal found for the government, saying that the government could do as it wished with reserve land, and had no legal obligation to act in the band's interest.

The Supreme Court did not agree. In his judgment Dickson gave a more favourable interpretation of aboriginal rights than ever before in a Canadian court. He described the Indians' interest in their lands as a "pre-existing legal right not created by the Royal Proclamation...the Indian Act...or any other executive order or legislative provision". He said aboriginal title had been recognized in the Nisga'a judgment of 1973 "as a legal right derived from the Indians' historic occupation and possession of their tribal lands".

Following this judgment, aboriginal people throughout the country began to insist with renewed vigour that their rights in Canada are "inherent" – that is, are not derived from any legislative act by a

Euro-Canadian, British, French or any other non-aboriginal institution, but flow from their occupation of their lands from time immemorial. When they joined the 1992 constitutional negotiations,
the native peoples' demand that their inherent right to self-government be recognized was at first peremptorily rejected by the federal
and provincial negotiators. But as the negotiations proceeded, the
need to include the aboriginal people in the proposed constitutional
changes became so obvious that halfway through the process, the
representatives of the federal and provincial governments changed
their minds: the inherent right to self-government was recommended
as part of the final constitutional package.

No doubt about it: this change reflected the judgment issued by
Chief Justice Dickson in 1984. It also reflected the skill with which
Ovide Mercredi and other aboriginal leaders argued their case
throughout these negotiations. The political and legal sophistication
of contemporary native leaders recalls what Dr. Oliver Brass told me
in Regina: the days are over when aboriginal people had difficulty
dealing with the complex structures of modern government. It would
be well for Canadians to realize that this change is permanent.

The Guerin judgment also confirmed that the federal government
has a fiduciary responsibility for Indian reserve lands, and gave rise to
some political soul-searching as to how that responsibility has been
fulfilled in the past. Within a few days of taking office in 1984, the
Minister of Indian Affairs and Northern Development, David
Crombie, asked his officials a list of sixty-four questions about how
the department had carried out its trusteeship role for Indian lands,
in light of the Guerin decision.[6] Crombie's questions implied long-
standing and persistent abuse of the trust relationship; but Prime
Minister Brian Mulroney removed him from the portfolio before the
bureaucracy provided the answers.

Always a weapon at hand
The examples just quoted are almost the sum total of the judgments
favourable to the aboriginal interest in the last decade. Even while
the Supreme Court was moving in a more sympathetic direction in
the '80s, lower courts were continually used by governments to frus-
trate the efforts made by aboriginal groups to defend their interest in
their traditional lands. Sometimes, as in the case of the Lubicon
Crees of northern Alberta, the law was even shamelessly rigged to

ensure that the aboriginals could not win. This happened in the 1970s when the Crees submitted a land caveat whose effect would be to freeze development over a large area while the case was argued. Alberta responded with a measure described by author John Goddard as "almost unheard of in a democracy",[7] refusing to accept the caveat, and referring the question to the provincial Supreme Court; and then, before the case came up, retroactively changing the law to ensure that the Crees would lose their case.

The courts to which the Lubicon kept appealing in the years that followed appeared to be under the influence of business interests (several key judges, for example, had once been lawyers for energy companies). While the legal arguments droned on, the oil companies rushed into the Lubicon lands, completely disrupted the traditional economy, and quickly reduced the people to poverty, disease, alienation, suicide and internal division, while scooping off more than $5 billion worth of oil.

Aboriginal efforts to defend their traditional hunting and fishing areas from the depredations of "developers" have brought them face to face with the capricious nature of the law in every part of the country. Some judges have appeared so firmly mired in historical Euro-Canadian assumptions that they have simply ignored the instructions handed down from the Supreme Court to give sympathetic consideration to aboriginal needs. For example, a group of three Quebec judges on the Federal Court of Appeal, in a 1992 judgment against the James Bay Indians of Quebec, placed the narrowest possible construction on Dickson's suggestion that the aboriginals should be given the benefit of the doubt of any ambiguities in treaties. "We must be careful...that we do not blindly follow the principles laid down by the Supreme Court...." commented the three judges.

Thus, for the aboriginals, any approach to the law is a kind of crap-game dependent on the attitudes of individual judges, who often take wildly differing approaches, even on the same case. The various judgments made in the Meares Island case in British Columbia are a good example. Meares is one of three large islands that form the backdrop to Pacific Rim National Park in the magnificent Clayoquot Sound, on the west coast of Vancouver Island. As in most of British Columbia, the aboriginal claim to Meares Island has never been dealt with. The huge firm of MacMillan Bloedel holds cutting rights to the island, and was preparing to clearcut.

Environmentalists invaded the island, stood in the path of the machines, and defied the loggers to do their worst. But they were obviously acting in a losing cause, because they did not have standing in the courts to interfere with the licensed rights of the company.

Most of the British Columbia forest has been divided up among multinational pulp and paper companies in a system known as tree-farm licences. These are like money in the bank for the companies, even if they never cut any trees: under each licence they are allowed a certain level of cut, and if the government ever wants to reduce that level by more than five per cent, compensation has to be paid to the companies. Thus, whenever an alternative use of the forest is proposed, the British Columbia taxpayer is put in the position of having to pay private companies not to cut trees that belong to the public. The courts have always stood ready and willing to enforce this ludicrous system at any time.

When the Meares Island battle was joined, I was making a film about the history of Canada's national parks. On Easter Saturday in 1984, a bitterly cold, wet day, environmentalists and natives from the Nuu-chah-nulth tribal council held a demonstration at Tofino, on the west coast of Vancouver Island, right opposite Meares Island, designed to draw attention to the irreparable damage that logging would do to Clayoquot Sound. The wind was too strong, the waters too rough, for a planned parade of small boats, but we shivered for hours on a barge in Tofino harbour as activists raised to a standing position a huge weeping statue designed to become the symbol of their campaign.

While this was dragging on, I went up in a light plane with a cameraman, and we bumped and ground our way behind Meares Island and deeper into Clayoquot Sound. I will never forget what lay before me: all around the sound, the steep mountains had been devastated by clearcutting; crude dirt logging roads had been hacked around these steep slopes, but had been abandoned and were now being flushed away by the rainwater, with enormous earth slides everywhere. The landscape looked as if nothing would be able to grow back for decades, if not centuries. It was hard to believe that any nation would allow this sort of thing to happen; or that any industry with any regard for its future would behave in such a way. This was what Meares Island too would look like if the cutting plans were carried out.

What eventually saved Meares was not the environmental struggle, but the presence on the island of a number of small Indian reserves.

The chiefs of the Clayoquot and Ahousaht bands, Moses Martin and Corbett George, asked the British Columbia Supreme Court to declare that logging would interfere with their aboriginal title on the island, and applied for an injunction to halt the logging until their claim had been dealt with.[8] The aboriginals thought they had an unbeatable case because of Chief Justice Dickson's judgment that the Indian interest in their lands predated the Royal Proclamation. But when the B.C. Supreme Court heard the Meares Island case, Mr. Justice Gibbs accepted the province's argument – customary in all such cases – that a halt to logging would have "potentially disastrous consequences" throughout the province; he said that financial damages could compensate the Indian bands for their interest in the land, if any.

Gibbs did not, apparently, believe that Dickson had meant what he said about aboriginal title. Indeed, he thought the claim to Indian title on Meares Island so weak that, as the Appeal Court later remarked, he felt "He could safely conclude that it could not succeed." The Appeal Court, however, supported the Indian case by a margin of three to two, and at least one judge expressed a view totally at odds with that of Mr. Justice Gibbs: "I cannot think of any native right that could be exercised on lands that have recently been logged," wrote Mr. Justice Peter Seaton, in the appeal judgment. "...The logger continues his steady march and the Indians see themselves retreating into a smaller and smaller area. They, too, have drawn the line at Meares Island. The island has become a symbol of their claim to rights in the land...."

As a result of that decision, the B.C. Supreme Court issued injunctions sought by Indian bands in half a dozen cases: to halt logging, to prevent railway expansion, and to stop general resource development on lands claimed by Indians. For every such judgment, however, there have appeared many judgments from justices who apparently still hold to the attitudes of superiority, shot through with cultural arrogance, that Europeans first brought to North America.

Temagami: back to square one
The two major cases of the 1980s in which native people asserted their land rights were resoundingly defeated at the level of provincial Supreme Courts, where judges rejected the notion that pre-European aboriginal societies had settled forms of government with their own established concepts of law.

The first of these was the judgment by Mr. Justice Donald Steele in Ontario Supreme Court against the claim of the Teme-Augama Anishnabai; the second that of Chief Justice Allan McEachern of the British Columbia Supreme Court against the Gitksan-Wet'suwet'en. Commenting on the second of these, historian Christopher Moore has expressed the dismay felt by many who have worked to improve understanding of aboriginals by Euro-Canadians. He said McEachern had "adopt[ed] the view that native societies were barbarous, primitive, and mostly irrelevant to Canadian history". [9]

It is instructive to examine both of these judgments briefly.

As mentioned previously in Chapter 14, the Anishnabai struggle to protect their Temagami lands began in 1973. Chief Garry Potts registered a caution against several townships covering 4,000 square miles, thus placing that land under a development freeze. The Anishnabai claimed entitlement to all these lands by virtue of their aboriginal rights, as well as by virtue of the rights reserved to them by the Royal Proclamation of 1763. But in 1978, the Ontario government sued in provincial Supreme Court to have the caution set aside, on the grounds that the lands in question were public lands, and the Anishnabai had no right, title or interest in them.

This case dragged its way through the courts until finally resolved by decision of the Supreme Court of Canada on August 15, 1991. In many ways the case was a disaster for the native cause in Canada, for the Anishnabai lost at every level.

In the Supreme Court of Ontario, the province argued that any rights the band may have had were surrendered in the Robinson-Huron treaty signed in 1850, or by treaty Number 9, of 1905-6, or were lost by various acts and statutes passed by Canada and Ontario. Mr. Justice Steele's preconception appeared to be that aboriginal societies at the time of European contact could not be called "organized", in the sense that European societies were organized. So he required the Anishnabai to prove that they had "an organized system of landholding and a system of social rules and customs distinct to the band", and that their occupation of the land had been continuous to the present day.

We have already seen in relation to the Algonquins how loose were the boundaries among various groups occupying eastern Canada at time of contact. The Algonquins, the Nipissing, the Ojibway, all considered themselves Anishinaabe (or Anishnabai), the differences between them apparently being limited to dialect chains. On the peripheries of their territories, some among them were always coming and going, moving between groups; the availability of game also dictated changing patterns of occupation and use. When I asked Gary Potts on one occasion where his people sat in this continuum, he said they were Nipissing, but added, "of course, we are all Anishnabai." The Nipissing were the people on the western edge of the Algonquin lands, mentioned in Chapter 9.

Steele, however, held that the ancestors of the Teme-Augama were not "an organized band level of society in 1763", and that it could be neither proven nor disproven that their ancestors had lived on these lands continuously since prehistoric times.[10] Even if they had so proven, he would have found against them, for he held that before the Royal Proclamation there were no Indian rights: they were created by the Proclamation, were limited in nature, and dependent upon the pleasure of the Crown (again, the St. Catherine's Milling case casts a heavy shadow). The colonists had obviously intended to occupy the aboriginal lands, Steele decided, and the purpose of the Proclamation was merely to ensure that the Indians accepted this occupation "with good grace and without bloodshed". After all, the general belief at the time, he wrote, was that Indians were "nomadic and wanderers" and all the Proclamation gave to the Indians was the "right to continue using the lands for the purposes and in the manner enjoyed in 1763".

Therefore, Steele said, if there were any aboriginal rights granted under the Proclamation, they were limited to such things as the right to hunt and fish for food, to trap for furs, to use herbs, berries and other natural products, to use dyes, to use stones for tools (but not for extensive mining), clay for pottery and pipes, trees for housing (but not for lumbering) and wood for fires, canoes and snowshoes.

However, all of this was more or less irrelevant to the main issue of ownership of the land. Steele also found that a leader called Tawgaiwene had signed the Robinson-Huron treaty in 1850 on behalf of the Indians living around Temagami Lake, and was paid $25 for this surrender. Steele admitted that the head man of the people living at Temagami appeared to be a man called Nebenegwune, who did not sign the treaty; but he found that Nebenegwune was too lowly a person to have expected to sign, and in any case he, too, was later paid treaty money. Steele thus rejected the claim of the Anishnabai that they had not signed the treaty. But even if they had not, he said, they had certainly adhered to it later, and had accepted treaty money for many years.

His judgment is peppered with legal *obiter dicta* revealing his complete acceptance of Europe's manifest destiny to occupy North America, regardless of who was here first. Many of his statements are similar to the legal arguments put forward by the province of Quebec in the James Bay case in 1972. For example, he says that "There is no legal trust relationship between the Crown and Indians. There may well be a high moral trust, but this is not one that is recognized at law." In that, he seems to be completely at odds with recent judgments of the Supreme Court of Canada.

Again: the government has a perfect right to extinguish aboriginal rights "by treaty, legislation or administrative acts".

And again: the Act establishing Canada in 1867 "did not leave to the Indians any independent rights or area of competence".

And again: "Parliament has exclusive power to define who are Indians."

And again: "Canada can totally ignore the band's internal rules as to who its members are, if Canada so chooses, and can deal only with those Indians or groups of Indians with which it wishes to deal."

It is worth quoting these legal opinions emanating from a highly placed judge, a highly educated Canadian, because these are the assumptions that natives must overcome as they struggle for their rights. However accurate Steele's dicta may be as law in the technical sense – no doubt they are descriptive of some sort of legal reality – they certainly pay scant attention to the changing climate of Canadian opinion, even within the legal system, in the last two decades.

Perhaps the most revealing of these opinions is Steele's decision that it was not the Teme-Augama who came to the conclusion that they had not signed the 1850 treaty, but

> ...rather it is the wishful thinking of a few well-meaning white people....
> In order to meet the aspirations of the...defendants, [this group] has pieced together a history from written documents, archeology and analogy...and then added to that history a study of physical features and other items, together with limited pieces of oral tradition....

Steele described the white experts who gave evidence on behalf of the Indians as "having lost their objectivity". In making these comments, he reverted to the infamous argument used by the Canadian

Parliament in 1927, when it concluded that the aboriginal claims of the Nisga'a of British Columbia were not only illusory, but were all got up by white agitators. The 1973 Supreme Court decision affirming the Nisga'a aboriginal rights showed how utterly wrong Parliament had been. Yet sixty years after Parliament made that terrible mistake, Mr. Justice Steele is still assuming that Indians are incapable of thinking for themselves.

Although Steele's judgment was at odds with the recent trend of Supreme Court pronouncements, once it had been uttered it seemed to have a weight that nothing could shift, not even the Supreme Court of Canada, when the Teme-Augama case reached that august body. The Supreme Court justices disagreed with many of Steele's conclusions. For example, unlike Steele, they found that the Teme-Augama had occupied the lands in question sufficiently to establish an aboriginal right; they also disagreed with Steele when he said that the Crown had no legal trust responsibility for Indians, for they found that the Crown had failed to comply with some of its fiduciary obligations. They did not, however, argue with Steele's basic interpretation of the facts: and they said that, whether or not the Teme-Augama had aboriginal rights, and whether or not they had signed the treaty, was irrelevant, because they had certainly adhered to the treaty afterwards and had accepted treaty money.

In this case, the bottom line of all the court decisions was that the aboriginal right had been extinguished.

Gitksan-Wet'suwet'en: failing to teach McEachern

Mr. Justice McEachern's judgment, delivered in 1990, was perhaps even more extraordinary than Steele's.[11] The 5,000 Gitksan and Wet'suwet'en people have always lived in the valley of the Skeena River in northern British Columbia, an area justifiably described by one local historian as one of the most beautiful places ever given to a people to live on.[12] Dismayed at the continued degradation of their life caused by the incursions of outsiders into their traditional lands, these people in the mid-1980s decided to seek a legal declaration that they own 22,000 square miles of territory, and are entitled to govern it through aboriginal laws that take precedence over the laws of the province.

Confident in the quality of their traditional forms of government and land management, the Gitksan-Wet'suwet'en decided to educate the court about their past. So, as they said themselves, they "opened up our treasure boxes of history" and spent nearly four years describing to McEachern how their social and legal system worked. In oral accounts brought into the courtroom they told of the hereditary titles, names and functions of their clans and Houses. They described how each House exercised control over its own territory, and how the Feast (sometimes called Potlatch) was the fundamental organ of government to maintain civil order, social equity and good relations among clan groups. But when the Chief Justice delivered his verdict, he gave no credence to anything the aboriginals had said. Like Mr. Justice Steele, he concluded that the aboriginals lived in a lower form of society than the Europeans who came among them.

> The evidence suggests that...[they] were by historical standards a primitive people, without any form of writing, horses or wheeled wagons.... The Gitksan and Wet'suwet'en civilizations, if they qualify for that description, fall within a much lower, even primitive order....
>
> ...Slavery and starvation were not uncommon, wars with neighbouring peoples were common, and there is no doubt, to quote Hobbes, that aboriginal life in the territory was, at best, "nasty, brutish and short".[13]

What the aboriginal witnesses had described as their law was, said McEachern, no more than "a most uncertain and highly flexible set of customs". He did not believe that they had "institutions", but that "they more likely acted as they did because of survival instincts which varied from village to village". In his view, the aboriginal people had become a conquered people "not by force of arms, for that was not necessary, but by an invading culture and a relentless energy with which they would not, or could not, compete".

Like Parliament in 1927 and Steele in 1984, McEachern completely discounted the evidence of Euro-Canadian witnesses who supported the aboriginals. He found anthropologists to be "more advocate than witness", and even went so far as to base this view on the code of ethics of the American Anthropological Association, which says that an anthropologist must do everything within his power to protect "the physical, social and psychological welfare" of those he studies, and "to honour their dignity and privacy". On these grounds, McEachern dismissed all anthropological evidence as biased and irrelevant.

Following the McEachern judgment, wrote Robin Ridington, a professor of anthropology at the University of British Columbia, "I experienced a deep sense of shame at the judge's failure to understand the teachings that the chiefs and elders had so generously given him. I knew they would feel deeply wounded by the callous and disrespectful language of his decision...." Ridington was not surprised that elders had said this would be the last time that the sacred boxes of their people would be opened for the white man to look at.[14] In his contribution to a conference that considered the McEachern judgment, Ridington isolated a number of McEachern's assumptions:

• Societies can be ranked on a scale from "primitive" to "civilized" (as we have seen in Chapter 4, this assumption was brought to North America by the first Europeans).

• Primitive societies were tiny, weak, unorganized and lost in an otherwise pristine wilderness.

• Written documents carry far more weight than oral traditions.

• Primitive societies did not fully occupy their lands and, unlike advanced societies, did not measure their occupation of territory by transforming or altering it.

• Aboriginal people of North America are all primitive relative to Europeans.

• Europeans tried to help the primitive Indians along the way to civilization.

• Indians must ultimately become civilized. Their problems arise from their lack of progress towards a state of civilization, not from their loss of lands and resources.

In fulfilment of this last assumption, McEachern took the extraordinary course in his judgment of lecturing the Indians, telling them they should forget about questions of ownership, sovereignty and rights, should "make their way off the reserves" and should join mainstream Canadian society.

I visited the Gitksan territories some months after McEachern delivered his judgment, and felt something of the crushed sense of bewilderment that the native people experienced. As one travels through the superb interior of British Columbia, it is easy to understand how they feel. Once they were the masters of this magnificent land. They lived well off its plentiful resources. They formed their lives around the yearly cycle of its seasons, the ebb and flow of its rivers and lakes, the movements of its animals, birds and fish. It has been said that these people could feed themselves for a year with the harvest from two months of fishing. That gave them time enough to build a unique form of government, and an impressive culture. They shared all these bounties with the newcomers: and yet it was all taken from them.

The snow still lay heavy on the towering mountain peaks as I drove up the valley towards the village of Kispiox, which sits on a point of land at the confluence of two rivers, north of Hazelton. Across the river, the valley floor lay towards the southern sun. The original inhabitants call the Skeena River the Xsan, or river of mists, and themselves the Gitksan, or people of the Xsan. Today the old Gitksan village of Kispiox has been largely rebuilt, with modern housing and a few public buildings, but it has a pleasing sense of individuality, stopping just short of disorder.

I talked to Jim Angus, administrator of the village school, a friendly, serious man of about sixty, president at the time of the United Church for British Columbia. Although apparently quite conservative, Angus could scarcely hide his anger over the court decision. He said the judgment couldn't have been more arrogant towards native people, or show more ignorance of them. "They have always said history began when we were discovered. But what about our history? There is going to be a certain amount of – bitterness is not the word – unhappiness." The years of the court battle had drained the people, he said. Locally, they had raised a million dollars to fight the case. Many now felt like abandoning the struggle. "But what about my children and grandchildren? For them there has got to be change: this can't continue."

Angus had heard an elder, a man who remembered when the people had been free to roam the land, say that they had all been herded into reserves like criminals. "I cried when I heard that." Angus had hoped the court would come halfway to meet them. Instead the court had shown there are still two systems of justice in Canada. "That is not a true justice system," he said. "I have no faith in it."

Indians became dependent on the government when confined to reserves. To break away from dependency, Angus said, they need self-government, which he compared to a bird with two wings. One wing is the knowledge and values of Indian people through their culture and languages; the other wing is formal learning about the modern world through the education system. "With both," he said, "we will be able to fly."

Angus is only one of many aboriginal people I have met in all parts of the country who insist that a fundamental change in the aboriginal condition depends on recognition by other Canadians of native traditions and cultures.

In the picturesque village of Hazelton, at the Gitksan-Wet'suwet'en headquarters, activist Herb George, who had travelled ceaselessly to explain his people's legal position, said many of them now realize that the remedy for their severe problems "lies within ourselves". Their programmes to improve education, to develop economically, and to pursue self-government, land claims and social development cannot work "until we become self-governing in our own minds".

George was known in the case as Sansat, his family's hereditary name, and his office was that of Speaker for the Office of the Hereditary Chiefs. He admitted a contradiction between what the Gitksan-Wet'suwet'en claimed to be and the way they actually lived. They claimed jurisdiction over a wide area, yet lived on reserves, were dependent on government, and had a band council under the Indian Act; they claimed they had their own laws, yet really lived under laws of general application; they claimed a spirituality based on their connection to the land, yet attended Catholic and United churches, and converted to revivalism.

The whole process of preparing the evidence and arguing the case had taken them back to who they really were, he said: as they argued, they began to live the way they were talking. They went off the reserves to confront loggers and government and assert their rights. They went into the rivers and began fishing in defiance of government regulations. Refusing to get permits, their people started to go out onto their traditional territory, "to manage it again", in George's words. When McEachern's judgment was appealed in 1993, a higher court accepted the existence of the aboriginal right, but placed a narrow interpretation on its meaning. No doubt the legal battle will continue.

Management the law won't accept

The Teme-Augama and Gitksan-Wet'suwet'en cases, embodying the colonialist attitudes of senior judges towards aboriginal peoples, suggest how dangerous it may be for aboriginals to look to the law for remedies. This is equally true, whether for defence of land title, access to traditional resources, or recognition of aboriginal management regimes.

The essence of the conflict over management is that for aboriginals, their methods of hunting animals are indistinguishable from their management of the animal resource. This is an idea strange to the European mind. Kenora lawyer Andrew Chapeskie has discovered that Euro-Canadian case law deals only with the right of access aboriginals may have to resources they have always used, but totally ignores the fact that native people have always managed their resources under a system of customary law.[15] Because of this, says Chapeskie, the courts have allowed government jurisdictions to encroach on aboriginal territories, leading inevitably to conflicts between the two systems of management, and creating enormous additional stress on aboriginal communities in northern territories.

Chapeski has described this issue in detail in a number of papers he has presented to international conferences. He uses the 1987 prosecution of an Ojibway elder, George Belmore, for hunting out of season, to show that in the Anishinaabe mind, to hunt according to customary practices is, *ipso facto*, to maintain an abundance of game, which to them is conceptually the same as game management.

Belmore came from the tiny Allanwater Bridge settlement, a few miles east of Savant Lake. Chapeskie reports that the thirty-five people there, members of the Saugeen band, were placed under surveillance during the waterfowl migration in April 1987 by officials of the Ministry of Natural Resources (MNR). On the evening of April 12, these officials watched while Belmore and his twelve-year-old grandson hunted in a canoe near his house. The boy shot a duck with his grandfather's shotgun, and when the officials found the bird in Belmore's canoe they charged him with "unlawfully hunting birds in contravention of the Migratory Birds Convention Act".

Later on the same evening, two adult sons of George Belmore, hunting with a younger brother, were charged with the same offence. They had shot twenty-five ducks, "to be shared out among themselves...for ceremonial purposes". Three other people from Allanwater who had shot nine ducks the previous day were also apprehended and charged, after they had shared the birds among them.

The plethora of Euro-Canadian regulations in this area still completely ignores native realities, and creates absurd confusions. Allanwater's customary hunting territory is bisected by two administrative regions and four separate districts of MNR, as well as two provincial electoral districts. Members of the band who live in

Savant Lake are in the Treaty 3 area, while Allanwater is in Treaty 9. George Belmore and his sons, though recognized as members of the Saugeen band, are not status Indians within the terms of the Indian Act. Nor are they ever likely to attain official status, since there is no record of Belmore's birth. Although officially not an Indian, he speaks Ojibway, understands little English, is literate only in Oji-Cree syllabics, and had to speak to the court through an interpreter. Taken together, these factors paint a picture of maximum confusion, with the aboriginal people caught in the middle.

Belmore and his family were hunting for waterfowl for a feast of thanksgiving "that forms a pivotal celebration in a cycle of celebrations based upon seasonal changes," writes Chapeskie. When interviewed about his offence, Belmore expressed anxiety that if the feast was not held

> ...the result would be the decline of game in the territory.... The game was put there for a purpose...to nourish certain animals of the forest and human beings. Unless the fabric of feasting and celebration was held, the relational balance between these animals and elder Belmore's indigenous people would be severed. By hunting with his grandson, Belmore was passing on the indigenous knowledge by which game in their region has been preserved to the present time. For the Anishinaabe people...conservation technique is learned through hunting, where, by direct experience, trans-generational indigenous knowledge is renewed...applied and updated.

In contrast to this delicate system, we appear with our regulations, surveillance and apprehension, turning a traditional ecological and spiritual experience into a criminal action. Chapeskie adds – not unreasonably, one would think, in the circumstances – that the non-aboriginal people who make the rules do not usually possess a knowledge of game sufficient to make responsible conservation decisions. The native methods of managing wildlife "resonate into the deepest aspects of...the political, social, cultural and informal legal institutions" of the Anishinaabe people, yet they have been "overrun and suppressed by the MNR rules". It is this, he writes, that has thrown Ed Machimity's Savant Lake community (and others) into crisis, with high rates of alcoholism, family breakdown, suicide and infant mortality.

Chapeskie's analysis of the Belmore case has convinced him that the Canadian courts have not understood the sophistication of aboriginal societies, their customary laws, and their regimes for management of wildlife, even when they acknowledge "traditional aboriginal use of the land".

Here again, the St. Catherine's Milling decision has had a critical influence. Its description of Indian tenure as "personal and usufructary" (that is, the aboriginals have a right to use something that is owned by someone else), says Chapeskie, "is not consistent with the communal practices of those societies and all that this way of life entails," and has blocked our courts from understanding indigenous law and management. Even the more sympathetic judgments of recent years, such as the Guerin and Sparrow decisions, leave the aboriginals subject to Euro-Canadian regulation of resources. Those decisions did not even try to deal with what Chapeskie says are the essentially different ways in which aboriginals and Euro-Canadians manage a resource. Chapeskie runs through every case that has come before the courts in recent years, and finds an underlying assumption by the judges "that others must manage these resources for the benefit of the Indians in the current Canadian context" – that is, within the context of a parliamentary democracy, and the federal division of powers.

This case law, he writes, "does not bode well" for the survival of indigenous wildlife-management regimes. He questions whether it is even worthwhile for aboriginals to argue their case for such management in Euro-Canadian courts, whose assumptions are so different from theirs. The implication of this analysis is that Euro-Canadians have far to go before we are ready to return to aboriginals powers that will enable them to recover their spirit, social coherence and economic prosperity. To date, only the very first, faltering steps have been taken along that path.

Sakej completes the picture

A few months after my visit to the Mikmaq village of Eskasoni, described in Chapter 5, I received a letter from Sakej Henderson (dated: "first snowfall"), enclosing a remarkable essay that further illuminates the differences between Euro-Canadian and aboriginal legal concepts. In the essay, Sakej turns the basic European assumptions on their head. He never goes quite so far as to say that aboriginals are civilized and Europeans savage, but he starts from the assumption, unheard of in non-native jurisprudence or historical writing, that when Europeans arrived in North America, they witnessed for the first time a system of government embodying personal liberties, social harmony, and freedom from rulers and elites, which was far superior to the systems they brought with them from Europe.

Sakej describes the writing of this essay – entitled "First Nations' Legal Inheritance" – as "my summer anguish". To compile it, he said, he had to search his soul so agonizingly that months later he was still not restored from the effort. I could imagine him at work: there must have been months of pacing morosely around the house as he dragged the written word out from within by main-force.

The essay is not easy reading. Sakej is very intuitive: he takes his impetus from the pulses arising from the North American land. He is a child of the realm of Indigena, and the written word is an agony for him. Nevertheless, he is trained as a lawyer, and his essay uses the legal concepts developed by Europeans, and the complex language of jurists, to reinterpret the consensual and non-authoritarian modes of pre-Columbian aboriginal life as they might have appeared, had they ever been defined in written form.

For the first Europeans in North America, Sakej writes, concepts of democracy and freedom going back to ancient Greece were "still entirely theoretical notions...since only monarchy and aristocratic structures predominated in Europe". Everyone, of course, he writes, loves freedom and individuality, but indigenous people had actually achieved a "higher political and legal development of these ideas".

Among the indigenous people whom the Europeans first encountered, their membership in a clan, territory, spiritual realm or race was secondary to their sense of a shared view of the world so strong it never had to be spelled out. Within their system of kinship relations, everyone had rights and responsibilities. The implicit order of this society was non-hierarchical: it could perpetuate itself without the need to accumulate more people, land or goods.

Using the Mikmaqs' cosmology as an example, the essay explains that their homeland was more than just a territory: it was a sacred order, with its own rituals for harmonizing the human, animal and spiritual realms. Inherent in these rituals was (and still is) the conviction that resources have to be renewed as well as shared. The family was the central and virtually the highest institution. Its shared values were reinforced by family opinion, and rewarded with honour and respect. By this means, individual passions were prevented from disrupting society. Many disputes that in other societies would be resolved by political bodies were resolved in the indigenous world within the extended family. Indeed, the very fact of having to seek a political solution to a situation was cause for concern, because it violated the harmony of the natural order and unleashed dangerous forces.

"Every family is equal, and every Mikmaw has an equal right to be heard and heeded by others. Coercive institutions are generally absent, if not vigorously opposed." Harmony, not justice, was the ideal, the priority being always to resolve conflict, not to determine guilt or innocence. Thus, the Mikmaqs did not have any inquisitional or adjudicative institutions, and no specialized professional elites, because they did not conceive of public wrongs. "There was only private tort, and families themselves were the courts."

In their relations with surrounding peoples, the Mikmaqs relied on indigenous federations, united by Nikmanen law (the word Nikmaq means allies or friends). These allies included the Beothuk, the Maliseet, the Passamaquoddy, the Abenaki and the Montagnais. When Europeans arrived, the aboriginals faced a constant struggle to stay neutral: "Europeans seemed to be constantly at war, and their need to take credit for victory when their wars ended was a source of further disharmony." For the Mikmaqs, peace was conceived as "a state of mind, calling for self-discipline and forgiveness". The Europeans appeared to define peace as "the humiliation and plundering of the defeated".

The concept of Mikmakik – the homeland – included the need for humans to live in harmony with the spirits of stones, trees, rivers, coasts, oceans and animals. Conceiving of their land as more than a territory to be occupied, they thought of it as having been "created by interactions and agreement between their ancestors and the ancestors of other species". It was an order in which a respectful human being could take part, but not possess or own. The Mikmaqs felt they were governed by the spiritual forces of the land, and so they developed rituals for harmonizing the human, animal and spiritual realms. These concepts emphasized stability rather than growth, minimizing risk instead of accumulating wealth.

The indigenous concept that resources should be shared, writes Sakej, has proven most elusive to British jurists: it seems inconsistent with the idea of property. "Among Europeans, sharing had traditionally been seen as a threat to personal autonomy or choice, and thus a threat to the enjoyment of legal rights. Altruism, the European conception of sharing and sacrifice...has usually been described as the antithesis of individualism."

Sakej says the treaties first signed with the Europeans recognized this customary, family-driven legal system. For example, a treaty of 1725 provided that "no private revenge" should be taken by either side, but wrongs or injuries should be submitted to the British government for remedy – an illustration, he says, of the indigenous habit of always seeking future harmony. District chiefs took personal responsibility for any outrage against the English, in an extension of customary laws.

Sakej's view is that this indigenous legal inheritance, as he calls it, has in fact influenced the European-based legal system: but in a multicultural Canada, the insistence on having one overriding system of law, superior to all others, has been used to "hold the indigenous people hostage". The resistance of the First Nations, their recent insistence on their aboriginal or treaty rights, has been met in such a way as to reveal "Canada's commitment to violence and terrorism, rather than justice".

Sakej says that to a certain extent, Canadian-trained indigenous leaders themselves have accepted the idea that native self-government requires coercive institutions. They have done so "without examining the elegance of the First Nations inheritance, or questioning the negative myths of the Canadian mind".

I have quoted this essay at some length because it brings us back to where we began this book – the state of mind of those who came here from Europe. Sakej's message is that elegant and ecologically sound aboriginal concepts of social and spiritual order, expressed more in actions than in theory, existed in the communities that Europeans encountered when they arrived in North America. The newcomers could have come to appreciate this order, and learn from it. They did not do so because their hierarchical notions, their racism, their assumption of cultural superiority, and their preference for authority over consensus blinded them to the aboriginal people whom they came among. They could not *see* them: and the evidence of my recent travels across the country is that only now, and only slowly, are we, the descendants of the colonists, beginning to see the people who were here first, and to appreciate that we have much to learn from them.

An exception to the rule

As several public inquiries into the justice system have shown, native people are often misunderstood, snubbed, insulted or treated with contempt by the lawyers, judges, policemen and justicial bureaucrats who deal with them. A notable exception in my experience was Mr. Justice Albert Malouf, a judge of Middle Eastern extraction, who was assigned by the Quebec Superior Court to hear the case of the Crees and Inuit who attempted to stop the James Bay hydroelectric project in 1972.

When the case came up, I was making a film about aboriginal rights for the National Film Board. A few days before the case began, we asked Malouf for permission to film in his court. We had recently spent three weeks filming a Cree hunting group, far in the northern Quebec wilderness. When my co-director Tony Ianzelo of the NFB and I met Malouf in his chambers – I remember he was dressing for a court hearing while we talked, buttoning his shirt, pulling on his pants, fixing his collar – he behaved towards us in a warm and engaging manner. He listened with such interest to our description of Cree hunting life, and spoke with such animation about the unusual nature of the participants in the case, that he entirely charmed both of us, and persuaded us that at least the Crees would be appearing before a human being of decency and goodwill. It is an indication of how little Malouf knew about aboriginal rights as he began the case that he referred to it throughout our conversation as "the Eskimo case".

He denied our request to film in his court.

As the case proceeded, Malouf's court was usually full of native people who knew no English or French, and were unaccustomed to the bizarre nature of court proceedings. Speaking always with the utmost deliberation, Malouf never failed to ensure that these people could see and hear, and, so far as was within his power, understand what was going on. If there were charts at the front of the court, he would ensure that they were clearly visible to everyone, and he never lost patience with the extremely laborious translation process.

The tall, shy Cree translator, Ted Moses, a youth scarcely out of his teens, had to wrestle with concepts that were simply unknown to Cree people. And he also had to feed back to the European sensibilities of the court ideas from the native witnesses which were not easily understood by non-natives.

Malouf never gave up trying to make things clear for everyone. Thus a hearing that the contemptuous lawyers for the Quebec government believed would last for only a few days stretched out for nearly six months, as Malouf laboriously turned the formal setting of his courtroom into a chamber in which a hunting people felt they could speak freely. All of this was in marked contrast to the way natives were, and still are, usually treated by the Canadian justice system.

Although he may not have known much about native cultures when the case began, somehow or other Malouf grasped that it lay within his power to create a sea-change, as it were, in the way that the justice system reacts to native people. At the end of this long process, he accepted the Cree and Inuit argument that their way of life depends on an untrammelled environment, and ordered Quebec to cease trespassing on the Cree lands. In doing so, he wrote a judgment that I am sure will always be among the finest humanist documents ever produced in Canada.

The prose of his central decision has an almost classical ring to it:

The Cree Indian and Inuit population occupying the territory and the lands adjacent thereto have been hunting, trapping and fishing therein since time immemorial. They have been exercising these rights in a very large part of the territory and the lands adjacent thereto including their traplines, the lakes, the rivers and the streams. Their pursuits are still of great importance to them and constitutute a way of life for a very great number of them.

Their diet is dependent, at least in part, on the animals which they hunt and trap, and on the fish which they catch. The sale of fur-bearing animals represents a source of revenue for them, and the animals which they trap and hunt and the fish which they catch represent, if measured in dollars, an additional form of revenue. The hides of certain animals are used as clothing.

They have a unique concept of the land, make use of all its fruits and produce, including all animal life therein, and any interference therewith compromises their very existence as a people.

They wish to continue their way of life.

Malouf's judgment was overturned within a week; the justice system reasserted its customary discriminatory attitude towards aboriginal people. But Malouf had done his work well. His judgment had such political weight that, under reluctant pressure from the federal government, Quebec was forced to enter into negotiations with the Crees and Inuit, which they had previously scorned as unnecessary.

A friend of mine who had known Malouf years before, when they were both engaged in the politics of the movement for returned servicemen, had told me that he was as straight and honest as the day was long; and that is exactly how he appeared both in his court and in his judgment. I have never felt that Malouf has been sufficiently honoured for what he did. No establishment honours have gone his way, and he would probably have been unable to accept any honours from the aboriginal people, even if they had been offered.

Malouf, however, has established his own reward: a judgment for which his name will always be honoured as a mighty stroke, both for natives and non-natives, towards the creation of a decent country.

21

Native self-government: escaping the tentacles

During the constitutional debates of 1992, as Canadian society moved closer to recognizing the aboriginal right to self-government, many critics took to the airwaves or the public prints to deplore the vagueness of the concept. Their fear appeared to be that native groups would use this right to declare independence from Canada; the country might find itself cut up into more than 600 ungovernable, impoverished little states, which would indeed be a kind of nightmare.

A more charitable (and realistic) interpretation of the native drive for self-government is that aboriginal people everywhere are fed up with the system of wardship that was imposed on them by the Indian Act in 1876. They have come to realize that their first task is to take control of their own communities.

The critics say that to grant aboriginal self-government is to enshrine a permanent division based on race within the Canadian body politic. (Not that there isn't one already, but that fact seems to have escaped their notice.)

Seen from the reserves, all this seems rather alarmist. What most aboriginal people have in mind is not the establishment of a patchwork nation of hundreds of powerless independent states, but something much more akin to the normal democratic situation in Canadian communities: one in which citizens exercise decision-making powers over their own lives through a hierarchy of institutions, established according to the functions they perform.

From that perspective, it is clear that significant movement has already been made towards self-government in many aboriginal communities. I have described some of these: for example, the takeover of education, or child and family services, by aboriginal institutions, and the many struggles to reassert control over their own economies. The work of the rice producers in Wabigoon, the effort of the Gitksan-Wet'suwet'en and Haida to control their fisheries, the attempt in Pukatawagen to obtain regional authority over wildlife management, are good examples. With few exceptions, aboriginals have so far won only powers to administer structures and regulations decided upon by higher levels of government – delegated powers, that is. Much closer to what they want, if they are really to take command of their communities and express their own social and cultural values, would be a new level of government that decides its own structures and rules.

At the broader level, aboriginals negotiating land claims have insisted, so far without much success, that the question of their jurisdiction is inseparable from the question of their ownership in the land, and should be negotiated at the same time. In other words, they are no longer struggling only for a defined territory, but are anxious to establish their rights within that territory, and the limits of their control over it.

The steps towards self-government take different forms, and are at different stages within each nation and community. In the Saulteaux community of Sandy Bay on the western shore of Lake Manitoba, they have been taking control of their own affairs by stages for the last twenty years. On the other hand, in a tiny Carrier community a few miles outside Prince George, British Columbia, the newly-styled Lheit Lit'en nation is just setting out on a bold programme to shake off the tentacles of the Indian Act which reduced them to poverty eighty years ago.

Self-government in action

I went to Sandy Bay to visit an old friend whom I had not seen in twenty years. I had first met Isaac Beaulieu in the late '60s, when he was secretary of the Manitoba Indian Brotherhood, an aggressive organization that was beginning to make the aboriginal voice effectively heard for the first time in decades. Its president, Dave Courchene, was a blunt, tough, working-class guy, typical of the aboriginal leaders who emerged in the '60s – men toughened by experience, who entered native politics because they were fed up with the way their people were being treated. As native political leaders, many of them faced far more complex and demanding tasks than they had ever faced before.

Dave Courchene and Isaac Beaulieu were an effective team, although quite dissimilar. Isaac was a short, plump, jovial fellow who loved to tell stories and looked and sounded as if he had just come off the reserve, but was really one of the best-educated native people in the country. Twenty years after we had last met, I ran into Isaac on Smith Street in Winnipeg outside the "rez". He was as amiable as ever, and a few days later I found myself driving west from Winnipeg across the gleaming-white, dead-flat prairie, on a cold day in early March, on the way to visit his reserve. I had heard on the grapevine years before that he had suffered some drinking problems, and had gone back to Sandy Bay, ninety miles northwest of Winnipeg, to recover.

Typically enough, Sandy Bay does not appear on most maps, yet the reserve has more people than the neighbouring towns. It is not one of those reserves that has begun to resemble an ordinary Canadian small town. Its houses are so widely dispersed that it does not have a real townsite. A few miles in from the highway, I came across a collection of larger buildings, and there, in a big, hangar-like structure that serves as the band office, I was soon being regaled with Isaac's irrepressible stories. The grapevine had been correct. Like many other leaders of aboriginal organizations in the 1970s, Isaac had had drinking problems, but they were long past. He wasn't alone in that, of course: leading the aboriginal movement as it was coming to life was a pitiless business that placed immense strain on those caught up in it. The communities were rent in a dozen ways: mostly impoverished, plagued with desperate psychological and emotional problems, uncertain of the best way forward, and for a long time powerless to resist the manipulations of governments. Little wonder that these leaders fell like nine-pins.

When Isaac returned home in 1972, he was still in his early thirties. He found plenty of work to do. The story he now told me was of a gradual movement towards self-government and self-reliance, first by using existing regulations, then by pushing them to their limits. The federal government was surreptitiously trying to implement the 1969 White Paper on Indian policy, although it had been officially withdrawn. Part of that strategy was the signing of master agreements by which the provinces would take over responsibility for services previously provided by the federal government.

Education was one of the main areas of federal control. Sandy Bay had for many years been the site of an Oblate residential school, much disliked and distrusted by the people on the reserve. The school had been buffetted by the many changes in government policies for Indian education. In the early '60s, to conform with one change in government policy, the Sandy Bay Oblate school was transformed into a federal day school (although the principal was still a priest). By the early '70s, to conform to another change in policy, the government wanted to close the school and send the children to the nearest provincial schools.

None of these changes improved the education offered. Only five Indian students had been graduated at Sandy Bay in 120 years; there was an annual staff turnover of 46 per cent, and an attendance rate of only 49 per cent. "They were running the school," Isaac said, "and we were running the cleaning services and buses." The band held a referendum to test opinion, and "One thing we knew was that the people did not want to lose their school. They wanted to keep it, but not the way it was."

Some government officials came to Sandy Bay with a proposed master tuition agreement covering the Turtle River school division. Isaac suggested a new, deadpan strategy. "Let's test the waters," he told the chief. At the next meeting, to the amazement of the officials, the natives accepted the master tuition agreement. Sandy Bay was the biggest school in the district, and they generously offered to accommodate in their school the white kids from the neighbouring districts. "That was the end of the conversation," said Isaac. He looked at me with an air of incredulity, and giggled from the sheer pleasure of the memory.

Before he returned to the reserve in 1972 Isaac had played a big role in writing a Manitoba Indian Brotherhood document called *Wahbung* (Our Tomorrows), a plan for the future that challenged Euro-Canadian control over aboriginal life at every level. Two decades later, the document still reads as a sensible plan for the improvement of native life in the province. "At Sandy Bay we started to implement it, and we've been doing so ever since."

Wahbung described the education of native children in Manitoba as "a complete disaster". As recently as 1959, only one Indian student in the entire province had made it into grade twelve from more than 1,000 who had originally enrolled in grade one; although this figure had risen to fifty-eight a decade later, nearly 95 per cent of those

316

who entered grade one still dropped out. At that rate, the Brotherhood figured, by 1980 only 10 per cent of native children would be making it to grade twelve. Clearly, something had to be done. Residential and reserve schools were described as overcrowded fire traps, poorly ventilated, with poor heating and lighting and cramped quarters. More than half the students entered school with no facility in English, and only 20 per cent were fluent. Dumped into a provincial school in a strange town or region, the Indian child was often embarrassed to participate in class work: "It isn't long," the report said, "before he begins to appear rather stupid to his fellow classmates. He realizes this and withdraws even further. The rest of the story is simple: frustration, loneliness, truancy, drop-out."[1] Of 337 teachers employed in Indian schools by the federal government in Manitoba, only seven were of Indian origin; and the rest were not encouraged to learn Indian languages.

"You are now the chairman"

Isaac was a little nervous about where he would fit in when he returned home in 1972. "We had been preaching community development," he told me. "People were hired to go onto the reserves to motivate the people. I was a consultant to Indian Affairs on that, but I came to the conclusion you can't do anything that way. You have to be part of the community to do anything. So when I went back home I asked, 'Do you have room for an extra guy, his wife and two kids?' I had some education in agricultural economics, and we had a fairly large ranch, so I thought I might fit in there."

One day Isaac took a drive around the broad expanses of the reserve, thinking about what he should do. He came across Angus Starr of the school committee standing beside his car, and stopped for a chat. Starr was trying to figure out the routes for the school buses. They spread the map on the hood of the car, and after a while Starr turned to Isaac and said, "Look, the school committee is me and two others. We try to maintain the school. Here, you take over. You are now the chairman of the school committee."

As he thought about how to wrest control of the school from the federal and provincial governments, Isaac spotted a section of the Indian Act that authorized the Minister to make agreements regarding the education of Indian children with other governments, public or separate school boards, and religious or charitable organizations.

Obviously, this section was not intended to include groups of Indians themselves, but he wondered what was to prevent the band from setting up its own Board of Education and applying for such an agreement? This was a pretty shocking idea for the Department of Indian Affairs; when the band announced its intention, the response was to assign a superintendent, Frank Verigan, to deal with the matter.

"Eventually he realized I'd been to college," said Isaac, "and we became good friends." A sympathetic Verigan carried Indian Affairs along, and the agreement was made. But there was one last hitch. Indian Affairs, unable to break the habits of generations, insisted that one of their officials should be a co-signer on behalf of the band. The chief would not agree. This must be all or nothing: a decisive move to self-determination. The chief argued that if an Indian Affairs official was needed as co-signer, the band was not taking real control. Finally the band was able to persuade the department to embark on a trail-blazing experiment – the Indians could run their own school.

From the beginning, the band members worked on two fronts: first, to transform the teaching staff, and, second, to make the curriculum culturally relevant to the students. They insisted the school should go to grade twelve. Older students who had been going out to Portage La Prairie schools were not doing well; lacking self-confidence in the city milieu, they complained of meeting discrimination within the schools. "When we began to hire teachers, we offered them a challenge. We asked them if they had any difficulty with the idea of working for Indians, not in the sense of being social workers, but as employees. We found most of them didn't mind; they were interested mainly in working with young children."

At a stroke of a pen, the band changed their Indian teacher aides into teachers-in-training, and persuaded Brandon University to set up a programme to educate them. "The most exciting were those first five years. We were able to hire a lot of misfits who weren't acceptable in the regular system. They had lots of new ideas. When we took over we had two of our own people working as teacher aides. Now we have fifteen of our own people as fully qualified teachers, and some native teachers from elsewhere as well. Thirty per cent of our staff are native people." In the first five years after the change, staff turnover dropped to one per cent. The band has had one of its own people as principal, and at the time of my visit, two aboriginals were working as vice-principals (one of them, as I later found out, the brother of National Chief Ovide Mercredi).

Cultural relevance in the curriculum was the key to the turnaround in Sandy Bay's school. From the beginning the band has worked to persuade the community that this is *their* school. The Ojibway language is introduced in the early grades, and native studies permeate the curriculum from the first grade up. The children are taught about the government of Sandy Bay, the meaning of the First Nations flag, the meaning of the nineteen eagle feathers, the history of the people lying in the village cemetery, the importance and meaning of their language and culture. The students get to know about the band council, who runs it, what they do. The students are also welcome in the band council offices. In high school, a formal native studies programme prepares the students for similar courses at university.

In the first five years, average attendance rose from 49 per cent to 85 per cent. The people of Sandy Bay are now better educated than those in the white communities surrounding them, said Isaac, with more than a touch of pride; as a mark of their growing confidence, they had once again alarmed government officials by proposing that they educate non-native children from neighbouring villages.

Isaac took me on a drive around the reserve. The houses are so far apart that everyone has plenty of space. There is a wonderful shoreline along the lake, but so far the people have preferred, Indian fashion, to keep it wild and natural rather than to cash in by creating a beach or marina. They realize that the cost of providing services to homes at modern standards will in future force them to build their houses closer together, and have begun to prepare a small townsite, which will eventually bring a big change in the Saulteaux pattern of living.

We finished the tour at the school. As I stepped through the doors, I could sense that cheerful spirit of inquiry by lively minds which is the mark of a good school. The corridors were ablaze with posters and drawings, many of them to do with a campaign that was underway against drugs, and the children seemed lively and outgoing. This is not the usual atmosphere in Indian reserve schools; often such schools have a strangely depressed and disoriented air, perhaps because in so many of them, people of one culture are imposing something on people of another. Isaac stepped into the school as if it was his.

No magic formula
Sandy Bay has begun to emerge from the hopelessness that has

afflicted so many aboriginal communities in Canada. The people have taken over administration of all their affairs; they have their own health, police and lottery commissions, and their own juvenile court. "I think we have reached the apex of mastering the bureaucracy," Isaac said. "Now we have to work ourselves out of that. Right now, in aboriginal communities across Canada there is a lot of rebellion because the chiefs and councils are becoming accountable to the people, instead of to Indian Affairs." He said the Assembly of First Nations has been created by Indian Affairs as a kind of parallel organ of government: "We are now having a big problem getting the government to understand that the AFN is only an arm of the Sandy Bay Indian reserve."

Many young people now hope to work in the reserve as opportunities expand. Graduating students have a new range of role models. "When I went to school," said Isaac, "all our role models were white. It seemed that you had to be white before you could do anything." Although there is still 65 per cent unemployment, that rate is low for an Indian reserve, and the day is fast approaching when those who leave will do so by choice, not because they are forced out through lack of opportunities at home.

Of course, for an aboriginal community to take control of its own decisions is not like waving a wand: profound problems arising from poverty, psychological alienation and cultural dissolution do not disappear overnight. A year or so after I visited Sandy Bay, shocking stories emerged of sexual abuse of children on the reserve. A thirteen-year-old boy, Lester Desjarlais, had hanged himself in 1988 after years of sexual abuse, and a provincial court judge in a 300-page report on the incident severely criticized the native-run Dakota Ojibway Child and Family Service agency for failing the boy.[2]

Wrote Judge Brian Giesbrecht: "His family let him down; his leaders let him down; then the very agency that was mandated to protect him let him down, and the government chose not to notice." In February 1993, charges were laid by the RCMP against some thirty residents of the reserve for allegedly molesting at least fifty children and young adults. Among the suspects were girls and women ranging from twelve to their early twenties, and several males younger than twelve.[3]

Judge Giesbrecht said the agency's workers were poorly trained and suffered from political interference by native leaders: sexual abuse of the boy had been covered up because it involved a prominent band member. This strong criticism of the first child-care agency in Canada to be run by aboriginal people themselves serves to remind us that self-government is no more a guarantee of impeccable behaviour in aboriginal communities than it is in our own. In fact, aboriginal people face a much tougher situation: inevitably, power will sometimes pass into the hands of people who are not fit to exercise it. This may be because they are themselves prey to the severe pathologies that afflict so many native communities; or because they are unfamiliar with the checks and balances that normally restrain politicians in the exercise of their powers; or even, as in non-native communities, because some individuals who get elected or promoted to positions of trust are not very good people.

I have heard aboriginal people argue passionately against self-government because in some places it has already led to authoritarian behaviour by corrupt leaders. Most aboriginal communities are very small, no more than villages, where a powerful person or family can easily seize control and use power for personal ends. Small communities can also become divided into bitterly opposed factions. Some native communities are already drifting in that direction. For example, in the Mohawk community of Akwesasne straddling the St. Lawrence River near Cornwall, Ontario, the large-scale smuggling of cigarettes, and big-money gambling, have created what appear to be almost irreparable divisions within a culture that for many years has been striving to recapture its ancient harmony through a return to traditional methods of government. Self-government is certainly no panacea: but with all its problems, it should produce better results than the physical and psychological chaos created by 150 years of Indian Act wardship.

An important change in Sandy Bay has been the revival in the authority of the elders. No amount of university learning takes precedence over their wisdom. "We have a number of university graduates, but when an elder walks into the room with something to say, everything stops," Isaac told me. "We have 280 elders on the reserve, and eighteen who are really active. We do not organize any committee without an elder."

Ojibway is the official language of Sandy Bay. "In public speaking I am more comfortable in English," said Isaac, "but if I start to speak English, an elder will get up.... The elders are the keepers of that spirit."

At the confluence of the rivers

The elders are also central to the self-government initiative under-taken by the Lheit-Lit'en Nation (meaning, "the people from where the rivers meet"). These are Carrier people who once lived where the Nechako River joins the Fraser – on the exact spot where the city of Prince George now stands in the north-central interior of British Columbia. There, Peter Quaw, a determined and charismatic chief, has taken charge of a tiny community of fewer than 200 people, and has begun to implement a long-range plan to hand back decision-making authority to the elders.

I found the reserve on a back road ten or twelve miles from the city, sitting almost alongside a huge abandoned sawmill, and only a few hundred yards from one of Prince George's three polluting pulp and paper mills. The reserve is just a collection of houses scattered among some trees along one single road. I walked into the band of-fice, said I was writing a magazine article, and a tall, rangy man im-mediately motioned me to a chair. "Sit down," he said, "you might be interested in this meeting we are having."

This was unusual. Aboriginal people tend to be somewhat guarded with outsiders, and with good reason. As a stranger walking into a re-serve, I could not remember having ever before been quite so imme-diately accepted as I was by Peter Quaw. Within moments I found myself listening to a fascinating conversation as two members of the Nechako Environment Committee from Prince George tried to enlist his help in preventing the logging and damming of a creek that runs through the heart of the Lheit-Lit'en lands.

As the two environmentalists waxed eloquent about the sunrise ceremony they would hold in the valley on Earth Day, I noticed an anxious, slightly patronizing tone enter their conversation. They ex-plained how the valley was full of grizzlies, caribou, mountain goats, many varieties of trout and salmon. This original ancient homeland of the Carrier people had already been the subject of a B.C. Hydro study for prospective damming and flooding, they said. Some log-ging had already started. The fisheries ministry declared there should be a 200-metre buffer zone for logging on all waterways, but the pulpwood company had cut down to the water's edge, with the approval of the Ministry of Forests.

The chief listened carefully as the visitors described the wonders of the Herrick Valley. Yes, he said finally, with a slightly sardonic air,

322

his people knew all about the valley. "Every year I make it a practice to go through the Herrick, and on up to the top of the mountain. We make it a practice to look after the Herrick. The most precious of all our medicines is found there."

The environmentalists wanted the area to be established as an ecological reserve; it would help achieve such a designation if the valley could be proven to have archeological values. They asked Chief Quaw if his people could proclaim the valley an area of traditional use, and prove their occupation of it by holding sweat lodges and ceremonies there. "Would our people be able to continue their way of life in an ecological reserve?" asked the chief. They answered that no logging, mining or hunting was permitted in an ecological reserve, but a local community could vary its uses. The question would be rather whether the native people could trap there.

"Trapping is a forgotten way of life for us," remarked the chief. "Hunting, fishing, medicines, they're important.... If we work with you on this, we want you to work with us on some of our projects."

The conversation turned to the overall pollution of the Nechako, the threat to the salmon, and the dangers of dioxins, which the environmentalists began to explain to him. Chief Quaw said: "We notice when we hang up salmon to dry, the skin of many of them will slip off and the flesh falls to the ground. This points to a skin sarcoma. But we need money. If we work with you on the Herrick, we want you to work with us on our court case to stop the pulp mills from discharging dioxins into the river. We've spent $122,000 of our own money. We've asked everybody and his dog, but no one will help us. We are in the discovery stage of the court case. We need $50,000 to proceed. If we don't get it, we are out, we'll have to drop the case."

Neatly, the tables had been turned. Two men who seemed to have arrived with the intention of explaining the modern world to the chief had been placed, as it were, in the dock. They agreed with him, of course, but he received no promises of financial help with the court case. When the two men had left he told me: "I tried for months to get these people to help us, but they didn't produce anything." Was I perhaps seeing something new here, a new relationship between aboriginals and Euro-Canadians, more equal than before, although still not entirely satisfactory?

Peter Quaw is now in his early forties. When he was away at residential school, his mother died and he was not allowed to go home for the funeral. His people were drifting away from the reserve at the time; his father left, and didn't return for many years. "My brother and I raised ourselves, either in the bush or on the streets of Prince George and Vancouver. That's where I learned about survival.... I could deal with things because as far as I was concerned, I was 15,000 years old, and I had the wisdom of the elders in me. People on the street kept telling me I wasn't meant for that life. To this day I owe them a debt for that, because these people who had no hope for themselves saw hope in me that I didn't see."

Quaw returned to the reserve and for a year worked in the sawmill; but what impressed him most was the hopelessness in the eyes of his people. "I decided I had to go back and finish my education." When he left home in 1971 to resume his education, he wrote down on a piece of paper what people on the reserve, then known as the Fort George reserve, were doing with their lives:

They were working from one paycheck to the next at the neighbouring sawmill. They stayed home during the week. On Fridays they went to town to buy liquor. On Saturdays and Sundays, they boozed. No one was getting an education. No one could look to a future beyond the sawmill.

"It was very sad," he told me. "It was a traditional Indian reserve – garbage everywhere, boozing, womanizing, gambling."

He returned eleven years later with a college degree and found his people were all doing the same things as when he had left. By that time, he was able to earn a good living as a consultant. But in 1986, he gave that up to become chief, as he had always intended. The Quaws had been leaders in a nation that once, he said, had been all-powerful throughout its traditional territory. The Lheit-Lit'en people had lived at the confluence of the two rivers from time immemorial. Many years ago, they were shoved onto three square miles selected for them out of town, and have lived on the margins of Canadian society ever since.

Peter Quaw's objective is to get rid of the system that overran his people, hemmed them in, cheated them, and destroyed their pride and confidence. "In the first four or five years, it was really difficult to get the message across. But gradually, the pride comes back," he said.

Quaw and the 200 people in his band have now banished the very idea of "the Fort George reserve", and declared themselves to be the Lheit-Lit'en Nation. This was the first step in his programme. They then set about creating a modernized version of their traditional form of government. To start, they declared jurisdiction over their traditional lands, a huge area of about 200 kilometres by 350 kilometres, nowadays inhabited by tens of thousands of Euro-Canadians in the city of Prince George and a dozen small towns. "The land is ours," said the chief.

The way the Lheit Lit'en people lost their land is not a pretty story. As the Grand Trunk Pacific Railway moved north, the authorities decided they needed the Indian land. So in 1908, their land was subdivided without their permission and advertised throughout the world as offering good lots for sale. An early offer came in at nearly $4 million, but the public officials ignored it. They also spurned a later offer of $1.3 million from a businessman. Then, with the help of a missionary, they cobbled together an offer from the railway company of $68,000. "There was no consultation, no reappraisal, no determination of market values, no follow-up of alternative offers, no negotiations on the railway's price, and to cap it all we have discovered the government was an interested party – they owned shares in the railway," said Chief Quaw.

The band refused two attempts to make them surrender the land, but finally agreed, under pressure, in 1911. For 1,366 acres, they received a total of $125,000 or $91.50 an acre. At the same time, land all around their village was selling for $1,625 an acre. It was the sort of transaction that has given rise to hundreds of claims of government malpractice in dealings with Indian lands, all across the country.

Peter Quaw told me his people are tired of waiting, and are ready to act as if they are already self-governing. On July 1, 1992, more than a year after my visit, they formally established an Elders Council as their highest governing body, and Quaw was chosen by the council as the first traditional chief (*Keyob-Whu-du-chun*, "the tree that people lean on for support") they have had since being forced under the Indian Act elective system in 1918. The band's action forced the Department of Indian Affairs to expose its claws: although the Lheit Lit'en changes were within departmental regulations covering customary elections, the Minister disallowed the band's proposed changes, froze its assets, and withdrew funding, in a draconian demonstration of who was boss.

But, said Chief Quaw, the changes have had a dramatic effect on the spirit of the elders. Having been pushed aside and ignored for much of their lives, he said, the elders "now swell with pride when they realize that the community is honouring them by once again placing trust in their judgment and wisdom."

Ancient and modern

Inevitably, for a chief who came of age in the streets of a big city, Peter Quaw's thinking is a mixture of traditional and contemporary. His tactics combine aggressive Indian nationalism with a willingness to co-operate with anyone who is friendly. He is unusually frank when he admits how desperately his people need help. They have all been affected by drug and alcohol abuse. In a survey a year or two ago, only one person said sexual abuse was not a problem, and the unemployment rate was 94 per cent. Most people were impoverished.

Although he likes much about the traditional Potlatch form of government, he has raised some hackles in his community by criticizing aspects of the traditional system. "How can we take a system from the past?" he asked. "We have to understand the contemporary system and integrate the two." But he added disarmingly, "We don't know exactly how we will do this."

To help him chart the way forward, Quaw cannily formed a fifty-eight-member advisory council, including fourteen non-native citizens of Prince George, "to create the policies and processes for a self-governing nation." The big problem is to find an alternative to government funding, somehow creating a self-sustaining economy to go along with the drive for self-determination.

Quaw has begun to move things. With the Community College of New Caledonia in Prince George, he initiated a salmon-enhancement course, which trained eleven people from the reserve in the skills of fisheries co-management. This enabled them to reduce their unemployment rate to about 40 per cent by 1992, and they are hoping to halve that rate within a couple of years through creation of other new enterprises. Chief Quaw wants to develop businesses "for which our experience over thousands of years of caring for the land, equips us very well.... We know how nature works. We know how and where the animals live and migrate. We know how long it takes a tree to grow. We know how much can be taken from an area without harming it. And we know what happens if so much is taken that nature ends up being too weak to replenish herself. By applying this knowledge we believe we can fill a valuable economic role in conjunction with the non-native business world."

The Lheit-Lit'en have declared that they will refuse to clearcut the forest, and will use horses instead of machines in any forestry operation they develop. They do not expect a non-native rate of return on investment. This could make it tough to attract outside capital, but Chief Quaw is optimistic. "We feel we can slow down this onslaught on the forest," he said.

He tried to light a fire under the Carrier-Sekani Tribal Council by accusing it of being a bureaucracy delivering only Indian Affairs programmes. When all twelve bands declared their willingness to pool their resources in creating a consortium to develop forestry, tourism and wholesale and retail trade, Quaw became for a time chairman of the tribal council's self-determination committee. The bands were planning to use their combined forest licences to buy two sawmills to produce timber for their own modular housing plant. But a year later, Quaw told me, "I have withdrawn from the consortium, because... they are stuck within a vacuum and cannot seem to get out of it, and the politicians are doing their usual thing, which is nothing."

The meeting I sat in on with the environmentalists led to the creation of a Local Resource Users Process covering the Herrick Valley. Under this agreement the Lheit Lit'en co-operated with hikers, naturalists, trappers, outfitters, lodges and environmental groups to seek preservation of the valley. After a year, Quaw withdrew from this, too: the aboriginals, he said, were not simply another "user group", and the other users were too ready to make deals with the paper company. He said no one could make decisions covering aboriginal lands until the treaty negotiations that have been started in British Columbia have been concluded. Until then, the Lheit Lit'en demand that the areas of the valley identified as "sacred" be unconditionally protected.

Unable to get substantial support to pursue the court case against the polluting pulp mills, Quaw switched his attack to the political level: one of the mills agreed to co-operate with the band, but the other company, he said (which also was interested in logging the Herrick valley) was unco-operative. Here is yet another of the many land-use conflicts I discovered on my trips across the country. At time of writing, the Lheit Lit'en people were gearing up for a physical confrontation in defence of a sacred place.

From time to time in my travels, I discovered a number of cultural misunderstandings that seem to symbolize the historic gap in outlook between natives and non-natives. There is one such in Prince

George, where the city has established a park on the site of a Lheit-Lit'en graveyard. The federal government and the city have both promised to take care of the graveyard, but not to the satisfaction of the Lheit Lit'en, who were outraged by a proposal to build a wash-room over the burial sites of their ancestors. The little houses that once stood over the graves have been vandalized. The chief said: "Unless our people are able to finish their journey properly through the circle of life, in our minds, their spirits will wander forever."

In many places, it seems, Euro-Canadians are still reluctant to respect the traditions of those who were here first.

To understand us...

Yet I am sure the aboriginal people do want to be understood by those who live around them. When the Lheit Lit'en held their first Potlatch for many years, in July 1992, they made an effort to explain them-selves to outsiders. They produced a moving statement that could stand as an aboriginal comment on much of the information in this book:

> To understand us is to understand a people who have lived in the place where we now live since before recorded history. Whose earliest known settlements date back to 8,000 years before the birth of a man named Christ in a far off land.
>
> A people for whom there were no such thing as minutes and hours, only the seasons – spring, summer, fall and winter. Each season being part of the cycle of life and our guide for living.
>
> Yet to understand us is also to understand a people whose joy was turned to overwhelming sadness.
>
> A people whose way of living was torn apart and thrown away like so much useless chaff.
>
> A people whose children were ripped from the arms of their mothers and fathers by strange men with white collars and with uniforms.
>
> To understand us is to understand men and women who, as it would be with anyone who had their lives and beliefs and families torn apart, walked for many years as if in a fog of disbelief and confusion, of fear and despair.
>
> A people who were cast aside for no reason and left to languish and perish in a dark world utterly without hope.
>
> To understand us as we are today is to understand a people who have just begun to awaken from a long and terrible dream and who are now rising once more.

The dream-like triumph of Elijah

Aboriginal communities are tiny, no bigger than villages for the most part; and many of them poor, forgotten villages at that, with little power or influence. Yet in 1989, the people from these villages had a heady experience of a kind they could scarcely have dreamed about. In that year, the people who run some of these tiny communities, the chiefs of Manitoba, orchestrated the rejection of the Meech Lake constitutional accord, and plunged the whole nation into a full-scale constitutional crisis.

This was the stuff of legend, making an obscure Cree member of the Manitoba legislature so famous, such a hero to native people everywhere in Canada, that he became instantly recognizable by his Christian name alone: Elijah.

In the week before the Meech Lake Accord was to be ratified by the Manitoba legislature, Isaac Beaulieu of Sandy Bay (whose story is told in the preceding chapter) was acting as chairman of a Winnipeg conference of chiefs and elders to discuss Indian health matters. In the course of the conference, they invited Elijah Harper to say a few words. "He said he had something to ask us," Isaac recalled. "He said they were in the process of ratifying the Meech Lake Accord, and he asked what we thought he should do.

"We immediately passed a resolution to support him in whatever he might do to stop the Meech Lake Accord. I think most of us really believed it was a foregone conclusion. We thought he might be able to delay it for three days. He managed to carry it on to the weekend, and from then on our health conference was totally about Meech Lake.

"We held workshops with the elders. We held healing workshops. That became the centre of the whole operation. From then on, it was always the elders who were in front. The leaders met with the elders every day. We had 5,000 people on the legislature grounds day after day. When I think of all the years we waited around for funding so that we could hold conferences.... We had no funding for this one, and yet people were there all the time.

"We had all kinds of people, black and white, coming into our office to offer support.... The press kept asking who was pulling the strings.... One afternoon I came home [to the Sandy Bay reserve on Lake Manitoba's western shore]. I stopped off in Portage La Prairie, and every person I met, white or otherwise, smiled or said hello and shook my hand, people who would usually ignore Indian people. The Manitoba government had promised to hold hearings, and by Saturday 6,000 of our people had applied to give evidence. It's almost like a dream. Meech Lake made the common people realize they have a lot of power. On the first day I don't think there was one person who thought we could stop it. All we wanted to do was make a deal, improve the deal. By the time the Prime Minister realized that's all we wanted, it was too late."

Perhaps the event that has stuck most firmly in Isaac's mind from that experience was a little thing that not too many other people would have noticed. The health conference where it all started was held at the Holiday Inn, so a lot of Indian officials from around the province were staying there, at the regular rate of $120 a night. As the events unfolded, and more and more Indian people crowded into the city, the hotel announced a special rate of $60 a night for all visiting Indian officials.

"I couldn't help thinking," said Isaac, "we've come a long way since the day when the Marlborough Hotel in Winnipeg announced that they would refuse to admit Indians.

"I wish I'd kept a copy of both those statements. They are part of our history."

22

Ovide Mercredi:
straddling two worlds

In spite of the many problems and setbacks described in this book, the past two decades have been a period of relatively hopeful change for the aboriginal people of Canada. The greatest change, perhaps, has been the emergence of so many articulate new leaders, some of whom have spoken in previous chapters. These leaders, with a mandate for action from their own people, ensure that the aboriginal agenda has become a permanent part of Canadian political life. It will not go away, as the Canadian establishment has wished since at least 1830; it cannot be ignored, as it was so brutally in the first half of this century; it can no longer be shuffled aside with tokens or short-term payoffs. The aboriginal agenda is here to stay: it has to be faced by Canadians, and taken seriously.

And in fact, Canadians have begun to pay attention. An earnest of this is the curiously intimate relationship we have established in the first years of the '90s with Ovide Mercredi, National Chief of the Assembly of First Nations. With his election in June 1991, Euro-Canadians accepted an aboriginal leader almost as one of their own for the first time since Confederation. It would scarcely be an exaggeration to say that Mercredi was lionized – sought after voraciously by the press, courted by political and business leaders, embraced by social activists.

Paradoxically, as 1992 ended, Mercredi's leadership was in question: the defeat of the national referendum on the Charlottetown constitutional accord was a setback for him personally and politically, as it was to many political leaders, since he had been party to the negotiations that produced the proposed amendments. But whatever happens to

Mercredi's leadership in the long run, the first two years of his mandate have represented a turning point for the acceptance of aboriginals within the Canadian political system. Why did this happen?

The explanation lies primarily in events that occurred before Mercredi was elected – especially the action of Elijah Harper in nullifying the Meech Lake constitutional accord, and the Oka crisis of 1990. These two events were themselves the fruit of the persistent refusal by the Canadian political establishment to deal seriously with the growing frustrations of aboriginal people, who had been gradually escalating their opposition to industrial developments that they once would have accepted with stolid fatalism. By the mid-'80s aboriginal leaders were warning that feelings were becoming so volatile in many communities, that, given a flashpoint of some kind, all hell could easily break loose. As the government kept stalling on aboriginal land claims, native groups in many places joined Temagami, Lubicon Lake and Barriere Lake in taking to the barricades, blocking roads and rail lines, or sitting in on airport runways, as they desperately tried to get the message across that they weren't prepared to give any more ground. Haida, Cree, Carrier, Dene, Nipissing, Innu, Mohawk, Algonquin – the message coming from them all was the same. All that was needed, it seemed, was the spark to ignite an explosion that would make Canadians sit up and take notice.

Elijah and his feather

Ironically, the first breakthrough into the consciousness of Canadians came not from one of these physical confrontations, but from the simple act of one man sitting on the back bench of a provincial legislature, holding an eagle feather in his hand and saying "No", in a voice so soft that it could scarcely be heard. Canadians saw this scene repeated time after time on television: Elijah Harper, the only aboriginal member of the Manitoba legislature, singlehandedly preventing the ratification of a proposed constitutional amendment from which the aboriginal people had been excluded. This was the first time in the history of modern Canada, the first time since the fall of Tecumseh, in fact, that native people had been able to intervene decisively in a matter of central importance to the dominant society. The strategy for doing this was carried out with such intelligence and dignity that, almost overnight, the image of native people among Euro-Canadians was transformed.

Not long afterwards, in the summer of 1990, the trigger was pulled igniting the expected explosion. The Quebec provincial police attack on a Mohawk barricade near Oka plunged the nation into a full-scale social crisis. Since at least 1781, the Mohawks of Kanehsatake, as they call their village, have been trying to prove that they are the real owners of the lands that were granted to the seminary of St. Sulpice in 1717 for the purpose of establishing an Indian mission. They repeatedly took their case to court, and lost; they tried to resolve the issue through political negotiation, and were rebuffed. In spite of everything, they have never ceased to believe the land is really theirs, even after the seminary sold much of it.

When the town of Oka decided to extend a golf course into a forest that the Mohawks considered sacred ground, the barricades erected by the Mohawks were simply the continuation of a 200-year policy of maintaining their claim. The issue was eerily symbolic of the historic relationship between Euro-Canadians and aboriginals: the product of years of paternalism and indifference on one side, and of an inextinguishable attachment to the land, of dogged resistance against all odds, on the other. The issue would have been resolved years earlier if Euro-Canadians had paid serious attention to the neglected rights and deteriorating living conditions of aboriginal people.

For some months the barricades sat harmlessly enough across a quiet country road, until the mayor of Oka unwisely lost patience and asked the police to clear the Mohawks out of the way. The Quebec police had already blasted their way into several Indian communities with blatant disregard for the civil rights of their occupants, but on this occasion they had forgotten, or didn't know, or perhaps were especially provoked by, the fact that behind the barricades were members of a recently revived Mohawk Warriors Society, armed and spoiling for a fight. The Warriors answered fire with fire; the raid collapsed in confusion and ignominy; a provincial policeman, Corporal Marcel Lemay, was killed, no one knows by whom.

The element of violence awakened the interest of the news media. And when other members of the Warriors Society blocked a major bridge that runs from the Mohawk reserve of Kahnawake into Montreal, the confrontation began to affect thousands of people directly. For three months, the Oka crisis, as this combination of events became known, was front-page and prime-time news all over Canada. Newspapers that had ignored the Oka land issue for 150 years now devoted four pages a day to the subject. The media appetite for detail, especially for anything to do with violence and confrontation, appeared to be bottomless. Whipped up by irresponsible, racist radio commentators, the Mohawks' neighbours along the south shore of the St. Lawrence River took to gathering in the evenings, waving their *fleur de lys* flags, emblem of resurgent Quebec nationalism, shouting racist insults, and burning Mohawks in effigy. On one terrible occasion some of them viciously stoned a line of cars for no other reason than that they were driven by Indians.

In solidarity with the Mohawks, aboriginals all across the country blocked roads and rail lines, and brought work to a halt in many places, demonstrating that they could seriously disrupt the workings of even so large a country as Canada, given the provocation. By the time the Mohawk Warriors emerged from behind their barricades and entered police custody at the end of September, Canadians understood something most of us had never grasped before: 150 years after the Indians had been consigned to oblivion, they were still very much alive, were not going anywhere, and sooner or later would have to be dealt with.

This was the context in which the Assembly of First Nations met to elect a new chief the following June. The election was unprecedented in the history of aboriginal Canada. It had all the hoopla, campaign organizing, floor hysteria, deal making and changing allegiances of a mainstream leadership convention. As the battle raged on the convention floor, it was reported in detail on television. This marked the first time that the national population or media had ever taken an interest in aboriginal politics.

In their usual aggressive fashion, the media began to chronicle the virtues and deficiencies of hitherto obscure leaders from hitherto disregarded nations – Salishan, Gitksan, Mohawk, Cree, Saulteaux – and to interpret the positions of the various candidates according to the customary, and largely inaccurate, stereotypes of Canadian politics. Mercredi's emergence from this process was unexpected. A slight, quiet figure, a young-looking Cree lawyer in his mid-forties, he came up through the middle against a couple of more favoured candidates. Perhaps because he looked and sounded so harmless and reasonable, mainstream Canada took to him immediately. In the next two years he was to become the most recognizable and quotable native leader in the history of modern Canada.

A visit to the Cree homeland

Mercredi was so much in demand after his election that to meet him I had to drive 600 miles north from Ottawa, where we both live, to the Mistissini[1] Cree reserve in northern Quebec. Twenty years earlier, when I'd been one of the few Canadian journalists writing regularly about Indians, it had been a simple thing to drop in on the leaders unannounced from time to time, to chew the fat. But times change; the appointment book of the new chief was so overstuffed with meetings, interviews, travel and negotiations that his staff couldn't find a spot for me, unless it could be worked in around the annual general assembly of the Grand Council of the Crees of Quebec, which Mercredi was attending in Mistissini.

It was a long way to travel, but I welcomed the chance. Mistissini is one of the most interesting aboriginal places in Canada. To reach it, you drive north in a long semi-circle from Montreal towards the mining district of the Abitibi, then northeast another 200 miles across a vast Canadian Shield landscape of lakes and forests, interrupted by the occasional French-Canadian small town built around its local mine, sawmill or pulp mill.

The Cree village is at the south end of Lake Mistissini, fifty miles north from the mining town of Chibougamau. The village sits on a peninsula dividing the southern reaches of the lake into two bays. It is a carefully chosen site that offers plenty of good fishing, excellent shelter from the unpredictable winds that can so quickly whip up the open lake to a fury, and miles of bay shoreline that the young can explore without danger.

At the time of my first visit in 1969, Mistissini was a collection of log cabins, mostly abandoned in the winter when people went into the bush to trap beaver. The Cree language was intact among all its residents, the subsistence economy still viable, and the cultural attachment to the ancient hunting ways far from broken. Most people made their living in the immense wilderness to the north, an area as large as Britain, virtually untouched by road, settlement or stranger. This was still not only the homeland, but the kingdom, of the Crees: Eenou Astchee as they called it.

The village is transformed now: the log houses have been replaced by smart suburban bungalows; several large insitutional buildings – band office, arena, two impressive schools – dominate the townscape; the population has more than doubled; people have begun to bustle around, carrying files, driving bulldozers, operating hi-tech communications gear, on the edge of hustling for a living, urban-style. Yet the felicities of Mercredi's visit, the formalities observed, were those of a hunting culture still intact. The village rambles down a hill overlooking the two bays. It was an appropriate spot to take the measure of the new National Chief, because he too is a Cree, who grew to manhood in a northern village where, as in Mistissini, people gathered when they returned from their own immense wilderness of trees and water, their own landscape of bays, lakes, islands, rivers and creeks, much like that of Eenou Astchee.

They have a new arena in Mistissini, big enough for any conference; but for this important meeting they turned away from the village to a spot across the water, where they erected a huge blue and white tent. Anyone who wished to take part in the meeting had to get into a canoe and move away from the village towards the bush, that natural element of Cree life. One did not have to move far, it is true, but far enough to catch the perfect symbiosis between aboriginals and nature. There on the edge of the forest — where only the night before a local shaman had conducted a shaking tent under a sky that yielded up a dramatic display of the northern lights — only a few feet from the bouncy muskeg, surrounded by the waters of the traditional transportation routes, the people gathered on the hillside and looked down to the shoreline where the new National Chief landed from his canoe and wandered in a relaxed fashion up the hill towards them. Welcomed for the first time to the Cree homeland, he had come to make his report to the people. The Crees greeted him with deep respect; they knew he was the first aboriginal leader to have become a significant figure in the political life of Canada.

A self-identifying status

The Crees had arranged for one of their talented artists, Glenna Matoush, to paint a portrait of Mercredi when the day's political discussions were done, and I was allotted an hour to talk to him as Glenna painted.

I soon discovered a surprising fact: the chief of all the on-reserve aboriginals in Canada has never lived on a reserve, not even for a single day, and is proud of it. In the nineteenth century his family moved north from Red River (later Winnipeg) and eventually settled in the village of Grand Rapids, on the northwest shore of Lake Winnipeg. There they lived as fishermen, trappers and hunters, and spoke Cree as their first language, but never had Indian status.

Ovide's grandfather was French, and may have come originally from Quebec. His grandmother on his father's side was a Cree woman, and on his mother's side, everyone was Cree. They were just one family among the many Mercredis scattered around the Canadian north. The origins of this large clan are unclear, but according to at least one tradition, the founder of the family was Joseph Mercredi, a Hudson's Bay Company employee, who died in 1893, and is buried at Fond du Lac in northern Saskatchewan. Mercredi could be, according to this story, a misspelling of a Scottish name – perhaps McReady.[2]

Ovide was born in 1946, one of nine children. When he was growing up, Grand Rapids was an isolated aboriginal community with only a few non-native inhabitants, who also spoke Cree, and few transients or visitors – fur traders, fish buyers, freighters. "My father was a freighter too," Mercredi told me. "He used to drive the tractor train to The Pas or Mafeking [west across Lake Winnipegosis towards the Saskatchewan border] for supplies in the winter." The family had been on their land for a long time, and when a reserve was created across the river, they refused to move. They had always identified themselves as Crees, but stood aloof from the identification rules of status and non-status imposed by the Indian Act. In the mid-'60s when the provincial Métis organization began to organize vigorously among non-status Indians, Ovide's father and mother joined the local; and later, at the University of Manitoba, from which he graduated with a law degree in 1977, Ovide himself became a Métis organizer. He became a status Indian only in the late '80s, after Bill C-31 allowed those many thousands of Indians who had lost their status to regain it.

Ovide grew into a world in rapid transition. His older brothers and sisters were brought up to know the trapline and the fishing camps, and to live within the traditional Cree culture. But in 1961, when Manitoba Hydro penetrated the north, it brought a new legal and political order, and a new language. The younger members of the family were exposed to English, to the changing lifestyle, the new wage economy. Ovide's father, at first a fisherman, now became a labourer. As the new economy caught hold, he became a trades helper, then a tradesman, and finally the sort of man who retired after twenty-five years with the company. In this new world, Ovide became the second or third boy in the village to enter high school, the first in the family to make it to grade twelve. The younger ones have followed the same route. One brother, mentioned in Chapter 21, is now a school principal, another is going to university.

Like many aboriginals, Ovide was also brought up under the influence of Christianity. As a child he was an altar boy, then an organist in a Catholic church. "I saw the inside of the church as much as the priest. I have been on my knees a lot when I was younger," he told me.

Thus he had an unusual preparation for leadership. A non-reserve Indian, he came to be head of the reserve organization. A devout Christian, he came to seek connection with the peace pipe, sweat lodges, prayer ceremonies, the reviving native spirituality sweeping through every aboriginal nation from coast to coast. He added: "I believe in the equality of all religions. While I still go to church and do not denounce Christianity, I now spend more time praying with the elders than as a Catholic."

I asked him how this eclectic background, embracing so many traditions, would affect the way he approached his leadership role:

"I see things from a different perspective from those leaders who have accepted the Indian Act identification. The fact that my mother was denied her inherent and treaty rights, and I also had no access to them, has made me more determined to defend those rights for people who are being denied them.

"Some people are very much into treaty and non-treaty. I challenge that concept when I talk about identity. I do not differentiate between Indians in British Columbia or Quebec who do not have treaties, and those who have treaties in Saskatchewan. The question is, who were we before contact? My sense of it is that even those leaders who have a strong identification with the Indian Act definition, and with treaty, are beginning to break away from the parochial view of who is an Indian."

Advocating civil disobedience

During the day's meetings, Mercredi made a superb intervention in the debate about the proposed huge addition to the James Bay hydroelectric project. Quebec and Canada had tried to evade their responsibility, assigned to them by the 1975 James Bay and Northern Quebec Agreement, to take account of the social and environmental impact on Cree life before embarking on any such development. The governments' arguments had been rejected by the courts, but Hydro-Quebec was threatening to go ahead regardless of Cree opposition, arguing that it could start to build the project, and discuss later any negative impact that might result.

The situation between the Crees and the Quebec government was tense as Mercredi stood to address the annual assembly that afternoon. He spoke in an extremely measured, calm tone, but his words were tough. He promised that if Quebec persisted in this attitude, and the Crees requested help, he would mobilize all the Indians of Canada to join the Crees in acts of civil disobedience. "The AFN has a new leader, and a new confidence, based on the strength of our people, and...we will be there to help you in every way we can, that is the commitment I give you today.

"Many government leaders think we are not capable of organizing anything.... But the idea is not so difficult to get across. All we have to do is say to our people, 'The Crees need your help, come on over'."

He recalled the experience of his youth in northern Manitoba, where Indian communities had objected to hydro flooding, but had not acted. This experience had convinced him that "It is important not to fight later, but now. Later means that they have already dammed the river. Later means they have destroyed the river. Later means we are begging for compensation. So the time to defend our rights, the time to act, is now." Civil disobedience, Mercredi said, does not mean destruction of personal, private or public property; it permits no violence, but must be "a morally justifiable action, a last resort", when all other legal and political avenues have been exhausted. And that last resort, he told reporters after his speech, "is almost here".

However softly they may have been spoken, these were not negligible words. As some advisers to the Quebec government quickly realized, Mercredi's promise held out the prospect of a social crisis of impressive dimensions, reminiscent of Oka. If Quebec persisted with its bullish determination to ignore all opposition to the James Bay II project, they could find themselves confronting thousands of aboriginals and their sympathizers from across the continent ready and willing to sit in the path of the bulldozers. If violent confrontation and mass arrests were to be the price of building the project, the situation could begin to look more like South Africa than Canada, and prospective New York investors would surely take fright.

Mercredi's message quickly sank in. Within a few weeks, Quebec had agreed to fulfil the responsibilities it had so long tried to evade, and to embark with the Crees on an environmental and social-impact study as demanded by the law. This meant a long delay in the proposed construction schedule: the first major victory of those, led by the Crees, who had opposed the project.

I could not remember a native leader in Canada ever advocating civil disobedience while invoking the names of Gandhi and Thoreau. I asked Mercredi where that inspiration had come from. "I read an article about Gandhi in a *Life* magazine that I found in the priest's residence. I was impressed that here was a man who had fought for the freedom of his country from the domination of white people," he said. "And there was a second influence: Pope John's encyclical on rights and duties – a very powerful idea." Civil disobedience, Mercredi said, is "very relevant" to the native cause, because "I don't think we will be able to make progress in rights and freedoms just because of other people's enlightenment. There will always be people like [Premier Robert] Bourassa and [Parti Québécois leader Jacques] Parizeau. They will always be in positions of power, and will have to be met with equal force. It's the only thing they understand." However, such action should be no more than a means to an end: "If a solution can be found, rather than carrying on the act of civil disobedience, you should take the solution."

The need for healing

I asked Mercredi what he considers to be the esssence of this crucial moment in the history of Canada's native people. "It's not really something tangible," he replied, "like a piece of land, or resources, or a river. It's a thought, it's reclaiming our past, it's what people call healing, it's the restoration of the culture, the way of life, but not necessarily referring to the past: the key is to move forward.... You cannot move forward if you are sick. You have to heal yourself. That's the climate in which I am involved as a leader."

To break the dependency on welfare, land rights and the traditional economy must be restored, and treaty obligations fulfilled. "But it's much deeper than self-help, and that's where Indian spirituality enters the picture. And even that does not necessarily have to be traditional."

When I asked him about relations with non-Indians, he was quick to build a bridge: "The human spirit is the same," he said. "The spirit of the aboriginal people has been dulled by pain, grievances, oppression, by – I don't like to use the word, but I have to – colonialism, rejection, exclusion. In the white community the spirit has been dulled, too. In Canadian society we have wholesale groups and many individuals who are seeking that same healing. But the sources are different – for them it is preoccupation with the economy, with the singular idea that the purpose of life is to be wealthy, you build a society around that objective. It is the separation of politics and religion. It is the same struggle."

He explained: "I am very combative. I like to debate and accept a challenge, but the advice I got from the elders was to be kind and generous." He explained how, when he had met Joe Clark, the Minister of Constitutional Affairs, the month before in Morley, Alberta, he had taken the elders' approach. "Joe Clark can help us, and we can help him. I have to lift him up so he can lift me up. He has to lift me up, so I can lift him up.... If you go into a meeting with that idea, you are going to couch your message in a different way than if you are going into combat. For the first time since he was appointed he was meeting a group who wanted to help him. It not only affected his decision, but mine.... It's different from being confrontational all the time. It's trying to arrive at a consensus."

At that meeting Mercredi had invited Clark to experience native spirituality in its current form through a pipe ceremony, and then through prayers read from the Bible by a Christian elder. "If you had been there, you would have seen I was flanked by the AFN executive, but on either side of me was the traditional elder and the Christian elder."

As we talked on in the failing light, Mercredi outlined some interesting ideas for future action to move the aboriginal agenda forward. Among these was a suggestion for a national aboriginal law-making body, which would define its own membership and pass laws that would then be applied within native communities.

"These laws do not have to become rigid, or to be applied uniformly. But they will stem from our own institutions, not from Parliament or the Indian Act. The strategy is to wrestle power away by creating parallel institutions." He said he had already hired four Indian lawyers as a qualified secretariat capable of drafting the needed laws. "I want to make the AFN into a change agent," he said, "to begin creating parallel institutions that can challenge the rights of Parliament."

I wonder if many of the Canadians who so warmly embraced Mercredi's leadership would be so enthusiastic, once they knew that he was hoping to make aboriginals the only people in Canada who stood outside and beyond the reach of Parliament.

That afternoon Mercredi had told the Crees: "The idea I am putting forward to you is to give Canada one more chance. If we can succeed in amending the Constitution in a way that guarantees our rights as a distinct people, and eliminates the past of exclusion, then every university and school will have to teach a new political and legal reality. In that way, we will break down prejudice, and eliminate the racism that flows from ignorance."

Triumph turns to ashes
In the year that followed the Mistissini conference, Mercredi – along with other aboriginal leaders such as Ron George of the Native Council of Canada, Yvon Dumont of the Métis National Council, and Rosemary Kuptana and Mary Simon of the Inuit Tapirisat – steered his people into and through the complex negotiations on the renewal of the Constitution. The native leaders succeeded in persuading federal and provincial leaders to recognize the inherent right of aboriginals to self-government. If approved, this would have been the first important change in the status of aboriginals within Canada since Confederation. Mercredi played his part, as most Canadians would probably acknowledge, with great skill. He demonstrated the efficacy of his consensual method of negotiation. When the Charlottetown Accord was completed in August 1992, Mercredi was riding a wave of success unparalleled for a native leader in Canadian history.

In his concentration on the Constitution, however, Mercredi may have moved too far from the people he was representing. As rumblings of discontent were heard from western chiefs worried about the impact of the proposed changes on their treaty relationships, Mercredi took Constitutional Affairs Minister Minister Joe Clark along with him to a gathering of chiefs in Vancouver; he had Clark explain the virtues of the accord to them, urging them to support it. This may have been a fatal error. When Mercredi appeared on the same platform with Prime Minister Brian Mulroney during the referendum campaign, and was seen to embrace Quebec Premier Robert Bourassa, he seemed to many aboriginals to have taken a step too far towards "the other side".

On the evening of the referendum vote, Mercredi appeared on television and bitterly blamed Canadians for having "rejected the aboriginal people". Six weeks later, he showed me a file containing hundreds of letters he received in the next few days from Canadians who wanted to reassure him that their vote against the accord had not represented rejection of aboriginals. "I made that statement deliberately. I discussed it beforehand with my advisers, and we decided to take that line," he told me. "We knew it would be contro-versial. But what was the alternative? If I had simply accepted the result without protest, we would have been forgotten. No one would have taken any notice of us." Still, a few days later he had to apolo-gize for the remark, when it became clear that even aboriginal peo-ple had voted solidly against the accord that he had put so much effort into fashioning.

Later, native leaders criticized Mercredi for having become a mem-ber of the Canadian political establishment, a member, as one chief put it, "of Mulroney's Yes team". Other leaders said that few of their people had voted because the proposals were never properly ex-plained to them, that there was just too much happening, too fast, for the aboriginal people to take it all in one hurried gulp.

In all the excitement about the Constitution, which dominated his first year in office, Ovide Mercredi laid aside his many other interesting and provocative ideas for the future. He forgot about his proposed parallel law-making body, did not carry forward his suggestion to convene tribal assemblies of the major nations, and appeared to back off from his support for civil disobedience. With the constitutional effort exploding in his face, he had to face a tense assembly of the forty-two chiefs who make up, in effect, the executive of the AFN. There he came under considerable criticism; and it began to appear that his very popularity with non-natives was being held against him.

This illustrates another of the many paradoxes we have met in the course of this book: to defend themselves adequately, aboriginal communities need leaders who understand and can relate to the Canadian political structure. What they are defending, however, is a value system and a way of life that is inimical to the very qualities they need if their defence is to be effective. To walk that fine line be-tween remaining true to aboriginal beliefs and traditions, and relating effectively to the power structure, is not an easy task: many native leaders have stepped over that line and been rejected by their peo-ple, while others have given up in despair.

The AFN chiefs were quick to look past the failed effort at constitu-tional reform. They adopted a three-pronged strategy – civil disobedi-ence, court actions and international pressure – to force the pressing changes that must come in the next few years. At time of writing, Ovide Mercredi's career as National Chief was entering a new phase; though he may have his detractors, he was clearly in no mood to quit.

23

Canada accused
before the world

It has always been obvious that some day Canada would face a reckoning for the "We're civilized, you're savage" policies imposed on the aboriginal people. In international terms, this reckoning began in the 1980s, when aboriginals began to turn up at United Nations meetings in Geneva and New York. There they exposed to the international community the racist assumptions that have always lain behind Canadian Indian policy. However much the Canadian government might deplore this, it is no more than just: at last we are reaping what we have sown.

The Grand Council of the Crees of Quebec was the first native Canadian group to obtain accreditation to the UN as a non-governmental-organization (NGO). The man who emerged as its representative was that same shy, lanky youngster who acted as the Cree interpreter in Justice Albert Malouf's court in 1972: Ted Moses. Now in his forties, Moses is typical of his generation. As a small child he was nurtured on the trapline of his Cree-speaking father and mother, Willie and Hattie (who are now in their late seventies, and among the most respected Cree elders), but was then whisked away to southern Canada and thrust into an ambience so completely different from the world of the bush as almost to defy description. With many other Crees of his generation, he went to a residential school in Sault Ste Marie (described earlier by Buckley Petawabano in his story), where he learned English and made it through high school. On his return to tiny, remote Eastmain on the James Bay coast, he was appointed band manager. The English he had learned in school had become essential for anyone who had to deal with government on behalf of the band. The emergence of this eager young man into the world of international diplomacy twenty years later could stand as a symbol for the changes that are transforming native life and politics in Canada.

In Geneva, the centre for aboriginal activity is a committee called the Working Group on Indigenous Populations, which has been busy for almost ten years publicizing what is happening to indigenous peoples around the world, and seeking to establish international standards for the way they are treated. The Working Group sits five levels down from the UN General Assembly. Early in the 1980s, a UN Sub-Commission on Prevention of Discrimination and Protection of Minorities received a report on the plight of indigenous peoples and established the Working Group as a consequence. Parent of the Sub-Commission is the UN Commission on Human Rights, which in turn is part of the UN Economic and Social Council. The Working Group consists of five experts under the leadership of an enthusiastic Swiss woman, Erica-Irene V. Daes. At the Working Group, governments have the status only of observers, as do indigenous people, so at this level aboriginals have their chance to influence decisions, and they have seized it with a will.

The Crees are one of the ten indigenous organizations accredited as NGOs, but by 1991 another eighty-seven indigenous groups (including twelve from Canada) were represented at the annual sessions. Also taking an active part are a collection of activist groups ranging from Amnesty International, the Anti-Slavery Society, the Bahais, Quakers, and World Council of Churches, to the Pro-Hawaiian Sovereignty Working Group, the Freunde der Naturvoelker, the International Scholars for Indigenous Americans, and the Bonded Labour Liberation Front. Since twenty-nine governments sat in on the session as observers, it can be seen that the Working Group attracts interest from virtually every corner of the globe.

To the Canadian government's astonishment, the Crees, Mikmaqs, Haudenosaunee, Six Nations, Inuit and others in Geneva have taken to denouncing Canada as an internally colonialist and racist regime – not much different, from their point of view, from the many other nations that routinely oppress their indigenous populations. This has proven to be an immense embarrassment to a nation that has always believed itself to be on the side of the angels.

Common problems, world-wide

Canadian native peoples began to forge an identity with other indigenous peoples only in the 1970s. George Manuel, the western community worker who became president of the National Indian Brotherhood, was the first leader to appreciate the potential of the international stage for advancing the indigenous struggle. Manuel visited a number of foreign countries, made contacts with a wide variety of peoples, and set in motion a movement that resulted in establishment of the first World Indigenous Congress. When they did get to know other indigenous peoples, Canadian aboriginals found an astonishing similarity in the problems they all face. In every country, without exception, the indigenous people are at the lowest level of economic and social acceptance; they are brutally deprived of land (and sometimes life), suffer from the destruction of their economic base, and are left to fester in poverty while non-indigenous people grow rich from the wealth taken from their territories.

There are some 300 million aboriginals in the world. Their lowly situation everywhere is indicated by the list of complaints they registered at UN meetings in Geneva as the 1990s got under way. These complaints came under several headings, and many of them are horrendous:

Health: Malnutrition, high infant mortality, extensive epidemics, and lack of basic food are almost the rule among indigenous people. Their death rates are so high that ill-health alone is having a genocidal effect in many places. Among one group in the Brazilian forest, 90 per cent of all deaths are caused by malaria brought into their territory by outsiders.

Education: Mainstream education systems do not cater to the special needs of aboriginal cultures, resulting in the psychological alienation of their young people. Curricula are normally designed for dominant cultures. Teachers are typically non-indigenous. Indigenous children are taught their own tongues as foreign languages, part of the systematic devaluation of indigenous cultures. Indigenous people have levels of illiteracy well above national averages. In some areas, there are no primary schools for indigenous children. Almost everywhere there are problems at secondary and intermediate levels, and little university education is available for indigenous students.

Unemployment: Reports of 80 to 90 per cent unemployment are common, resulting in a high incidence of alcoholism, suicide, wife and child beating and sexual abuse, among many other consequences.

Child labour: Use of indigenous child labour is common, the children working for practically nothing in conditions similar to slavery. Many are forcibly taken from their parents, do not receive an education, and are often used in religious schools for cheap labour. Girls and young women are bought and sold as child prostitutes. On the pretext of adoption, a pattern of trafficking in indigenous children has emerged.

Women: Indigenous women have less access to education, and are economically exploited, oppressed and marginalized. Their work (mostly in the informal or black-market economy) is unprotected by law. There are frequent reports in many countries of forced sterilization. Women are not even fully supported within indigenous societies, although they carry the burden of survival of the race, and do much of the work in factories, fields and homes. They are considered unproductive because their work in the fields does not produce cash or profit. Many become the victims of sex trafficking and prostitution, and even in developed countries like Canada, indigenous women suffer extraordinary levels of physical and sexual abuse within their own damaged communities.

State terror: Indigenous organizations in some countries report frequent arbitrary detentions, disappearances, summary executions, and torture. Military attacks on indigenous villages have taken place, resulting in summary executions, rape and brutality, and forcing people to flee to neighbouring countries or into the jungle. Other countries report police brutality, appalling prison conditions, deaths in custody, and attacks by paramilitary, military and police squads. In one country in the last ten years, 80 per cent of the 15,000 people who have been killed, or who disappeared, were indigenous.

Effects of development: Governments continually try to force indigenous peoples into the mainstream economy. In the name of modernization, aboriginals are forced to abandon pastoral, hunting and gathering traditions and take up farming. In the name of progress, their traditional lands are taken from them, often resulting in famine and mass suffering. They are exposed to soil, water and air pollution and the general devastation of their natural surroundings. They are primary victims of deforestation, damming and flooding of traditional lands, disruption of fishing or hunting, forced relocation and displacement. Result: mental anguish, alcoholism, prostitution, and high suicide rates.

Land: For almost every group of indigenous people, the persistent assault on their land for resource extraction is the major problem in this terrible catalogue. That was true when George Manuel made his first contacts, and it remains true. Today throughout the world, indigenous people are desperately trying to defend themselves against those who would "develop" their lands.[1]

There are four major problems around land:

• Intensive **logging** has prompted direct action not only in British Columbia, Quebec and Ontario, but among the Dayaks of Sarawak and the Penan of Borneo in Malaysia, and among aboriginal groups in various parts of Latin America.

• Thousands of aboriginals (not to mention peasants and small farmers) have been **displaced** to make way for dams and reservoirs. Canadian displacements, such as those in James Bay and northern Manitoba, are on a minor scale compared with the likely result of dams proposed in Brazil and India, where hundreds of villages and hundreds of thousands of people will be displaced.[2]

• **Mining** and the extraction of gas and oil have raised issues in Brazil as well as Canada. In Australia, clashes over the effect of uranium mines on sacred sites led the country's Aborigines to send their first delegation to the United Nations.

• **Transmigration** – the movement of settlers into aboriginal lands – has led to appalling violence against aboriginals in Brazil and other Latin American countries. The indigenous population of Brazil, once five million, is now a mere 220,000.

At the beginning of the 1980s, a consultant called Martinez Cabo produced for the UN a study of discrimination against indigenous peoples around the world. He reported that the land question was the key issue. His study persuaded him that indigenous peoples have "a natural and inalienable right to retain the territories they possess, to call for the return of lands of which they have been deprived, and to be free to decide as to their use and development". His report gave a tremendous impetus to the international recognition of these problems.

Not a pretty story

Canadian indigenous representatives at the UN have made common cause with aboriginal people from Malaysia, Brazil, Guatemala and many other countries over their common plight. They have described Canadian policies at international meetings in terms similar to those used to condemn repressive regimes.

In July 1991, Ted Moses, as the self-styled Ambassador of the

Crees to the UN, told the Working Group that the James Bay hydro-electric project was imposed on an unwilling people with "catastrophic effects". He reported that the Crees' 1975 treaty has not been fully implemented, that Quebec is threatening to build even more dams and flood even more land, and that both Quebec and Canada have tried to have the courts invalidate the treaty, and three courts have stated that the governments are trying "to illegally escape" from the binding provisions of the treaty. Moses said:

> The construction of this project affects the Cree peoples' right to life, right to subsistence, right to use and benefit from their own resources, right to the expression and manifestation of their own culture, as well as numerous other rights.... The proposed projects have been condemned by the world's major environmental organizations.

Faced with these embarrassing denunciations, the Canadian authorities began by assuming there really wasn't a case to answer. At first Canada assigned only one civil servant, based in Ottawa, to attend the early meetings of the Working Group. But as the attack on Canada escalated, Canadian representation was expanded to a team of seven diplomats, headed by an ambassador. Even then, the commitment seemed less than wholehearted: at time of writing the ambassador is an expert in trade, not human rights.

When the Oka crisis erupted in 1990, the Canadian government finally realized it could no longer ignore the international dimension of its Indian policies. Much to Canada's embarrassment and irritation, the UN Sub-Commission (the immediate parent of the Working Group) asked Canada to report on its actions. Ted Moses thanked the international body:

> You acted when the Premier of Quebec had issued an ultimatum to the indigenous peoples, when our people were surrounded by hundreds of heavily armed police, when the threat of force had already been invoked, when food, water, medicine, and advisors were being denied to our people solely on the basis of race.... [Your] act forced Canada and Quebec to realize that any act of violence against the indigenous peoples of Canada would be seen and heard by the whole world.... I believe that this Sub-committee's interest is what averted further violence against the people of Kanehsatake and Kahnawake.

Moses says Canada's diplomats tend to wave off aboriginal problems by spouting figures about money spent, negotiations under way and principles adhered to in domestic policy. "We have been able to create awareness that you can still run into difficulties even with governments that are supposed to be the most democratic in the world." He believes that Canada has become more careful in what it says about native people in international forums.

Certainly the government no longer ignores this international dimension of Indian policy. In June 1991, this once-shy youth from the tiny village of Eastmain, whose dad is a trapper, was invited by the Department of External Affairs to brief Canada's diplomatic heads of post. Moses gave it to them with both barrels. Much of Indian reserve land has been taken from native people, he said. The federal government has violated its trust responsibility by using Indian lands and resources for its own ends. Federal and provincial governments do not even respect their own laws when it comes to Indian rights:

> As Indians we live in a dictatorship every bit as real, every bit as offensive as the dictatorships that were overthrown in Eastern Europe. Many native Canadians watched that situation with intensity, sympathy and understanding. They hope that they too will some day be liberated.

This is harsh stuff, but certainly heartfelt.

The Crees, of course, are not the only aboriginal nation to approach the UN. A case was taken by the Maliseet woman, Sandra Lovelace, to the UN Human Rights Commission, complaining of sexual discrimination in the Indian Act. Her success eventually led Canada to reinstate as Indians thousands of women who had lost their Indian status.

The Lubicon Crees of Alberta also used the UN forum to draw international attention to their struggle with the federal and provincial governments in the 1980s. And ever since 1979, the Mikmaqs have been conducting a running battle with Canada at the UN Human Rights Commission, as mentioned in Chapter 5. They have argued that their right to self-determination was recognized and affirmed by their eighteenth-century treaties with Britain, and that consequently their constitutional relationship with Canada can be changed only with their consent. They claim that when Prime Minister Mulroney excluded the Mikmaq Grand Council from the constitutional conferences in the '80s, in effect non-Mikmaqs were given authority to exercise the Mikmaq right.

The Mikmaqs have won minor victories in this long struggle: in

1990, the UN agreed, over the objections of Canada, to accept the Mikmaq communication; but in November 1991, the committee concluded that Canada's refusal to admit Mikmaqs to the constitutional table did not constitute "discrimination" or "unreasonable restriction" of their rights. The Mikmaqs said this decision appeared to give the state the right to decide who should represent them, that this was incompatible with "the recognition of the special and collective character of indigenous rights" by the UN General Assembly, and they asked that the matter be referred to the International Court of Justice. It seems, however, that the sympathy of governments for the principle of self-determination began to evaporate when ethnic groups in eastern Europe and the former Soviet Union began to fight each other, and this has affected determination of the Mikmaqs' case.

Canada has had to argue strenuously that the Mikmaqs are not a "people" within the international meaning of the term, even though the 1982 Constitution refers to the rights of Indian, Metis and Inuit "peoples". The Mikmaqs, says the government, are a tiny group scattered among four provinces in which two million other people live. By no means can they be considered a "people". Yet that has not prevented Canada's representatives from also arguing that the Mikmaqs are threatening the "national unity and territorial integrity" of the country. This must have seemed rather a feeble and mechanistic argument in the ears of foreigners accustomed to thinking of Canada as the nation that engineered the expulsion of South Africa from the Commonwealth, and practically invented the concept of international peacekeeping. More pertinent, perhaps, was that Canada's own Human Rights Commissioner, Max Yalden, was almost simultaneously denouncing his country's treatment of natives as a "national disgrace".[3] The idea that the Mikmaqs are threatening to break up the country is surely one that only government lawyers out of touch with the real world could take seriously.

All of this activity in Geneva has given Canada rather a new international image: one more closely connected to reality. Although claiming to be progressive and tolerant of diversity, in fact Canada has a 200-year record of legislated racism, not only against natives, but against non-white immigrants from other parts of the world. Only now, because of the persistence of the aboriginal attack at the UN, has Canada's human-rights record come under international scrutiny. The South African apartheid regime was certainly quick to get the point. When a chief in Manitoba invited the South African ambassador to take a look at the appalling conditions of his people, Canada's embarrassment went clanking ponderously around the world.

This is no more than the country deserves, as Ted Moses forcefully told the Canadian heads of post:

> Canada's national interest will best be served when there is no longer anything to be embarrassed about.... Imagine a Canada where the native peoples live as long as everyone else, where they have the same quality of housing, where they are educated...[as] doctors, lawyers, accountants, scientists. Imagine a Canada where the native people have a fair share of the wealth, live on lands and have a share of the resources that would permit them to participate fully and equally in the economy. Would that not be in the national interest?
>
> Indians do not ask that our inherent right to self-determination be respected because we want to separate from Canada...[but] because our internal right to self-determination has been historically denied. You have not taken care of our health and education; you have not defended our land base; you have not protected our wealth. It is a fundamental principle of democracy that a people can best look after their own interests. No wonder we have not done well!

In 1991 the Crees compounded Canada's embarrassment by taking the domestic squabble between Quebec and federal Canada to the international body. In an intervention that rattled the dovecotes of External Affairs back in Ottawa, and alarmed Quebec nationalists, the Crees complained that in the event of a unilateral declaration of independence, Quebec intended to "assume sovereignty over the indigenous peoples living in the province". The Crees said this would abrogate treaty relationships undertaken by Quebec and Canada; and they warned that they would not passively surrender their lands and rights to a new state. Canada's refusal to discuss this threat to native self-determination, while entertaining Quebec's claim, said the Crees, "reflects a double-standard based on racial prejudice".

Snail-like momentum for change

Governments fight like tigers to avoid fundamental change that might commit them to act decently to aboriginal peoples; and when forced into it, they do everything possible to avoid actually carrying out such commitments. It is already more than thirty years since the

International Labour Organization passed the world's first "Indigenous and Tribal Populations Convention" in 1957. The agreement didn't have much effect, and was revised in 1989. The revised version came into effect two years later, after the first two nations, Mexico and Norway, ratified it.

Canada has not yet ratified the convention, and it is not difficult to understand why: the country is grossly in violation of many of the articles setting standards for the treatment of indigenous peoples.. For example:

<u>Article 7:</u> *(1) The peoples concerned shall have the right to decide their own priorities for the process of development....and to exercise control...over their own economic, social and cultural development.* (In Canada, Indian development issues are still entangled with the bewildering red tape of the Indian Act, the ultimate instrument of government control over Indians.)

(2)...Improvement of the conditions...of the peoples concerned...shall be a...priority in plans for the overall economic development of areas they inhabit. (In Canada, most traditional aboriginal lands are being mined, clearcut and otherwise exploited over the strenuous objections of the aboriginals.)

(3)...Governments shall ensure that...studies are carried out...to assess the social, spiritual, cultural and environmental impact on them of planned development activities. (This is almost never done, anywhere in Canada. A prime example was the total lack of such assessment before the building of the $23-billion James Bay hydro project in the 1970s. Nor have governments changed their attitudes: in the '90s, Canada and Quebec strenuously resisted fulfilling their legal obligation to carry out such studies before construction starts on the second phase of this enormous project. The Crees had to go to court to have the obligation enforced.)

<u>Article 8:</u> *(1) In applying national laws and regulations...due regard shall be had to their customs or customary laws.* (Recent official inquiries into education, child care and the justice system prove that the contrary is the case in Canada.)[4]

<u>Article 10:</u> *(2) Preference shall be given to methods of punishment other than confinement in prison.* (Thousands of aboriginals languish in Canadian prisons, far out of proportion to their numbers in the population. Usually they are jailed for minor, liquor-related crimes, often without properly understanding the nature of their crimes.)[5]

<u>Article 14:</u> *(1) The rights of ownership and possession of the peoples concerned over the lands which they traditionally occupy shall be recognized.... Measures... shall be taken to safeguard the right of the peoples concerned to use lands not*

353

exclusively occupied by them.... (Provincial governments frequently deny such ownership rights, and try, through wildlife, game, forestry and land-use regulations, to prevent native people from using traditional lands they do not now exclusively occupy.)

Article 20: *(1) Governments shall...adopt special measures...with regard to recruitment and conditions of employment of workers belonging to these peoples....* (In Canada, such measures are rare. Even where promised, as in many major resource projects, they are not carried out: for example, in both the James Bay and northern Manitoba hydro developments.)

Article 23: *(1) Traditional activities...such as hunting, fishing, trapping and gathering, shall be recognized as important factors in the maintenance of their cultures and in their economic self-reliance and development.... Governments...shall ensure that these activities are strengthened and promoted.* (In Canada, with rare exceptions such as the income security programme for trappers in James Bay, the opposite is true: governments do everything possible to undermine the traditional life, to herd the people into a sedentary life in villages, and attach them to the wage economy.)

Article 27: *(1) Education programmes...shall incorporate their histories, their knowledge and technologies, their value systems and their further social, economic and cultural aspirations.* (With rare exceptions, Canadian educational curricula either ignore or denigrate native history, knowledge, technology and value systems.)

Article 28: *(1) Children shall, wherever practicable, be taught to read and write in their own indigenous language.... Measures shall be taken to preserve and promote...[these] languages.* (Outside the Northwest Territories, and to a lesser extent Quebec, no significant encouragement is given by any Canadian government to indigenous languages.)[6]

Article 31: *Education measures shall be taken among all sections of the national community... with the object of eliminating prejudices that they may harbour in respect of these peoples.* (If such programmes exist in Canada, they are well hidden.)

Canada is not within a country mile of meeting these minimum standards. Where the recommended policies have been introduced, it has been by the native people themselves (for example, by using native practices in child-care services, encouraging native languages in native-run schools, and applying their own values to native-run justice systems).

If Canada were to ratify the ILO convention, it would have eighteen months to begin implementing its provisions, in default of which it could be called on the carpet in Geneva and told to clean up its act. The government, of course, can ignore such demands, as it has done in the past, yet such condemnation would be embarrassing for Canada. The convention describes principles of just and decent behaviour towards native peoples that should, in the coming decades, eventually become the accepted international standard. By changing its policies and practices, Canada would be showing leadership in a vital area – human rights – in which the world expects us to be showing the way.

Building a convention of hope

The Working Group in Geneva has been trying for some years now to take the ILO Convention one step further by creating a Universal Declaration of the Rights of Indigenous Peoples. This, it is hoped, will eventually take its place alongside the Universal Declaration of Human Rights as a global standard, applicable to all nations, by which improvement in social equity and justice can be measured. It takes a long time to achieve such a declaration. And even after it is passed, the fact that there are new rights common to all human beings percolates slowly into public consciousness.

Still, such declarations of general principle have proven to be far from insignificant. For example, the signing of the Universal Declaration of Human Rights in 1948 added impetus to a movement already underway in Canada for abolition of legal discrimination against minorities. Since then, Canada has been obliged to provide regular international reports about the treatment of minorities, an obligation that has created a continuing, official recognition of the need to keep working for improvements. Progress may be slow, but it has been steady over the last three decades. Something similar can surely be hoped for from the Universal Declaration of the Rights of Indigenous Peoples.

The rights to self-determination, land, culture and spiritual freedom, and to a fair share of the resources and opportunities within their nations, form the heart of the draft declaration. The indigenous peoples who have become involved in the work at the level of the Working Group, like the Crees, have had a considerable influence on the thirty proposed paragraphs. But as the declaration moves to higher levels in the UN Human Rights Commission, the Economic and Social Council, and finally the General Assembly itself, decisions about it will be made only by governments.

As may be imagined from their reaction towards the Mikmaq case,

Canada's UN representatives have been uneasy about any entrench-
ment of the right of indigenous self-determination, which they insist
"must be put in the context of not implying any right to threaten the
boundaries or political integrity of existing states," according to an
External Affairs department document issued in reaction to the draft
declaration. This right to self-determination was left out of the first
drafts; but by 1991 the very first paragraph of the draft declaration,
as approved by the Working Group, stated:

> Indigenous peoples have the right to self-determination, in accordance
> with international law. By virtue of this right, they freely determine their
> relationship with the States in which they live, in a spirit of coexistence
> with other citizens, and freely pursue their economic, social, cultural
> and spritual development in conditions of freedom and dignity.

Whether this will survive the declaration's later passage through
the higher UN bodies, at which only governments are represented, is
anyone's guess. In its response to early drafts, the Canadian government claims to be in favour of greater levels of self-government for
indigenous people; but what it means by that is a willingness to hand
over some form of municipal powers. It is interesting to see that in
the horsetrading over the declaration's wording, Canada's federal
government never pretends to be anything else but a defender of the
nation state, not a defender (as it is constitutionally supposed to be)
of the rights of the indigenous people within Canada.

Even in relation to health and education rights, Canada would
rather be obliged only to consult with indigenous peoples about
state programmes affecting them, rather than to obtain consent for
such programmes. This has always been the Canadian formula: father knows best. Any written guarantees about indigenous access to
traditional lands finds Canada frankly worried. Our government, in
its reaction document, states:

> Those articles relating to land are more difficult than many of the others
> for...Canada. Indigenous rights over land must be balanced with those of
> third parties, and problems would be caused by recognizing rights "to lands
> once used by" indigenous people, rather than "those currently occupied".

(It is easy to understand this position: Canada has always tried to
squeeze indigenous people onto a few acres of land, so that "third
parties" can be allowed to exploit their larger traditional territories.

And we are still doing so).

On the environment, Canada favours "shared decision-making or a consultative mechanism". This echoes the consultation process set up in the James Bay Agreement, which has been consistently violated by the governments of Canada and Quebec for fifteen years. But the government is so pleased with this flawed process that it is now recommending it for all other countries.

Canada has also demurred from clauses that would confirm cultural and language rights, saying that the state's financial obligation to promote such rights is problematic.

Most governments have been drawn kicking and screaming to the table in this effort to affirm aboriginal rights. But there is no doubt that this international movement has given great hope to many indigenous peoples, particularly those from nations where they have no rights and are fighting daily for their survival. During the Indigena 500 conference in Ottawa described in the Prologue to this book, South American delegates made repeated references to "Convention 169", urging everyone at the conference to work for its ratification. They were talking about the revised version of the ILO Convention; but it would probably be no exaggeration to say that most natives in Canada would not have known what they were referring to. However little-known this convention may be in Canada, the people from Latin America spoke of it as a lifeline, a source of hope that the international community might find a way to stop their governments from oppressing them.

This chapter has outlined the recent transformation of aboriginal people from a forgotten, neglected minority to an international force. Personally I have no trouble putting faces to this transformation. I have in my mind's eye a group of partially educated, partially deracinated Cree kids, victims of Canada's vicious "We're civilized, you're savage" ideology, who in 1971 are sitting in a greasy-spoon restaurant in Chibougamau, Quebec, when they read the scary news that their homelands are to be flooded, and nobody has bothered to tell them about it. Twenty years later, in company with their indigenous compatriots from around the world, these same kids appear in the ornate and impressive halls of Geneva, where they expose to global view the truth that Canada has systematically worked to destroy their cultures, languages, and economies.

It's a start: and a great start, at that.

24

Goodbye indifference,
hello goodwill

I hope it is clear by now that the Indian Act, redolent with the crude racial and cultural prejudices of Victorian times, has been a disaster, and must be changed. This disaster has been evident, of course, for much of this century. But the essential ingredients for change have been missing: first, for decades the aboriginal people had no means of expressing themselves politically with sufficient coherence and force to make Euro-Canadians take notice; and secondly, Canadian public opinion about aboriginals has been notable more for indifference than goodwill.

When I began my excursions into aboriginal Canada in 1968, that public indifference was compounded by profound ignorance and prejudice. It is good to be able to report, a quarter of a century later, that indifference has given way to a vague sympathy, and the ignorance has lessened, although much prejudice remains. There is, however, a definite momentum for improvement in the situation of aboriginal people, powered by the native reawakening and the growing goodwill of Canadians, and I would not be surprised if the changes in the coming five years are even greater than those of the previous twenty-five.

The aboriginals began to overcome their political powerlessness in the late '60s. Funding by the federal government of their political organizations allowed them to build an organizational base they had never had before. Simultaneously, there began what has since become an extraordinary increase in the number of aboriginal people receiving a formal education at colleges and universities. As the aboriginal political organizations have shaken down – very often breaking up, then regrouping – they have come into the hands of the first generation of aboriginal leaders who are capable of engaging the Euro-Canadian political structure with some hope of changing it to their advantage.

The pathway to this transformation has not been particularly smooth. The native political groupings that emerged from the 1960s mirrored the structures of Canadian government, with umbrella national organizations of the three major groups – status, Métis and non-status, and Inuit – and provincial associations at the lower level. This was a neat and manageable structure for bureaucrats and politicians, but unfortunately it did not correspond to the realities of aboriginal life.

Although some of the provincial organizations were aggressive and effective, eventually many nations within their membership found them too remote. For example, the opposition to the James Bay project in Quebec in the early '70s was first undertaken by the Indians of Quebec Association (dominated by the Mohawks of Kahnawake and the Hurons of Loretteville); but within a year or two, the northern Crees found the association's other priorities interfered with its dedication to the Cree fight. The Crees broke away to form their own Grand Council of the Crees, which spelled the end of the provincial association. Similarly, in Manitoba, the provincial organization could not adequately represent both southern and northern nations, who eventually formed two separate associations. In British Columbia, the well-established Union of B.C. Indian Chiefs foundered in the '70s and was replaced by various tribal organizations – Nisga'a, Nuu-chah-nulth, Carrier-Sekani, Gitksan-Wet'suwet'en, and so on. At various times, associations of prairie natives quit the national organization altogether, but it was revamped into the Assembly of First Nations (AFN), and by the late '80s most status Indians were again members, about half a million of them organized into nearly 600 bands, occupying 2,000 reserves throughout the country. The AFN remains the solidest native organization, and was an effective leader in the negotiations leading to the Charlottetown Accord.

The Native Council of Canada (NCC), whose founding meeting I described in Chapter 19, could not contain the impatience of some of the long-established prairie Métis organizations, which split off to form their own Métis National Council. In British Columbia, one of the founding organizations of the NCC, the B.C. Association of Non-Status Indians (BCANSI), collapsed in the 1970s and was replaced by the United Native Nations, which opened its membership to both status and non-status Indians. After all these defections, the NCC regrouped and emerged as an organization for non-status and urban Indians (although including some status Indians).

There is a paradox in the acceptance of federal funding by native organizations whose mission in life is to force the federal government to make policy changes. Many native people regard the AFN as an arm of government, and it is common to hear them say that the National Chief "has been put in there" by government, and is essentially the creature of government. The fact is that native people in Canada are, for the most part, poor in resources; they do not have the capacity to generate the large sums of money needed to run a modern political organization. As they are constituted now, native associations live always with the knowledge that government can, to quote Dr. Oliver Brass, "pull the rug out from under them" at any time. And, in fact, Ministers of Indian Affairs have tried to do so from time to time, whenever they have felt that the native organizations are getting out of hand.

Getting a national profile

At first, the new native politics made little impression on the average Canadian; the impact on public awareness grew slowly. But by 1979 a study of the aboriginal presence in the media showed that the stereotyped image of disoriented and dependent native people had been replaced by an image of articulate native leaders making cogently argued statements about the needs of their people.[1] Slowly, what Harold Cardinal, the Alberta Indian leader of the 1960s, once described as the "problem problem" (that is, the problem of being regarded only as a problem), was being overcome.

Still, the native profile in Canadian politics remained low until Prime Minister Trudeau's attempt to amend and repatriate the Constitution in the early '80s. Aboriginal leaders became nervous that repatriation might affect the treaties their forebears had signed with Britain. At one point, more than 500 chiefs gathered for a major lobby in London. They asked the British Court of Appeal for a declaration that responsibility for Indians be left with the Crown. Lord Denning ruled that the Royal Proclamation was equivalent to an entrenched provision in the Constitution of the American colonies, and was binding on the Crown "so long as the sun rises and the river flows".

The provincial Premiers and Prime Minister first agreed to entrench aboriginal rights in the new Constitution, then had second thoughts and casually dropped the aboriginal references from the final package of amendments agreed on November 5, 1981. This retreat from principle brought an outburst of criticism and furious lobbying. Justice Thomas Berger of the British Columbia Supreme Court, a long-time supporter of aboriginal causes, publicly attacked the change, and later had to leave the bench for his temerity in doing so. Eventually, the provisions were restored so that "existing" aboriginal and treaty rights of the "Indian, Métis and Inuit peoples" (including the Royal Proclamation, thanks perhaps to Lord Denning), were guaranteed in the 1982 Constitution. The casualness with which the nation's political leaders had dropped the aboriginals off the page, was, however, a warning that native people never forgot: nothing was going to come easily for them.

From this brief outline, it can be seen that the new prominence of aboriginals in Canadian political life today is no overnight thing, nor is it temporary. By the beginning of the '90s they had become a considerable presence and played a large role in the latest round of negotiations for an amended Constitution, which resulted in the Charlottetown Accord. For most Canadians the proposed constitutional changes held the promise of a complete renewal of the relationship with aboriginals, and although there were vociferous opponents of this renewal, most public opinion appeared to favour it, at least so far as that opinion was clearly articulated during the constitutional debate and referendum campaign.

Perhaps too much to swallow

Although the Charlottetown Accord provided for aboriginal self-government as an inherent right, there was a great deal of criticism from aboriginals themselves, especially from treaty Indians on the prairies, and from those groups, such as the Mohawks and Six Nations, who have always insisted that they are still sovereign nations. Many First Nations refused to allow referendum polling to take place on their reserves, but even those aboriginal people who had the opportunity to vote stayed away from the polling stations in droves. The AFN's own figures suggest that only 20 per cent of people in reserves where there were polling stations bothered to vote, and of these, 60 per cent voted against the proposed changes.

This is really not surprising, given the complexity of the proposals.

In the section covering "First Peoples", the accord had fourteen clauses, written in legalistic language that is not particularly easy to follow. "The inherent right of self-government within Canada" was to be interpreted "in light of the recognition of aboriginal governments as one of the three orders of government in Canada." This certainly would have been a major change, but its exact meaning would not be known for many years. This right to self-government would not have been justiciable (that is, no one would have recourse to the courts to enforce it) for five years, and after 1996, conferences would be held every two years until 2004 to discuss aboriginal constitutional issues.

This was a programme and a timetable so vague and remote that people in the reserves could be forgiven for wondering what it really meant. Much would depend on the goodwill of future governments with which the negotiations would take place. And (as we have seen) what reason do aboriginal people have to place their trust in the goodwill or integrity of governments? If that goodwill should fail (as it did in similar circumstances following the 1982 accord, when Prime Minister Mulroney wiped his hands of the problem one afternoon in 1987), then the aboriginal people would have to depend on the courts to interpret the agreement, and virtually to decide the constitutional position of aboriginals. They would just have to hope, presumably, that the judges involved would not be like Justices Steele, McEachern, or any number of others who have in recent years brought down neanderthal pronunciamentos about aboriginal life and rights. Not much of a bargain, there.

There were, of course, positive features to the proposed changes affecting aboriginals. Issues of jurisdiction, lands and resources, and economic and fiscal arrangements, were specifically included as subjects for future negotiation. It was provided that treaty rights should be interpreted "in a just, broad and liberal manner taking into account the spirit and intent of the treaties and the context in which the specific treaties were negotiated". (This wording echoes some of Chief Justice Brian Dickson's liberal Supreme Court judgments of the mid-'80s.) The government of Canada undertook, in fact, to "clarify treaty rights", and "rectify terms of treaties when agreed to by the parties", and to have regard for the spirit and intent of the treaties "as understood by aboriginal peoples". These proposals certainly went far to meet the demand, formulated by aboriginal organizations in the late 1980s, that the treaties should be reinterpreted in terms of modern Canadian life. But again, the commitment was scarcely more than a promise to negotiate in good faith, and anyone who has seen what such promises have meant to Canadian governments in the recent past – for example, in negotiations with the Lubicon Crees of Alberta, the Crees of James Bay, the Algonquins of Barriere Lake – could be forgiven a healthy scepticism.

Then the accord contained puzzling references that seemed to place native self-government definitively under the umbrella of general Canadian law, while apparently disavowing that this was so. This seemed to many aboriginal people to run counter to the idea that their right to self-government is inherent in their prior occupancy of the Americas, and has not been granted to them by any Euro-Canadian legislature. For example, it was provided that any law passed by an aboriginal government "may not be inconsistent with those laws which are essential to the preservation of peace, order and good government in Canada". Probably most Canadians would agree with this as a practical limit on the meaning of the term "self-government". But then this sentence was added: "However, this provision would not extend the legislative authority of Parliament or of the legislatures of the provinces." It is hard to discern what this means. If aboriginal laws have to be consistent with the laws of Parliament (and if not, presumably, they could be struck down by the courts), how could it be argued that this does not extend the authority of Parliament over aboriginal legislatures? How must this contradiction have struck people in aboriginal communities who are not used to interpreting such arcane concepts (especially those for whom English is not their first language)?

Whatever the rights and wrongs of this particular clause, and many others in the Charlottetown Accord, it has since been generally admitted that aboriginal people were not given enough time to absorb the new proposals, discuss them, and decide on them. "Too much, too fast," one Saskatchewan chief told me a month after the vote. "Only thirty-one people in my reserve voted. Most people felt it was just too much for them to take in." The nature of the referendum also offended many native people. They had used their customary consensus politics as the deal was hammered together. But when the final decision was to be taken, consensus went out the window. It was either to be yes, or no.

The big winners from the Charlottetown Accord, if it had been passed, would have been the Métis people. The accord committed governments to negotiate "a legally binding, justiciable and enforceable accord" on Métis issues in Ontario, Manitoba, Saskatchewan, Alberta and British Columbia, covering self-government agreements, land and resources, and "transfer of the portion of aboriginal programmes and services available to Métis" to their own governments. For the first time since 1870, the federal government would have acknowledged an obligation to Métis people, similar to its obligations to Indians; and the provinces would be able to devise special arrangements similar to those already in Alberta (the only place where Métis have a land base, as we have seen in Chapter 19).

A continuing process of change

There is no ideal moment to finish an examination of the history and contemporary circumstances of the aboriginal people of Canada. However much an author might wish to do so, it is not possible to conclude this story by wrapping it into a neat package, and sending the reader off with a few comforting homilies about the future. The aboriginal people are preparing for an era of rapid and dramatic changes in their relationships with non-aboriginals. No one can be certain exactly what form these changes will take. Many of them are already underway as aboriginal communities assume greater control over their affairs. We have met some of the people who are leading these changes in a great variety of places. For every one mentioned in this book, there are hundreds of others working every day to restore their nations to something like their former glory.

Canadians at the half-dozen citizens' conferences held during the 1992 constitutional process consistently expressed sympathetic feelings towards aboriginals. But as my travels in aboriginal communities have shown, it is one thing to express a generalized sympathy, and quite another to translate that sympathy into concrete action for change. "When it comes to Indian people, it is the bureaucracy that holds back change," Ovide Mercredi told me, "even when we get a good Minister of Indian Affairs. We cannot rely on policy decisions to make change. Cabinet decisions on our rights depend on what is in the law. That is why we need fundamental change in the supreme law." And it is why he placed so much emphasis for so long on trying to change the constitutional situation of his people.

Nevertheless, the debate over the Constitution appears to have taught Mercredi that many aboriginal leaders are stuck in the assumptions of the past, as are many Euro-Canadians. He spoke of the need to "decolonize" his people. He said the people were "too fragmented" to enable him to call the national law-making assembly, a native parallel to Parliament, of which he had spoken to me a year before. "Many leaders have accepted the Indian Act system of government, and the challenge of asserting the inherent right to self-government is threatening to them," he said. The sobering reality is that in many places, the aboriginal people have no leverage: no control over their land or resources, and no independent revenue. In fact, they are totally dependent on government to keep functioning.

Many have assumed that the promises made to aboriginals in the constitutional accord could still be implemented through the normal process of political life; but that may not be so easy. Mercredi and others have pointed out that federal and provincial legislatures continue to have primacy over aboriginal communities, which still have to negotiate within that framework – as Peter Quaw's Lheit Lit'en so rudely discovered when they tried to break out of the Indian Act strait-jacket.

Thus, although aboriginal nations have taken control of their child-welfare services (to use a common example), with the exception of one British Columbia band they all have to administer laws and regulations that have been handed down to them from provincial governments. The logical consequence of this is that in some places, native social workers employed by these agencies through sheer force of circumstance begin to be perceived as representatives of an outside authority, imposing alien rules on a reluctant people. "When provincial governments impose laws on us," said Mercredi, "we find we are at the bottom of the hierarchy of rights. That's the reality." And that is what he was hoping the Charlottetown Accord would change: aboriginal communities would have become free to establish and administer their own systems for child welfare, education, health, and so on, according to their own values and traditions.

Following defeat of the Charlottetown Accord, aboriginal organizations decided to press on with their plans for change, just as if the accord had been agreed to. Mercredi, scrambling to overcome the setback to his leadership, talked again of engaging the AFN in local actions of civil disobedience, of "getting into the trenches" with people who have taken to the barricades to defend their fisheries or forests, thus giving them the national profile they need if their protests are to be effective. In addition to such direct action, he said, the AFN would become involved in helping aboriginal nations, many of whom could not afford to hire lawyers, to prepare litigation in defence of their rights.

Mercredi was not alone among aboriginal leaders in saying that in the next five years, aboriginal people would be "asserting *de facto* self-government" without waiting for permission or agreement or any change in Canadian law. As I have tried to show in this book, this may not be an orderly process, and certainly will not be a painless one. The struggle over access to resources (already the central issue for the Haida, Mikmaqs, Algonquins, Ojibway, Crees of Manitoba, and many other groups) is sure to become even more intense.

Frontiers in this coming war are opening up almost every day. The Supreme Court's Sparrow decision gives aboriginal access to traditional fisheries high priority; but provincial governments have tended to ignore the decision, and future conflict over fisheries seems inevitable. Early in 1993, a protest meeting attracted 2,000 British Columbia fishermen to Vancouver against the "special privileges" given Indians by federal policies arising from the Sparrow decision.

At the time of writing, a group of Cree elders in northern Saskatchewan, calling themselves the Protectors of Mother Earth, have maintained a blockade against clearcut logging of their traditional lands for more than six months. Significantly, their struggle is against a band council that had acquiesced in European-style "development" of the forest. The Barriere Lake Algonquins are gearing up for another major struggle. In Restigouche, Quebec, Mikmaqs who believe the provincial government has violated their salmon-fishing rights are preparing for a challenge in the spring of 1993 (which Mercredi said he would join). Aboriginal people in Fort MacKay, north of Fort McMurray, Alberta, are preparing to challenge a Syncrude mining lease in traditional aboriginal lands which has generated more than a billion dollars to the provincial government, while paying nothing to the aboriginals. And in the prairies, the ground is being prepared for a legal challenge to the Natural Resources Transfer Agreements, under which land and resources were handed over to the provincial governments in 1930.

Some of the grounds for this coming assertion of self-government by aboriginal nations may seem strange, and even antipathetic, to

their non-native supporters. The right to establish gambling on reserves has already become a flashpoint in several places across the
country. The aboriginals argue that since their traditional economies
have been wilfully destroyed by Euro-Canadian society, they have
no option but to create an alternative economy; and in many places,
gaming – high-stakes bingo, casinos, and so on – ideally suits their
situation. They claim to be free of federal or provincial jurisdictions
limiting the establishment of gaming places. Some bands say this
issue is a test of the sincerity of Canadian politicians who agreed to
guarantee aboriginal self-government in the Constitution. For example, at time of writing, a war of words was under way between a New
Brunswick Maliseet band and the provincial government, with the
band threatening to open a casino, and the government warning that
casinos are illegal in the province, and in violation of the Criminal
Code of Canada.

"Gaming is not the issue I would have preferred for the assertion of
rights," commented Ovide Mercredi, when I talked to him in early
1993. "But it is the issue that is in the forefront now." Consequently,
he said, the AFN's lawyers would be working with chiefs to establish
a code of laws covering gaming, which would guard against potential
abuse either by outside investors or by community leaders. "It will be
very difficult for courts to ignore the inherent right, particularly if
our people go with a rational, reasonable law that takes into account
the public interest," Mercredi said. "But the chiefs who are asserting
this are very militant, they are not pussycats. My approach is one of
peaceful reconciliation."

Questions for the future
Throughout 1992, the constitutional negotiations and their impact
on aboriginals monopolized public attention, overshadowing the
work of the Royal Commission on Aboriginal Peoples, chaired by
Justice René Dussault and Georges Erasmus, former National Chief
of the AFN. Receiving little attention in the media, the Commission
in its first round of hearings visited thirty-six communities, and heard
from more than 800 people. Not surprisingly, these preliminary hearings left the commissioners with dozens of unanswered questions,
which they placed before the public in a discussion paper before beginning their second round of hearings in December 1992.

I hope that the answers to some of those questions have been at least indirectly suggested by the information in this book. Will aboriginal self-government require more land and resources to be placed under the control of aboriginal people? Assuredly, yes. But, if so (to quote another of the Commission's questions) "are Canadians willing to ensure that aboriginal people achieve this?" Only time will tell. I hope that the public sympathy now felt towards the aboriginal cause will be translated into meaningful action of this kind. Much will depend on whether the Canadian public continues to accept that the injustices of the past must be redressed. If Canadians are as tolerant and pragmatic as we like to think, we should have no difficulty in recognizing that we cannot indefinitely maintain our own Third World of poverty, discrimination and injustice, while still aspiring to fulfil a moral role in global affairs.

A modern Indian

As they grow to adulthood, people do not always develop in the way one would expect. The generation of those confused Cree kids who first heard about the James Bay project in the greasy-spoon restaurant in Chibougamau in 1971 has already given rise to aggressive entrepreneurs, statesmanlike politicians, effective social workers and talented artists, in addition to Ted Moses, who treads the halls of international diplomacy; and of course, as one would expect, a good number of hunters, fishermen and trappers.

But when I try to summon up the image of a modern Indian, the person who immediately comes to mind is another of that generation: an old friend of mine, Gilbert Herodier of Chisasibi, the new town created at the mouth of the La Grande River by the James Bay project.

In his late teens and early twenties, Gilbert was almost preternaturally handsome – a glowing, laughing presence with shining copper skin, long black hair and a radiating warmth that attracted people to him like bees to honey. Life was a tremendous romp for him, and he transmitted his enjoyment of it to everyone who knew him.

In the late '60s Gilbert attended the National Theatre School in Montreal, was later part of the first Indian film crew at the National Film Board, and seemed destined to become an artist. One year, the small community north of Montreal where I lived in the summer hired him as a counsellor in a day camp for our children, and we had a summer-long demonstration of Pied Piper-ism: the children loved him. My youngest son in particular followed him around everywhere he went, for to be with Gilbert was very heaven for him. When I went north in 1972 to film *Job's Garden*, that alarming and hilarious expedition that I describe in Chapter 2, Gilbert saved us from total disaster by smoothing our way, setting up contacts for us, and using his skills as assistant cameraman to keep our volatile and unpredictable crew together. Without him we would never have got the film made.

Later Gilbert married the prettiest girl in the Cree dominion, Daisy Bearskin, and they settled down in Chisasibi and produced a family of six children. I went on to do other things, and lost touch with them. I heard that, surprisingly, Gilbert was running the gas station. Even more surprisingly, when over the succeeding years I inquired of Gilbert, people usually said, "We never see him," or, "He seldom comes out of his house." It seemed scarcely credible that this was the same laughing, glowing Gilbert I had known in Montreal. I heard that he had become a computer enthusiast, and his house was jammed with every computer programme under the sun.

I was not back in contact with Gilbert until 1989, when, after an absence of fourteen years, I returned to Chisasibi to make another film. I phoned excitedly, hoping that he could join us in the enterprise, as in the old days; he was more than willing, as helpful as he had always been. But a few weeks after we talked, he was struck down with what seemed to be a severe heart attack, and was unable to do any strenuous activity.

When I visited Chisasibi with my youngest son, the one who had followed Gilbert everywhere, now grown to manhood, we had a great reunion with our old friend. But the glowing teenage Gilbert had given way to a rather paunchy middle-aged man who clearly had not taken care of himself. He introduced us to his vigorous children, who had inherited their parents' good looks. But one of them, Jeremy, was not able to move, and his immobility was what had kept Gilbert in his house for all those years. At the age of two, Jeremy had suffered an attack of meningitis, accompanied by a series of seizures, each of which had damaged his brain more severely than the last. Ever since, Gilbert had devoted much of his life to caring for the child. And when I saw Jeremy, I was even more deeply impressed with Gilbert and Daisy than I had been when they were young. Although Jeremy's body was immobile, his eyes were sparkling, his expression alive. He was obviously a child who had been surrounded with love all his life, and it showed. "He is an angel," said Gilbert, and I think he meant it literally.

Although everyone said he seldom left his house, Gilbert was still an amazing character, who was having a remarkable impact on his community. He ran his gas station virtually from the small office in his house, one wall of which was full of sophisticated computer equipment. On the other wall, he had his telephone, and he moved between the two of them on a swivel chair, almost the only exercise he had taken for many years – a neglect that he was now paying heavily for.

It was an experience just to sit in Gilbert's office and watch him at work. His phone rang constantly, the callers usually asking for advice, or wanting to discuss village affairs. Few of the conversations lasted more than half a minute. Then people would arrive and sit with Gilbert, talking. Gilbert used his computer to print out their wedding invitations, Christmas cards, notices of meetings and anything else they wanted; he would instruct young men and women, some of them left almost illiterate by their poor schooling, in how to master this essential tool of modern life, the computer. He was a kind of unofficial community adviser, whose office had become a centre where everything in the village came under his thoughtful and encouraging gaze.

I did not have to talk to him for very long to realize that here was a most unusual man in Canadian life: a man who, by sitting in his room in this small village, devoting himself to his children and his community, without any apparent thought of reward, was still able to draw people to him by his sincerity and generosity, just as he had years before when he was glowing with youthful health and high spirits.

Gilbert, the father of six, was now a non-drinker, worried about the impact of liquor on the children and teenagers, and acting as a catalyst for a movement to get something done about it. Gilbert, the computer whiz, was worried about the decline in the Cree language, the damage caused to Cree culture by the hydro project, and the devastating impact that money was having on the spiritual qualities of Cree life. When I asked him what the Crees needed, he said, "A spiritual leader." And by that he meant an elder steeped in the Cree hunting life and the Crees' traditional spiritual link with the land and the animals.

Gilbert was adamant that the Crees had to hang onto their culture. He meant the belief system, the sharing ethic, the devotion to the land, the instinctive Cree desire to maintain themselves in balance with other life forms. He did not think that one necessarily had to practise the hunting culture to defend these values: the Crees had to find a form that would ensure the survival of their ethic and their culture in the modern world. He regarded his computers as a tool in this search.

Since that visit, I have kept in touch with Gilbert regularly. He has become my computer guru – it always surprises people when I tell them I'm learning about computers from a Cree in James Bay – and I have become one of the many recipients of his extraordinary generosity of spirit. He has lived through three or four tough years as he has struggled to regain the physical health that he neglected for so long. And then, to the great distress of Gilbert and Daisy, Jeremy died in his early teens, unable to resist the onslaught of disease.

From the time he fell ill, Gilbert had begun to re-emerge into the village, taking long walks every day for the sake of his health. Then someone called me to say that Gilbert had been elected deputy chief. "I didn't even know I was nominated until the day before the election," he told me, when I phoned to congratulate him.

So there he is: a modern Indian. So much charm, so much talent, so much commitment and compassion. So much grief and sadness. And so much hope.

1
Celebrating Survival
1 Neidhardt, 1961: 199.
2 Jennings, 1975: 22.
3 Neidhardt, 1961: 43.

2
The education of an urban Canadian
1 Richardson, Dec. 1968: 21.
2 Trigger, 1986.
3 Myers, 1984: 12.

4
We're civilized, you're savage
1 Jennings, 1975: 5.
2 Moore, 1991.
3 Jennings, 1975: 75.
4 Ibid., 74.
5 Ibid., 78.
6 Ibid., 60.
7 Ibid., 12.
8 Ibid., 127.
9 Cassidy, Frank,199: article by Brian Slattery, "Aboriginal Sovereignty and Imperial Claims." See also Sanders, 1989.
10 Ibid., Slattery: 208-9.
11 Op. cit., Sanders.
12 Gisday Wa and Delgam Uukw: 1990.

5
Mikmaqs: in the path of the invaders
1 There are several acceptable spellings. The most common in Canadian usage is *Micmac*. The form used by the tribe's Grand Council, in its name and documents, is *Mi'kmaq*, in which the accent indicates a long vowel. Another spelling accepted by some is *Miqmaq*. Sometimes the accents are omitted, and sometimes written with a colon instead of an accent. Although the Grand Council has adopted *Mi'kmaq*, it also occasionally writes the word without the accent. The Micmac Association of Cultural Studies retains the more common form. I am told that a conference some fifteen years ago failed to come to an agreement about a common spelling, so all those forms in use appear to be acceptable to at least some members of the tribe. Many native peoples across Canada have reverted to traditional names in recent years, and I have chosen to use the more unfamiliar spelling favoured by the Grand Council as a written symbol of the cultural renewal and affirmation that is underway. Since the word will be pronounced by most readers as written, quite differently from the Mikmaq pronunciation, I have chosen to omit the accent as irrelevant to English-speaking readers.
2 Trigger, 1976: 177-178.
3 Whitehead, 1991: quoting Lescarbot, 1907-14, 47-48. Marc Lescarbot was a French lawyer who in 1606-7 spent a year in the French colony of Port Royal in Mikmaq territory, and who after his return to France published his history in 1609. According to Trigger, 1985: 21, Lescarbot "portrayed the Micmacs as noble savages whose exemplary way of life was free from all the vices of civilized France".
4 Ibid.
5 Mikmakik, "the land of friendship", is the traditional land of the Mikmaw Nation, inhabited by the Mikmaqs, "the allied people".
6 Battiste, 1989: 63-70.
7 Mikmaq Grand Council (Sante' Mawi'omi wjit Mi'kmaq), 1986.
8 *Canadian Encyclopedia*, 1985. Vol.I: 253.
9 Trigger, 1985: 124.
10 Berger, 1991: 15-25.
11 Whitehead, 1991: 15, quoting Lescarbot, Vol. II: 324.
12 Thwaites, 1896, Vol I: 109-111, Extract from the Register of Baptisms in the Church of Port Royal, New France.
13 Op. cit. footnote 7.
14 This is usually spelled Malecite in English, but the people themselves have recently agreed on Maliseet as the preferred spelling.
15 Thwaites, Vol III: 87, L'abbé Biard as quoted in Battiste, *Indian Historian*, 4.
16 Whitehead,1991: 335.
17 Battiste, *Indian Historian*, 8.

18 Ibid.

19 Ibid., 3-13.

20 Trigger, 1985: 239. Also Richardson, ed. 1989: 77, Marshall et al, estimate the original Mikmaq population at 100,000.

21 Trigger, 1985: 238.

22 Daugherty, 1981: 45-47.

23 Cumming and Mickenberg, 1972: 95.

24 Op. cit., footnote 22.

25 Stagg, 1981: 259

26 Mikmaq Grand Council, 1986: 9.

27 Whitehead, 1991: 198.

28 Ibid., 218.

29 Mikmaq Grand Council, 1986: 10.

30 Ibid.

31 Whitehead, 1991: 228

32 Ibid., 237-8.

33 Ibid., 238.

34 Ibid., Foreword by Peter Christmas, Micmac Association of Cultural Studies.

35 Whitehead, 1991: 238.

36 Ibid., 330, quoting Inverness County Court, King vs Sylyboy, Minutes 1928, Public Archives of Nova Scotia.

37 Cumming and Mickenberg, 1972: 98.

6

Colonials and the Policies they made

1 Brown and Maguire, 1979: 25-28.

2 Special Joint Committee of the Senate and House of Commons appointed to examine and consider the Indian Act, 1947: 32-33. These treaties are also listed in Brown and Maguire, 1979: xviii-xxiv.

3 Brown and Maguire, 1979: 21-25.

4 Josephy, 1969: 131-173.

5 Journals of the Legislative Assembly of Canada, Appendix EEE. This appendix lacks page numbers.

6 Ibid.

7 Indian and Northern Affairs, 1978: 17.

8 Ibid., 15.

9 Dickason, 1992: 238.

10 Patterson, 1972: 121.

11 Journals of the Legislative Assembly of Canada, quoting Lord Glenelg's dispatch to the governors, August, 1838.

12 Indian and Northern Affairs, 1978: 18-22.

13 Op. cit., footnote 5.

14 Ibid.

15 Ibid.

16 Richardson, Dec.1989: 15-20.

17 Indian and Northern Affairs, 1978: 24.

18 Miller, 1989: 110.

19 Indian and Northern Affairs, 1978: 28-30.

20 Ibid., 26-27.

21 Ibid., 53. See also Miller, 1989: 114.

22 Indian and Northern Affairs, 1978: 54.

23 Ibid., 55.

24 Ibid., 60.

25 Indian and Northern Affairs, 1978: 61.

7

Mikmaqs: the trauma of government help

1 Special Joint Committee of the Senate and House of Commons appointed to examine and consider the Indian Act: Vol. 21-41, 1947, No. 41, Appendix GN, 2010-11.

2 Ibid.

3 *Halifax Chronicle-Herald*, March 6, 1964, 15

4 Battiste, 1989: 63-70.

5 Richardson, ed. 1989: 93.

6 Henderson, 1991: Note 111, 42.

7 Ibid., 28.

8 Op. cit., footnote 4.

9 Ibid., 93-95.

8

The land is lifted, nimbly

1 The precise wording of the Order-in-Council, admitting Rupert's Land and the North-western Territory to the Confederation: "14. Any claim of Indians to compensation for lands required for purposes of settlement shall be disposed of by the Canadian Government in communication with the Imperial Government; and the Company shall be relieved of all responsibility in respect of them."

2 Cumming and Mickenberg, 1972: 90.

3 For a more detailed account of these legal arguments, see Richardson, 1991: 18-28.

4 Tennant, 1990: 61.

5 Ibid., 59.

6 Ibid., 89-91.

7 Ibid., 112.

8 Berger, 1991: 140-156.

9

Algonquins: at the heart of Canada's history

1 This account is based on Trigger, 1987: 275-287.

2 Ibid., XX, Preface to 1987 edition.

3 This historical account draws on Richardson, ed. 1989: 167-200, article by Greg Sarazin, Chief of the Golden Lake Algonquins, "220 Years of Broken Promises"; and also on an unpublished article prepared for the Algonquins by lawyer Paul Williams, Toronto.

10

The fantastic world of the Indian Act

1 Indian and Northern Affairs, 1978: 67.

2 Ibid., 68.

3 Morris, 1880: 297.

4 Special Joint Committee of Senate and House of Commons appointed to examine and consider the Indian Act: Minutes of Proceedings and Evidence, May 30, 1946: 11, evidence of R.A. Hoey, Director of Indian Affairs.

5 Indian and Northern Affairs, 1978: 107.

6 Ibid., 110.

7 Section 4, 1918 amendment to the Indian Act (S.C. 1918, chap. 6, 8-9 George V).

8 Gambill, 1968: 2 (typed version, quoting petition to Governor-General of Canada, October 29, 1888).

9 Richardson, ed. 1989: 118, article by Mike Mitchell, Grand Chief, Mohawk Council of Akwesasne, "An Unbroken Assertion of Sovereignty."

10 Section 1, 1884 amendment to Indian Act of 1880 (S.C. 1884, chap. 27, 47 Victoria).

11 Carter, 1990: 149-156.

12 Section 2, 1884 amendment to Indian Act of 1880 (S.C. 1884, chap. 27, 47 Victoria).

13 Indian and Northern Affairs, 1978: 80.

14 Sections 1-3, 1881 amendment to Indian Act of 1880 (S.C. 1881, chap., 17, 44 Victoria).

15 For a full account of this policy see Carter, 1990: 209-229.

16 Sections 94-105, 1886 amendment to Indian Act (R.S.C. 1886, chap. 28, 43 Victoria), and Sections 135-146, 1906 amendment to Indian Act (S.C. 1906, chap. 20, 6 Edward VII).

17 Section 11, 1894 amendment to Indian Act, amending sections 137-139 (S.C. 1894, chap. 32, 57-58 Victoria).

18 Special Joint Committee of the House of Commons and Senate appointed to examine and consider the Indian Act: Vol. 21-41, 1947, No. 27: 1448-49.

19 Rev. Doug Crosby, OMI: address of July 24, 1991 to annual religious pilgrimage at Lac Ste-Anne, Alberta.

20 Section 6, 1914 amendment to Indian Act (S.C. 1914, chap. 35, 4-5 George V).

21 Section 5, 1918 amendment to Indian Act (S.C. 1918, chap. 26, 8-9 George V).

22 Section 3, 1920 amendment to Indian Act (S.C. 1919-20, chap. 50, 10-11 George V).

23 Section 20, 1880 amendment to Indian Act of 1876 (S.C. 1880, chap. 28, 43 Victoria).

24 Section 5, 1884 amendment to Indian Act, amending Section 20 of 1880 (S.C. 1884, chap. 27, 47 Victoria).

25 Section 1, 1894 amendment to Indian Act (S.C. 1894, chap. 32, 57-58 Victoria).

26 Gisday Wa and Delgam Uukw, 1990: 7.

27 Indian and Northern Affairs, 1978: 82. La Violette, 1961: 4-97.

28 Section 149, 1906 amendment to Indian Act (S.C.1906, chap. 20, 6 Edward VII).

29 Section 8, 1914 amendment to Indian Act (S.C. 1914, chap. 35, 4-5 George V).

30 Section 16, 1930 amendment to Indian Act, amending section 140 (S.C 130, chap. 25, 20-21 George V).

11

Barriere Lake: people of the Stone Weir

1 Richardson, ed. 1989: 140, article by Chief Jean-Maurice Matchewan, "Mitchikanibikonginik Algonquins of Barriere Lake: Our Long Battle to Create a Sustainable Future."

2 Affidavit by Lena Jerome, sworn on March 20, 1990, entered into Quebec Superior Court, March 30, 1990, in support of an application for an injunction by the Algonquins of Barriere Lake ordering the Quebec government not to sign Timber Supply and Forest Management Agreement (known as CAAF Agreements) for management units 73 and 74, covering the Algonquin lands. The application was refused.

3 This overview of the history of Barriere Lake's traditional lands is largely based on Aird.

12

Harvest of a failed policy

1 Indian and Northern Affairs, 1978: 114

2 Fumoleau, 1973: 266.

3 Ibid., p 267, quoting an article by Jim Cornwall in the *Edmonton Journal*, August 7, 1934.

4 Ibid., 275 (see Appendix 14, 370 for text).

5 Ibid., Appendix 15, 379, quoting article from the *Toronto Star Weekly*, May 28, 1938.

6 LaViolette, 1961: 153.

7 Special Joint Committee of Senate and House of Commons appointed to examine and consider the Indian Act: Minutes of Proceedings and Evidence, No. 9, June 27, 1946.

8 Ibid., No. 1, May 30, 1946, table 3, 10. Evidence of R.A. Hoey, Director of Indian Affairs. For slightly different figures, see 1964-1966.

9 Ibid., Vol. I, No. 21, May 12, 1947, 1080.

10 Ibid., No 1, May 30, 1946, Appendix G, table 5, 211.

11 Op. cit., footnote 8.

12 Ibid.

13 Ibid., No. 3, June 6, 1946, evidence of Brooke Claxton, Minister of Health, 1947, Appendix B, 91. See also brief of Canadian Welfare Council, and Canadian Association of Social Workers, Vol. I, 1947, Appendix BO, 154-161.

14 Ibid., Appendix F.

15 Ibid., Vol. I, 1947, Appendix BO, 154-161.

16 Ibid., Vol. 21-41, 1947, 1806 et seq., evidence of H. Lariviere, Abitibi agency.

17 Ibid., Vol. I. 1947, No. 4, 121-125, evidence of L.J. Raymond, MP for Wright, Quebec.

18 Ibid., Vol. I, 1947, No. 4, 125 et seq., evidence of T. Farquhar, MP for Algoma East.

19 Ibid., Vol. I, 1947, No. 21, Appendix EV, 1123-1129, brief from James Smith's reserve No. 100.

20 Ibid., July 25, 1946, 685 et seq.

21 Ibid., Vol. I, 1947, No. 4, 117, evidence of Douglas Harkness, MP.

22 Larner, 1972: 189.

23 Ibid., p 191.

24 Ibid., p 197.

25 Ibid., p 311.

26 Special Joint Committee of Senate and House of Commons appointed to examine and consider the Indian Act: Vol. 21-41, 1947, No. 41, Appendix HG, 2064-6, brief from Stoneys of Morley reservation.

27 Ibid., 1946, No. 5, Appendix G, 1934, table on pupil enrolment, evidence of R.A.Hoey, Director Indian Affairs. Table in Vol. I, 1947, No. 7, Appendix DO, 340-341, shows slightly different figures.

28 Ibid., Vol. I, 1947, No. 9, Appendix DZ, 461, table on school population.

29 Ibid., Vol. I, 1947, No. 16, 777.

30 Op. cit. footnote 9.

31 Ibid., Vol. 21-41, 1947, No. 25, 1338, brief of Manitoulin Veterans Association of Wikwemikong.

32 Ibid., Vol 21-41, 1947, No 33. 1710, evidence of Mathew Lazore, spokesman for hereditary chiefs.

33 Ibid., No. 19, 1946, 749-750.

34 Op. cit., footnote 32.

35 Op. cit., footnote 31, 1337.

36 Op. cit., footnote 19, p 1124.

37 Special Joint Committee of Senate and House of Commons appointed to examine and consider the Indian Act: Vol. 21-41, 1947, No. 33, 1743-45.

38 Ibid., Vol. I, 1947, No. 9, 430-438.

39 Ibid., Vol. I, 1947, No. 7, 310.

14

Our wealth, taken from their lands

1 Richardson, ed.1989: 6-7, Introduction

by Georges Erasmus, "Twenty Years of Disappointed Hopes."

2 Project Report Mill-by-Mill Listings, 1990, published by Project Report, San Francisco.

3 Statement, Colleen McCrory, Valhalla Society, July 1990.

4 Claude Emery, 1991, "Share Groups in British Columbia," Research Branch, Library of Parliament, Ottawa.

5 Valhalla Society, Submission to Ministry of Forests Hearings on Pulpwood Agreement No. 9, July 5, 1990.

6 Greenpeace Statement, 1990: "Cutting Down Canada: the giveaway of our national forests."

7 World Commission on Environment and Development, 1987.

8 Richardson, 1987: quoting Whiteside, 1981.

9 This account is based on a private communication from Martin Loney, Ottawa policy consultant, who has worked on the issue for northern Manitoba native communities.

10 Cheslatta Band, "The Story of the Surrender of the Cheslatta Reserves on April 21, 1952."

11 Mike Robertson, 1991. "Chronology of the Cheslatta Lake Flooding,...as Gleaned from Original Letters, Documents, Interviews, and Other Printed and Written Material," quoting letter from Indian Agent Robert Howe to W.S. Arneil, BC Indian Commissioner, April 28, 1952.

12 Robertson, 1991: Quoting letter from W.J. McGregor, Regional Supervisor of Indian Affairs, to Ottawa headquarters. (Undated).

13 Quoted in Robertson, 1991.

14 Cheslatta Band, Op. cit. footnote 10, 5.

15 Quoted in Robertson, 1991: 14.

16 Cheslatta Band, Op. cit. footnote 10: July 25, 1992 update.

17 Vancouver Sun, July 9, 1990, B1: "Haida gain allies in war over fishery," by Terry Glavin.

18 The Daily News, Prince Rupert, July 12, 1990: "Haida gain blockade support," by John Farrell.

19 The Daily News, Prince Rupert, July 13,

1990: "Fishcharter feels squeeze in huge blockade," by John Farrell.

20 Vancouver Sun, August 3, 1991: "Haida leader freed in fishing dispute."

21 The Daily News, Prince Rupert, October 21, 1991: "12 Haida now face criminal charges," by John Farrell.

22 Richardson, ed. 1989: 5, Introduction by Georges Erasmus. A detailed account of these questions is contained in that same book in the article "Unflinching Resistance to an Implacable Invader," by N.J. Sterritt.

15
Ojibway: being watchful was not enough

1 Special Joint Committee of the Senate and House of Commons appointed to examine and consider the Indian Act: Vol. 21-41, 1947, No. 47, 1308-1312.

2 Kagiwiosa Manomin Inc. presentation to Ad Hoc Canadian Wild Rice Council, with respect to wild rice grading system, Jan 10-11, 1990. In this paper, Pitchenesse argues that the so-called scientific attitudes embodied in wild-rice grading regulations are not value-free, but "are used to support a system of values that maximizes production, efficiency and profits, and pays no respect to the Anishinaabe way of dealing with Nature. Science in this context...is being used as part of the larger dynamic of the non-indigenous society to tear apart Indian peoples and cultures."

3 Letter to the Times-News, Thunder Bay, April 19, 1990.

4 Grand Council, Treaty 3, 1986: 2-5.

5 Holzkamm and Waisberg, 1991: 1-2.

6 Ibid., 28.

7 Grand Council Treaty 3, 1986: 13-14.

8 Holzkamm and Waisberg, 1989: 24.

9 Grand Council Treaty 3, 1986: 19.

10 Holzkamm and Waisberg, 1991: 21.

11 Whiteside 1981: 48, quoting The Globe, Toronto, Dec. 16, 1857.

12 Whiteside, 1981: quoting The Globe, Toronto, Sept. 22, 1859.

13 Grand Council Treaty 3, 1986: 20-21.

14 Dickason, 1992: 267-268.

15 Holzkamm and Waisberg, 1990: 33.
16 Morris, 1880: 44.
17 Ibid., 1880: 62.
18 Ibid.
19 Ibid., 7-8.
20 Holzkamm and Waisberg, 1991: 3-4.
21 Holzkamm and Waisberg, 1990: 26.
22 Ibid., 8.
23 Grand Council Treaty 3, 1986: 25-26.
24 Ibid., 30-31.
25 Ibid., 20.
26 Dickason, 1992: 279.
27 Morris, 1880: 322.
28 Ibid., 75.
29 Holzkamm and Waisberg, 1991: 4.
30 Holzkamm and Waisberg, 1989: 13.
31 Grand Council Treaty 3, 1986: 40.
32 Ibid., 37
33 Sections 1-3, 1881 amendment to the Indian Act (S.C. 1881, c. 17, 44 Victoria).
34 Holzkamm and Waisberg, 1989: 16.
35 Holzkamm and Waisberg, 1991: 8.
36 Grand Council, Treaty 3, 1986: 44.
37 Grand Council, Treaty 3: *These Indians are All Good Axemen and Good Workers*, pamphlet, 4.
38 Holzkamm and Waisberg, 1991: 17.
39 Op. cit., footnote 34.
40 Holzkamm and Waisberg, 1991: 18.
41 Grand Council Treaty 3, 1986: 44.
42 Special Joint Committee of the Senate and House of Commons to examine and consider the Indian Act: Vol. 21-41, 1947, No. 47, 1308-1312.

16
"Without land our people will be nothing"

1 Bighetty, 1986: 153.
2 Ibid., Introduction.
3 Ibid., 8.
4 Ibid., 49.

17
The aboriginal city

1 *Justice on Trial:* Report of the Task Force on the Criminal Justice System and its impact on the Indian and Métis People of Alberta, March 1991. Submitted to Solicitors-General of Canada and Alberta, and Attorney-General of Alberta.

2 Assembly of First Nations, 1990. Also, House of Commons Standing Committee on Aboriginal Affairs, 1990,

18
Healing, teaching, learning

1 A Canadian Press article in *The Toronto Star*, April 27, 1991, tells the story of Richard Muksoyak, one of a number of children sent south for treatment in the 1950s and 1960s, and never sent home again. After a difficult life on the streets of Montreal, he was reunited with his father on Baffin Island in 1989, but after a couple of years he returned to Montreal, having decided that human beings are less a product of culture and genetics than of their own experience, and that he would like to work as a volunteer among the homeless.

19
Superbly mixed up: the Métis

1 Richardson, Nov. 1970.
2 Richardson, Feb. 1971.
3 Macleod and Morton, 1974: 38-42.
4 Sealey and Lussier, 1975, quoting A.S. Morton.
5 Ross, 1856: 244. For rules of the Métis buffalo hunt, see also Sawchuk, 1981: 11-12.
6 Howard, 1952: 41-42.
7 Ross, 1856: 193.
8 Fryer: 42.
9 *Alaska Highway News*, Nov. 28, 1990: 14. "Native Leader all wrong," says local man.
10 Richardson, Dec. 1970.

20
The Law: a doubtful ally

1 Cassidy, Frank, ed. 1991: 249, article by Roland Penner, "Power, the Law and Constitution-making."
2 Ibid.
3 Nowegijick v. The Queen (1983), 1 S.C.R. 29.
4 R. v. Sparrow (1990), 1 S.C.R. 1075.
5 Tennant, 1990: 222-224.
6 Richardson, Dec. 1989.
7 Goddard, 1991: 51.
8 Tennant, 1990: 222-223.

9 Moore, 1991.

10 Attorney General for Ontario v. Bear Island Foundation (1984), 49 O.R. (2nd) 353, affirmed 1989 68 O.R. (2nd) 394 (O.C.A.), further affirmed (1991) 3 C.N.L.R. 79.

11 Delgamuukw v. The Queen (1991), 79 Dominion Law Reports (4th) 286 (B.C.S.C.).

12 Cassidy, Maureen, 1984: 7.

13 Delgamuukw et al. v. The Queen et al. (1991.) "Reasons for Judgment of the Honourable Chief Justice Allan McEachern in the Supreme Court of British Columbia." Number 0843, Smithers Registry.

14 Cassidy, Frank, ed. 1991: 207, article by Robin Ridington, "Fieldwork in Courtroom 53, A witness to Delgamuukw."

15 Chapeskie, 1990.

21
Native self-government: escaping the tentacles

1 Indian Tribes of Manitoba, 1971: 96, quoting "Indians: Canadians, Plus or Minus?," A resource book for teachers, published by Project Canada West.

2 *Toronto Star*, September 5, 1992, "Abused Teen Let Down by All, Manitoba Judge Finds."

3 *Toronto Star*, February 9, 1993, "30 on reserve face sex assault charges."

22
Ovide Mercredi, straddling two worlds

1 Most maps spell the name Mistassini, but the reserve's band council recently decided to adopt the spelling Mistissini, as being closer to the correct Cree pronunciation.

2 This hypothesis was suggested by Professor W.A. Fuller, of the University of Alberta, in a letter to the editor, *Canadian Forum*, December 1991, in response to an article I had written about Ovide Mercredi in the October issue of the magazine. Prof. Fuller said he had seen the grave of this Joseph Mercredi about 40 years before, and

had been told by the man in charge of the Hudson's Bay Company store, also a Mercredi, that Joseph was the original Mercredi.

23
Canada accused before the world

1 Sanders, 1989, gives an overview of these impacts, and an appreciation of their legal consequences.

2 For a detailed account of the proposed displacement of 100,000 "tribal" people by construction of the Sardar Sarovar dams and canals in India, see the 1992 report, *Sardar Sarovar*, published by Resource Futures International, Ottawa. An independent review of these projects was carried out for the World Bank under the leadership of Bradford Morse and Thomas R. Berger.

3 *Annual report*, Canadian Human Rights Commission, November 1990.

4 Assembly of First Nations, 1988.

5 *Justice on Trial*: Report of the Criminal Justice System and its Impact on the Indian and Metis People of Alberta, March 1991.

6 Assembly of First Nations, 1990 and 1991. Also House of Commons Standing Committee on Aboriginal Affairs, 1990.

25
Goodbye indifference, hello goodwill

1 Peggy Vogan, 1979: *Indian Coverage in Canadian Daily Newspapers, 1978: a Content Analysis*. Research Branch, Department of Indian Affairs, Ottawa.

Aird, Rebecca. "Alienation of Traditional Lands Through Conflicting Uses." Research paper prepared for Algonquins of Barriere Lake.

Assembly of First Nations. 1988. *Tradition and Education, Towards a Vision of Our Future.* Ottawa.

—— 1990. *Towards Linguistic Justice for First Nations.* Ottawa.

—— 1991. *The Challenge.* Report on Aboriginal Languages and Literacy Conference, Jan 29-30 1991. Ottawa.

Battiste, Marie. 1989. "Different Worlds of Work: The Mi'kmaq Experience," in *Ethnicity and Oral History.* Proceedings of a conference at Baddeck, 1988. Halifax: International Education Centre.

—— "Cultural Transmission and Survival in Contemporary Micmac Society." *The Indian Historian,* Vol. X, No. 4.

Berger, Thomas R. 1991. *A Long and Terrible Shadow.* Vancouver: Douglas and McIntyre.

Bighetty, Marie Adele. 1986. *Missinippi Ethniwak (Big River People),* Pukatawagen: Pukatawagan Cree Language programme.

Brown, George, and Ron Maguire. 1979. *Indian Treaties in Historical Perspective.* Ottawa: Treaties and Historical Research Centre, Department of Indian Affairs and Northern Development.

Canadian Encyclopedia. 1985. 3 vols. Edmonton: Hurtig Publishers.

Cassidy, Frank, ed. 1991. *Aboriginal Self-Determination: proceedings of a conference held September 30-October 3, 1990.* Lantzville: Oolichan Books, and Institute for Research on Public Policy.

Cassidy, Maureen. 1984. *From Mountain to Mountain, a history of the Gitksan village of Ans'pa yaxw.* Kispiox: Ans'pa yaxw School Society.

Carter, Sarah. 1990. *Lost Harvests.* Montreal: McGill-Queen's University Press.

Chapeskie, Andrew J. 1990. "Aboriginal Customary Hunting and Trapping Law and State-defined Aboriginal Hunting and Trapping Rights in Canada: a case study in conflict creation." Paper delivered at sixth international Conference on Hunting and Gathering Societies, May 27-June 1, 1990, Fairbanks, University of Alaska.

Cumming, Peter A. and Neil H. Mickenberg. 1972. *Native Rights in Canada,* second edition. Toronto: General Publishing and Indian-Eskimo Association of Canada.

Daugherty, W.E. 1981. *Maritime Indian Treaties in Historical Perspective.* Ottawa: Research Branch Corporate Policy, Indian and Northern Affairs Canada.

Delgam Uukw, and Gisday Wa. 1990. *The Spirit in the Land: the Opening Statement of the Gitksan and Wet'suwet'en Hereditary Chiefs in the Supreme Court of British Columbia, May 11, 1987.* Gabriola Island, B.C.: Reflections.

Dickason, Olive Patricia. 1992. *Canada's First Nations: a History of Founding Peoples from Earliest Times.* Toronto: McClelland and Stewart.

Fumoleau, Rene, OMI. 1973. *As Long As this Land Shall Last: a History of Treaties Eight and Eleven.* Toronto: McClelland and Stewart.

Fryer, Harold. *Stops of Interest in Alberta: Wildrose Country.* Aldergrove, B.C.: Frontier Publishing Co.

Gambill, Jerry. 1968. "How Democracy Came to St.Regis." Paper prepared for *Akwesasne Notes.*

Goddard, John. 1991. *Last Stand of the Lubicon Cree.* Vancouver: Douglas and McIntyre.

Grand Council, Treaty 3. 1986. *The Fishing Rights of Treaty 3 Indians.* Kenora, Ont.

Henderson, James (Sakej) Youngblood. 1991. *First Nations Legal Inheritance.* Eskasoni, N.S.: Unpublished manuscript.

Holzkamm, Tim F. and Leo G. Waisberg. 1991. "The Creation of Economic Underdevelopment Among Treaty 3 Ojibway: the impact of government intervention 1800-1980." Paper delivered to Economic Development Conference, Dryden, Ont, Jan. 1991. Kenora,Ont.: Treaty and Aboriginal Rights Research (TARR), Grand Council, Treaty 3.

—— 1990. "Their Gardens Mostly on Islands: Ojibway Agriculture in Northwestern Ontario 1805-1875." Paper delivered to American Society for Ethnohistory, Toronto, November 1990. Kenora, Ont.: TARR.

—— 1989. "Our Land Here is Not as on the Plain." Paper delivered at American Society for Ethnohistory, Chicago, November, 1989. Kenora, Ont.: TARR.

House of Commons Standing Committee on Aboriginal Affairs,1990. *You Took My Talk: Aboriginal Literacy and Empowerment.* Ottawa: Department of Supply and Services.

Howard, Joseph Kinsey. 1952. *Strange Empire.* New York: William Morrow.

Indian and Northern Affairs Canada. 1973. *The Canadian Indian, Quebec and Atlantic Provinces.* Ottawa.

—— 1978. *The Historical Development of the Indian Act.* Ottawa: Treaties and Historical Research Centre, Policy, Planning and Research Branch.

—— 1979. Brown, George and Ron Maguire. *Indian Treaties in Historical Perspective.* Ottawa: Treaties and Historical Research Centre, Policy, Planning and Research Branch.

—— 1981. Stagg, Jack. *Anglo-Indian Relations in North America to 1763.* Ottawa: Policy, Planning and Research Branch.

—— 1981. Daugherty,W.E. *Maritime Indian Treaties in Historical Perspective.* Ottawa: Research Branch, Corporate Policy.

—— 1981. *Indian Acts and Amendments 1868-1950.* Ottawa: Treaties and Historical Research Centre, Policy, Planning and Research Branch.

—— 1981. *Contemporary Indian Legislation, 1951-1978.* Ottawa: Treaties and Historical Research Centre, Policy, Planning and Research Branch.

Indian Tribes of Manitoba. 1971. *Wahbung (Our Tomorrows).*

Jennings, Francis. 1975. *The Invasion of America.* New York: W.W. Norton.

Josephy, Alvin M. Jr. 1969. *The Patriot Chiefs.* New York: Viking Books.

Journals of the Legislative Assembly of Canada. (8 Vic. March 20, 1845). *Appendix EEE. Report on the Affairs of the Indians of Canada, 1844-45. Section II: Past and Present Condition of the Indians.*

Larner, J.W. Jr. 1972. *The Kootenay Plains Land Question and Canadian Indian Policy.* Unpublished Ph.D. thesis, West Virginia University.

LaViolette, Forrest E. 1961. *The Struggle for Survival: Indian Cultures and the Protestant Ethic in British Columbia.* Toronto: University of Toronto Press.

Lescarbot, Marc. 1907-14. *History of New France,* 3 vols. (1609). Toronto: The Champlain Society.

Lussier, Antoine S. and D. Bruce Sealey. 1975. *The Metis, Canada's Forgotten People.* Winnipeg: Manitoba Métis Association Press.

Macleod, Margaret and W.L. Morton. 1974. *Cuthbert Grant of Grantown.* Toronto: McClelland and Stewart.

Mi'kmaq Grand Council (Sante' Mawi'omi wjit Mi'kmaq). 1986. *Communication under the Optional Protocol to the International Covenant on Civil and Political Rights Regarding the Right to Self-Determination,* Submission to the United Nations Commission on Human Rights.

Miller, J.R. 1989. *Skyscrapers Hide the Heavens: a History of Indian-White Relations in Canada.* Toronto: University of Toronto Press.

Moore, Christopher. 1991. "The Gitksan and the Wet'suwet'en." *The Beaver*, Vol. 71:4, Winnipeg.

Morris, Alexander. 1880. *The Treaties of Canada with the Indians.* Toronto: Belfords, Clarke and Co.

Myers, Norman, ed. 1984. *Gaia, An Atlas of Planet Management..* New York: Anchor Press/Doubleday and Co.

Neidhardt, John. 1961. *Black Elk Speaks.* Lincoln: University of Nebraska Press.

Patterson, E. Palmer II. 1972. *The Canadian Indian, a History Since 1500.* Toronto: Collier-Macmillan.

Richardson, Boyce. 1968. "Indian Lives Could Make Good Novels." *The Montreal Star*, Dec. 20, 1968.

—— Nov. 1970. "Métis organize to fight for recognition." *The Montreal Star*, November 21, 1970.

—— Dec. 1970. "Hard work fails to bring prosperity to Métis." *The Montreal Star*, Dec. 26, 1970.

—— Feb. 1971. "Métis Becoming Proud of Their Heritage." *The Montreal Star*, Feb. 6, 1971.

—— 1987. "The Indian Ordeal: A Century of Decline." *The Beaver*, Vol. 67:1.

—— Dec. 1989. "Concealed Contempt." *The Canadian Forum*, Vol. LXVIII, Number 784.

—— 1989. ed. *Drumbeat: Anger and Renewal in Indian Country.* Toronto: Summerhill Press and the Assembly of First Nations.

—— 1991. *Strangers Devour the Land*, Vancouver: Douglas and McIntyre.

Ross, Alexander. 1856. *Red River Settlement.* Edmonton: Hurtig Publishers.

Sanders, Douglas. 1989. *Indigenous Participation in National Economic Effects of Racism and Racial Discrimination on Social and Economic Realities before Indigenous Peoples and States.* UN Docu. No. E/ON. 4/1989/22.

Sawchuk, Joe. 1981. *Métis Land Rights in Alberta.* Edmonton: Métis Association of Alberta.

Sealey, D. Bruce and Antoine S. Lussier. 1975. *The Métis, Canada's Forgotten People.* Winnipeg: Manitoba Métis Association Press.

Special Joint Committee of the Senate and House of Commons appointed to examine and consider the Indian Act. 1946-47.

Stagg, Jack. 1981. *Anglo-Indian Relations in North America to 1763.* Ottawa: Research Branch, Indian and Northern Affairs Canada.

Tennant, Paul. 1990. *Aboriginal Peoples and Politics, The Indian Land Question in British Columbia, 1849-1989.* Vancouver: University of British Columbia Press.

Thwaites, R.G., ed. 1896-1901. *The Jesuit Relations and Allied Documents*, 73 vols. Cleveland: Burrows Bros.

Trigger, Bruce. 1976. *The Children of Aataentsic, A History of the Huron People to 1660.* Montreal: McGill-Queen's University Press.

—— 1985. *Natives and Newcomers.* Montreal: McGill-Queen's University Press.

—— 1986. *Archeology and the Future.* McGill Arts Faculty Distinguished Lecture, November 11, 1986.

Wadden, Marie. 1991. *Nitassinan, The Innu Struggle to Reclaim their Homeland.* Vancouver: Douglas and McIntyre.

Whitehead, Ruth Holmes. 1991. *The Old Man Told Us, Excerpts from Micmac History, 1500-1950.* Halifax: Nimbus Publishing.

Whiteside, Don and Scott Douglas Whiteside. 1981. *Articles Pertaining to Indians in The Globe, 1844 to 1867.* Ottawa: Aboriginal Institute of Canada.

World Commission on Environment and Development. 1987. *Our Common Future* (The Brundtland Report). Oxford and New York: Oxford University Press.

Williams, Guy 139
Wilson, Bill 278
Winneway, Que. 87-8
Winnipeg 17, 184, 191, 210, 216, 260-1,
274, 315, 329, 336
Aboriginal Council of 235-6; Argyll
High School 245, 247-9; first urban re-
serve 236; lack of ghettos in 244; Mayor
of 235; Native Family Economic
Development (WNFED) 238; native or-
ganizations in 237-9; native population
of 236; Original Women's Network
238-9; Treaty Council of 236
World Council of Churches 345
World Indigenous Congress 346
Wright, Bob 179
Wyandots 52

Yalden, Max 351